THE
NORTHWARD
EXPANSION
OF CANADA
1914–1967

MORRIS ZASLOW

THE NORTHWARD EXPANSION OF CANADA 1914–1967

The Canadian Centenary Series

McClelland and Stewart

Canadian Cataloguing in Publication Data

Zaslow, Morris, 1918–
The northward expansion of Canada,
1914–1967

(The Canadian centenary series ; 17)
Includes bibliographical references and index.
ISBN 0-7710-9071-4

1. Canada, Northern. I: Title. II: Series.

FC3963.Z38 1988   971.9′03   C87-093385-X
F1090.5.Z38 1988

Printed and bound in Canada

McClelland and Stewart
The Canadian Publishers
481 University Avenue
Toronto, Ontario
M5G 2E9

A History of Canada

Ramsay Cook, EXECUTIVE EDITOR

†ALSO AVAILABLE IN PAPERBACK

*Volumes I, III, VII, and XII of The Canadian Centenary Series
were published with the help of grants from the Humanities
Research Council of Canada.*

CONTENTS

The Northward Expansion of Canada

MAPS

James Loates and Josef Gardisch, Cartographers

The Canadian Centenary Series

Half a century has elapsed since *Canada and Its Provinces*, the first large-scale co-operative history of Canada, was published. During that time, new historical materials have been made available in archives and libraries; new research has been carried out, and its results published; new interpretations have been advanced and tested. In these same years Canada itself has greatly grown and changed. These facts, together with the centenary of Confederation, justify the publication of a new co-operative history of Canada.

The form chosen for this enterprise was that of a series of volumes. The series was planned by the editors, but each volume will be designed and executed by a single author. The general theme of the work is the development of those regional communities which have for the past century made up the Canadian nation; and the series will be composed of a number of volumes sufficiently large to permit adequate treatment of all the phases of the theme in the light of modern knowledge.

The Centenary History, then, was planned as a series to have a certain common character and to follow a common method but to be written by individual authors, specialists in their fields. As a whole, it will be a work of specialized knowledge, the great advantage of scholarly co-operation, and at the same time each volume will have the unity and distinctive character of individual authorship. It was agreed that a general narrative treatment was necessary and that each author should deal in a balanced way with economic, political, and social history. The result, it is hoped, will be an interpretative, varied, and comprehensive account, at once useful to the student and interesting to the general reader.

The difficulties of organizing and executing such a series are apparent: the overlapping of separate narratives, the risk of omissions, the imposition of divisions which are relevant to some themes but not to others. Not so apparent, but quite as troublesome, are the problems of scale, perspective, and scope, problems which perplex the writer of a one-volume history and are magnified in a series. It is by deliberate choice that certain parts of the history are told twice, in different volumes from different points of view, in the belief that the benefits gained outweigh the unavoidable disadvantages.

W.L. MORTON
Executive Editor
D.G. CREIGHTON
Advisory Editor

Executive Editor's Preface

W.L. Morton and D.G. Creighton, two of Canada's most distinguished historians, together conceived the Canadian Centenary Series, divided the work, recruited the authors, and presided over the publication of fifteen volumes. Regrettably, neither lived to see the final four books through the press. That responsibility has fallen to me. I intend to carry it through according to the letter and the spirit of the introductory statement written by the first editors, which will continue to appear in each volume. The series remains theirs, an appropriate reminder of the seminal contributions that they made to the understanding of Canada's past. Having served my apprenticeship as a historian with each of them, in different ways, it is a signal privilege for me to be able to oversee the completion of this fine series of Canadian historical volumes.

In *The Opening of the Canadian North, 1870–1914* (1971) Morris Zaslow described the first phase of Canadian development in the North after Confederation. That was the story of a rather tentative probe into areas that were often still uncharted. In this new volume he analyses the more powerful developmental thrust that in the subsequent half century brought the North more firmly into the Canadian orbit. It is the story of the expansion of transportation and communications, the exploitation of natural resources, and the slow growth of European settlement. Paralleling these changes Professor Zaslow describes the struggles of the native peoples to preserve something of their culture.

This volume concludes the Canadian Centenary Series. In nineteen volumes, the Series brings together the whole history of Canada and reveals much of what has been achieved by historians of Canada over the past twenty-five years. Successive editors and the authors have endeavoured to provide Canadians with a thorough, well-written account of their past. We believe that we have succeeded, and that the Series will stand the test of time.

Two participants deserve special mention, now that the series is concluded: Janet Craig, an editor of unsurpassed skill, and Jack McClelland who, though he must often have despaired about the pace of the project, never wavered in his belief that the game was worth the candle. The completed Series, then, is a monument to Jack McClelland, D. G. Creighton, and W. L. Morton.

RAMSAY COOK

PREFACE

The aim of this volume is to describe and analyse the development
from 1914 to 1967 of the Subarctic and Arctic parts of Canada that
measure over three million square miles in extent and occupy some
three quarters of its land surface. Most people have been taught (and
this is widely reflected in popular writings) to see Canada's northward
expansion purely in terms of the feats of explorers, fur traders, gold
seekers, whalers, missionaries, policemen, bush pilots, and other
glamorous figures. The valuable contributions of these individuals certainly cannot be gainsaid, but the far greater part of the work of
expanding Canada's frontiers has been done by the myriad persons
who moved with their families into the North to participate in developing its unexploited or underused natural resources. To treat the
experience and accomplishments of these many thousands of pioneer
settlers and hundreds of industries and agencies, and also the thousands of Indians, Métis, and Inuit who were the main casualties of the
expansion process, let alone the exploits of the adventurers listed
above, would require not one but a series of volumes.

Such a detailed narrative approach being out of the question, this
book has adopted one that has analogies with preparing a first map of
a little-known land on a scale small enough to depict and identify only
its largest, most significant features. Indeed, so vast is the scale of this
subject that every single word of the text represents more than a half
century's history of a twenty-square-mile segment of Canada's northlands. This volume does try to deal with the most important topics,
the key happenings, the persons who "made history" by their actions
or through the force of their personalities. The main aim, though, is
to distil the experience of the innumerable individuals, agencies, and
institutions and set them into their proper perspectives for more specialized future studies.

In *The Opening of the Canadian North, 1870–1914*, of which this
volume is the continuation, northward expansion was examined on a

xiii

region-by-region basis. Expansion followed a progression from the south, where the primitive economy and society were almost completely displaced by modern industry, whereas in more northerly districts the process was just getting under way, or had not even begun by 1914. Investigating northward expansion since 1914, however, requires a different approach in that the "discovery" phase was largely completed except for parts of the Arctic Archipelago, while much of the Subarctic was being occupied by modern industries striving to exploit the agricultural, forestry, hydro-electric, and mineral resources of the land. The features and effects of each industry were almost the same whether observed in Northern Quebec or Yukon. This also applied to the agricultural frontier, where thousands of pioneer farmers carried on as individual operators, for each farmer throughout the Subarctic had to meet similar climatic, physical, and other challenges. Above all, the presence of government agencies imparted an important common element to each industrial frontier, especially as their control was intensified, their roles became increasingly active and their operations more centralized and standardized. The present work will examine northward expansion around three main aspects: the sweep of the industrial frontiers across Subarctic Canada; the changing situations of the native populations and the wildlife industries; and the economic, social, and political maturation of the Northwest Territories and Yukon.

Since most of my research, teaching, and writing over a forty-year period has centred on the matters treated in this volume, it would be very difficult to list and properly acknowledge my indebtedness to all the institutions and individuals that assisted me while this book was in the making. Rather, I must single out a very few from among the many whose contributions were especially important: the Public Archives of Canada, the Arctic Institute of North America, the Scott Polar Research Institute, and the research libraries and archives of the Universities of Toronto, Western Ontario, and Calgary. My researches were assisted by sabbatical and study leaves and reduced teaching loads from the Departments of History at the Universities of Toronto and Western Ontario that were made possible through the generosity of the Nuffield Foundation, the Canada Council, the Social Science Research Council of Canada, and the Social Sciences and Humanities Research Council of Canada. The Killam Foundation with true munificence underwrote my two study-year leaves plus another two years, one as a research scholar at the Arctic Institute of North America and the other as a visiting professor at the University of Calgary. A grant from this foundation also enabled me to employ five students as summertime assistants at an early stage of the research. Travel allowances from these and other sources, such as the Rockefeller Fund, helped me both to work at many archives and libraries and to interview numerous persons during several northern visits. Through special favour of Eldorado Mining and Refining Limited and the Department of Energy, Mines and Resources I was privileged to travel the length of the Mackenzie waterway system on Northern Transportation Company vessels and to spend a week visiting the Polar Continental Shelf Project, where I also enjoyed several flights around the Queen Elizabeth Islands. I offer heartfelt thanks to these and my many other benefactors for their assistance with the research side of this study.

Turning to the writing phases, I must first extend thanks to my typists, in particular Annemarie Marriner, who typed the earliest tape-recorded drafts (1976–77), and Christianne Speed, who typed the several drafts of chapters and the final text (1984–86) on the word processor of the Department of History, University of Western Ontario. James Loates and Josef Gardisch prepared the maps, and the Photographic Archives of Canada supplied most of the illustrations. Professor G. Ramsay Cook, the editor of the Canadian Centenary Series, and Janet Craig by their careful, thoughtful editorial work on the manuscript and guiding it through the press contributed in a major way during the lengthy publication stage.

I close by expressing gratitude beyond words to my wife, Betty, for having borne the separations and years of neglect, frustration, and disappointment that are prominent features of the academic wife's lot with such unselfishness, understanding, gentle forbearance, and never-ending devotion.

MORRIS ZASLOW

CHAPTER 1

Middle North and Arctic in and after
the Great War

On Armistice Day, 1918, no street cars were running in Toronto. Vilhjalmur Stefansson, in the city to lecture on his Arctic experiences and views, walked downtown from Joseph and Edith Tyrrell's home to address an Empire Club luncheon and a non-academic audience of servicemen and civilians at Massey Hall in the evening. His presentations were made romantic and fascinating by the novelty of his experiences and his provocative opinions, but at the same time his message was greatly at variance with the current realities – a glimpse of a past that had been altered beyond recognition in the years since 1913, when Stefansson had buried himself in the islands and seas of the Western Arctic.

For the style of Arctic living Stefansson described – and for years advertised in lectures, articles, and books – harked back to the timeless methods by which Arctic nomads had survived for millennia in their harsh environment. The technique he extolled, of living off the land, while appropriate for a man or two investigating the human and physical aspects of a little-known region, had little in common with the war-induced fashion of directed, organized mass actions attacking difficulties head-on with the latest technology. Again, the view he expressed of the present and potential value of Arctic renewable resources was wildly naïve, wholly ignoring economic and technical realities. When his statement that "all of northern Canada used as a grazing land for the musk ox would produce as much wool, meat and butter as Argentina"[1] was put to the test it revealed no end of difficulties and created endless disappointments, not least for Stefansson himself. How far could all the foodstuffs the Arctic was capable of producing go toward solving the bottomless needs of mass markets in the South? How feasible was it to ship meat and butter from the Arctic to such markets and expect it to compete with supplies from other sources? Seen in the cold light of reality, the natural resources of the

1

Arctic lands (apart from furs) were neither capable of being developed for world markets nor economically worth developing for decades to come.

When some fifty years later western man returned to the scene of Stefansson's exploratory triumphs it was not to exploit its food resources but its newly discovered gigantic fossil fuel occurrences under the conditions of late-twentieth-century civilization, "hurling a massive, highly capital-intensive, and technological assault against the problems of remoteness, cold, and economic backwardness of the area."[2] The drive to develop these resources for world markets would certainly demonstrate western man's impressive technical capabilities but also his unbridled hunger for exploitable energy and other natural resources that could leave no supply untapped, however remote and inaccessible. The intervening stages by which Canada's industrial frontiers advanced from the southern margins of the Subarctic forest in 1914 to the barren Arctic islands and seas in 1967 will be examined in the pages that follow.

I

The challenges of the Great War immeasurably hastened the trend to organized, mechanized, mass action. The war put more than half a million of Canada's most productive workers in uniform and gathered the bulk of the remaining population into the service of the Allies' war effort. For the first time, the full weight of the nation was harnessed to the requirements of a long war of attrition. The federal government emerged as the manager of the national life, directing manpower, controlling distribution of foodstuffs and fuel, marketing farmers' grain, allocating crucial materials to industry. In this many-sided war effort the settlers and the industries of the frontier districts were called on to contribute according to their capacities.

Footloose, venturesome young men who had recently been drawn to the frontier districts responded enthusiastically to the call to the colours, partly out of patriotic motives but mainly, perhaps, because of a wish to exchange humdrum everyday lives for the excitement and adventure of foreign travel. "I think we have all decided to enlist and get the war over with as soon as possible,"[3] was a statement that expressed a common mood. The news of the outbreak spread to some remote sections with surprising rapidity. It reached Fort McPherson in less than a month, on September 3, when "Jacquot returned from Dawson, with news of terrible European war,"[4] and sped along the Arctic coastline through the autumn and ensuing winter of 1914–15.

Stefansson heard of the event on August 1, 1915, when, emerging from his prolonged drift across the Beaufort Sea ice, he encountered the ship *Polar Bear* at Banks Island. Isolated Hudson's Bay Company inland posts, like that on Lac Mistassini in Nouveau-Québec, also received the news at much the same time as Stefansson, along with the next year's outfit for 1915–16.

Recruiting centres such as Sault Ste Marie, the Lakehead cities, Prince Albert, or Edmonton that drew heavily upon northern regions reported gratifyingly large enlistments for the First Contingent and subsequent drafts. Other pioneers, among them Archie Belaney (the future Grey Owl), John Hornby, the recluse of the Barrens, Warburton Pike, the aging explorer of the Northwest, and Louis Romanet, the Revillon fur trader, returned to their homelands to enlist in the armies there. Recent immigrants from all the Allied countries – Frenchmen, Belgians, Serbs, and, after 1915, Italians and Romanians – responded to the call and departed for the outside world, as did many Canadian-born recent settlers in the North and over 3,500 of Canada's Indians. Only a few armed units were actually stationed along Canada's frontiers, notably at internment camps and a few industrial centres. At Kapuskasing, 1,259 detainees – mostly Slavs, Magyars, and Turks – toiled to clear a 1,280-acre tract for the future Dominion Experimental Farm. Released on parole in July 1916 to work in war factories, they were succeeded at the camp by German prisoners of war. These proved far more intractable, even going on strike in the autumn of 1917 against the cutting of firewood lest their captors would benefit as well as themselves.

The men from the frontiers were distributed throughout the forces of Canada and her allies. Rarely were they assigned to identifiable units, such as the Yukon Machine Gun Battalion toward which J.W. Boyle, the Klondike mining developer and wartime adventurer in the Balkans and Russia, donated $75,000. They served in disproportionate numbers, however, in activities that utilized their peacetime experience or skills. Many Indians were used as snipers (an especially hazardous assignment) because of their experience of hunting and travelling in the bush. Lumberjacks found their way into the Canadian Forestry Corps, which secured 70 per cent of the Western Front's needs from the forests of France and Britain. Former railway workers served in the railway construction battalions commanded by the Western Canadian railway contractor J.W. Stewart and did excellent work bringing supplies and munitions forward almost to the rim of the trenches. Others found themselves repairing and maintaining railway lines as far afield as Palestine and doing water transport duty in Mesopotamia. But most recruits from the North participated in the long, agonizing nightmare of the Western Front, and many became casualties of that bloody struggle. The travellers, migratory trappers, and industrial workers had left behind few traces of their sojourns in the North. The pioneer farmers who had been in the process of developing homesteads and pre-emption lands were a different matter. The government of Saskatchewan, for instance, had to appoint an administrator to handle the melancholy duty of making the best possible settlements of the estates of more than fifteen hundred Saskatchewan soldiers, many of them participants in the latest drive to extend the farming frontier into the woodlands of the province.

A few northern centres eventually were permitted to participate in producing the manufactured goods required by the gigantic war effort. Shawinigan Water and Power Company's plant at Shawinigan Falls on the St Maurice supplied electric power for the pulp and paper, calcium carbide, aluminum refining, textile, mining, and other plants engaged in war production. At the industrial complex of Sault Ste Marie in Northern Ontario, Algoma Steel produced specialty steel, from which other plants processed two hundred high-explosive shells per day, as well as a large fraction of Canada's toluol, an essential ingredient of TNT, which was manufactured at plants opened at Nobel and Renfrew, Ontario. Several steel ships were built at the Lakehead cities, where the Canadian Car and Foundry plant also produced railway boxcars and other vitally needed transportation equipment. Hence Northern Ontario's manufacturing capacity was significantly increased as a result of the Great War.

Other centres scattered along the frontiers responded to the inflated wartime markets for timber, woodpulp products, minerals, or foodstuffs. One special activity was the manufacture of aircraft-grade spruce lumber from the Sitka spruce stands along the coasts of British Columbia. At five main centres in the Queen Charlotte Islands contractors felled the giant trees and hauled the logs down steep slopes to the coast, where they were formed into rafts and towed as far as 600 miles across frequently choppy seas to sawmills on the mainland. Even after careful selecting, culling, and milling of the logs, barely 30 per cent of the resulting lumber proved suitable for the intended purpose. The 35.3 million foot board measure (FBM) that were accepted, however, represented 40 per cent of Britain's total requirements of this vital material. Numbers of wooden ships also were built at West Coast shipyards for war transport work.

Notwithstanding the many farmer enlistees, every part of the agricultural frontier across Canada responded to both the higher prices for cereals, meat, and dairy products and governmental exhortations to disregard the dangers of overworking the land and bring every possible acre under cultivation. Western Canadian farmers put record acreages under cultivation in 1915, 1917, and 1918 and hurried to buy or rent as much land as they could; they also mechanized their operations to help overcome the growing shortage of farm labour while expanding production. Immigration also continued to enlarge the frontier farming districts. A few hundred settlers located in Northern Ontario each year, while colonization proceeded more rapidly in Quebec, notably in the newly opened Abitibi district, the population of which increased from 1,254 in 1915 to 9,401 by the war's end. In Western Canada settlers took up homesteads along the wooded fringe district from the Manitoba lakes to west of Edmonton and especially in the Peace River district, which became very attractive after a railway reached that region in 1915–16. Immigration from the United States revived in 1916, encouraged by the opportunities for securing good cheap lands in a time of rising prices for farm produce. American immigrants moved into the Peace River district in 1916 to homesteads in the Battle River area and to the Peace River Block, where 2,000 settlers were reported in 1918. The district was favoured with bountiful crops, and the railhead at the town of Peace River received wheat shipped by river from as far north as Fort Vermilion and cattle driven overland from Hudson Hope and Fort St. John to the west. As the Great War came to an end, the region seemed on the verge of a renewed wave of agricultural settlers like those that had filled the prairie West before the war.

Mines along the northern frontiers were drawn on to supply American factories working on lucrative war contracts. For instance, two-thirds of British Columbia's output of copper was secured from the northern region, notably from the large Granby Consolidated plant at Anyox on Observatory Inlet, an arm of the Portland Canal. Important quantities of molybdenite ore were extracted from the Dolly Varden mine in the same region, while hand-picked copper ore or copper-gold-silver concentrates were shipped from other mines near Hazelton and on the Queen Charlotte Islands. The high wartime prices also greatly stimulated the economy of the Sudbury district, where production of copper and nickel soared to record heights.

A noteworthy development of the war years was the conclusion of a prolonged campaign to bring the crucial refining stages of this industry under greater scrutiny and control. The two operators, the American-controlled International Nickel Company (INCO) and the British-owned Mond Nickel Company, that shared the production in a three-to-one ratio, smelted the ore into matte at Sudbury, which they shipped to New Jersey or to Wales to be refined into its varied components. Every previous effort to persuade or cajole INCO to refine its ore in Canada had proved unavailing. Frequent accusations that refined nickel was making its way to enemy countries via the United States up to 1917 resulted in investigations by two royal commissions. The appearance also of the British American Nickel Company with a proposal to establish its refinery in Ontario finally turned the tide; INCO consented to build a refinery at Port Colborne in the Niagara district and expand the smelting operation at Sudbury. That step effectively silenced complaints, although Sudbury residents remained disappointed that their centre had not progressed in any appreciable degree into the refining and manufacturing sides of the industry. The move, however, was a significant step toward giving Ontario and Canada a better share of the benefits from this rich provincial resource.

The pulp and paper industry of the northern woodlands of Ontario and Quebec continued to expand during the war thanks to greatly increased consumption of newsprint paper and specialty pulps, coupled with the closing of European sources of supply. The earlier trends of United States operators to move to Canada and the Canadian industry to become increasingly integrated with that of the United States continued. Pulp and paper shipments continued to rise until Canada by 1920 was supplying 30 per cent of the pulp and paper needs of the United States, the world's largest single market. The largely Canadian-owned lumber industry, which had been in the doldrums since 1913, also experienced higher prices and greatly increased demand from 1916 onward. Operators expanded into the rich forests opened by the recent round of railway construction, encouraged by carefree wartime attitudes toward resource granting and timber harvesting and by relaxed enforcement of the regulations intended to safeguard the public interest. Along with increased activity at Canadian lumber mills and pulp and paper plants went a great rise in exports of unprocessed pulpwood, sawlogs, and, after the war, wood pulp and newsprint paper to the United States, where much higher prices prevailed.

These responses to the challenges and opportunities presented by the Great War came from the recently settled Subarctic fringe and were largely controlled and directed by Canada's wartime government. Still almost completely beyond its control were the small but important hunting, trapping, and fur-trading industries of the unsettled wildernesses of the Middle North and of the Arctic regions beyond, where Canada's authority was almost non-existent. These industries, like the others, were strongly affected by wartime developments and were badly in need of governmental oversight, for the war years wrought tremendous changes in the traditional fur trade, which before 1914 had been largely dominated by established firms, notably the Hudson's Bay and Revillon Frères companies. The major companies' trading sys-

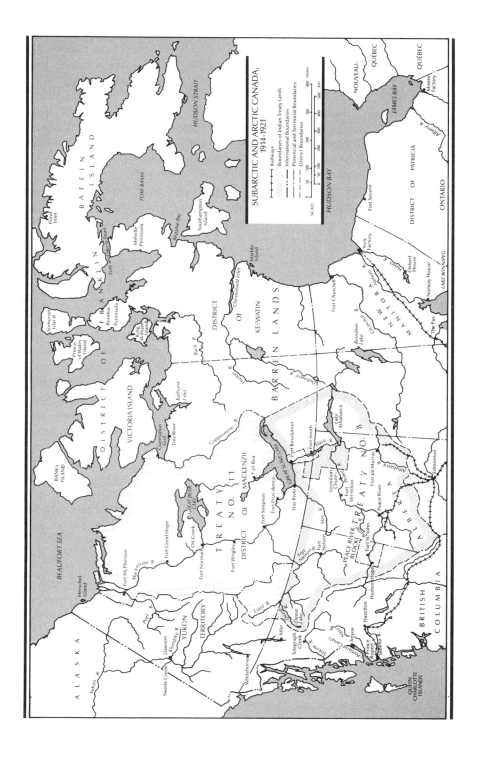

SUBARCTIC AND ARCTIC CANADA, 1914-1921

Railways
Boundaries of Indian Treaty Lands
International Boundaries
Provincial and Territorial Boundaries
District Boundaries

SCALE

0   50 100   200   300   400 Miles

0   50 100   200   300   400   500 km

BAFFIN ISLAND

HUDSON STRAIT

FOXE BASIN

Fury and Hecla Strait

Pond Inlet

Melville Peninsula

Repulse Bay

Southampton Island

DISTRICT OF FRANKLIN

Somerset Island

Boothia Peninsula

Prince of Wales Island

King William Island

Marble Island

Chesterfield Inlet

DISTRICT OF KEEWATIN

BARREN LANDS

HUDSON BAY

JAMES BAY

QUÉBEC

QUÉBEC

NOUVEAU-

Moose Factory

Albany R.

Fort Severn

DISTRICT OF PATRICIA

ONTARIO

York Factory

Oxford House

LAKE WINNIPEG

Norway House

The Pas

MANITOBA

Nelson R.

Hayes R.

Fort Churchill

Churchill R.

Reindeer Lake

Dubawnt R.

Thelon R.

Back R.

BANKS ISLAND

VICTORIA ISLAND

Coronation Gulf

Tree River

Bathurst Inlet

Coppermine R.

BEAUFORT SEA

Fort Rae

GREAT BEAR LAKE

Oil Creek

Fort Good Hope

Fort Norman

Mackenzie R.

Fort Wrigley

DISTRICT OF MACKENZIE

TREATY NO. 11

Fort Providence

Fort Simpson

Hay River

GREAT SLAVE LAKE

Fort Resolution

Fort Smith

Slave R.

Lake Athabasca

TREATY NO. 8

Fort Smith

Vermilion Chutes

Fort Vermilion

Hay R.

Fort McMurray

Athabasca R.

Peace River

ALBERTA

Edmonton

PEACE RIVER BLOCK

Fort St. John

Hudson Hope

Herschel Island

Fort McPherson

Peel R.

Dawson

Klondike R.

Swede Creek

YUKON TERRITORY

Whitehorse

Liard R.

Fort Nelson

Fort Nelson R.

Dease Lake

Atlin

Telegraph Creek

Stikine R.

Nass R.

Anyox

Hazelton

Prince Rupert

Skeena R.

Portland Canal

BRITISH COLUMBIA

QUEEN CHARLOTTE ISLANDS

ALASKA

Yukon R.

tems were severely disrupted by the closing of European markets, the commandeering of their ocean-going ships for war service, and the enlistment of many of their most experienced traders in the armies of Britain, France, and Canada. The outbreak of the war ushered in two years of such low fur prices that the companies reduced their credit advances to trappers to discourage them from taking more fur.

Then in 1916 came a sudden surge in prices that continued until 1920, spurred by a burgeoning market for fur in the United States centred on New York. Sir Robert Kindersley, the new governor of the Hudson's Bay Company, informed his first annual meeting as early as August 2, 1916, of

> . . . a considerable incursion of American traders, who, for the time being, have been keen competitors in our districts, and their efforts have been the more energetic owing to the fact that the principal demand for furs has largely shifted from the European markets to that of the United States, and this has enabled these traders to dispose more rapidly of their goods, and therefore to run less risk of loss.[5]

Native trappers turned to the free traders who invaded every district of Northern Canada and profited from the fierce competition for their furs that ensued. These traders substituted cash trading for exchange of goods, leaving the natives the burden of securing their wants from available suppliers. Sometimes fur buyers met native trappers at the camps with showy but shoddy goods that did not have anything like the proven utility of the merchandise carried by the established traders. Some natives spent their unaccustomed earnings on intoxicants smuggled into the country, on expensive but impractical goods from among the glittering array of modern manufacturers, or on such new needs as gasoline motors, rifles, and ammunition. Thus the wartime fur-trade boom seriously affected the native way of life across Subarctic Canada.

The newcomers, having few of the heavy transport and trading expenses of the established traders, found it easy to dispose of their furs at good profits to dealers or at fur auction centres in New York, Vancouver, Montreal, or Winnipeg. New York interests, in fact, even chartered the Lamson-Hubbard Canadian Company to operate a string of trading posts and related transport system along the waterways of the Mackenzie basin. Fortunately for the older companies, however, the newcomer had only incompetent traders they had discarded, overextended its credits to trappers, and operated in altogether too elaborate and expensive a fashion, so that its long-term survival was problematical.

The wartime expansion of the fur trade was aided by the recent round of railway construction, some of it still under way during the war years. In Central Canada the National Transcontinental and Canadian Northern systems traversing the forests and Clay Belts of Quebec and Ontario opened rich grounds to incoming traders and large numbers of white trappers, while the Grand Trunk Pacific had a similar effect for central and northern British Columbia. Particularly important, however, were the extensions of the province-sponsored lines to heads of river navigation on the Athabasca (near Fort McMurray) and Peace (town of Peace River) rivers in Northern Alberta. By this means easy entry was afforded to the vast trapping hinterlands of the Slave and Mackenzie river systems in the Northwest Territories, which were also being invaded by trappers and traders from Alaska. Lamson-Hubbard based itself at Peace River and acquired a river fleet that included the large stern-wheeler *D.A. Thomas* for the Peace River, the smaller *Slave River* for the lower Peace and upper Slave rivers, and the queenly *Distributor III*, built at Fort Smith in 1920, to operate all the way to the Mackenzie delta. In addition, the company introduced automobiles, trucks, and tractors to transfer freight and passengers across the two portages around the Vermilion Chutes and the Slave River rapids. The Hudson's Bay and Northern Trading companies operated their fleets from Fort McMurray, a route requiring only the single portage at Fort Smith, where the brothers Mickey and Pat Ryan started their own freighting business. Both fur companies added to their fleets to cope with the increased traffic, the chief innovation being Northern Trading's *Northland Pioneer*, the first oil-burning steamer along the waterway. Its appearance in 1921 heralded the passing of the wood-burning steamboats, for no more of these were placed on the northern waters thereafter, though the picturesque roomy stern-wheelers, eventually converted to oil, continued operating until the Second World War.

II

The involvement of the Canadian government and government personnel in the Canadian Arctic Expedition of 1913–18 had drawn the Western Arctic fitfully into the national limelight and attracted public scrutiny to its problems.[6] Among them was the new one created by the expansion of fur-trading activities into that remote region, for alongside the scientists of the Southern Party and in the wake of the whalers went eager fur buyers in search of the white fox pelts that had recently begun to enjoy good commercial markets. Following a pioneer supply voyage from Vancouver in 1914, the Hudson's Bay Company quickly opened a new trading district between Herschel Island and Tree River, 500 miles farther east, where its half-dozen posts faced competition from a number of independent traders, mostly former whaling personnel, and from the H. Liebes Company of San Francisco. As early as 1917 the Royal Northwest Mounted Police reported: "The most striking feature in the Arctic is the extension of trade eastward into Coronation gulf as far as the mouth of the Coppermine river. Along the coast from Nome to Herschell island the lure of new trading fields has attracted traders and trappers with the hopes of profitable trading among the Eskimo, hitherto untouched."[7] Two years later Constable Cornelius, patrolling from the new post at Tree River, observed that "practically every native on the mainland is the owner of a rifle now" and noted a new trading development on the adjacent island coast: "At the Eskimo villages which we visited on the Victoria Land coast we met a number of Eskimo fur runners who were employed by the traders on the mainland. Some of these fur runners are entrusted with an outfit amounting to four or five hundred dollars at outside prices, and so are able to do quite a business with their native friends."[8]

The Hudson's Bay and Revillon firms also extended their trade into the Eastern Arctic, opening posts on the west side of Hudson Bay and Foxe Basin as far north as Repulse Bay, and along both sides of Hudson Strait. On Baffin Island the Hudson's Bay Company competed with a number of rival trading interests, including the Robert Kinnes and Sabellum Trading companies from Great Britain, the Arctic Gold Exploration Syndicate, with which the British traveller Henry Toke Munn and Captain J.E. Bernier were associated, and R.S. Janes, a Newfoundlander who operated his post on Eclipse Sound.

Expansion of activity by the traders naturally led to larger numbers of hunters and trappers and more intensive hunting. Inuit hunters, armed with rifles, ravaged the herds of muskox and especially caribou for their hides. Police officers commented almost immediately on the diminution in numbers of caribou, "in all probability caused by the great numbers of rifles in the country."[9] Stefansson and Inspector G.J. Jennings were in rare agreement in 1914 in suggesting that export of polar bear skins and muskox robes and sale of caribou meat or skins be prohibited; both proposed regulation of trapping seasons and entry of whites into the region by permit only, for reasons of health and because "the less the eskimo has to do with the white man, the better for them."[10]

Concern for wildlife was widespread everywhere in Canada among well-educated, outdoors-loving members of the public, and wildlife protection was one responsibility of the Commission of Conservation that continued unabated during the war.[11] The commission organized a conference on the conservation of fish, birds, and game in Ottawa in November 1915, studied the subject further at its annual meetings in February 1916, and sponsored a First National Conference on Wildlife Protection that met shortly after the end of the war in February 1919. The movement was organized and directed particularly by J.B. Harkin, Commissioner of Dominion Parks, Dr. C.G. Hewitt, Dominion Biologist, and the other members of the federal government's Advisory Board on Wildlife Protection (established in December 1916), and it was sustained by influential federal and provincial officials responsible for parks, game resources, and related fields. With such close rapport among administrators, virtually every province passed legislation or issued regulations during the war years to limit the hunting of endangered species and control the commercial exploitation of wildlife. Their measures included establishing limited, or closed, seasons for hunting and trapping various species, prohibiting the sale of game, licensing non-native trappers and fur dealers, and imposing royalty fees on all furs traded. Two pieces of federal legislation enacted in 1917, the Northwest Game Act and the Migratory Birds Convention Act, were especially significant for the northern territories.

The Northwest Game Act prohibited the hunting of buffalo, muskoxen, wapiti, and white pelicans altogether, of swans and eider ducks for the time being, and set the seasons when other species could be hunted or trapped. It banned the use of poisons and other undesirable methods of hunting or employment of natives by whites to circumvent restrictions. The act instituted licence fees, from which natives were exempted, and made it lawful for Indians or Inuit "who are *bona fide* inhabitants of the Northwest Territories" to take game and birds' eggs but illegal for non-natives to do so unless "actually in need of such game or eggs to prevent starvation."[12] The intended protection of the native peoples, however, was in part undermined by the Migratory Birds Convention Act, which implemented an agreement with the United States. This act, which applied everywhere in Canada, imposed closed seasons on migratory insectivorous and non-game birds and on the rare swans and cranes, and restricted hunting seasons for ducks and geese. There were exceptions when the protected birds were needed to sustain life, while the scarcity of policemen and game wardens made enforcement ineffective in northern districts. Nevertheless the measure could be invoked anytime even against natives, since the courts held it to be superior both to provincial laws and regulations and to the terms of the Indian treaties.

The wide dissemination of firearms among the Central and Eastern Arctic Inuit was accompanied by a significant increase in violent crimes during the period 1916–21 that brought a greater police presence to the Inuit country. The increase may be attributed in part to the fact that previously unnoticed and unrecorded crimes now were being reported to the authorities, but the main reasons undoubtedly were the presence of larger numbers of white men and of firearms in Inuit hands. Earlier murders, like those of two Oblate priests on the Coppermine River in 1913 and of two hunters at Bathurst Inlet in 1912,[13] had occasioned long, arduous police patrols to those localities. The accused in the first case, Sinnisiak and Uluksuk, were tried in Edmonton and acquitted of one murder, then retried and convicted in Calgary for the other. But the mandatory death sentences were commuted to life imprisonment at Fort Resolution. Then, after just two years, the men were returned to their own country where it was hoped they would "exert a salutary influence on their tribe as they will be able to inform them of the power and justice of the Government."[14] Instead, they returned as heroes who lorded it over their fellows until Uluksuk finally was murdered (1925). Sinnisiak, on the other hand, was later employed as guide and interpreter by the RCMP at Tree River. The perpetrators of the Bathurst Inlet murders were released from custody without trial, as having been provoked by the deceased and acted in what they considered to be self-defence.

The hoped-for remission from further acts of violence did not follow. Instead, police patrols were needed in 1920, 1921, and 1922 to investigate homicides of white men and of Inuit by other Inuit coveting their women. The unlucky trader Janes fell out with his clients in 1920; abandoning his post, he fled for safety toward Chesterfield Inlet, only to be pursued and killed. Worse still occurred near Tree River, where one Inuk was murdered by another named Tatamigana who desired his woman, abetted by the young and possibly mentally deficient Alikomiak. Then, when the two men were arrested and brought to the post, they murdered the unsuspecting Hudson's Bay trader Otto Binder and RCMP Corporal W.A. Doak. By 1922, as a result of these and other episodes, nine Inuit were in custody at Pond Inlet, Tree River, and Herschel Island for complicity in the murders of ten Inuit and the three white men. Drastic action clearly was needed to uphold the law and bring order and authority to this newest, most primitive of Canada's frontiers.

The Arctic Archipelago also aroused concern in the Canadian government because Canada's sovereignty over some of the northern and western islands discovered by Norwegians and Americans prior to 1905 still remained in question. That uncertainty was underscored by the four-year (1913–17) Greenland-based expedition of D.B. MacMillan, a teacher at Bowdoin College in Maine who had been with Peary on his last expedition and regarded himself as Peary's successor.

The MacMillan Expedition spent most of its time exploring the northern parts of Ellesmere, Axel Heiberg, and other islands of the Sverdrup Group. When MacMillan returned from Greenland after his unauthorized exploration in the Canadian Arctic on July 29, 1917, he had challenged Canada's sovereignty, ignored its game laws, and made no effort to account for the mysterious deaths of an Inuk and a white member of his party.

Greater concern was felt, however, over the activities of a Greenlander, Knud Rasmussen of Thule Station near Cape York. Reacting to the large-scale killing of muskoxen by the Peary, MacMillan, and other expeditions, the Advisory Board on Wildlife Protection first had a closed season proclaimed on hunting muskoxen throughout the archipelago, then proceeded to try to halt hunting by Greenland Inuit on Ellesmere Island. Having advised Rasmussen of the new regulation, the government received a letter in 1919 stating that Rasmussen was willing to try to wean his people from the practice by importing reindeer hides for their needs but rejecting Canada's offer to station officers on Greenland to achieve the objective. His reply, though no doubt meant to be conciliatory, contained a statement the Canadian authorities found unacceptable: "It is well known that the territory of the Polar Eskimo falls within the region designated as 'No Man's Land', and there is therefore no authority in the district except that which I exercise through my station."[15] Worse still, the covering letter of the Danish government stated: "Having acquainted themselves with the statement in question my Government think that they can subscribe to what Mr. Rasmussen says therein."[16]

The Canadian government grew progressively uneasier when Denmark made no reply to their letter protesting the implication that Ellesmere was a "No Man's Land" and when Stefansson reported that Rasmussen had informed him "there is no question of our breaking Canadian Game Laws because we are not coming into Canada but a part farther north. It is not under Canadian jurisdiction."[17] Moreover, Captain G. Hansen, acting on Rasmussen's behalf, ranged across Ellesmere Island during the winter of 1919–20 on a commission from the Norwegian government but without so much as a by-your-leave from the Canadian government, depositing supplies at predetermined points in connection with a proposed transpolar sledge journey of Roald Amundsen. The Canadian government's suspicions were rekindled early in 1921 when it learned Rasmussen was preparing an expedition to study the Central Arctic Inuit of Baffin Island and Hudson Bay; in this plan it detected once again evidence of his "disposition to question our sovereignty over Arctic Islands, particularly in respect to Ellesmere Land."[18]

The government's interest in the Arctic sovereignty question was

heightened by the dynamic, ambitious, self-assured, incredibly energetic Vilhjalmur Stefansson, who made frequent visits to Ottawa to
persuade or cajole civil servants, parliamentarians, cabinet ministers,
and three successive prime ministers into adopting a vigorous role in
the Arctic. His message, based on experience, reading, reflection, and
a fertile imagination, was strengthened by an onerous schedule of
lecturing, correspondence, and writing – notably three books that
appeared in swift succession, *The Friendly Arctic, Hunters of the Great
North,* and *The Northward Course of Empire.* This last volume was
strongly appealing to a nation and government looking for appropriate
tasks to engage the energies of its victorious sons. The Arctic lands and
waters were the frontiers of Canada's future, a region destined to be
exploited as its resources became better known and as more southerly
regions were occupied. The Arctic Ocean then would come into its
own as a Polar Mediterranean, bordered by major countries across
which lay the shortest distances between great cities. Its skies would
be traversed by aircraft, its waters by cargo-carrying submarines. Arctic lands would gain undreamed-of importance, and nations would be
envied for their good fortune in possessing them. Canada should hasten to affirm its authority over all the territories it claimed and add to
them by further explorations.

While he lobbied behind the scenes in Ottawa, Stefansson gained a
public forum for one of his more practical theories – the development
of a ranching industry in tundra lands. He considered the muskox far
more suitable than the reindeer, since a single animal furnished twice
as much meat or milk as a reindeer in addition to excellent wool; the
muskox was also hardier and better adapted to thrive in an Arctic environment and was apparently far easier to manage and domesticate. But
the public and the government were dazzled by the potentialities of
the reindeer-herding industry, which was enjoying highly publicized
success in Alaska. There, 171 animals introduced from Siberia by Dr.
Sheldon Jackson in 1892 had multiplied into nearly one hundred herds
totalling 100,000 reindeer by 1918, and reindeer meat was being
shipped to Seattle and other West Coast cities. In July 1918 the Department of the Interior leased out a huge tract in Northern Manitoba and
the District of Keewatin (75,850 square miles) for three years for a similar Canadian experiment. Arthur Meighen, the Minister of the Interior,
arranged for Stefansson to address members of the Senate and House
of Commons on the subject, then secured a royal commission to investigate the possibilities of establishing reindeer and muskox herding in
Arctic and Subarctic Canada. Stefansson was one of the four appointed
commissioners but resigned almost before the commission got under
way in order to put his ideas into practice. With the backing of the

Hudson's Bay Company he secured from the Department of the Interior a thirty-year lease of Baffin Island south of 68° N (113,900 square miles) on which one thousand reindeer were to be located by 1924 and ten thousand by 1932. A new company was chartered for the purpose, the Hudson's Bay Company supplying the capital and Stefansson direction of the enterprise through his associate Storkerson as manager.

Stefansson also presented very highly regarded testimony in the spring of 1920 before the Special Senate Committee Appointed to Report on the Navigability and Fishing Resources of Hudson Bay and Strait. In its final report on June 9, 1920, that committee could not "too strongly endorse" his suggestion "as to the cultivation of the Reindeer and the Musk Ox," and undertook to lecture the government on Stefansson's services to Canada: "The Committee ventures the hope that the Canadian Government will not be unmindful of the great services performed by Mr. Stefansson, whose reward so far has not been commensurate with the national importance of the work he has accomplished."[19]

The chairman, Senator G.W. Fowler, pleaded with Sir Robert Borden on Stefansson's behalf, and Borden, in turn, took the matter up with Meighen, the new prime minister, who eventually had an order in council promulgated tendering the thanks of the government of Canada and formally honouring Stefansson "in recognition and appreciation of his distinguished services." Besides praising his contributions to exploration and to science, the minute also referred to his role in publicizing the Arctic:

> By developing a method new in arctic exploration, the method of living on the country by forage, he has called strikingly to the attention of the world the fact that the north is not so barren, nor its climate so hostile to comfort, as had previously been regarded as true. He has thus foreshadowed an important extension of the boundaries of human habitation. In his writings and speeches he has been assiduous in calling to our attention the great natural resources of the north that we had previously undervalued. He has turned men's minds towards the north country as a possible source of food supply and a home for colonists, and his work and advice have proved the greatest incentive in promoting public and private development of our northern resources.[20]

Thus Stefansson gained the official recognition he craved. The next three months saw him attain the height of his influence with government and also begin a precipitous fall from its favour.

His loss of influence arose in part from continuing rancour against him among certain civil servants over the Canadian Arctic Expedition, kept alive by controversies over that expedition's reports.[21] Stefansson had complained to Prime Minister Borden during a luncheon on July 10, 1919, that he was not being accorded the supervising authority over the publication of the reports of the expedition to which he was entitled as its commander. He said the Geological Survey's decision that expedition scientists should describe only what each had personally collected or done perversely restricted the reporting to the accomplishments of the Southern Party. Stefansson felt he had won his point when he left Ottawa, but the original plan continued to be followed, and R.M. Anderson, his former second-in-command but now his implacable enemy, remained in charge of the project. In fact, the Canadian Arctic Expedition, for one reason or another, never did receive the full, complete report it merited despite the heroic efforts of Diamond Jenness and some of the other contributors who carried the work on into the 1940s. Stefansson, annoyed by the delays and concerned that the work of his own Northern Party would pass almost unnoticed if Anderson and his colleagues had their way, went ahead and filled the gap with one of the best books to come out of Arctic exploration – *The Friendly Arctic*, published in 1921. That book, whose provocative, misleading title Stefansson attributed to Gilbert Grosvenor of the National Geographic Society, was more than a definitive account of the Northern Party's work; it was replete with the author's scientific theories and his versions of the controversial episodes of the expedition. Its publication only fanned the animosity against Stefansson within the civil service, which continued to smoulder until the deaths of Anderson in 1961 and Stefansson in 1962.

Mainly, however, Stefansson's fall from grace resulted from his ambitious plan to persuade or coerce the Canadian government into actively affirming and extending its authority over the Arctic lands it claimed and enlarging those claims by further explorations and acts of occupation. His own efforts, directed at the top levels of the federal civil service and Cabinet, were pushed with unprecedented vigour and ultimately to unacceptable limits. As early as 1915 and 1916 he had written to Sir Robert Borden pleading for support for the work of discovering new lands for Canada "by Canadians in the service of the Government."[22] Later, on October 2, 1920, while in Ottawa, he enlarged on his plan: Canada should set up a revenue cutter service to carry government agents as far north as possible each year and establish police posts on islands where Canada's claims needed strengthening. It should also undertake a vigorous program of mapping and economic surveying on the northern islands, search for others still undiscovered, and encourage private enterprise to develop their resources. Scientists and hardy young men skilled in Arctic journeying should be recruited to live off the country as he had done, operating from fixed bases and covering the area within a 300- or 400-mile radius, then moving on to new bases. In this fashion, he estimated, the unexplored ocean north of Canada could be completely investigated within a five-year period and at a cost of below $500,000. Still later, on January 8, 1921, he proposed to lead an expedition to establish police posts from which parties could explore the surrounding districts during the winters. As he had done with the Canadian Arctic Expedition, he offered his services gratis at considerable personal sacrifice, since he would have to cancel a lucrative thirty-five-week lecture series contract for 1921–22.

At the same time Stefansson was trying to involve the government further in his personal project of claiming and occupying Wrangel Island, the forbidding island north of Siberia that some of his party had reached after the *Karluk* disaster and that two of them had sanctified with their lives. Stefansson, apparently misled by the report of one survivor, depicted the island as possessing rich food resources, possibly valuable minerals, and a very strategic location in relation to future world travel patterns. He suggested the Canadian government should follow two courses of action simultaneously. Along the eastern fringe of the Arctic Archipelago it should assert its claims to Ellesmere and other islands against other powers openly and decisively, while in the west it should pursue its interests stealthily by supporting "exploration by a scientific expedition," and "encouraging the quiet, unostentatious settlement of Wrangel Island by a Canadian development company" as "a basis for a subsequent assertion of Canadian title to the island."[23]

The government, confronted with challenges on the eastern margin and the supposed opportunity on the west, referred the matter to the newly appointed Advisory Technical Board on Canadian Sovereignty, comprised of a group of civil servants concerned with northern matters. The board, which devoted its first meeting to the Wrangel Island question, threw cold water on any involvement there. Sir Joseph Pope termed it "essentially . . . an Asiatic island"[24] and no concern of Canada's, while the board reported:

It was generally considered that any pretensions we might have to this island must be of a very unsubstantial character, and could only result in weakening our legitimate claims to the Arctic islands contiguous to our own territory, for if we can go so far afield as Wrangel to take possession of islands, unconnected with Canada, what is there to prevent the United States or any other power, laying claim to islands far from their shores but adjacent to our own?[25]

By the end of 1920 the board had decided that the best procedure lay in "quietly but effectively establishing its sovereignty" along the eastern flank by opening a string of police posts to "close up what might be called the front door of the Arctic Archipelago."[26] This should be done during the 1921 shipping season, and the veteran government ship *Arctic* should be outfitted for duty and returned to service. In the meantime, if any emergency arose, an airship could be summoned from Britain from which men and supplies could be parachuted onto Ellesmere Island.

While these plans were proceeding Stefansson was pushing ahead with his own campaign to have Canada acquire Wrangel Island. First he approached the Hudson's Bay Company with a suggestion that it would be desirable for the company to establish a trading post there. Then he advised Prime Minister Meighen that the company wished to open a post on the island but needed some indication of support from the Canadian government. Meighen put the matter before the Cabinet on February 19, 1921, then dashed off the following note to the waiting Stefansson:

> I have discussed the matters which you laid before me today and desire to advise you that this Government purposes to assert the right of Canada to Wrangel Island based upon the discoveries and explorations of your expedition.
>
> I believe this is all that is necessary for your purposes now.[27]

Stefansson hastened to inform the Hudson's Bay Company that the Canadian government supported the company's plans for Wrangel Island "and would look with the greatest favour" on its going ahead since "their plans for making secure the claim of Canada to island would be materially helped if a British concern were to start a post there in the summer of 1921."[28]

Unfortunately for Stefansson the government quickly had second thoughts. Faced with strenuous objections from Pope and his colleagues, Meighen abruptly withdrew his endorsement on March 1, after just ten days – "The Prime Minister asks that pending further advice you make no use of his letter to you of February 19th about Wrangel Island."[29] The project seemed lost, but Stefansson remained undaunted and continued to make plans to have the island occupied by a private Canadian expedition in the hope of compelling the government to support a *fait accompli*. He organized a small expedition of three American protégés and a young University of Toronto undergraduate, Allan Crawford, to occupy the island in 1921. Despite his inexperience, Crawford was named commander to sustain the fiction of Canada's involvement, the flag was immediately hoisted over Wrangel Island, and Stefansson tried unsuccessfully to manipulate the federal government into resupplying the expedition on humanitarian grounds. The ship he himself sent out in 1922 failed to reach the island, and the resupply ship for 1923 found that the men had perished.

A second party of fourteen Americans was landed on the island while Stefansson attempted to persuade either the British or the United States government to appropriate Wrangel Island. He eventually transferred his own interests in the island to a wealthy Alaskan businessman. The USSR, alarmed by the interest of these powers in territory it considered its own, protested the unauthorized occupation and sent an icebreaker in 1925 that seized the Americans as intruders and deposited them in a Siberian prison from which they eventually made their way home to Alaska. It followed this action on April 15, 1926, by proclaiming its sovereignty over all lands inside the sector formed by extending its easternmost and westernmost boundaries northward to the North Pole, in keeping with the Polar Sector Principle first suggested by Senator Poirier in 1907. The Wrangel Island fiasco of 1921–24 completed the ruin of Stefansson's influence with Canadian governments and turned an important segment of the Canadian public against him, too.

In the meantime the urgency for maintaining Canada's authority along the eastern flank of the Arctic had been eased in 1921 by the successful outcome of negotiations with Denmark respecting Rasmussen's proposed Arctic expedition on Canadian territory. The Colonial Secretary reported that Rasmussen had been given Danish government support for a purely scientific enterprise to conduct a study of the Inuit and their culture in the Fury and Hecla Strait district of Foxe Basin and collect pertinent ethnological data and artifacts over a three-year period. The Canadian government was reassured that Denmark was a reliable friend to the British Empire and that Canada need have no fear of its sovereignty being challenged from that quarter. No airborne occupation of Ellesmere Island would be needed after all. A further telegram from London helped persuade the Canadian government and induced it to extend its full co-operation:

> My telegram 8th June Rasmussen, Danish Minister has submitted memorandum containing definite guarantee by Government of Denmark that expedition has no political or mercantile aims but is of entirely scientific character and that no acquisition of territory whatsoever is contemplated in regions in question. He adds that expedition leaves Copenhagen for Greenland June 16th and asks that consent of Canadian Government may be given to landing and further progress of expedition.[30]

Following approval from the relieved Canadian government, Rasmussen could go ahead with a valuable many-sided study of Canadian

Inuit bands that ranged as far south as Churchill and along the Arctic coastline west to Alaska.

Meanwhile, the Eastern Arctic Patrol voyage first considered in 1920 underwent still further changes early in 1921 following the sudden appearance in Canada of Sir Ernest Shackleton, the noted Antarctic explorer, with a highly attractive proposal for executing the government's plan at considerably less cost than refitting and sending the *Arctic* would have entailed. Stefansson was highly incensed by this new competitor, feeling Shackleton had stolen the idea from him when they met in London in April 1920. (Shackleton, however, seems to have discussed a plan of working in the Canadian Arctic with the council of the Royal Geographical Society in February 1920.) The Canadian government at first demurred at Shackleton's approach, perhaps out of sympathy with Stefansson's claims or from fear of his reaction if he were cast aside. But Shackleton proceeded with his plan by negotiating with Canadian officials, raised a $250,000 fund, and outfitted his recently purchased wooden auxiliary-powered 204-ton Norwegian whaling ship. His submission to the government included a *curriculum vitae* crammed with awards and full details of his meritorious service in the South African and Great wars. With his rival in mind, perhaps, Shackleton asserted he had never lost a man under his direct command and proposed to insure his expedition with Lloyd's of London so that come what might, it would not have to be rescued at public expense. He suggested a staff of fifteen officers, nine of them from his own teams and six recruited from the Canadian universities, plus a few "French-Canadian and North-West dog-drivers."[31] While in Ottawa he also agreed to transport the gear for one police post in return for a grant-in-aid for his expedition and to resupply the post in the following year, eliminating the need to send the *Arctic* altogether. The offers tipped the balance; just two months after the order in council in praise of Stefansson and one month after the débâcle over Wrangel Island, the government accepted Shackleton's proposal and halted the refit of the *Arctic*. Stefansson was left perforce to carry on with his strenuous lecturing and writing schedule and overseeing his Baffin Island reindeer and Wrangel Island occupation enterprises.

Then, suddenly, Shackleton reported from London that he could not perform the proposed operation without chartering an additional ship to carry all the supplies the police deemed necessary for their Arctic station, and he proposed three alternative courses of action. The change of plan apparently was the straw that broke the camel's back; Meighen refused to listen to any new proposals and savagely rejected any further overtures: "Our arrangements now do not admit of assistance your expedition this year," (May 9) and "Cannot give any definite promise for next year," (May 16) were his chilling replies to Shackleton.[32] To put his ship and men to work, the despairing Shackleton was forced to improvise an ambitious Antarctic oceanographic expedition for the coming winter, for which a single British patron subscribed the cost. That expedition sailed from London on September 17, and crowds lined the banks of the Thames to view the departure of what was to be Shackleton's last voyage. For just after *Quest* entered Grytviken harbour in South Georgia, Shackleton suffered a heart attack and died in the ship's cabin on January 5, 1922, to be laid to rest in that lonely place so far from home.

Meighen's decision not to negotiate with Shackleton, perhaps because of the now gloomy economic situation and the amounts already spent on the *Arctic*, came too late for a government expedition to go north during the 1921 season. The *Arctic* simply could not be made ready in time, and the expedition to uphold Canada's Arctic sovereignty would have to wait until 1922. By then changes in command had occurred; the Nova Scotian Captain H.C. Pickles, whom the Meighen government had designated to command the *Arctic*, had died, and the sponsoring administration had also expired in the interim. Instead, the *Arctic* sailed on its mission in 1922 under the auspices of the newly elected Mackenzie King government and under its former skipper, the bluff, venerable Captain J.E. Bernier, who had kept his interest in the Arctic alive since 1911 by a variety of mining, herding, and publishing activities and plans. The tangled, confused, shifting character of Canada's Arctic policy in the early post-war years pointedly demonstrated the vital need for a permanent federal government agency that would give continuous study to, and advice on, northern matters and prevent any repetition of the hasty, uninformed actions of the winter of 1920–21.

III

While the fate of the Eastern Arctic Patrol was being settled, five senior civil servants representing the federal Departments of the Interior and of Mines and the RCMP met on Thursday, April 28, 1921, in Ottawa to hold the first session of a Northwest Territories legislature in over fifteen years. This Council of the Northwest Territories was the direct successor of the appointed council that had first met in 1877 and afterwards evolved into a territorial assembly and two provincial legislatures. What lay behind the resurrection of this moribund institution? What did its revival signify?

When Saskatchewan and Alberta were carved out of the settled parts of the original Northwest Territories lying south of the 60th parallel, the question of providing a government for those parts north of the new provinces and the areas awarded in 1912 to Manitoba, Ontario, and Quebec was left in limbo. By an act of 1905 the functions of the former territorial legislature were transferred to a commissioner who was responsible to the Minister of the Interior, assisted by an appointed four-man council, and Ottawa was named the seat of government. Lieutenant-Colonel Frederick White, the comptroller of the RNWMP until his retirement in 1912, was appointed commissioner and was retained in the position until his death in 1918, since the duties were negligible. No council was appointed, no new ordinances were promulgated, and after White's death the position was simply reabsorbed into the federal administration by the appointment of W.W. Cory, the deputy minister of the Department of the Interior, as commissioner in 1919.

The most immediate force behind the decision to activate the council was the recently awakened hope that the mineral resources of the District of Mackenzie would provide some spectacular discovery that could touch off a repetition of the rush to the Klondike twenty-five years earlier. The end of the war had revived interest in the region, typified by the restaking in 1920 by J. Mackintosh Bell of the 1909 lead-zinc claims at Pine Point. In the main, however, it centred on the petroleum possibilities of the district hinted at by the samples T.O. Bosworth had brought out in 1914 from the vicinity of Fort Norman. Many petroleum and natural gas claims had been staked along the north shore of Great Slave Lake in 1914 and 1915, and the Geological Survey had investigated and mapped the area surrounding the western arm of the lake in 1916 and 1917. The Northwest Company, a subsidiary of Imperial Oil, followed up the earlier find by sending in a drill rig in 1919 to a site selected by T.A. Link at Oil Creek, forty-five miles north of Fort Norman, where the crew spent the winter of 1919–20 preparing for an early start in the spring. They struck oil on August 24, 1920, when a flow strong enough to gush to the top of the mast was tapped at a 783-foot depth and flowed for forty minutes before the well was capped. Work was halted on September 20, and by mid-October Link had carried the news of the discovery outside.

The success was something of an embarrassment, for the program had been strictly exploratory and experimental. But Imperial's reminders that the find had no immediate commercial value and that production would have to await greatly improved transportation facilities were brushed aside as company propaganda. Rumours had the oil field extending to the Arctic Ocean and being perhaps the largest in the world. ''Nature may have provided along the Mackenzie Valley for a thousand miles or more in length a vast reservoir of oil, whose possibilities may eclipse any of the romances of modern discoveries," a Toronto *Globe* writer fantasized.[33] Such speculation inspired a small, highly publicized staking rush during the winter of 1920–21, first by trappers and traders of the district, then by experienced wintertime travellers from outside. The winter also brought grandiose transportation plans, some based on the new-found capabilities of the airplane and airship, and ambitious projects of building railways from Hudson Bay across the Barren Lands to the site of the oil discovery. More modest ones would merely span the Slave River portage above Fort Smith, the main bottleneck of the water route from Alberta to the District of Mackenzie. In the meantime the federal government, Imperial Oil, and other private interests made preparations for the coming onslaught in the summer of 1921.

The most noteworthy innovative response to the transport problem was one undertaken by Imperial Oil. Aviation had been in the experimental stage before 1914, but under the impetus of the Great War the airplane had been greatly improved in effectiveness. As early as February 1919 the possible use of aircraft in the North had been described in the House of Commons, and Parliament in May 1919 had passed the Air Board Act to regulate the industry and place it under national control. The Canadian Air Board was empowered to build and operate all governmental air services, stations, and aircraft; license pilots, airplanes, and airports; regulate commercial air services; and generally supervise all aspects of the new industry. From the start, it aimed to develop facilities and aircraft appropriate for working in unsettled, unimproved parts of Canada. Experimental flights quickly demonstrated the immense value of airplanes for topographical and geological surveys, forestry patrolling and fire prevention work, and transport services. But the limitations of operating in unsettled districts were revealed by other attempts. For example, a United States Air Force flight by four De Havilland biplanes from New York to Nome, Alaska, required 112 flying hours that extended over six weeks (July 15–August 23, 1920) because of inclement weather and accidents.

Imperial Oil's experiment exemplified these difficulties. The company had acquired two Junkers monoplanes to make possible an early start of work at the new oil discovery. In late March 1921 the planes flew north in relays from Peace River toward Fort Norman, stopping to refuel at various points. One smashed its skis and propeller during a landing at Fort Simpson while the other was damaged when it hit thick snowdrifts during a takeoff, leaving both planes immobilized at that isolated post. An ingenious carpenter at the fort with incredible patience and skill used oak sledge boards to carve two wooden propellers that enabled the planes to resume their flights. By that time, spring was at hand and the Mackenzie River was breaking up, so the experiment no longer was required; instead, the company's men and supplies proceeded to their destination by river transport and the planes were returned to Peace River. The experiment demonstrated the ingenuity of the pilots, air mechanics, and craftsmen and the imaginativeness of the oil company. But it also graphically underlined the tremendous difficulties aviation in the North faced at this time from lack of accurate maps, weather reports, proper landing and repair facilities, parts and radio communications, to say nothing of deficiencies in the aircraft themselves. Still, all these were quickly being overcome, and within a decade improved planes would routinely make both hundred-mile flights between posts and thousand-mile journeys and Canada's northlands would be laid open to investigation, travel, and development as never before.

To help plan the 1921 exploration and developmental activities and oversee future development in the Northwest Territories, the Department of the Interior was reorganized, effective April 1, 1921, by the formation of a new agency, the Northwest Territories Branch: "All indications pointed to an oil stampede into the Mackenzie district on the opening of navigation in 1921, and it was deemed advisable to establish the Northwest Territories Branch in Ottawa for the purpose of administering the natural resources and transacting departmental business pertaining to those territories."[34] That departmental business, according to the subsequent annual report of the Auditor-General for 1921–22, included mainly administration of the District of Mackenzie in the field, exploration (chiefly refit of the *Arctic*, with more to come in 1922–23), plus the usual small outlays on school subsidies ($1,500) and relief ($7,040) on behalf of non-Indian persons.

On April 20, 1921, the four-member council provided for by the act of 1905 was finally appointed by order in council: R.A. Gibson, assistant deputy minister of the Department of the Interior, J.W. Greenway, commissioner of Crown lands in the same department, Charles Camsell, deputy minister of the Department of Mines, and Colonel A.B. Perry, the veteran commissioner of the newly reorganized RCMP. The first session of the council, eight days later, took charge of the department's program, which included the movement of settlers into the area, arranging for a permanent administration under its control within the District of Mackenzie, and considering new ordinances for proper governance of the region. One new ordinance, indeed, already had been published under the authority of the federal government by simple order in council to deal with the anticipated rush – the Entry Ordinance of March 18, 1921:

> No person shall enter, or attempt to enter, the Provisional District of Mackenzie, Northwest Territories, without first having satisfied the officer or non-commissioned officer in charge of the Royal Canadian Mounted Police at one of the following places, namely, Edmonton, Peace River, or Fitzgerald in the Province of Alberta, Whitehorse, Dawson, or Herschel in the Yukon Territory, or MacPherson in the Provisional District of Mackenzie, that he is not likely to become a public charge while in the Territories.[35]

Following the swearing in of the councillors the council set to work. The validity of the Entry Ordinance was questioned in view of its non-parliamentary, non-council origin. Reports were received on the organization of the Northwest Territories Branch and the proposed expansion in the field, banking arrangements were announced, and notaries public were appointed. Plans were made to revise the entire corpus of ordinances inherited from the pre-1905 territorial legislature and to receive authority to enact new ordinances to license and regulate businesses, trades, and callings in the Northwest Territories. A recommendation was made to enlarge the council to six members, one of them to be deputy commissioner. By a subsequent order in council of June 16, 1921, R.A. Gibson was promoted to the new position, and two more officials of the Department of the Interior were added to the membership – H.H. Rowatt, superintendent of the Mining Land and Yukon Branch, and O.S. Finnie, chief mining inspector. And so, at last, a distinct administration and legislature had come into being for the Northwest Territories.

In keeping with the announced field program, a staff of twenty-five, headed by Finnie, was sent to Forth Smith, the designated administrative centre, with some thirty tons of records, furnishings, and supplies. The crush on the main access route via Fort McMurray was so great that the Hudson's Bay Company's fleet was said to have rejected 1,200 tons of freight even before the season opened. The government party, as well as three Geological Survey parties, therefore travelled by rail to Peace River and then proceeded north by river, the surveyors in a scow, the Northwest Territories administrative party by the Lamson-Hubbard Company's steamers and portage transport service. One adventurous Topographical Survey party even journeyed up the Peace to Fort St. John, then travelled cross-country 150 miles to the Fort Nelson and Liard rivers to avoid being delayed by the ice on Great Slave Lake in reaching its work site. That plan was so successful that other survey parties adopted the same route in 1922, as did fur traders.

Arriving at Fort Smith, Finnie's party found the portable sawmills of the Fort Smith and Fort Simpson Indian agencies waiting for them, but not the logs or lumber that were to have been prepared for their use. The Indian agent had been unable to procure labour for these tasks because of the boom conditions. So the entire party set to work building and furnishing the headquarters, and then after the ice left Great Slave Lake (around July 1) various officers proceeded to their inspections of the more northerly settlements and the oil industry. When Hawthorne Daniel, an American journalist, visited Fort Smith in June, he found the administration under "Governor Finney" occupying a double row of tents. The Crown Lands and Timber Office was under construction. The Mining Recording Office, which was moved from Edmonton, opened for business at Fort Smith on Dominion Day under Major L.T. Burwash, a former mining officer in the Yukon; a little later sub-recording offices followed at Forts Resolution and Norman. The Administration Building was ready by August 15, 1921, after which work continued on the living quarters, stable, and other buildings.

All the while settlers, prospectors, and tourists were being dealt with and timber regulations were drafted and put in effect. The settlements along the waterway were inspected, and one or two lots were reserved for government purposes at each. Hospitals and residential schools also were inspected, and the annual liquor applications were processed. The staff also administered the Northwest Game Act (for the present on behalf of the Dominion Parks Branch), the experimental farming operations of the local Indian agency, and the future Wood Buffalo Park. At outside points the administration was represented by notaries public, who were mostly government officials but included a few leading residents, fur trade officers in particular. The inspections yielded a rough census of the major settlements along the waterway: 3,838 Indians and 650 others.

Other federal agencies were also active, studying the waterway from a navigational standpoint, starting a topographical survey of the Mackenzie River from its source in Great Slave Lake and mapping the geology down to Fort Wrigley, including also the new oilfield. The RCMP checked twenty-four parties that made winter journeys to Fort Norman and the summer travellers along the waterway. That same summer the police accompanied H.A. Conroy, who had been commissioned to negotiate a treaty with the Indian bands along the Mackenzie River north of Treaty No. 8 of 1899. Conroy, who administered that earlier treaty, had often advocated extending it northward and on occasion had visited as far north as Fort Simpson. But though the Indian Affairs Branch provided relief assistance, school grants, and even for some years stationed an agent and farm instructor at Fort Simpson, it had seen no need for a treaty of surrender. Now, in view of the anticipated change in the region's future, that important step finally was taken. During the summer Conroy met with the Indians at seven major centres along the waterway between Fort Providence and Fort McPherson and at Fort Rae. All told, 1,934 persons – seven chiefs, twelve headmen, and 1,915 other Indians – joined Treaty No. 11.

Under the treaty, as published, the Indians agreed to "cede, release, surrender and yield up to the Government of the Dominion of Canada, for His Majesty the King and His Successors forever, all their rights, titles and privileges whatsoever to the lands included within the following limits." Its terms included promises of reserves for each band on the basis of 640 acres for a family of five, per capita annuities of five dollars (with a larger initial payment on signing the treaty), small annual grants for twine, ammunition, and other hunting, fishing, and trapping equipment, tools for "a band that selects a reserve," assistance to Indians who wished to follow agricultural pursuits "as is deemed necessary for that purpose," and payment of the salaries of teachers to instruct their children "in such manner as His Majesty's Government may deem advisable." It acknowledged the right of the Indians

> . . . to pursue their usual vocations of hunting, trapping and fishing throughout the tract surrendered as heretofore described, subject to such regulations as may from time to time be made by the Government of the Country acting under the authority of His Majesty, and saving and excepting such tracts as may be required or taken up from time to time for settlement, mining, lumbering, trading or other purposes.

For their part, the Indians agreed to observe the treaty, respect and abide by the laws, keep the peace towards all subjects "now inhabiting and hereafter to inhabit any part of the said ceded territory," to refrain from molesting or interfering with travellers, and to assist in bringing any Indian violators of the treaty or the laws to justice.[36]

As published, Treaty No. 11 carried the marks of the chiefs or headmen of the eight communities visited, the signatures of Conroy and Inspector W.V. Bruce, RCMP, at all eight points, of Bishop Gabriel Breynat at seven of them, and of others – usually Hudson's Bay Company officers – at several posts. In the statement that accompanied the treaty Conroy reported reassuring the bands that their freedom to hunt, trap, or fish would not be curtailed and that "the Government will expect them to support themselves in their own way," that any game laws imposed were for their benefit, and that "whether they took treaty or not, they were subject to the laws of the Dominion." He assured them that signing the treaty did not make them liable for military service or confine them on their reserves – rather that "the reserves mentioned in the treaty would be of their own choosing, for their own use, and not for the white people, and that they would be free to come and go as they pleased."[37]

But for all these efforts, only 360 oil and gas claims were staked and only four drilling outfits were imported in 1921, three by Imperial and the fourth by the Fort Norman Oil Company of Toronto. That company had brought only 1,500 feet of well casing, which was completely used up on a site eight miles south of the discovery well without finding oil. Imperial's well at Windy Point on Great Slave Lake was abandoned as a dry hole at 1,806 feet, and two additional wells drilled near the discovery well to depths of 2,080 and 3,057 feet were likewise unsuccessful – demonstrating how small an area the original oilfield occupied. As a further blow, the flow from the discovery well – reported as 100 barrels a day – was slowed to a trickle by a cave-in. Such were the disappointing results of Imperial's program in 1921. By the end of the season most of the company and government employees had departed, and the summer of 1922 brought only one new oil company to the region. That company selected a location sixteen miles up Hay River and drilled a well that encountered salt water at 712 feet and was abandoned.

In fact, commentators concluded in 1921 that the boom had been grossly exaggerated and that the government had over-reacted on very slim evidence indeed. Hawthorne Daniel noted that no more than seventy-five of the original claims had been staked by outsiders and entitled his article on the season "The Canadian Oil Rush Limited."[38] J. Ness described the rush at the annual meeting of the Natural Gas and Petroleum Association of Canada as "almost wholly a newspaper boom" made glamorous only because of the inaccessibility of the site and attributed its collapse to the stakers' inability to sell their claims at inflated prices to reputable oil companies.[39] Apart from the small continuing activity of Imperial Oil in the vicinity of the discovery, the District of Mackenzie appeared to relapse into preoccupation with the fur trade. The Entry Ordinance was cancelled at the end of the season, because of its doubtful legal validity and because it was no longer needed.

Indeed, the creation of a separate administration for the Northwest Territories in Ottawa and in the North in 1921 would seem a ludicrously inappropriate reaction to an ephemeral situation if it had been based solely on the boom inspired by the Imperial Oil discovery. But it was a response, besides, to such long-standing goals as protecting the native inhabitants and the wildlife resources, upholding and extending Canada's Arctic sovereignty, providing a more effective government for the region, and above all, establishing a permanent, informed basis for administering a developing region in keeping with territorial and national interests. Hence, though the oil-boom bubble was quickly pricked, the innovations of 1921 remained in being and were increased in ensuing years. Fort Smith was retained as the regional capital headed by a District Agent, Treaty No. 11 was extended to the remaining Indians of the District of Mackenzie, while the RCMP and other branches of government gradually expanded their activities in the settlements along the Mackenzie waterway, the tiny trading posts hugging the shores of Hudson Bay and the mainland coasts, and the remote, wind-swept Arctic islands.

In Ottawa the arrangements made in 1921 were consolidated and enlarged by further legislation, notably an act of 1922 that empowered the federal government to make ordinances for the peace, order, and good government of the Northwest Territories. In turn, an order in council of May 4, 1922, issued under this act authorized the Northwest Territories Council to pass, and the branch to administer, ordinances within the same range of jurisdiction as the legislature of the North-west Territories had enjoyed in 1905. Administration of the Northwest Game Act was transferred from the Dominion Parks Branch to the Northwest Territories Branch in 1922, of which O.S. Finnie was appointed director. Then in 1923 it received the added responsibility of overseeing the affairs of the Yukon Territory and was renamed Northwest Territories and Yukon Branch accordingly. Whatever the government's motives, a separate, distinctive legislative and admin-istrative structure had been created for Canada's northlands, one with the capacity both for directing and co-ordinating the administration of that vast region from Ottawa and for evolving into the present legis-lative assembly of the Northwest Territories.

The activities of the new branch, however, were strictly restrained as a consequence of the federal general election of December 1921. Prime Minister Meighen, burdened by the liabilities of the war and early post-war years, unrepentantly sought approval for a powerful centralist, interventionist, *dirigiste* style of government that tried to manage the national economy in peace, as in war, in the interests of the nation rather than those of occupational or regional groups. But the public considered Meighen's past rule entirely unacceptable, and a large section of it demanded an end to federal government encroach-ments in spheres that traditionally belonged to the private sector or constitutionally to the provinces. The attitude that had swept the Republicans into office in the United States was espoused in Canada by the revived Liberal party, led since 1919 by W.L. Mackenzie King. With a narrow Liberal victory at the polls there departed much of the visionary, northward-expansionist quality that had so strikingly characterized the first two decades of the twentieth century. The concept of a strong federal government that might put national concerns such as northern development ahead of the politics of consensus vanished, and the nation settled down under Mackenzie King to apply the enhanced powers of the post-war state to the tasks of satisfying the concerns of the south-living, southward-looking electorate.

CHAPTER 2

Agricultural Frontiers of the Middle North, 1918–1940

I

That farming should be extended as far as natural and economic conditions permitted was an article of faith during the twenties for those Canadians who looked back to the pre-war prosperity and concluded that high rates of immigration and frontier settlement were the sure recipe for national success and greatness. Railway companies regarded immigrant settlers as customers for their lands and revenue for their transport services. Immigration and colonization companies, including the Hudson's Bay Company, which had received lands in the Peace River district under a recent arrangement, hoped to sell land to these newcomers, while religious and ethnic organizations were eager to resettle their fellows in Canada. Manufacturing, commercial, and financial interests saw immigrants and their farms as customers and markets, clients and patrons. Governments, too, welcomed additional settlers as a means to improve the prospects of the developing regions and communities, enhance their own records, and contribute to a rising tide of prosperity that would redound to their credit and be rewarded by political success.

A central attraction for intending immigrants, the one governments stressed above all, was the opportunity of becoming proprietors of larger, better farms than they worked in their homelands. Traditional "free" homesteads drew scores of thousands of land-poor British, European, and Canadian farmers to the homesteading districts. Many from Eastern Europe wished besides to leave behind religious discrimination, economic and social ostracism, repressive regimes, and incipient or actual persecution. New settlers looked to becoming their own masters, bringing up their children in a peaceful, healthful environment and opening doors for them to advance according to their merits in a land that was comparatively free of hereditary or religious

31

privilege. For many, an added incentive was joining with fellows of similar religious, linguistic, and social backgrounds. Moreover, the attractiveness of settling in Canada was greatly enhanced after 1923 when the United States introduced its quota system for immigrants.

To attract settlers to the tasks of converting brush-covered lands into prosperous farms, the federal government relied especially on the well-publicized merits of the lands themselves. Tens of thousands of quarter-section (160-acre) lots of every imaginable description lay practically free for the taking in a farming empire that stretched 1,200 miles from Lake of the Woods to beyond Fort St. John: "You put up ten dollars ($10) with the government against that 160 acres, on which you must sleep six months of the year; and you must do this for three years . . . break fifteen acres, put up a shack, eat flapjacks."[1] To secure the patent an alien homesteader also had to become a British subject, which usually was a formality. The homestead's attractiveness was supplemented by the availability of adjoining land, which could be purchased, rented, or leased cheaply from the government or from private owners, or which war veterans or holders of half-breed scrips could have free. The settler was left virtually free to choose from among a bewildering diversity of locations:

> I know people have been crossing the Peace river and going as far north as Fort Vermilion almost 100 miles or perhaps more from a railway. . . . There is no doubt that this is a mistake, but they are doing it and what can you do about it? They are free people; they can do as they like. They have the spirit of adventure and if they are making a mistake, they will find it out in the future. But that is what they do, and no department of immigration will prevent their doing it. The same thing occurred on the prairies; when good land could be secured near a railway, you would find people going twenty or thirty miles away just to find the piece of land they wanted at that particular time. The same thing will happen again and you cannot prevent people from doing this.[2]

In the provinces that administered their own lands, intending settlers no longer were offered free homesteads but were required to purchase their lots, although on easy terms – at sixty cents an acre for 160-acre lots in Ontario, 100-acre in Quebec, payable in six annual instalments. To encourage farmers to develop their holdings Ontario introduced a variant in 1926 by restricting the initial lot to eighty acres, with a right to purchase a further eighty at fifty cents an acre when thirty-five acres of the original lot were under cultivation. The residence duties were more onerous in these provinces, taking the heavier tasks of clearing, draining, and improving the lands into account. In

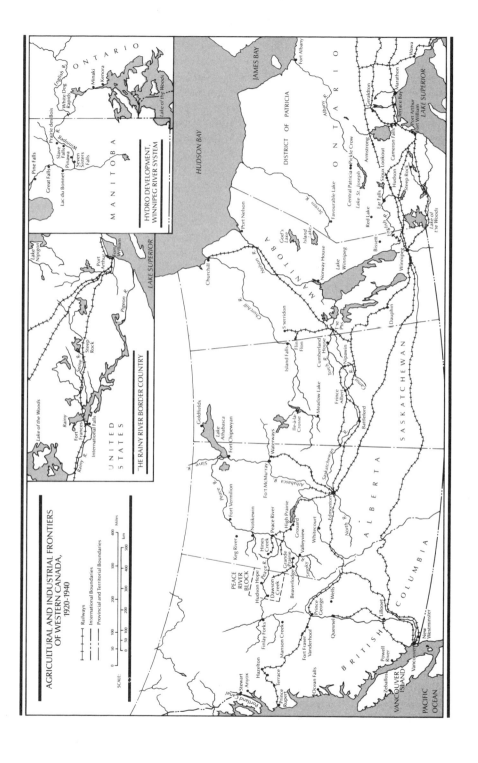

AGRICULTURAL AND INDUSTRIAL FRONTIERS
OF WESTERN CANADA,
1920-1940

Railways
International Boundaries
Provincial and Territorial Boundaries

SCALE:

0   50 100   200   300   400 Miles
0 50 100   200   300   400   500 km

HYDRO DEVELOPMENT,
WINNIPEG RIVER SYSTEM

THE RAINY RIVER BORDER COUNTRY

PACIFIC
OCEAN

VANCOUVER
ISLAND

BRITISH COLUMBIA

ALBERTA

SASKATCHEWAN

MANITOBA

ONTARIO

DISTRICT OF PATRICIA

HUDSON BAY

JAMES BAY

LAKE SUPERIOR

UNITED STATES

PEACE RIVER BLOCK

Quebec, for instance, a settler would need far more than three years to build a house of the specified size and to place a thirty-acre block (fifteen in Ontario) under cultivation – a task that usually proceeded at a rate of three to five acres a year. Ontario allowed its pioneers to diversify their activities, even to harvest the trees on their farms for income, and encouraged pulp and paper companies to buy the logs offered by the settlers – despite the well-founded fear that this policy encouraged bogus settlement and timber piracy rather than the building of permanent farming communities.

What were the northern limits of the arable land, the frontier to which farming could be successfully extended? Optimism continued to run very high indeed. After visiting the gardens along the Mackenzie in 1930 and 1932, W.D. Albright, the noted director of the Beaverlodge agricultural sub-station, became convinced that the Liard would become the next farming frontier after the Peace River district. The famous geographer Isaiah Bowman, influenced no doubt by his friend Stefansson, even foresaw a vast pastoral frontier extending beyond the limits of cultivation: "Beyond the grainfields are the pastures. The Arctic or sub-Arctic prairies will carry settlements as far north as grass grows. There can be no doubt of this. . . . The moss-covered plains of sub-Arctic Canada suitable as ranges for caribou or reindeer are of vast extent."[3] Governments maintained experimental farms in their northern sections to test possible paying crops in the localities, develop improved varieties of plants and animals, and encourage farmers to adopt the most suitable practices. The Dominion Experimental Farms constantly tested new crops and farming methods not only in settled districts but also at remote places in the District of Mackenzie (Forts Providence and Good Hope), Yukon (Swede Creek), and Quebec North Shore area (Betsiamites).

Despite visionary opinions as to the limits of successful agriculture, economic and technological conditions confined commercial farming to potentially arable districts along the southern rim of the Canadian Shield and in the Clay Belts of Quebec and Ontario, the northern fringe skirting the prairie and parkland regions of the Prairie Provinces, and certain sections of the valleys and plateaus of northern interior British Columbia. Even within these areas the percentage of land capable of being farmed successfully was and is far smaller than in the established farming districts, and the soils, moreover, usually require special treatment to overcome organic or chemical deficiencies. Furthermore, pioneer farmers had to contend with adverse climatic conditions, such as short summers, cold winters, and unseasonal frosts. In Northern Ontario and Quebec relatively heavy autumn rainfalls frequently delay harvesting until crops are overtaken by frosts or snow. These conditions increase the risk of losses, reduce the yields, lower the quality of crops harvested, and restrict the varieties of plants that can be cultivated successfully.

A continuing effort was made to develop hardier, more productive, quicker-maturing cereal strains, especially of wheat that might repeat the success of Marquis in extending the range of wheat culture in Western Canada. Garnet, a variety developed by the Dominion Cerealist in the twenties and highly regarded for its hardy qualities, was widely distributed to northern farmers during the decade 1925–35 only to be found unsuitable for bread flour, so that it had to be discontinued except for animal fodder. More satisfactory results were achieved with forage crops, notably brome, western rye, timothy, and other grasses, legumes such as alfalfa and clovers (which improved the soil and provided a good basis for beekeeping besides), field corn, sunflowers, and root crops.

Settlers in northern districts also faced economic handicaps. Operating costs were higher because of larger outlays on shelter and heating, feeding livestock indoors for longer periods of the year, and the greater risks of small or low-quality crops. Clearing away trees and brush and preparing the land for cultivation (including sometimes draining and "sweetening" the soil) were very expensive in both labour and capital. The scattered pockets of arable soil and often rough terrain also restricted full use of labour-saving machinery, while the remoteness and isolation increased the costs of transportation and reduced the farmer's net income, especially when the produce had to proceed to distant markets yet remain competitive in price.

The tasks of helping settlers establish themselves on the land fell to a variety of government agencies, mainly at the provincial level, even though the federal government retained control of the natural resources of the Prairie Provinces until 1930. Indeed, those provinces complained that the federal government derived all the benefits and heedlessly increased the provinces' difficulties by its recklessness in permitting unrestricted homesteading while leaving them the burdens of satisfying most of the settlers' needs. Provincial departments of agriculture and of public works were mainly involved with settlers' economic problems, though practically every department was concerned with the various aspects of settlement. In British Columbia the settlers were looked after by the various departments, but a broad range of activities devolved upon district agents, who administered the sets of regulations in the light of local conditions. Ontario made special provision for pioneer settlers, notably through the Colonization Roads and Northern Development branches of the Department of Lands and Forests, which were combined as the Department of Northern Development in 1926. This essentially road-building department with additional responsibilities toward new settlers in due course (1936) was absorbed into the Department of Highways.

In Quebec, a single department was responsible for new settlements and settlers: the Department of Colonization, Mines and Fisheries (after 1934 the Department of Colonization). It alone attended to colonization and immigration, agricultural lands, colonization roads, and aids to settlers. Consolidating these functions under a single department helped co-ordinate colonization activities and made it easier to adapt to changing conditions, while ministerial status ensured that colonization concerns would be aired before the provincial cabinet. The ministry was both a handy focus and channel for representations, complaints, and pressures by the colonization lobby and a vehicle for assisting and directing the work of that powerful interest group.

By the early 1920s governments had made large numbers of farm lots available for intending settlers in most frontier regions. The federal government had conducted massive land surveys of northern sections of the Prairie Provinces during the late war years as part of its postwar reconstruction program. No fewer than 235 newly surveyed townships of potential farmlands, about three-quarters of them in the wooded districts fringing the open prairies and in the greater Peace River district, were made available for homestead entry in 1920 and 1921. There seemed little point in adding to their number for the time being when so many good lots adjacent to existing communications remained unoccupied. The federal survey also subdivided twelve to sixteen new townships each year in the Peace River district so to have some six million acres available there for incoming settlers. Quebec also kept the area of land surveyed for settlement fairly constant, and new subdivision surveys closely matched the amounts of land actually granted for farming. British Columbia, similarly, arranged subdivision surveys in particular districts in line with actual or anticipated settlement trends. The federal branch, and no doubt the others as well, also made additional subdivision surveys when settlement outran the existing limits, "to provide for the requirements of squatters on unsurveyed land."[4]

The evident eagerness to accommodate squatters' wishes clashed with another trend – ensuring that settlers occupied lots that could afford a satisfactory livelihood to a capable farmer and not, as in times past, leaving would-be settlers to choose lots with "soils and slopes that resembled those back home that were known to be good."[5] An important study, *Unused Lands of Manitoba*, by R.W. Murchie and H.C. Grant, demonstrated the close relationship between poor soils and rural poverty. Land classification work was carried out as an aid to settlers by the Topographical Survey Branch, which in 1917 began assigning annual parties to classify several million acres in all three Prairie Provinces. The provincial agencies also joined in; for instance, in 1928 the Alberta Research Council started a series of studies of the lands from Lesser Slave Lake west and north to the limits of the province. These quickly dispelled the wildly optimistic views of the grain-growing capabilities of the northern soils, notably by revealing the limited quantity of first-class soils even in the renowned Peace River district. More important, the surveys helped farmers select good land and gave them guidance to make the best use of lands they worked.

Because access to and transport from the individual farm were essential for its operation and for the settler's well-being, every survey plan bounded each farm with a road allowance. In Northern Ontario and the western provinces those allowances criss-crossed plains and forests, swamps and lakes along north-south and east-west lines regardless of topographical, engineering, travel or traffic considerations, making it almost impossible to use them in their unimproved state. Indeed, the first farmers preferred to follow the convenient trails across unoccupied lots to visit the post office, send the children to school, or haul produce to the nearest market town and return with supplies. Once settlement got under way, transformation was very rapid. A few months after her arrival in the Battle River district in the northern Peace River region, Dr. Mary Percy Jackson observed that "there are great stretches of the district that were unbroken bush when I came in, and now I find houses, fences, and patches of land cleared. I hardly ever ride over the same trail twice; everywhere people are fencing the land, and forcing the trails to follow the road allowances."[6]

The automobile in particular made it necessary to channel traffic onto improved dirt roads that in the main followed the road allowances except where that proved too impractical. Eventually some roads were ditched, widened, straightened, graded, and bridged, greatly reducing the costs of moving produce off the farms. The building and upkeep of such roads also provided work and income for needy pioneer settlers. Quebec and Ontario each spent in the neighbourhood of $1 million a year on colonization roads, and in the late thirties Quebec was spending up to $5 million. The local transportation networks might include a navigable waterway, such as the Peace River, which was used to convey local farm produce from river ports between Fort Vermilion and Hudson Hope to the railhead at Peace River, Alberta. Such traffic declined as the road network was extended to centres along the river and was largely ended by 1940.

The provincial governments also improved their trunk road systems for long-distance travel to and from the northern farming districts.

Among them were the Quebec-Chicoutimi highway, Ontario's Ferguson Highway from North Bay to Cochrane and west to Hearst (opened September 1927), and British Columbia's trunk road from Quesnel to Prince George and west toward Prince Rupert. Most trunk roads tended to follow existing railway routes because these ran through more settled, prosperous districts that were better able to contribute to building and maintaining their sections of highways. The extreme case of this was the Edmonton–Peace River district highway. Not until the late thirties was travel from the capital to Grande Prairie shortened one hundred miles by running the road due west from High Prairie to avoid the long northward jog via the town of Peace River. A truly direct highway link via Whitecourt and Valleyview had to await the 1950s. Yet the inter-war highways, some of them paved, assisted passenger travel by automobile and bus and were far more convenient for moving dairy and other perishable farm produce to distant markets or processing centres.

Branch railways, however, were unquestionably the lifeline of commercial farming. Agricultural economists, in fact, related the practicability of grain farming to the farm's distance from a railway shipping point, the figure varying from fifteen to twenty miles. Railways also were important in attracting settlers to a locality, for, it was said, "the appeal of cheap or free land and of promised or expected roads and railways are among the powerful motives which make the land-hungry march into fringe areas."[7] Expansion of agriculture northward went hand in hand with branch railway construction. The return of prosperity and the impressive expansion of homesteading in the wooded grey soil districts north of the North Saskatchewan River in the late twenties inspired considerable additional construction, notably the extension of the Peace River district's line to a terminus at Dawson Creek within the British Columbia boundary. This was the work of the Northern Alberta Railways (NAR), a company formed in 1928 and owned jointly by the CNR and CPR systems to take over the provincial lines, the very unprofitable Edmonton-Waterways branch as well as the highly prosperous roads in the Peace River district.

A main element in the campaign for lower freight rates consisted of organized efforts to secure more direct, shorter (and cheaper, since the rate was based on distance) routes to convenient ocean ports. Between 1917 and 1927 success was achieved in securing very low export rates on grain and flour moved over the existing railway network to Great Lakes, Atlantic, and Pacific ocean ports. But western farmers sought further reductions, those in Manitoba and eastern Saskatchewan looking to completion of the Hudson Bay Railway as the ideal solution to their export freight problem. Construction of that government-built line had been started in 1912, then halted in 1917 when only a short distance from its intended terminus, and when most port facilities at Port Nelson had been completed. Farmer pressure for completion of the branch, mobilized by an On-to-the-Bay Association, mounted, and during the political stalemate in Ottawa in 1925–26 the hard-pressed Liberal government announced its readiness to complete the railway "forthwith."

After that government's return to power in 1926, the road was rehabilitated and the ocean terminus and port were again investigated. Sir Frederick Palmer, a British engineer sent to examine the relative merits of Port Nelson and Fort Churchill, was emphatic in favour of the latter, which had a far superior, sheltered deep-water harbour and could be put in operation more cheaply and quickly than its rival. The Department of National Defence, in addition, conducted a year's aerial survey of ice conditions in Hudson Strait and Bay in 1927–28 (a very important experimental Arctic flying and communications operation) that prompted setting up a network of direction-finding stations to assist shipping over the route during the three or four months' open-water season. When construction resumed, the railway was diverted from Mile 356 northward to Churchill, and the considerable investment at Port Nelson was simply abandoned. The railway was sufficiently completed for a token wheat shipment to be sent from Churchill on the *Nascopie* in 1929, but the first commercial cargo of wheat destined for Britain departed only on August 31, 1931, following completion of the two-million-bushel grain terminal. The grain farmer secured somewhat lower freight rates, but Churchill never became more than a minor outlet (less than 5 per cent) for western grain, while its function as an import centre remained almost non-existent. Nonetheless, the railway proved helpful in developing the mineral, forest, hydro, and fishing resources of its hinterland, and Churchill became a useful base for administrative and economic activities around the coasts of Hudson Bay and Foxe Basin.

Peace River farmers, a far smaller, less influential group than the one mobilized to achieve the Hudson Bay outlet, pinned their hopes on securing a similar, more direct railway outlet to the Pacific Coast – or outlets, for several were proposed. Their inability to settle on any one route, the differing interests of the provincial governments on the outlet question, and the unwillingness of either the railway companies or the federal government to make the large investment required ensured that no construction would be undertaken for a generation and more.

Governments for the most part were content to let agricultural expansion proceed in accordance with economic and social forces and individual settler's plans. But the crisis of the Great War caused them to participate actively in the process to help war veterans to return to productive life. In the West the Dominion government reserved all its lands within fifteen miles of a railway or along the routes of certain projected but unbuilt railways for the time being for veterans, a step copied by British Columbia. A war veteran was also allowed to file for a second lot in return for fulfilling the regular residence and improvements conditions. Ontario and Quebec gave their veterans a similar privilege except that the extra land had to be purchased at the standard sixty cents an acre. More than 10,000 soldier's grants were taken out on the federally controlled western lands, two thirds of them in the six Dominion Lands Agencies having appreciable northern frontier lands to settle – Dauphin, Prince Albert, Battleford, Edmonton, Grande Prairie, and Peace River. These same districts also attracted a like proportion of the regular homestead applications.

The federal government extended important aid to other farmer veterans through the medium of the Soldier Settlement Board established in 1917. By purchasing school sections, Indian Reserve lands, Hudson's Bay and other lands in private hands it acquired acreages for resale to veterans and made loans available to assist them to buy farms, livestock, and farm equipment. By the end of 1921 more than $80 million had been lent to 19,771 veterans, 71 per cent of whom had been helped to purchase land. British Columbia also created a special fund from which veterans could apply for loans towards improvements, while Ontario offered soldier settlers the same generous loan fund privileges available to all settlers in Northern Ontario.

The Ontario government also sponsored a highly publicized organized settlement at Kapuskasing, along the railway west of Cochrane, where six townships were to be settled along co-operative lines. Each veteran was to clear the front ten acres of his hundred-acre lot and was to be paid for his labour. He would receive one quarter of the cost of his house plus a $500 loan toward the purchase of farm equipment. Horses, wagons, and implements also were made available for his use. Disputes quickly arose between the more skilled or harder-working men and their less able fellows, and single and married men were at odds because of the higher pay given the latter. When the government responded by starting a contract system, further resentment arose over alleged differences in the quality or amounts of work performed for equal pay. Discontented soldier settlers bombarded the press and the newly elected United Farmers government with their grievances and complained over the delay in opening the promised pulp mill that would furnish a market for their produce and help make farming a paying proposition. A provincial commission of inquiry minimized the physical and climatic conditions the farmers faced and concluded that the project was intrinsically sound; instead, it found most of the men unsuited to farming because of their military experience. The commission recommended that the government buy the assets of those who wished to leave. No more than twenty veterans were still on the land when the pulp and paper mill went into operation to give the colony a proper economic foundation. Clearly the Ontario experiment was a failure. On the other hand, a comparable experiment away from the limelight in the Porcupine Forest Reserve of eastern Saskatchewan, where 150 veterans cleared the bush and worked together to improve common facilities before taking up their individual farms, proved completely successful.

II

The 1920s were a period of adapting frontier agriculture to the natural conditions of soil and climate and to current market trends. These directed northern farmers towards using low-grade field crops as fodder for livestock and poultry and deriving their main income from the sale of animal products. An exception was the growing of registered quality seeds in certain districts that were free of weeds and insect pests and whose climate would test the seeds' hardiness, so that they would command good prices. Determined efforts were made to introduce strains of livestock that promised better returns. Carloads of high-grade dairy cattle were sent to Northern Ontario for sale at cost to farmers, quality bulls and stallions were made available to farmer co-operatives, farmers were urged to raise hogs with proper conformation to produce quality bacon for the British market, and beekeeping and fur-farming were encouraged as profitable sidelines.

As northern farming districts became settled, new regulations were introduced to facilitate the shift to better-grade stock and poultry. Dairy and poultry farmers were urged to keep production records and cull low producers and poor-quality breedstock. Commercial distribution of unpasteurized milk products began to be restricted, while farmers were encouraged to keep tuberculosis-free herds and organize districts free of the disease from which dairy products could be shipped direct to markets. Eggs intended for sale had to be graded for size and freshness according to federal standards; national standards also were applied to butter and cheese, bacon-grade hogs, beef carcasses, and registered seeds. These were instituted mainly to satisfy domestic and export market requirements and to assist efficient processing and packing of the produce. Compliance was secured through mandatory regulations but was helped by the higher prices good-quality produce commanded. Thus incentives were provided to improve the grades of northern crops while farmers were still free to raise whatever they wished for their own use or for private exchange. The overall result was to encourage northern farmers to move toward becoming specialized producers of animal products.

If the northern farmer was to adjust to the special characteristics of his land, information and demonstrations of methods were also required. Regional agricultural colleges at centres like New Liskeard, special programs at Guelph or St Hyacinthe trained farmers to operate under northern conditions, and extension work spread the latest techniques of a rapidly changing industry throughout the agricultural frontier. University-trained agronomists and agricultural representatives advised farmers on their problems and organized them for group activities such as "the sow thistle war." Farmers visited demonstration farms and attended regional fairs and exhibitions to improve their education; the railways co-operated by offering those attending instructional programs low fares, and carried travelling exhibits to demonstrate new equipment and techniques to farmers.

By the late twenties, established frontier farmers had accepted commercial farming to a greater or lesser degree. The logic of the industry drew them toward this market-oriented, specialized style. The direction that specialization took, or how completely the farm operation was devoted to it, depended on more than the properties of the lot – its soils, topography, climate, location with respect to transportation and markets. Other important considerations included the training, skills, and preferences of the farmer and the relative profitability of farm commodities at a given time:

> Far more mixed farming than elsewhere is found in those grain-growing districts of the Peace River that have been settled by Germans and Southern Europeans. The most successful creamery of the north is maintained by a homogeneous Norwegian settlement. But in time wheat culture has threatened the very existence of this dairy venture. In due course there will be an adjustment between natural conditions and an imported culture – a compromise between nature and nurture.[8]

Technological advances, particularly the introduction of new implements and machinery, were another factor. New labour-saving, cost-reducing equipment appearing in the twenties induced many farmers to adjust their operations: "In general, western agriculture is in process of being motorized to a great extent. Tractor and truck sales increase year by year. Implement manufacturers are continually requested to produce larger and larger implements. The very evident result has been a vast increase in the volume of production and a decided decrease in the cost of production.''[9] Milking machines and improved cream separators were similarly helpful innovative equipment for farmers specializing in dairying.

Not all the new machinery was well suited to the frontier farm: combine harvesters, for instance. Trucks were uneconomic for a single farm unless that farm was exceptionally large and wealthy or unless the truck could help the farmer earn extra revenue. As for tractors, the agricultural economist R.W. Murchie concluded that in most frontier situations horses were more economic and efficient: "It would appear that the majority of fringe areas in the Prairie Provinces possess natural features more adapted to the production of cheap horse feed and to diversified farming than to machine operation, and are sufficiently distant from the distributing points for fuel to emphasize the advantages of horse-farming methods.''[10]

Tractors, along with heavy brush-breaking ploughs, were extremely helpful for clearing, breaking, and bringing new land under cultivation, however, greatly reducing the time and effort needed to develop the farm to the point of affording an adequate livelihood to an efficient farmer. The pioneer settler unaided and with little equipment could break perhaps five acres each year – and that only by forgoing income-earning work outside. On the other hand, with proper equipment the task could be completed relatively quickly, sparing the farm family years of privation and struggle with the attendant social and emotional problems. Small wonder, then, that powerful tractors quickly made their appearance in wooded areas being prepared for farming:

> There will be a tremendous lot of land broken this year, probably 20,000 acres! It's all being cleared and burnt off now. Lots of new tractors are coming in and are working 18 hours a day! I can hear a tractor at work across the river – it will be going at 11 p.m., and will be on again before I wake. Very different from breaking with horses, though, of course, lots of them still do it that way. I love seeing them at work, one man driving 4 to 6 horses and guiding the plough too; it is a great picture, but the breaking is rarely so even as when they use a tractor.[11]

After the Second World War, in fact, some provinces financed large-scale land-clearing and breaking operations in advance of settlement to relieve some of the severe hardships that had accompanied earlier agricultural pioneering.

The trend toward specialization in animal husbandry was especially appropriate to the frontier districts in Central Canada, whose farmers were less concerned with distant markets than with supplying the needs of nearby industrial communities for vegetables, eggs, meat, dairy, and other products. Besides, stock-raising and dairying were the established farming pattern in the older pioneering districts of Quebec and the earlier settlements in the Clay Belts, which the region's experimental farms and agricultural agents continually emphasized in their research and educational efforts.

The Quebec and Ontario governments offered financial incentives to keep pioneer farmers at work establishing themselves on the land. Ontario lent new settlers $500 to assist them to purchase stock and equipment, then provided further loans once the land patent was secured, for building, purchasing additional land, and the like. Quebec's solution was a system of incentive grants. Responding to pressures from settlers and colonization societies, in 1923 it instituted premiums for clearing land – four dollars an acre to a maximum of five acres in a given year, with a twenty-acre limit on any lot. The bonus was increased in stages to twelve dollars in 1928, when a "first ploughing" premium of twelve dollars for up to five acres also was introduced; the province's spending thus rose to the $200,000 level by the late 1920s.

Despite these inducements, expansion of the farming frontier proceeded slowly in Central Canada, and then mainly through resettlement of surplus farm population from regions already occupied. Ontario strove vigorously to attract immigrants from outside, and Premier Howard Ferguson co-operated with the plans to recruit British farm settlers for Canada, advertising his government's welcome to such settlers: "We meet him at North Bay and we look after him until he gets settled on his land; we feed and care for his livestock and house his implements until he gets settled. We build roads for him; we locate him on good land and try to find him congenial neighbours; we help him to get started and lend him money if necessary. . . . Settlement is now our most important task."[12] But the measure of success was limited. Between 700 and 900 land sales involving some 150,000 acres of land were recorded each year, with new settlements growing up around Kapuskasing and Hearst and in the Thunder Bay district, while (contrary to the government's hopes) French Canadians continued to move westward into the Timiskaming and Cochrane districts. To relieve rural distress in areas like Haliburton and increase the number of experienced farmers in the North, the province arranged for farmers to exchange unsuitable farms for new ones in Northern Ontario. Unfortunately, relatively few restrictions were put on where newcomers might settle, so that some moved into townships poorly supplied with roads, schools, and other facilities. The subsequent high level of farm abandonments further aggravated the difficulties of supplying adequate services for the settlers that remained.

In Quebec, the progress of frontier settlement, apart from a small Franco-American immigration from the United States, depended almost wholly on the indigenous rural population. The movement, as in the previous century, still enjoyed powerful support from culturally and nationally motivated societies that pressed the Quebec government to join in a co-ordinated drive to establish new parishes in the Lac St Jean and Abitibi regions. The pace of settlement, however, tended to reflect nationalist propaganda less than general economic conditions. In times of prosperity, as in the late 1920s when colonization had to compete with industrial employment or emigration to the United States, it fell off markedly, whereas during times of economic recession, as in the early twenties and especially the 1930s, it tended to increase. Thus ten new parishes were established in 1921–22 and six in 1922–23, but only three in 1927 and none at all in 1929. The slow pace of colonization in the late twenties intensified fears for the survival of the French-Canadian nationality in an increasingly urban and industrial Quebec. The Rev. A. Dugré complained in 1926 that enough young people to settle thirty new parishes a year were leaving the rural parishes, that there was less than a single train daily to the colonization areas but twenty each day south to the United States, and that 105,000 Quebeckers, double or triple the natural increase, had expatriated themselves to that country in 1925–26, constituting a "suicide de race, tuberculose nationale."[13]

Settlers continued to take up lands in the valleys of the tributaries of the Ottawa and St Maurice rivers, in remoter parts of the Lac St Jean district, below Tadoussac along the North Shore (in 1929–30), in Témiscamingue, and especially in Abitibi. That county recorded between 500 and 1,000 farm lot sales each year during the twenties. Settlement spread along the railway and the paralleling roads between Senneterre and the Ontario border, fanning out along the north-trending rivers. The number of parishes increased from fourteen (1921) to twenty-five (1927), and the population of the still predominantly agricultural county doubled from 11,823 in 1921 to 23,692 in 1931. The early emphasis on feed grains and potatoes to serve the region's lumber camps was succeeded by greater concentration on dairy products and the opening of new creameries and cheese factories. In the now largely occupied Saguenay–Lac St Jean region, oats and hay, raised as fodder for horses, pigs, and especially dairy cows, were the main products in 1931. It was the same in the Districts of Timiskaming and Cochrane in northeastern Ontario, where the number of cattle rose by 60 per cent over the decade, perhaps reflecting growing French-Canadian presence in those districts.

Far greater success attended the settling of the mostly wooded parkland that constituted the newest agricultural frontiers of Western Canada. This result reflected mainly the far larger immigration attracted to the western provinces and the periods of prosperity and profitability that western grain and livestock exports enjoyed at intervals between 1918 and 1930. The rising price of wheat after the Armistice meant that new lands even in remote marginal districts were planted in wheat, and settlers rushed to purchase so much additional land that in 1920 the railway companies sold nearly 8 million acres and the Hudson's Bay Company a record 178,301 acres. To clear their acreages quickly, farmers in frontier areas experimented with controlled burning of light brush cover. The higher prices for grains also encouraged mechanization of farm operations, and progressive farmers adopted threshing machines, tractor-driven ploughs, and seeding equipment. Indeed, in 1919 the horse seemed on the way to being phased out in favour of the tractor.

In the autumn of 1920 farm prices, heretofore protected by unlimited wartime and post-war markets in Europe, abruptly collapsed. The Canadian Wheat Board, which had regulated the marketing of wheat for the crop year 1919–20, withdrew altogether from marketing the 1920 crop, which encountered drastically reduced prices. In ensuing months similar declines occurred in the prices of other agricultural products. In the northern farming districts of the Prairie Provinces the situation was worsened by the well-meant 1918–19 governmental program of assisting northward transfer of livestock from drought-ridden southern areas. Many frontier farmers, having been encouraged to raise livestock on a large scale, faced ruin in the dull, low-price markets that prevailed in 1920, 1921, and 1922 when it came time to sell their cattle.

For the next few years frontier agriculture languished. The pace of new settlement slowed and was more than offset by a high rate of farm abandonments, mainly in poorer districts such as the Manitoba interlake region, but also in rich ones such as the Peace River district. As the *Peace River Record* observed on January 23, 1924: "Given another year such as the past, and there will be a bigger colony of Peace River farmers in California than in Alberta. Will our governments stand by until the remainder have gone? The north will not always ask for this relief. Before long . . . there will not be enough left of the north to raise the call for help." The collapse was especially hard on the soldiers and other recent settlers. When they had started out, prices of land, stock, and equipment – mostly purchased on credit – and interest rates were at their peak. Now loans had to be repaid at a time when prices for produce were below the costs of production. Many veterans, besides, found it hard to adapt to the primitive conditions, unfamiliar routines, shortages, and deprivation that every pioneer farmer faced.

Although interest charges were waived for a time, over one fifth of the nearly 20,000 soldier settlers had given up their farms by 1924. The Soldier Settlement Board salvaged its investments by reselling the properties, often to British settlers coming to Canada under the various assisted immigration and colonization schemes of the twenties.

For notwithstanding the clouded economic situation, special efforts were launched to assist British war veterans and qualified civilian families to re-establish themselves on farms in Canada. The Canadian and British governments in so doing were implementing a war-inspired grand design to encourage fuller development of the resources of the Empire and bind the member countries closer together by strengthening their economic and cultural ties. The Three Thousand Family scheme inaugurated in 1924, the most important of these, secured settlers mainly for the unoccupied or repossessed Soldier Settlement Board properties, especially in the Peace River district and along the fringe of settlement north of the prairies. The board helped finance the land purchases, while the British government lent each family $1,500 to help with livestock and equipment. Similar schemes were sponsored by the Hudson's Bay Company, the Scottish Immigrant Aid Society, the Royal Naval Association, the Salvation Army, the United Church of Canada, and the Grand Orange Lodge of British America, to name a few. Several provinces made similar efforts, especially Ontario, whose agent general in London secured farm labourers and occasional agricultural capitalists for his province's farmlands.

Greatly reduced government-subsidized railway and shipping fares were offered the intending immigrants from Britain, with ocean fares as low as £2 for approved travellers under the Empire Settlement Program (1927) plus "a £3 ocean passage rate for the wife, and a free passage for children under seventeen."[14] Training assistance was provided for teenaged British boys, who were placed with selected farmers. During the twenties, groups of British farm labourers were also brought out in hopes that they would decide to settle in the West. The plan did not always succeed: an 8,000-man party made up chiefly of unemployed Welsh miners aroused so many complaints in Canada that Lord Lovat, the administrator of the Oversea Settlement Committee, visited Canada's colonization districts to observe conditions for himself and negotiate further programs with Canadian officials.

The low wheat prices of the early 1920s had brought a shift to mixed farming and dairying, but a sudden upward surge in the price early in 1925 inspired an immediate rise of 20 to 30 per cent acreage planted in wheat. Further expansion continued so long as good results in terms of prices and yields prevailed. Those from 1926 to 1928 encouraged farmers to bring more land under cultivation and invest heavily in land

and machinery, while, in the blaze of new prosperity, "mortgages were lifted, houses painted, cars bought. The horse and buggy now rarely rattled by on the road, and on Saturday nights the streets of the towns were jammed with farmers' cars."[15] Districts that previously had concentrated on ranching sent large amounts of wheat to railway shipping points across seventy miles and more of winter sled trails. Farmers reduced or abandoned their livestock, dairy, and poultry operations, with one exception – production of hogs increased in the remoter sections, since farmers found them a profitable way of utilizing their low-grade, often frost-tinged grain crops.

Homesteading revived in the late twenties to something approaching pre-war days, particularly along the northern fringe, where a person without much capital could still find a good quarter-section that could be developed into a successful farm by dint of hard work and some good luck. Approximately twenty million acres were added to the occupied farmland of Western Canada in the 1920s, nearly all of it in the homesteading districts of Saskatchewan and Alberta. The Dominion Lands Agencies reported new homesteads taken up in Northern Saskatchewan to the numbers of 4,341 in 1928, 6,212 in 1929, and 4,258 in 1930, figures that were surpassed by those for the Peace River Agencies – of 6,608, 6,895, and 6,246. Settlers tended to prefer lands that were only lightly brush covered: "Matters such as relief, drainage, character of soil, water supply, in some cases even transport, appear to have been items of minor consideration with many settlers."[16] Occupation of the frontier districts in the area drained by the Carrot and Torch rivers east of Prince Albert and west from Prince Albert to Edmonton was aided by recent road and railway construction. Some of the settlers there and in the Peace River district had been defeated by frequent crop failures in the Palliser Triangle and were permitted to take new homesteads upon surrendering their original ones. The federal and provincial governments and the railways shared the cost of moving the settler and his belongings, and the option seems to have been offered more than once.

The Peace River district, the strongest magnet for new settlement, was as early as April 1927 drawing farmers from the South: "You can hardly pick up a paper at the present time in western Canada but you find that families are moving from the dry belt of Alberta to the Peace River country."[17] From the autumn of 1926 onward a torrent of favourable publicity boosted the region, inspired especially by the achievements of Herman Trelle of the Grande Prairie district in winning grand championships in both hard red spring wheat and oats at the International Grain and Hay Show in Chicago. Trelle followed these victories with more at Chicago and Toronto, and other Peace River district farmers joined the winners' circles to add to the evidence "that the northern sections of Alberta are exceptionally adapted to the growing of high quality seed."[18] Effective also were reports of high yields and rare crop failures in the publicity released during the agitation for the Peace River railway outlet and the directed settlement schemes. Numberless articles published in Canada and abroad extolled the district's magnificent agricultural prospects. Governments, railways, and others issued publicity releases and arranged for tours by important visitors, whose reports and comments brought even more favourable notice.

So many settlers were attracted that additional Crown lands had to be surveyed and subdivided, more land was removed from forest reserves, and other acreages were thrown on the market through auctions of school lands and surrendered Indian reserve lands. Earlier settlers who had accumulated large holdings sold out at high prices, in some cases to group settlements of Russians, Mennonites, and Ukrainians. Scenes reminiscent of pre-war times were repeated as applicants streamed through the doors of the land agencies or camped for days outside to secure first rights to particularly desirable parcels of land. By 1929 the new settlement was advancing in columns from the already settled districts, bypassing heavily timbered sections, which later arrivals would attack. It proceeded along the west side of, and parallel to, the Peace River, north to the several open "prairies" and to Fort Vermilion; and west along the Peace to the new railway terminus of Hines Creek and beyond. Settlers took up land west and north of the new terminus of Dawson Creek in the Peace River Block in British Columbia and moved eastward from Grande Prairie across the Smoky River to Valleyview. In spite of the harder times that had arrived by 1930, settlers continued to pour into the same remote districts and into British Columbia, where new farming communities sprang up south and west of Dawson Creek. Some even passed beyond the federally controlled Peace River Block into lands controlled by the province, which at this time also received numbers of settlers in the Prince George, Fort Fraser, Vanderhoof, and Terrace districts along the railway to Prince Rupert, and south from Prince George.

The census of 1931 for the Peace River district, in fact, showed that the achievements of the five years just past far exceeded those of the previous twenty and that its population had more than doubled (from 22,591 to 50,777), the increase in occupied farm acreage and improved acreage was 226 per cent, and in acres in field crops nearly 228 per cent. The 1931 census also revealed that immigrants from Central Europe (70 per cent of whom were farmers, as compared with 37.7 per cent of settlers from the British Isles) had become a significant element in the northern fringe districts of all four western provinces. In fact, one quarter to one third of the more than 30,000 farming families occupying those districts were recent migrants from Europe.

This was an unsought, and in some quarters unwelcome, result of Canada's immigration program in the 1920s, which had striven mainly to recruit British, French, and U.S. (especially ex-Canadian) farmer settlers. By contrast, many obstacles were thrown in the paths of intending settlers from the non-preferred countries of Eastern and Southern Europe, who had first to apply, then meet increasingly stringent medical, financial, and other inspections at one or other of the offices the government or transport companies maintained at selected overseas centres. Yet the numbers of continental immigrants, particularly from the non-preferred countries, continued to rise steadily after 1926. These persons found the frontier lands of the western provinces very attractive. In fact, Murchie saw such settlers as particularly suited to these districts, which ". . . if settled at all, [are] likely to be colonized only by those who will be content with a standard of living lower than that demanded by the average English-speaking settlers in Western Canada. . . . It is highly probable that, beyond the present fringe, agricultural settlement will largely be made by Central and Southeastern Europeans, who have shown in the past a lower rate of assimilability."[19]

Opponents of the government's efforts to promote farmer immigration during the 1920s varied in their approaches. Some were against immigration in general, such as the historian A.R.M. Lower, who compared Canada to "a ship which can carry only a fixed number of people, crew and passengers" and concluded with a sardonic version of Gresham's Law: "Cheap men will drive out dear."[20] Others begrudged government spending to recruit immigrants. A United Farmers of Alberta meeting of January 1926, for instance, asserted: "Be it resolved that we do not oppose the coming of suitable immigrants of their own free will, but that we oppose the spending of our money in order to induce them to come, by the same government which allows conditions to exist which drive present settlers out."[21] The heavily subsidized low transportation rates for intending immigrants from Britain were a particular target of resentment. Farmer organizations demanded equal treatment for Canadian farmers seeking to re-establish themselves in other parts of the country, and nationalist spokesmen in Quebec contrasted the federal government's support for European immigration with its alleged indifference toward assisting colonization of the Quebec frontiers by "ces robustes Canadiens qu'on proclame toujours les premiers défricheurs du monde et qui ont si peu de chances de se faire valoir."[22]

Further racist criticism was voiced by a segment of the English-speaking population, who became alarmed in the late 1920s that government-assisted immigration from Central Europe was growing strong enough "to threaten the dominance of British ideals and institutions in the Western provinces."[23] The General Synod of the Church of England in Canada heard allegations that the government was biased in favour of Roman Catholic immigration and that its pattern of 60 per cent "foreign" immigrants to 40 per cent British settlers was undermining the British character of the Prairie Provinces. Conservative newspapers joined in a campaign to force the government to recruit British settlers and take measures against continental Europeans, while G.E. Lloyd, the Anglican Bishop of Saskatchewan, in an article headlined "British Australia: Mongrel Canada," called on Canada to institute a quota system under which of 100,000 allowable maximum immigration, 75 per cent would be British, 5 per cent French, 10 per cent Scandinavian, and 10 per cent "others" in proportion to 1901 census figures.[24]

In the West, these immigrants brought out the long-ingrained prejudices of established Canadians against the newcomers' Old World practices and standards – against the sod-roofed, plastered, mud-floored, unventilated huts in which many of them had to live; the evident signs of poverty reflected in the lack of warm clothing and healthful nutrition for the children; the sometimes harsh, domineering conduct of fathers; the correspondingly inferior status of their women and children, and the heavy tasks these performed; the odd-sounding languages, strange foods, decorative arts, and costumes, and the scandalously uninhibited manner of celebrating festivals and funerals. Others, however, regarded the newcomers not as annoying, troublesome foreigners, nor as objects of scorn or pity, but as useful additions to Canada. S.J. Latta, Saskatchewan Minister of Education, observed that "the very polyglot nature of our population by wise and sympathetic policies may become our greatest asset."[25] Men of this view looked at the immigrants' positive virtues and set about integrating them into Canadian society through commercial and other contacts but especially through the provincial schools that introduced their children to Canadian values and ways.

Robert Forke, responsible as federal Minister of Immigration and Colonization for bringing "the landless man to the manless land,"[26] responded in 1928 to these criticisms with this statement of government policy: "There was no restriction whatever on British immigration and the same was practically true of the Scandinavian countries and certain other countries whose people were considered desirable immigrants. These people were in the majority and press reports that foreigners were flooding the country gave an erroneous impression."[27] He hoped immigration from non-preferred countries could be reduced by two thirds in 1929. Nonetheless, the numbers of immigrants from Eastern Europe driven by pressures in their homelands continued to mount in 1929 and only began to decline with the onset of the Depression. When the Conservative government elected in 1930 acted to limit farmer immigrants from non-preferred countries to persons with capital or relatives of farmers already established in Canada it was but reacting belatedly to a situation that no longer existed.

III

The Depression of the 1930s, when the price of wheat fell disastrously and that of other farm commodities followed suit, sharply altered the course of agricultural colonization. On the one hand, immigration from abroad, a principal source of settlers for the frontiers of the Prairie Provinces, virtually ceased except for rare individuals and groups such as the Sudeten German refugees who were settled by the CPR in the Peace River district in March 1939. Instead, an intensified drive was begun to resettle displaced Canadian farmers or ex-farmers on unoccupied agricultural lands of the Middle North. At first the advertising and resettlement programs of the railways and federal Land Settlement Branch were directed at persons who could make the move largely by their own means. By the spring of 1932, however, widespread urban unemployment led business leaders and politicians to reduce their cities' relief rolls by encouraging ex-farmers to return to solvency and contentment in rural settings. Yet even this sort of settler needed considerable assistance to make a new start.

Accordingly, in May 1932 the federal government inaugurated the so-called Gordon Plan (named for the Minister of Immigration and Colonization, W.A. Gordon) under which federal, provincial, and municipal authorities would each contribute $200 to help resettle a farmer, the provinces undertaking to administer the programs, select the farmers and the lands to be settled, and locate the settlers on their farms. The $600 given each settler was to help with resettlement and start-up expenses; in Ontario, for instance, the allocation was $80 for transportation, $110 for housing, $200 for stock and equipment, and $200 to help maintain the family for the first two years. The arrangement was renewed in 1934 and 1936. The subsidies varied from province to province; Quebec, for example, increased the amount to $1,000 so as to furnish monthly rations to the settlers for four years, the province contributing the extra $400 and usually the municipality's $200 share also. The settlers were, of course, eligible for the loans, premiums, paid work on roads, and other aids provided by the respective provinces.

The most striking resettlement drive occurred in Saskatchewan, where thousands of farmers saw their investment and years of hard work destroyed by the relentless drought that overwhelmed so much of the southern part of the "wheat province." Many of these dried-out farmers tried their luck farther west; excluded from Alberta, they formed a large part of the new settlers in the British Columbia Peace River region. In the main, however, they tried to re-establish themselves in the northern woodlands of their own province. At least 2,000 families made the move under a 1930 resettlement plan giving them $500 loans from the province. The credit terms subsequently were eased, federal participation raised the size of the grants, and transportation costs were reduced by means of subsidies. As a result, the movement rapidly accelerated, so that between 1933 and 1936 some 35,000 settlers made the northward trek.

Many farmers together with hundreds of railway carloads of settlers' effects journeyed by train. Others arrived more picturesquely in horse-drawn wagons and "Bennett buggies," plodding in unending streams along the highways twenty miles a day, their campfires stretching for miles lighting up the skies at night. Families often travelled by stages, some members remaining to manage the old farms while others left to examine the new territory and prepare the way for eventual migration of the whole family. Typical of this sort of movement was a 400-mile, month-long journey of two families from southern Saskatchewan to the White Fox district north of Nipawin. The group used two covered wagons, had three wagonloads of goods and machinery, drove sixteen horses and eighteen cattle (some cows in milk), and was assisted by two men who helped as drivers and planned to return to settle on their own account. A few settlers formed homogeneous groups, such as the French Canadians who settled at Cabana in the Meadow Lake area. Most of the newcomers had English-Canadian backgrounds. The first settlers were mainly second-generation Ukrainians or Germans who had taken up farms here, north of their home districts, when they reached adulthood. Still, as English was the common language most newcomers found it easy to work together in farmer organizations or schools and at such group endeavours as fence-building, road-making, and digging drainage works.

Because a number of forest reserves dotted the province, the settlers were forced to occupy the tongues of land between them. Many, in their haste ignoring forest reserve or Indian reserve boundaries, even the limits of the surveyed land, simply squatted on the first patch of likely ground without searching for the best possible location. Unable to direct the settlers away from designated reserves, the province in the end regularized squatting and abandoned the idea of confining holdings to the square survey lines. The Northern Settlers Re-Establishment Branch directed settlers instead to blocks of land where there was enough good soil to promise successful farming and stable farm communities. In addition, the Rehabilitation Branch directed drainage projects and other common works as a means of providing employment and making the land more suitable for settlement. Although most of the settlers were experienced wheat farmers, few if any were familiar with the situation to which they had come. Government agents helped them adjust by encouraging them to raise livestock, develop reasonable crop rotation systems, grow legumes and clovers, and produce honey.

These pioneers, as well as those already on the land, were held back from developing successful farms by the long-continuing low prices for their produce and the lack of opportunities for outside income from other work. The price situation did begin to improve after 1932, first for dairy products, poultry, honey, and especially hogs, but not until after 1935 for cattle and grain. The result, accordingly, was further encouragement for the mixed farming economy. Responding to financial incentives, western farmers concentrated increasingly on raising livestock, and cattle and hog marketings were extremely heavy in 1936 and succeeding years. On a single day (October 16, 1937), 162 railway carloads, three complete stock trains, left Peace River town for Edmonton markets.

In Northern Ontario and Quebec (and in a very small way in the District of Mackenzie), expanding mining, aluminum refining, and pulp and paper industries created markets for foodstuffs and draft animals and employment opportunities for frontier farmers in mines, mills, and camps. The provinces did what they could to help their pioneer settlers. Ontario, for instance, voted another $5 million in 1931 to the Northern Development Board to continue building roads and bridges, and paid small subsidies to creameries and to farmers to raise cattle or grow seed grains. A further $7 million was voted in 1934 as Northern Ontario's share of a province-wide highway expansion and maintenance program. In Quebec, the annual spending on colonization road construction increased from below $1 million in the twenties to $4.9 million in 1937–38 and $5.6 million in 1938–39, about 25 per cent of the outlays being in Abitibi and another 25 per cent in Témiscamingue and Charlevoix-Saguenay combined.

Recognizing that farmers might need to exploit other resources besides land, and desperately concerned for their success, the various governments assisted their efforts at diversification. Saskatchewan readily issued fishing, hunting, and trapping licences to settlers and permits to cut timber for sale to small local sawmills, ties to the railways, even pulpwood and logs to be shipped by rail to distant mills. Ontario and Quebec abandoned their forest conservation programs by authorizing colonists to market the wood from their own lots or cut logs from Crown lands under permit. Quebec also encouraged parishes to organize co-operative lumber camps and forestry associations, which many did, each providing seasonal work for 100 to 300 men. But the relaxation of regulations often hindered fishing and forestry concerns struggling to survive and sometimes wasted or abused the resources since the unpoliced licences undermined proper conservation and resource management programs. Also, as always, they encouraged farmers to neglect the less immediately rewarding tasks of developing their own farms.

To keep its farmers on the land and at their primary work, Quebec revised and greatly increased its system of premiums. Adjustments were made in 1933 to take families into account. A single man, for instance, could claim the land-clearing and cultivation bonuses for up to fifteen acres, a married man for thirty, and a father of six minor children for up to forty acres. The premium for bringing an acre under cultivation was increased to $25 in 1937, to $30 in 1942. In 1937 a special additional premium of $15 an acre was offered for up to five acres of land that had been broken or were newly worked that season, while 1937–38 brought many special premiums for building a house ($250), a bake oven ($10), drains ($2 an arpent), purchasing livestock and farm implements, or producing honey, maple syrup, or maple sugar (each 5¢ a pound). Most of these were speedily abolished, but in 1942 a similar system of grants for rearing livestock or poultry, keeping bees, or like activities was inaugurated. In the 1936–49 era Quebec spent about $850,000 yearly on these aids, which were paid directly to the farmers. With outside work so scarce, settlers threw themselves with a will into the premium-earning tasks of developing and upgrading their farms.

The Depression gave renewed vigour to the colonization movement in Quebec and more direct government participation in it. Higher spending on agricultural development, colonization roads, and subsidies and premiums for colonists were forthcoming from both Liberal and Union Nationale governments. The outlays of the Ministry of Colonization soared from $2.2 million in 1931–32 to $10.5 million in 1937–38 and 1938–39. Much of this was in support of the clerically dominated colonization movement that suddenly sprang to life in 1930 when a society at Ste Anne de la Pocatière undertook to sponsor settlement of a district in Abitibi, and, as though on cue, diocesan interest in this work was rekindled. In 1934 the province brought the dioceses into the picture by assigning them specific colonization areas. Each diocese selected colonists from among its own communicants and recruited Franco-American and other immigrants from abroad. These they directed to the reserved lands, providing missionaries to organize and take charge of the settlements. They also opened colonization roads, helped colonists fence their lands, and arranged for seed grain and other supplies and equipment.

Unfortunately, even government-assisted and clerically sponsored colonization was not proof against settler disillusionment and frequent farm abandonment, for many colonists gave up and sought futures elsewhere. Many simply considered life on the land too difficult or unsatisfying; others found work in mines, mills, or cities more congenial. Nearly half the colonists who settled under the Gordon Plan in Témiscamingue and a quarter of those in Abitibi quit, as did about two thirds of those recruited under the 1934 agreement, while even the 1936 program reported a one-sixth shrinkage by 1940. Similarly with the acreages sold for settlement – they did indeed reach record heights in 1933–34 (556,606 acres and 5,989 lots) and 1938–39 (459,846 acres and 5,064 lots), but so did the acreages repossessed. In 1935–36 there was an actual reduction in land in private hands, and the net increase in 1937–38 was negligible.

Despite these losses, the Quebec drive achieved considerable success. No fewer than 145 new parishes were formed between 1931 and 1941, a sharp contrast with the experience during the prosperous late twenties. As many as 29 new parishes were started in 1931 and a record 33 in 1935. The populations of the northern frontier counties increased strikingly as well – Témiscamingue from 20,609 to 40,500, Abitibi from 23,692 to over 64,000. Of course, much of the increase, in Abitibi at least, was the result of concurrent expansion in the mining industries. Still, by 1941 no fewer than fifty townships in Abitibi (of seventy-two surveyed) had acquired settlers, sixty-one parishes and missions were developed, and because of widespread clearing of land the climate of the district had become significantly warmer.

Farming also was becoming more specialized into dairy and livestock production and in potato growing. While Abitibi still seemed an immature farming region, Témiscamingue was approaching maturity. In both counties farming villages appeared amid the ever-widening clearings, with improved houses and barns, well-fenced fields, and dirt roads linking the farms to the villages and their shipping points. With a return to somewhat better economic conditions, the farmer's success was reflected in more purchases of farm machinery and automobiles, increasing specialization in cash crops, greater attention to crop rotation and to improving the soil by raising leguminous crops, and wider use of chemical fertilizers. Advances in dairying were indicated by the establishing of more tuberculosis-free cattle districts and competitions among farmers to encourage better livestock and improved crops.

In contrast with Quebec, the Depression led Ontario finally to abandon the generations-long program of actively promoting and assisting colonization of the arable northern lands of the province. Despite the government's efforts and the assistance settlers received under the federal-provincial agreements, the success record of land settlement remained exceedingly low. The numbers of farm lots purchased each year fell steadily from 1,351 in 1930 to 386 in 1939, and the results of the Relief Land Settlement Scheme were equally unfortunate. The failure rate among these last settlers was as high as 70 per cent in the Hearst and Kapuskasing districts, though only 33 per cent in the Cochrane and Matheson districts, the locale of considerable French-Canadian immigration and of mining growth and prosperity. The difficulty apparently began with the choice of settlers; the local boards that selected them were interested primarily in removing them from the relief rolls, not in their suitability for northern pioneering. They took up their farms with little capital beyond the remainder of their $600 subsidy, which was wholly insufficient to develop a successful farm, especially in a time of economic crisis and in usually difficult surroundings. Poor choices of land were frequent, some settlers were content to wait passively for further assistance that never came, and cultural differences created distress in districts originally settled by French Canadians whose institutions already were in place.

The record of these years, however, differed little from that of the previous thirty. A study claimed that of 38,160 land sales made in Northern Ontario after 1912, up to 64.7 per cent of the purchases and 72 per cent of the land area had been abandoned or cancelled by 1937. Small wonder then that the election of the Ontario Liberal party on July 19, 1934, should have been followed by virtual termination of the colonization programs that the new premier, Mitchell Hepburn, had long pilloried as a waste of public money. The public had become convinced that assisted settlement was a hopeless failure and accepted the new government's writing off the program without protest. On September 18, 1935, Hepburn announced: "We are going out of the business of colonisation. It is unsound in principle and simply throwing good money after bad."[28] Colonization henceforth would follow, not lead, economic advance. Instead, the government would improve the northern farmers' position indirectly by encouraging expansion of the mining and forestry industries. Local markets for farm produce would then revive, and farmers would gain employment working in the woods or cutting logs and pulpwood for sale. Thus an era that stretched back to Ferguson, Whitney, Ross, and Mowat came to an end, and Ontario's northern farmers were left largely to their own devices.

Alberta was another province where pioneer farmers had to face down the Depression by their own efforts. The provincial government participated in the joint programs to resettle farmers driven by drought from the South (many had already moved during the twenties) and ex-farmers from the cities or coal towns on new farms along the northern or western farming frontiers. Above all, Alberta had to cope with the serious difficulties faced by recently settled pioneers, starting the arduous tasks of carving successful farms out of the northern brush, for whom it became responsible when it finally gained control of its natural resources on October 1, 1930. The new administration decided that Albertans alone (including seventeen-year-old youths and women heads of families) would be permitted to take up homesteads and closed many areas to settlement. Eventually in 1939 it terminated the free homestead policy altogether, replacing it with a system of leases of 320-acre lots on which no rent had to be paid for the first three years and only small rents thereafter. The leaseholders, for their part, were required to reside on the land for six months of the year, build a house worth $200 within five years, break 160 acres, and have 90 acres in crop by the fifth year.

Because of the virtual cessation of new settlement the farming frontier expanded slowly. During the decade the population of the Peace River district increased only from 50,000 to 60,000 and the population on farms from 34,234 to 40,643. The book value of the farms shrank from ten dollars an acre to seven, and declining cash incomes forced some established farmers to cancel recent purchases of school or Indian reserve lands and others to have their debts scaled down by the Farmers' Creditors Arrangement Act. Many disposed of their lands to more fortunate neighbours, significantly increasing the numbers of tenant-operators. These consolidations raised the average size of farms by 25 per cent to 320 acres (and to 352 acres in the British Columbia part of the district) – a condition that facilitated introduction of more mechanical equipment when times improved. On the farms the improved acreage soared by a remarkable 50 per cent during the dec-ade, 525,248 acres being placed in cultivation, particularly in recently settled sections along the northern and western fringes. Four addi-tional acres on average were won for cultivation on each farm each year (as much as eight in areas of lighter forest cover), and by 1941 the average frontier farm contained sixty acres of cleared land, enough to give the farm family a livelihood in normal years. Despite physical and climatic difficulties, long years of low prices for farm produce, and lack of paying work between farming seasons, the homesteaders of the 1927–32 era achieved economic security by their own strenuous efforts.

In spite of hardships and numerous tragedies, considerable increases in occupied and cultivated lands were recorded in the thirties north of the Saskatchewan River in Saskatchewan and Alberta, in the Peace River district of Alberta and British Columbia, and in central British Columbia along the CNR's Prince Rupert branch. In Ontario and Quebec, French-Canadian settlement expanded steadily down the lower St. Lawrence, along the edges of the Lac St Jean country, and especially in the Clay Belts along the former National Transcontinental Railway in Abitibi, Témiscamingue, and westward in Ontario. Indeed, the Quebec geographer Esdras Minville credited French Canadians with a unique talent for conquering forested wildernesses, and he saw their mission as spreading themselves across the Middle North of Quebec and adjacent provinces.

The sufferings of the thirties, however, made it evident that more positive steps from government were needed if colonization were to succeed. As had been proposed elsewhere, Minville advocated state-sponsored clearing operations using efficient, large-scale machinery in advance of settlement to reduce the cost of bringing land into production. He also put his finger on another difficulty facing future farm pioneers in Quebec and elsewhere – the growing scarcity of 100- or 160-acre units of land capable of providing a livelihood for a farming family. Minville advocated a new form of landholding for Quebec that would allow for part-agricultural, part-forestry, part-fishery units to utilize the poorer soils that still remained for colonization. For the thirties had fully demonstrated that agricultural pioneering pure and simple in the Subarctic was scarcely a viable long-term proposition. Farmers might accept the privations that went with carving traditional farms from thin soils during a time of acute economic depression. But would they persist in doing so when alternative paying employment became available, and when attainment of a comfortable standard of living became the overriding goal for every Canadian?

IV

Settlers of the farming frontiers during the interwar years fitted into one or other of two widely differing societal patterns – an individualistic type, under which each settler conducted a family enterprise, in his own interests and according to his own wishes as best he could, and a group settlement form, in which an agricultural community was organized along predetermined lines to achieve desired social, religious, ethnic, or other goals. The individualistic system – that mainly followed in Ontario and the provinces to the west – left each pioneer to provide for his social and other needs by co-operating with his neighbours in voluntary or state-directed activities. The system tended to foster a form of farming that was not only inefficient and wasteful of labour and resources but also largely ignored social considerations. By offering only enough land to sustain one family the system segregated the agricultural community into discrete family-sized units. The haphazard character of the free homestead system also resulted in great ethnic and religious diversity among settlers that made it harder to build firm social relationships and co-operative institutions. In addition, widespread poverty, the large recently settled immigrant populations, and the low density of rural settlement led to deplorably inadequate educational, health care, and other services that brought hardship and suffering to many settlers.

Most of these conditions improved as pioneers started to clear away the brush and bring additional acres under the plough or into pasture, erect buildings, acquire implements and stock, and attain a comfortable if not affluent livelihood. In fairly well settled districts, rural neighbourhoods became able to support local public improvements, schools, churches, and amenities that had formerly been beyond the pioneers' reach. Unfortunately, in hard times other districts regressed through widespread farm abandonments, making it more difficult for the survivors to maintain existing services. This occurred in Southern Saskatchewan and Alberta through drought, and in the interlake district of Manitoba – where much submarginal land occupied during and after the Great War had to be abandoned in the early 1920s – through unwise settlement. A more general cause everywhere was the wretched Depression-era conditions. So many farms were abandoned in the Middle North during the thirties that the governments of Ontario and British Columbia had to gather isolated farm families and consolidate them in more favourable localities where they might better sustain their social as well as economic positions. Another socially inhibiting force whose effects grew more pronounced from the twenties onward was technological change, particularly mechanization; this increased the optimum size of farm while reducing rural population density and, consequently, the social amenities available to the settlers of the agricultural frontier.

Co-operation and collective action were especially important for individual farmers attempting to establish themselves along the northern frontier. Administrators saw co-operatives as an important tool to enable such farmers to combine forces to achieve goals beyond the abilities of each, and provinces made it easy for all sorts of co-operatives to be formed under the benevolent supervision of their departments of agriculture. In the West, locals of the provincial wheat pools extended into the northernmost grain-growing districts, and the rosters of provincial farm associations included farm women and youth clubs, beekeeping, floriculture, and poultry-raising associations and even farmers desiring to share the costs of acquiring pedigreed livestock. Quebec's farmers were especially well organized, the Union catholique des cultivateurs (UCC), formed in 1924, including no fewer than ninety-one agricultural societies and 723 farmers' clubs by 1929. The co-operative farmer groups were more than economic organizations. The vast majority performed educative functions by encouraging adoption of improved practices and properly kept accounts and records, besides social and acculturative functions of bringing together persons of differing backgrounds.

The group approach gathered intending settlers in concentrated colonies of farming families that occupied contiguous districts and functioned as religious, linguistic, and ethnic entities. In Quebec, where this system was the most prevalent and officially favoured, new settlements were made up of relatively homogeneous groups of families under the direction of specially trained curés. These were well adapted for coping with the physical challenges, for the colonists could be readily mobilized for group tasks such as clearing forest cover and draining the soil and could procure specialized equipment for these purposes beyond the means of the individual farmer to acquire. The consequent solidarity and sense of security also kept members from giving up in times of adversity. Quebec-style colonies were found along the frontiers all the way to the Peace River district; in addition, some other religious and ethnic minorities established substantial compact settlements, sometimes grouped around central villages. The Hutterian Brethren even lived together in communal buildings and collectivized their farming operation.

The *raisons d'être* for the group settlements were to maintain their people's way of life by reuniting scattered followers into communities that could survive economically and where their adherence to the group's traditions would be intensified, with contamination from outside reduced. The great desire of most of these people was to be left alone, and they were content to make the best of whatever situation they faced. Their religion, which played a large part in the efforts to maintain their separate identity, was quite secure; their churches could function effectively without challenge or distraction and maintain control over many social and cultural as well as religious functions.

Despite their best efforts, however, group settlers found it increasingly difficult to maintain their distinctive characters, for the trend was against the self-sufficient style of farming that alone could effectively insulate the group from outside contacts. Even in Quebec the rise of specialized farming, cash markets, mechanization, advanced technology, and farming organizations interfered with preserving the traditional values of family, church, language, and rural way of life. Colonists were drawn into relationships with outsiders through schools, sports activities, farmer organizations, political parties, and periodic visits to predominantly English towns. Sometimes the larger population applied pressure to the group settlements to hasten the process of acculturation, usually kindling suspicion and resentment that perhaps intensified their determination to survive as distinctive entities. Indeed, "Assimilation [might] be facilitated . . . if administrations learned how to work with the inevitable tide rather than against it."[29]

A frequent source of concern for the group settlements in the English-speaking provinces was control and operation of their schools in the face of pressures to make them conform to the standards of the departments of education. Some religious instruction could generally be accommodated under the existing regulations, particularly by establishing a Separate School district. Teaching in languages other than English was a more difficult privilege to obtain, although a sympathetic administration and school inspectors could go some way to meet the desires of French, German, Ukrainian, or other peoples. Even such support, however, had its limits, for the officials, like the public, considered it the primary purpose of state-supported schools to acculturate pupils to the English-Canadian pattern. They accomplished this by imparting facility in English expression, modern ways of thought, and exposure to English-speaking classmates and other influences. Segments of the majority community periodically expressed alarm at the persistence of ethnic differences and pressed for an end to leniency in school administration in order to hasten the assimilation of immigrant populations. That attitude persisted during the twenties, thanks to passions generated by the Great War, concern over the scale of continental European immigration, and the activities of politicians hoping to profit from the emotions aroused by the issue. The threatened groups reacted by using what means they could to work for their rights as they saw them – which in the case of the French-Canadian colonies could be quite considerable.

As frontier-style farming advanced from primarily home-consumption operations to the stage of commercial production for outside markets, communities developed that served the surrounding farm populations and were sustained by their patronage. Most of these were small centres with a general store or two, a post office, and usually a livery barn, gasoline station, hardware, lumberyard, blacksmith and machine shop. Those on railway lines also served as collecting points for farm produce to be shipped outside, which called for station agents, grain elevators, restaurant and hotel, perhaps a part-time bank branch. Where railways were still under construction buildings often were built on skids, ready to be moved to the official townsite once the route was fixed. By the time the steel arrived, the town was already in being, with substantial hotels, stores, poolroom and barbershop, movie house, bank, lumberyards, grain elevators, stock pens, garages. Of course, many railway stations remained mere shipping points with but an elevator or two plus a stock pen.

Many small communities, especially in Northern Ontario and Northern Quebec, also boasted small manufacturing industries: creameries, cheese factories, sawmills, or woodworking plants. At divisional points, railway payrolls supported sufficient numbers of mechanics and trainmen to require communities with a full complement of public utilities and services besides the usual stores and offices. District capitals such as Grande Prairie had several dozen stores, service industries and businesses, doctors, lawyers, bank branches, weekly newspapers and movie houses, churches of several denominations, multi-roomed elementary and secondary schools, court houses, immigration halls, police detachments, branches of federal and provincial government departments, and the like. Thanks to the growth of automobile traffic, these independent trading centres drew upon increasingly wider districts and were patronized by farmers whenever they needed a special service, made an expensive purchase, or desired to attend church or lodge meetings and entertainments, movies, or visit the beer parlours. The smaller local centres continued to meet the day-to-day needs of the farmer, but the automobile restricted their functions and their prospects for growth.

A major force in the evolution of farming areas was the apparatus of local self-government. Frontier settlement usually took place within townships or parishes that already possessed some form of municipal structure, at least on paper. In sparsely settled districts, provincial officials set the local rates and arranged for public works and social services. After the populations reached a certain size, they became improvement districts, whose residents were empowered to elect reeves and councillors and levy taxes on property for local purposes. Still later, they advanced to municipal district status, with wider powers of local self-government administered by an elected reeve and six councillors. The municipal government could levy both property and poll taxes and licence fees and issue bonds to finance capital projects. They appointed secretary-treasurers, hired public works and maintenance men, and collected the requisitions levied by the school districts and those for the support of hospitals. Villages were organized along similar lines except that their governments had somewhat wider powers. Whatever their functions, these local government organizations were important agencies of democratic action, transcending differences among residents and enabling localities to progress at the pace the majority of inhabitants desired.

Education was organized still more democratically, for school districts were no more than twenty-five or thirty square miles in extent (to limit the distances children had to travel) and the schools were of immediate interest to every settler. The school board members usually built the first school with their own hands and boarded the teachers among their families. The school's cost was the largest single burden on taxation raised in the locality; its conduct concerned all, for the public school

> . . . signifies the presence of children, family life, and the development of stable settlement in new areas. It serves the whole population, regardless of race, creed, or language, and it is therefore one of the chief means by which a variety of population elements become assimilated to one language and a common culture. The fact that it is supported by funds from local taxes as well as from provincial grants makes for greater stability than is commonly found among voluntary institutions. Moreover, the role of the school as a social centre, especially in rural areas, and the interest which is shown in its work by various organized groups, makes the school one of the basic institutions of a prairie community.[30]

Establishment of a school district usually required only four resident taxpayers and at least eight school-aged children as pupils. A petition from at least three residents was required, but more often the local school inspector decided when a school was needed, set up the district, and acted as trustee until a local board could be elected. Typically the first rural school was built of logs by volunteer labour with a small provincial grant to help pay for purchased items. The province initially supplied special operating grants, but when these aids ceased the rural schools often had difficulty raising enough revenues because homesteaders were exempted from local taxation until they received their patents. The boards reacted by reducing teacher salaries, shortening the school term, and taking taxes in kind for such services as heating or maintaining the school or boarding the teacher. An unsatisfactory standard of education often resulted because the schools had to hire beginner teachers, who seldom stayed more than one year, and children who had to travel long distances over almost impassable trails were often absent on account of inclement weather, lack of proper clothing, or parental indifference. When in school, the children received very little individual attention to their particular needs because all the grades were taught in the single classroom.

The obvious shortcomings of the rural schools aroused calls during the twenties to reorganize them into larger, centralized, consolidated districts that would lessen inequalities in revenues, provide graded schools and their facilities, attract better teachers, buy needed equipment, offer additional teaching services, and be operated along business lines. Yet this important reform was held back by the communities' strong determination to retain control of their schools (mainly for selfish reasons, unfortunately), coupled with lack of proper transportation to convey pupils to centralized schools. Alberta did introduce such a system in 1936, but other provinces did not follow suit until after the Second World War. The quality of education was undoubtedly improved by this means, but local school boards were reduced to figureheads, for the running of the schools passed almost completely into the hands of professional superintendents and full-time secretary-treasurers.

The situation was seldom as bad in hamlets and villages, where enrolments might warrant graded classes and taxes were sufficient to secure experienced, qualified teachers, teaching of technical and commercial subjects, and teaching aids, and to provide medical examinations. Even rural school districts sometimes joined together to operate a rural high school for their own senior pupils, many of whom were boarded in dormitories far from home. In Northern Ontario railway car schools provided schooling in seven systems along a thousand miles of railway by 1938. Children in other isolated areas or in places where they were too few to warrant a school often were accommodated by correspondence lessons furnished by provincial departments of education.

Above all, special attention was paid to providing a satisfactory level of public education to children from language groups other than English and to winning their parents' co-operation. The inspectors who oversaw the new settling districts often were specialists in dealing with the educational needs and problems of ethnic communities, such as the large Ukrainian blocs that had recently settled across the West. Parents in such groups who had little or no schooling themselves often failed to see the value of learning, and resented losing control over their children. But as they discovered the importance of education they sent their children more readily and for longer periods. During the twenties the average number of years of schooling increased in the western provinces until it surpassed that of Quebec and approached the level of Ontario.

The serious health needs of the populations of the new farming districts were a continuing challenge that became an increasing cause for concern. General A.D. McRae (M.P. for Vancouver North), for instance, complained that the new settlers in the Peace River district could not take proper care of their families and that "women and children die there for lack of medical attention."[31] In that district, as elsewhere, doctors and dentists were free to choose where to set up their practices and secure most of their income from private patients or occasionally from private hospitals they owned and operated. In addition, they received payments from the federal government for work with Indian patients, from the province or municipality for indigent patients, from municipalities and school boards for serving as health officers or school doctors. These services usually were adequate in settled areas, but they were far from meeting the needs of fringe districts where travel arrangements were primitive and the bulk of the people were penniless homesteaders, palpably unable to pay for medical attention, many of them being bewildered newcomers to Canada in the bargain.

By now, however, Canadians viewed health as a public concern and pressed governments to assist privately operated health services and establish public health facilities. Governments and philanthropic agencies began stationing district nurses and doctors in frontier locations. Thus Dr. Mary Percy Jackson, one of three English medical personnel the province of Alberta secured in 1929, was stationed at Meikle River on the northern margin of the Peace River district. There they were in a position to treat diseases, serious illnesses, maternity cases, and the accidents associated with clearing land or handling unruly livestock. Preventive action was supplied by periodic travelling clinics of doctors, nurses, and dentists who examined the children in the schools and investigated whatever local health problems were reported to them. Unfortunately, little as yet was done about the many threats to mental health resulting from the hardships, privations, isolated living, and limited outside contact that were the fate of the pioneering farm family, particularly the farm wife.

Hospitals were often available in frontier districts, for a goodly number had been opened by missionary organizations to treat their native clients and others were provided by the Victorian Order of Nurses, the Red Cross Society, Women's Institutes, and similar agencies. These last usually considered their role an interim one pending transfer of the responsibility to the local communities, which could transform them into municipal hospitals supported by public taxes and able to borrow for modernization and expansion. The church hospitals on the other hand, especially the Roman Catholic ones, continued to be maintained by the sponsoring orders as expansions of their earlier charitable work for native congregations. As districts became more settled and developed, new hospitals were built and operated by public authorities, though even then many local authorities found it advantageous to encourage a religious organization to open and operate a hospital in their area.

Both education and health were areas in which one-time private activities were becoming increasingly regulated or operated by public authorities. Socio-cultural organization and behaviour, in contrast, still remained a field for non-governmental concern, particularly of the churches. Because of the religious diversity that prevailed in many homesteading areas, churches found it difficult to maintain contact with followers widely dispersed as small minorities within the areas in which they dwelt:

> In almost every direction large settlements of foreigners are found who retain their national and religious faith and customs. Our own Church people are for the most part scattered – a few here, one there, here a small settlement, and there a wide area without any of our people. Hence our mission districts are large and the Missionary is required to spend much time getting over the ground, while the majority of our people are still in the "homesteading" stage, and little actual financial support can be secured either for the maintenance of the Missionary or towards the general needs of the Diocese.[32]

To serve these scattered groups, clergymen were stationed in the larger centres, churches were built at strategic sites, and "preaching points" were arranged where ministers could hold meetings and conduct services as often as other responsibilities permitted. Theological students became missionary assistants during the summers, gaining experience while they relieved the hard-pressed clergymen for other duties. Volunteers often aided the work in their neighbourhoods; the local Baptists at Grande Prairie, for instance, established a small church in 1928, which was followed by organization of a district church at Beaverlodge by "one of the converts of Grand Prairie Church" who "was evangelizing in the district . . . where his labors were attended with blessing to many."[33] The Church of England benefited from the efforts of Miss F.H.E. Hasell, who organized a van system to operate through the frontiers of Western Canada, visited remote districts, held sessions among Anglican families, enrolled their children for Sunday School correspondence lessons, arranged for clergymen and missionaries to follow up her work, and spoke widely in Eastern Canada and Britain to raise money and recruit volunteer workers.

Gradually, more ministers were secured, and the religious work was able to meet the needs of more of their people. Regular meetings began to be held at rural schools; then churches were built, until the larger denominations had church buildings and resident ministers or priests in most of the large villages of the farming frontier. Smaller villages often had one or more resident ministers, and visiting ministers cared for members of other denominations. Because of the scattered settlement, many residents rarely received visits from ministers of their own faith and often had to participate in other churches not too distant doctrinally from their own. The same pragmatic interdenominationalism had played a large part in the Church Union movement consummated in the 1920s.

Communicants of the Roman Catholic Church did not attend the meetings of other denominations and hence did not have to be "recaptured" from earlier mixed congregations, as was often the case when other churches came to establish new stations. Moreover, every settlement area already was part of a missionary apostolic prefecture or vicariate, and the clergy was present when the first settlers arrived; the missionaries simply applied their experience and outside support to serving white congregations while continuing their work with the native peoples. A single parish or centre often had to serve a community comprised of British, French, German, Polish, Ukrainian, Italian, Dutch, and other language groups, so that preaching and instructing sometimes had to be provided in three or more languages until, it was hoped, English would come into general use. Here lay a new difficulty, for the Catholic missionary orders in the frontier areas were predominantly French speaking. Many missionaries and their earlier congregations resented shifting to English. These language problems created many difficulties and occasional crises in frontier dioceses. Gradually, however, the Roman Catholic Church in Northern Ontario and the West became essentially English speaking except for certain parishes that remained French Canadian and Métis in composition or where members of a particular language group – such as the Italians – succeeded in securing priests of their own tongue. The religious situation of the Ukrainians was met by special missions to the "Ruthenes" by Ukrainian-speaking priests of the Uniate Church, in addition to which United Church and Church of England clergymen tried to win Ukrainians to their own flocks. There were also many proselytizing efforts among other Protestants, particularly by the smaller, more aggressive, recently founded sects.

The churches were by far the most important voluntary social organizations at this time, and they also sponsored some of the associations that formed part of the social life of the frontiers: Boy Scouts, Girl Guides, Canadian Girls in Training, Women's Auxiliaries, and Knights of Columbus. Many non-church associations also were active, among them the Great War Veterans' Association, the Canadian Legion, the Orange Lodge, the Masons, Oddfellows, Elks, Buffaloes, Rotarians, and Kiwanians, the St-Jean-Baptiste Society, and temperance societies. Local businessmen formed boards of trade and chambers of commerce; farmers formed locals of the provincial United Farmers movements and the parallel women's and youth groups. The Women's Institutes deserve special mention as a major multifunctional organization directed especially at the needs of the farm women. All these groups had further value in that they linked the small frontier populations in important cultural and fraternal ways with larger Canadian, even international, communities, resulting in support and badly needed aid.

Important socially at the local level were the schools and later the community halls, where musical, dramatic, literary, and athletic activities could be carried out. Sports were a strong socializing force, attracting members of all groups to join in local activities and exercise their skills as individuals by participating in baseball, hockey, soccer, and other team sports, in athletic competitions, horse races, and the like. In all these ways the inhabitants of the agricultural frontiers responded to the changing social, cultural, and technological situations of the period.

Thus expansion of the agricultural frontier meant more than bringing virgin lands under cultivation and harvesting their fruits. It represented a move forward of a complete civilization, imprinted with the technical, governmental, social, religious, and cultural features of the nation at large and of its many parts. Exploitation of the other great resources of the frontier required a mobile, nomadic society, or gave rise to small, isolated, sometimes impermanent centres of population organized along hierarchical or class lines. But agriculture constituted the planting on new soil of a permanent, essentially egalitarian civilization. In Northern Ontario and Quebec in particular, the agriculture *ecumene* affected the northern limits of forest, mining, and manufacturing frontiers over the long term, for the farms of the Middle North provided the foodstuffs and manpower and generated the year-round transportation facilities that enabled the other industries to become established and function. The agricultural frontiers may have been confined by climate to southerly parts of Subarctic Canada, but their repercussions extended much farther afield, turning Canadians' thoughts and many of its people to untapped resources awaiting development farther north.

CHAPTER 3

Forestry and Hydro Frontiers of the Middle North, 1918–1940

North of the St.Lawrence Lowland and the western prairies the Subarctic and Cordilleran forests extend across the Middle North of Canada in an unbroken band that is up to 400 miles wide. While pioneer farmers were nibbling at the southern margins of the woodlands, the forestry industries waged a far more extensive onslaught on this rich resource that occupies at least a third of the country, many times greater than the area of arable land. In Quebec, the forested lands alone are about twenty times as extensive as those devoted to agriculture. At various times the total area of the commercially exploitable forests has been estimated as 310,000 square miles of merchantable timber (1930), 450,000 square miles of productive and accessible forest (1955), and, more recently, 920,000 square miles of forest suitable for regular harvesting (1974). In short, the area considered productive forest almost trebled over this forty-year period, mainly because access and economic conditions improved, but also because utilization patterns changed drastically. Areas of forest, of course, do not tell the whole story, for productivity varies as much as twentyfold between Clayoquot on Vancouver Island and inland centres such as Cochrane, Fort McMurray, or The Pas.

I

As was true of other natural resources, during the interwar years extension northward of the forest industries was the result in part of the harvesting of larger quantities of certain kinds of wood, but mainly of the exhaustion of the best timber in the more accessible southerly parts of the forested region. In Quebec and Ontario, the red and white pine that had been mainly used in the manufacture of lumber had become

70

seriously depleted through heavy exploitation. The output of the Ottawa valley district by 1936 was only one fifth that of 1900, and scarcely any of the region's twenty large lumber mills were still operating. It was the same along the CPR west of Ottawa; Manitoulin Island had been completely stripped of sawlog material, and sawmilling at Callander, Bruce Mines, and Sault Ste Marie was only a shadow of its former self. Much the same could be said of the St Maurice and Saguenay–Lac St Jean districts in Quebec and the smaller accessible mixed-wood forests along the Saskatchewan River of the Prairie Provinces. Only in British Columbia did the lumber industry still thrive and expand. Thanks to the enormous quantities of excellent sawlog material in the southern parts of the rich, dense Pacific Coast Forest, huge sawmills were still kept busy at Vancouver, New Westminster, and other Lower Mainland centres, and on Vancouver Island.

The lumber industry shifted its focus to the new districts opened by the recently completed railways and expanding mining operations, but it was the remarkable expansion of the pulp and paper industry that affected forest utilization most during the twenties. As the big sawmills ceased operating, the stands left over from lumber operations were utilized for pulpwood. Pulp and paper mills sprang up along the railways crossing Northern Ontario to exploit the extensive forests of that region, while in Quebec the industry spread down the North Shore of the Gulf of St. Lawrence and into the fringes of the Lac St Jean district. From Shelter Bay, Pentecôte, Betsiamites, and other locations on the North Shore large quantities of pulpwood were cut, barked, and shipped by water to mills as far west as Cornwall, Thorold, and Fort William. One Trois-Rivières concern acquired Anticosti Island from its French owners, the $6-million purchase assuring the company of 450,000 cords annually. A large modern paper-manufacturing plant was established at Corner Brook, Newfoundland, at the mouth of the Humber River.

Expansion was greatly facilitated by the policies of governments that controlled forest and hydro power resources. During the 1920s a strongly pro-business stance supported their conviction that the way to promote the public interest was to assist the speediest, fullest development of their natural resources. The provinces readily granted generous concessions to resource developers, imposing few conditions on their plans for exporting the products of the resulting industries. By 1929 virtually all the accessible forest lands of Quebec, 80,188 square miles in total, had been granted or leased out to private holders; by 1940 Ontario had assigned an even larger portion (92,870 square miles) of its timber lands to pulp-making or lumbering concerns. The generosity, laxity, or reckless optimism of the forest-leasing policies of these two governments led directly to a newsprint industry débâcle after 1928.

Nor were these governments greatly concerned to generate revenue from their forest and power resources. The day had long passed when these could be regarded as a major revenue source; by the twenties the income was minor, even insignificant, in terms of current levels of government finance. Furthermore, ever-increasing fractions of what revenue was secured were being spent in administering the resources, especially in protecting the forests themselves – over 50 per cent in the case of Ontario. Only British Columbia – whose forests accounted for 36 per cent of its primary production – derived a significant part of its revenue from that source. Its forests in 1927–28 and 1928–29 yielded slightly better than one sixth of the provincial revenue, 25 per cent of which the provincial government devoted to administering them. The level of public spending reflected the larger scale and improved efficiency of government operations and the higher professional attainments of the staffs concerned with administering the resource.

During the Great War years the opportunities for easy profits, coupled with the shortage of qualified administrators, had encouraged widespread flouting of the laws and corrupting of public officials. In northwestern Ontario a powerful ring of lumbermen had shipped vast quantities of logs and pulpwood to the United States. These they secured, with the connivance of political confederates and local officials, by purchasing so-called settler lands, blanketing the country with bogus mining claims that allowed holders to clear the brush from the land, or simply raiding Crown lands. G. Howard Ferguson, Minister of Lands and Forests in Ontario from 1914 to 1919 and premier from 1923 to 1930, was accused of selling timber berths to a favoured company at below half the going rates. (The company eventually was fined $1.5 million for having underpaid its timber dues as well.)

After the war, and throughout the 1920s, there was a marked increase in professionally trained government foresters, and their better qualifications were reflected in the gradual assumption of greater authority in areas that had previously been left to private initiatives. By 1923, for example, the Ontario staff was setting up timber limits and estimating the prices to be secured from them instead of, as formerly, permitting the companies to locate and estimate desirable tracts and approach the government to set these aside for their convenience. Later legislation empowered the minister to expropriate land for forest purposes, expanded the forest reserves system, and obliged pulp and paper companies to furnish full information on their holdings and submit plans for conducting their operations on the sustained-yield prin-

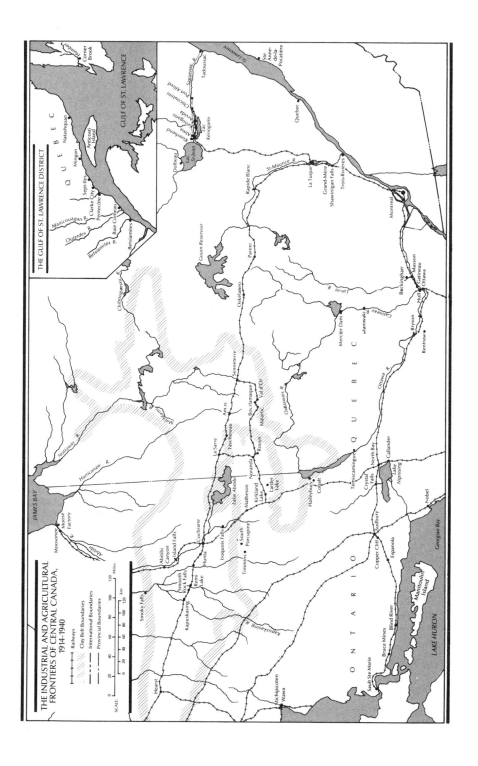

THE INDUSTRIAL AND AGRICULTURAL
FRONTIERS OF CENTRAL CANADA,
1914-1940

SCALE:

Railways
Clay Belt Boundaries
International Boundaries
Provincial Boundaries

THE GULF OF ST. LAWRENCE DISTRICT

GULF OF ST. LAWRENCE

QUEBEC

ONTARIO

LAKE HURON

Georgian Bay

JAMES BAY

ciple. E.J. Zavitz, who had reorganized the forest fire protective service, was given charge of a new forestry branch, which he turned into a research agency by expanding the tree nursery and seed farm services, starting ambitious reforestation projects, and subsidizing important research projects.

An example of greater governmental involvement that represented considerably more expenditure was Ontario's Provincial Air Service, established in 1924 chiefly for forest fire prevention work following an experimental program in conjunction with the Canadian Air Board and a broader contract in 1923 with Laurentide Air Service. The Department of Lands and Forests bought fourteen HS2L amphibious air-craft from Laurentide and appointed W.P.R. Maxwell, that company's manager, to direct the new service. The fleet was speedily enlarged to twenty planes, a headquarters was established at Sault Ste Marie with regional airbases at Remi Lake, Sudbury, and Sioux Lookout, and fliers and mechanics were recruited. Float-equipped planes patrolled threatened areas to detect incipient fires and transport firefighting crews, pumps, and other equipment to active fires. Control measures were helped greatly in the thirties by steadily improved meteorological reporting and broadcasting of hazardous weather conditions. The air service was of great benefit to forestry companies, relieving them of heavy expenses and doing useful aerial photography and mapping while patrolling their limits as well as other parts of the forest domain.

The air service was the most important single advance in the long-standing campaign against depredations caused by forest fires. In addition the provinces expanded their ranger services and tightened their regulations against travel in the woods, burning of brush by farmers and prospectors, and spark emissions from railway engines, steam boilers, and camp stoves. These efforts enjoyed some success in reducing forest fire losses, though they were undone during the Depression when governments reduced their protective staffs to economize. Countermeasures against the damage caused by insect pests and plant diseases were more difficult to devise and carry out. The main recourse available was the use of airplanes to dust infected areas with insecticides. The effectiveness of that procedure was already recognized as limited in comparison with methods of biological control such as introducing useful parasites. But practical solutions were still wanting, and research into the problem was proceeding in government and university laboratories.

Behind the increasing public involvement in research and forest management was concern over the ability of the forests not only to sustain the heavy annual commercial harvests but also the considerable losses caused by fires, parasites, and insect pests, estimated at upwards of 25 per cent of the annual depletion in 1936. In 1929 the governments started preparing a national inventory of the forests as an essential first step in determining future plans and programs. An improved forest classification was developed for the purpose, and the RCAF conducted extensive aerial photographic surveys to "estimate the volume of standing timber with an accuracy that compares favourably with ground surveys."[1] The resulting inventory, 273,656 million cubic feet of timber (170,144 million of which were classed as being in accessible forests), was shown as being depleted at an annual rate of approximately 4,000 million cubic feet in the later twenties. It was somewhat less during the thirties when annual commercial cuts declined drastically but losses from insects and parasites were on the increase and forest fires were at a high level, particularly in 1936 and 1938. The annual depletion rate of over 2 per cent of the accessible forest was dangerously high, and probably exceeded the annual growth rate of the entire resource. It was far higher, of course, in districts actually being utilized for logging and lumbering operations.

Such findings reinforced a growing conviction that stronger, more effective measures were needed to regulate the activities of companies and arrest the depletion of the forests. Informed scientific opinion was increasingly coming to the view that forestry, like agriculture, should be put on a sustained-yield basis and that administrative policies to put this into practice should be developed. The Rowell-Sirois Report (1940), for instance, suggested that forestry companies institute effective management and conservation programs and conduct operations on the sustained-yield principle rather than the traditional "cut-and-run" approach. Since the companies generally failed to adopt proper conservation practices, persons concerned for the forests' well-being felt it was incumbent on governments to take steps to maintain the resources over the long term on behalf of the community as well as of the industry. After 1945 governments would take stronger measures to direct the development of their forest resources along sounder, more responsible lines.

The forests gave rise to three major industries: logging, sawmilling, and manufacturing pulp and paper. In the provinces east of the Rockies, work in the woods was largely seasonal, geared to wintertime cutting operations on normally marshy ground and the use of icy sleigh roads to haul the logs to watercourses. Every winter thousands of men would leave farms and towns to work in the forests at the camps of timber operators or of jobbers filling contracts for pulp and paper concerns. The winter months would be spent felling the trees, chopping or sawing the trunks into eight-foot lengths for lumber mills or four-foot lengths for pulp mills, and moving the logs by horse-drawn sleds to the banks of lakes, rivers, and creeks. During the spring freshets the logs would be floated down to larger rivers, to be driven by the current or towed in rafts by tugs. As many as 240,000 men and up to 30,000 horses were employed in the woods operations at their peak. The drives by river were still very important, though in some regions the logs were usually sledded to a railway or highway point for shipment to their destinations.

Fundamental changes were impinging on the traditional mode of operation by the end of the thirties. Portable power saws began to be used, especially to cut logs into suitable lengths or fell small trees. Automotive transport became far more extensive: tractors for hauling in the woods, trucks for long-distance road transport, and motorboats and tugboats on the lakes and rivers. Mechanical graders and bulldozers were used in making forest trails and roads; mechanical cranes helped load and unload the wood supplies. These, while considerably increasing the output per man, reduced woods employment, made many traditional axemen and river drivers redundant, and demanded a new workforce dominated by skilled machine operators and mechanics.

Pacific Coast logging was a very different proposition because of the size of the trees and the mild climate that permitted virtual year-round activity. Logging was done by specialized companies that employed much machinery as well as horses and oxen to fell the giant trees and haul them to marshalling points in secluded coves for shipment along the coastal waters to the mills. To move the heavy logs down the steep slopes donkey engines were often needed, and the spectacular ''high lead'' system also was employed:

> Later it was found that by running the cable through a pulley attached to the top of a spar tree 100 or more feet above the ground, the logs could be ''skidded'' to the main line of transportation – railway or road – more easily and cheaply. With this method the front end of the log is lifted to some extent so that at least some of the obstructions are avoided. . . . In some cases, such as in crossing a ravine, a cable is stretched between two spar-trees and the logs are elevated to a travelling carriage. There are many methods of setting up these cable systems to suit the topography and lay-out of the operations.[2]

Coast logging was very wasteful because the operators cut down the mature trees and left them to roll down the slopes or dragged them through the underbrush, either way ruining new growth and destroying the area for future logging. Moreover, the slash often was left behind to impede new growth and create a serious fire hazard during the hot summer days. Very little attention was paid to reforestation.

The quantities of timber logged from Canada's forests during the interwar period reflected the changing markets for wood and ranged from 3,091 million cubic feet in 1929 to as little as 2,378 million cubic feet in 1922. The principal use was for lumber, fuelwood was the next largest category, pulpwood represented a smaller but growing share, and the final 5 per cent was comprised of railway ties, posts, round mining timber, fence rails, and other products. By 1939, when production of pulpwood was setting new records, equal amounts of timber were being used for each of the three main purposes. Quebec was the largest source for pulpwood and for fuelwood, its annual cut being around one third of Canada's total. A sizeable fraction of the pulpwood, incidentally, moved to the United States in unprocessed form, the amount being 1,294,000 cords in 1929 (nearly a fifth of that year's pulpwood cut), and during the thirties 1,020,000 cords were exported annually from Quebec alone.

The lumber industry, centred mainly in Quebec and Ontario in 1919, achieved an interwar production record of 4,299,000 M. ft. b.m. in 1920 at the crest of the post-war boom, which was not to be reached again until 1941 and 1942 but has been far exceeded since 1950. The declines in lumber prices of 25 per cent in the autumn of 1920 and in 1921, and a further 20 per cent in 1922, drastically curtailed lumber production, which only began to recover in the mid-twenties. The industry expanded into appropriate forested areas opened by recently completed railways, for example along the National Transcontinental and Canadian Northern routes in Quebec and Ontario, along the Hudson Bay Railway, and west and north of Edmonton. Usually the big operators arrived first to harvest the largest, richest stands for distant markets, exhaust them, and move on to other locations, leaving the field to numerous small, mobile milling companies, serving largely local markets, that cut the smaller, sparser, more remote tracts that had not been worth the big companies' while.

While production of lumber and minor wood products increased in Alberta and Manitoba in the 1920s, the larger lumber industries of the central provinces were unable to follow suit. They were affected by the increasing demand for pulp logs and, after 1924 and 1925, by competition from British Columbia. Lumber there, drawn mainly from the southern coast and interior forests and only marginally (about one eighth) from the northern Prince Rupert and Fort George Forestry Districts, was of very high quality and could be produced cheaply enough to capture markets in the Prairie Provinces and, thanks to the Panama Canal, in the larger markets of the Eastern United States and Canada, too. Ontario's lumber production recovered somewhat during the twenties, but Quebec's fell by one third and did not regain its previous volume, for operators turned to producing pulpwood and fuelwood instead. By 1930 the Quebec lumber industry numbered 1,883 small mills, and each typically employed two to five men working for three to four months in the summers. The small operators of the thirties mainly served expanding mining and construction activities in the Lac St Jean and Abitibi areas of Quebec, the new gold mining camps of Northern Ontario, industries along the Prince Rupert branch of the CNR, and numerous isolated mining camps scattered across the North all the way to the District of Mackenzie and Yukon Territory.

II

The pulp and paper industry and its related hydro-electric power developments assumed important positions in the Canadian economy during the twenties and profoundly affected many parts of Canada's frontier, where the industry was mainly located. Pulpwood, wood-pulp, and newsprint paper exports became leading components in the national trading pattern, even rivalling wheat as a major export staple. Newsprint paper output doubled every five or six years after 1913, when 350,000 tons were produced. The total reached 1,400,000 tons in 1924 and soared to 2,725,000 tons (valued at $150.8 million) in 1929. Then, after declining to a low point of 1,919,000 tons in 1932, it moved to new records of 3,673,000 tons in 1937 and 3,503,000 tons in 1940. The reasons behind the spectacular tenfold increase in less than a generation are readily apparent. The industrial and financial might of the United States was growing immensely, and its domestic supplies of woodpulp and papers steadily fell farther behind the accelerating demand. Newsprint paper especially was in short supply as a result of the heightened worldwide consumption of newspapers and magazines, and an endless market for the products of Canada's forests seemed assured.

The Subarctic forests recently opened by the pre-war round of railway construction contained both the vast woodlands and the valuable hydro-electric power sites needed by the pulp and paper industry, and the provincial governments were eager to see these resources developed. The government of Ontario, seeing the mills as the spearhead to opening new districts and making successful farming possible, stood ready to collaborate with the companies in their work of regional development. Quebec refused to yield even to powerful Sunday Observance groups pressing it to make the mills comply with the statutory day of rest lest such a step might arrest the expansion of the industry in the province. Governments in both provinces were downright lavish in awarding new timber and hydro grants in exchange for commitments to establish new pulp and paper industries and carry them forward to the most advanced stages of activity. The concessions, in turn, became instant assets against which the recipients could float large loans and raise new share capital to carry out their undertakings.

This process was already under way in 1914 and was stimulated by the trends of the war and post-war years. During the war, U.S. interests continued to enter Canada to take advantage of the greatly increased wartime markets for newsprint and specialty pulps, the absence of European sources of supply, and technological advances that were making large-scale operations and the manufacture of newsprint paper more profitable. Paper companies hastened to acquire additional timber limits from the provinces, while leases transferred between companies commanded ever increasing prices. New grants included one by Quebec in the Shelter Bay district on the North Shore to the Ontario Paper Company, controlled by Colonel Robert McCormick, the publisher of the *Chicago Tribune*, the *New York News*, and the *Detroit Mirror*, who already operated a newsprint mill at Thorold. Ontario companies, notably Abitibi Power and Paper and Spanish River Pulp and Paper, secured additional limits, the latter to supply its newsprint mill at Espanola.

Even though they could not undertake costly waterpower development projects during wartime, entrepreneurs continued to secure concessions to valuable sites for future development. The vast hydro potential of the Saguenay–Lac St Jean district began to be assembled by Price Brothers and J.E.A. Dubuc, who jointly formed the Quebec Development Company in 1914 to exploit the huge site at La Décharge de Lac St Jean. The Quebec Streams Commission also continued its program of assisting forestry companies by building works to divert Lac Kénogami to create a larger power source for the Price Brothers and Dubuc pulp and paper mills at Chicoutimi, and started work in 1916 on a very large storage dam on the upper St Maurice River, behind which the massive Gouin Reservoir began filling with water. That dam, together with smaller ones on the tributary Manouane River, added 50 per cent more power potential to every hydro plant on the St Maurice.

The rush to secure Canadian forestry and waterpower resources became a torrent when the war ended, especially as prices of newsprint paper and specialty pulps soared to triple the pre-war levels. In the east, on the Gulf of St. Lawrence, British press lords secured exploitable Crown forests in Newfoundland and Quebec and took over the pioneer Gulf Pulp and Paper Company of Clarke City. The Southern Labrador Pulp and Lumber Company, a Boston organization, also obtained a large timber limit in that region. Much new investment went into reorganizing companies and financing their progression to the production stage. The 1,740-square-mile concession on the Kapuskasing River, granted in 1918, was speedily taken over by the Kimberly-Clark Corporation of Wisconsin, which chartered the Spruce Falls Pulp and Paper Company to develop the property as a source of supply for the parent concern. The giant International Paper Company entered Quebec by acquiring the St. Maurice Lumber Company and its properties, securing two large waterpower sites on that river, and building a huge modern pulp and paper mill at Trois-Rivières (1920). With the aid of U.S. capital, the Saguenay district industrialist J.E.A. Dubuc reorganized his properties there, including four pulp mills and a hydro site at Port Alfred. Quebec also leased out hydro sites on the Batiscan River to Price Brothers and on the Ottawa to the Kippawa Company. The I.W. Killam financial interests of Montreal reorganized the Whalen Pulp and Paper Company on the Pacific Coast, and engineered the most ambitious merger of all, the $53 million Riordon Pulp and Paper Company, which took over the Edwards and Gilmour properties in the Ottawa valley, including the pulp mill at Kipewa and waterpower sites rated at 150,000 horsepower. In northwestern Ontario E.W. Backus – a powerful Minnesota financier and entrepreneur who already controlled vast forests in the United States, pulp and paper mills at International Falls and Fort Frances, and waterpowers of the Rainy Lake region and one of the outlets of Lake of the Woods – received a large timber limit on English River and a lease of White Dog Rapids on the Winnipeg River twenty-four miles below its source in Lake of the Woods, which gave him a virtual power monopoly in the district beyond the Lake Superior watershed.

All these arrangements were made possible by a buoyant market for the companies' shares, some of which rose by as much as 600 per cent between 1917 and August 1920. On August 14, 1920, the first major break in the stock prices occurred, and serious declines set in during the ensuing winter as investors finally realized the difficulties that confronted the industry. By early 1921 the markets for forest products had also fallen and production of woodpulp and newsprint paper dropped by almost 20 per cent in that year. The companies were left with large quantities of logs purchased at ruinously high prices. The jobbers who purchased logs from settlers also were hurt, and farmers in the spring of 1921 suddenly found themselves unable to dispose of their winter's cuts. Some pulp and paper companies laid off hundreds of men; others cut the wages of their employees to bring down operating costs. The recently organized Riordon Company went bankrupt in 1921, throwing its labour force out of work and spreading distress across Abitibi, where it had secured large amounts of pulp-wood from private suppliers.

But the recession soon lifted, and from 1923 the pulp and paper industry seemed to move ahead following a dynamic of its own. The improved market for newsprint caused firms to upgrade their manufacturing from groundwood, sulphite, and kraft pulps to the more remunerative newsprint and other papers and the widening range of specialty pulps needed in the manufacture of rayon and other industrial products. Some raised new capital and built up-to-date establishments to exploit the forest and hydro wealth being offered to them. Much of the expansion was inspired by American newspaper interests, which signed large-volume long-term contracts with producers to secure their wants and often invested in the companies as well; some of them, in fact, set up their own newsprint-producing subsidiaries, as Colonel McCormick had done earlier.

The assured markets encouraged manufacturers to expand production by installing bigger, more efficient machinery and set them on a course of acquiring still larger timber limits on the ground of needing adequate supplies of pulpwood for their enlarged operations. A good illustration is the Spruce Falls Pulp and Paper Company at Kapuskasing, which produced woodpulp for manufacture in Kimberly-Clark's U.S. plants. The owners secured the *New York Times* as a new partner, applied for and received a larger pulpwood tract and a bigger hydro-electric power site from the provincial government, and then proceeded to expand the newsprint output from 115 to 550 tons a day by adding a modern newsprint mill to serve the needs of the two owner companies. All told, the owners' investment in the plant, timber limits, power station, local railway, and community amounted to $30 million, mostly borrowed from American financial institutions and repaid out of company profits.

The same process was under way in much of the Middle North, creating a great series of pulp and paper mills that reached the stage of production during the middle and later 1920s. In Quebec there were plants at Riverbend, Dolbeau, and Port Alfred in the Saguenay district; at La Tuque on the St Maurice; and at Gatineau and Buckingham in the Ottawa sector. In northeastern Ontario there were mills at Iroquois Falls, Smooth Rock Falls, and Kapuskasing, and at Fort William in the west; still other plants were at Pine Falls, Manitoba, and Corner Brook, Newfoundland. These produced, or were preparing to produce, enormous quantities of pulp and paper products for U.S., British, and Canadian markets. To bring order to the headlong expansion a new trend set in after 1926 – consolidation of individual concerns into large corporate combinations. The earliest of these, in 1926–27, brought together nine paper mills of the Abitibi and Spanish River companies – six in Ontario, two in Quebec, and one in Manitoba. The new corporation controlled over 30,500 square miles of forests and operated facilities with a reported 2,100 tons of newsprint capacity daily, 25 per cent of Canada's total. An even more impressive combination, the Canada Power and Paper Corporation, was organized by the Montreal financier Sir Herbert Holt. Holt merged half a dozen large organizations of the St Maurice and Lac St Jean districts to form an empire with over 24,000 square miles of forest land and a daily manufacturing capacity of 2,464 tons of newsprint plus 260 tons of other pulps.

By 1931 these two giants, together with Canadian International, Price Brothers, St. Lawrence Corporation, and Backus-Brooks Company, controlled nearly 80 per cent of the total newsprint capacity east of the Rockies. Some combinations, however, were more impressive on paper than in reality. Abitibi, apart from its two modern plants at Iroquois Falls and Smooth Rock Falls, was made up mostly of old, inefficient plants. At the other extreme the large, aggressive Canadian International Paper Company, the subsidiary of the giant International Paper Company of the United States, made the bankrupt Riordon Paper Company's assets acquired in 1925 the basis for a large, modern milling and power operation on the Gatineau River, enlarged its original mill at Trois-Rivières to the point where it was producing more newsprint by 1926 than the Price Brothers' three plants combined, and in 1928 acquired the promising partly developed enterprise at Corner Brook.

The merged corporations could produce more effectively by redistributing their timber and power holdings, devote individual plants to products for which they were best suited, and introduce more up-to-date, efficient machinery to the mills. The larger companies might even be able to regulate markets and prices. The speculative mood of the times undoubtedly fostered the trend; company officials and financiers were able to reap large profits by organizing the mergers, refinancing the component companies at inflated figures, and issuing large amounts of watered stock that was readily sold to eager speculators. The result ultimately was to weight the companies with heavy debts that could be carried only if the mills operated at near capacity and their products enjoyed good markets. But all the while more mills coming into operation created so much excess capacity and competition that prices were depressed below the operating costs of many of the least efficient plants.

To gain still more leverage, companies representing about half the Canadian capacity combined in 1927 into a loose cartel, to make contracts and pro-rate sales among its members in proportion to their newsprint-making capacities. Competition between this combination and Canadian International Paper became acute. In 1928 the latter undercut the cartel's price of $60 a ton by $10 to win the business of the Hearst newspaper chain. William Randolph Hearst, who headed a similar organization of newspaper owners, gladly accepted the offer, and the whole industry, which had to match the new $50 price in their own sales contracts, was plunged into serious difficulties. The Quebec and Ontario governments, concerned over the impact of low prices on their own revenues and on provincial economies, persuaded a still larger group of manufacturers (but not Canadian International Paper, whose president insisted on following an independent line) to join in another common front in November 1928. This time the member companies agreed to set a price of $55.20 a ton and to restrict production to about 80 per cent of capacity, and Canadian International was forced to cancel its $50 contract. In 1930, however, the companies failed to bring the price back to $60, and when members quarrelled among themselves, each was left to face the Depression as best it could on its own. An influential group of financiers headed by Sir Edward Beatty of the CPR had no success in re-establishing co-operation among the companies in 1931, and the price of newsprint went down and down to $40 a ton delivered in New York and was prevented from sinking even lower only by the National Recovery Act (NRA) program of Franklin Roosevelt's New Deal administration.

The premiers of Ontario and Quebec, G.S. Henry and L.A. Taschereau, met to concert some plan of action and to plead with the companies and with the federal government, but all to no avail. Producers' efforts to advance the New York price beyond the $40-level were stalled when one company signed new contracts for 1935 at the old price, forcing the others to accept the old rate for another year. Though the Quebec government withdrew some of the company's privileges to show its displeasure, the damage had been done. Working out a division of production between the Ontario and Quebec paper mills and changes of government in both provinces also further delayed concerted action. Finally the premiers threw their support behind the new Newsprint Association of Canada, headed by Charles Vining. His drive and vigour, plus the premiers' threats of punitive action against recalcitrants, enabled the association to negotiate a series of agreements rated according to capacities of the various plants that the companies grudgingly accepted. The effective policing of the member companies by the association, backed by the provincial governments, was a prelude to the Second World War when the federal government was able to take full control over every detail of supplies, costs, prices, production, and manpower.

In the meantime many of the companies and mergers proved unable to carry on in the face of the shrunken markets and the disastrously low prices. The Backus-Brooks Company went bankrupt in 1930, while Canada Power and Paper Company survived only by a drastic capital restructuring that wrote off much of its bonds and shares and reorganization as the Consolidated Paper Company. In 1932 it was the turn of the ungainly Abitibi Power and Paper Company, which proved unable to meet the instalments on its bonds or complete the construction of the large hydro-electric enterprise it had begun at Abitibi Canyon through a subsidiary. The company was placed in bankruptcy in September 1932, and a liquidator was appointed to manage its operations. Several of its mills were closed for long periods, notably those at Pine Falls and Espanola. The latter, a town of 2,700, went through years of suffering and declining population, with unemployment so widespread that at one point 80 per cent of the inhabitants were receiving provincial assistance. The mill was not reopened, nor did the town revive, until a new owner, Kalamazoo Vegetable Parchment Company, took control after 1945.

The historic Price Brothers firm also went under in 1932, and two of its newsprint mills remained closed until 1934, with resulting local unemployment. In the meantime the creditors entertained offers from the Bowater organization of Britain, and from the Duke-Price Power Company to take over the firm and return it to operation. Other companies also were reorganized at this time. Indeed, the only firms that remained solvent throughout the Depression were those that were tied to American owner-customers (such as Ontario Paper, Canadian International, and Spruce Falls) or that enjoyed a protected market in Canada for fine papers (E.B. Eddy). For the remainder, the thirties was a decade of great difficulty. Recovery came with the Second World War and post-war boom, which carried the whole industry into a new period of prosperity and growth. It paid a heavy price over many years for the unwise overexpansion and speculative financing of the boom years of the twenties, however. As. A.R.M. Lower, who investigated the industry, observed:

> At no other time has Canada seen such a rapid industrial development as was based on the pulp and paper industry in the ten years following the war . . . but it was not long before the industry got into the clutches of the masters of high finance and then a series of amalgamations, new flotations, and grandiose projects were initiated which had the inevitable result of bankrupting most of the companies concerned, ruined thousands of investors, and abruptly halted the march of settlement in pioneer areas.[3]

Throughout the thirties the provincial governments kept close watch over the agonies of the pulp and paper industry with whose survival and speedy return to health they were vitally concerned. After all, they had to protect the companies both because they were important contributors to the economic health of whole regions and the mainstays of numerous communities and because of their own involvement as sponsors and partners of those enterprises. To ease the companies' burdens they reduced the Crown royalties on logs, stumpage dues, and ground rents on leased timber limits and allowed operators to pay their dues in instalments. The Hepburn government in Ontario, however, also redistributed idle timber limits without tender to pulpwood exporters and eased the regulations against exporting logs from Crown lands to maintain as much activity as possible in the forests. Although some did result, the pulp and paper mills were hurt and the industry was undermined, especially when at the same time the provincial protective staff was drastically reduced. The ailing giant Abitibi was protected from being sold by its creditors, and an Ontario royal commission was appointed in 1940 to work out a system for keeping the vast organization in being under trustees until such time as it could regain its financial equilibrium. Premiers Hepburn and Duplessis also tried to use the Newsprint Association of Canada to press companies to co-ordinate their policies of resource management and accept new goals, such as maintaining labour standards and adopting proper forest management programs.

Even in the 1930s, in spite of or because of these governmental efforts, some recovery began, and production first reached, then passed, previous records, though prices remained disappointingly low. Many of the mills that had been closed down were reopened while others began expanding operations. From 1936 onward Marathon Paper Mills, a new concern from the United States, developed a townsite and carried on logging operations preparatory to going into production on the limit of the former Pigeon Lumber Company in the Pic River section north of Lake Superior. The Ontario Paper Company also began in 1935 to develop the large timber and waterpower concession acquired a dozen years earlier in the Shelter Bay district of the North Shore of Quebec, with assistance from the provincial Department of Lands and Forests, anxious to encourage colonization in that region. The small hydro-electric power plant on the Outardes River was enlarged, a model town named Baie Comeau was built and incorporated in 1937, and pulpwood logging was begun. The town and plant were in operation in 1938, by which time the project had been reorganized, at the insistence of the provincial government, as a Quebec corporation, the Quebec North Shore Paper Company.

As the pulp and paper industry recovered, production of woodpulp, its basic raw material, soared from the low levels of 1932 and 1933 to a record 5.1 million tons in 1937. Then, after a setback during the recession of 1938, a new record of 5.2 million tons was attained in 1940. Production of paper, particularly newsprint, hit new peaks in 1936, 1937, and 1940. Employment did not recover in the same proportion, however – from 24,037 in 1933 to 33,205 in 1937, and 34,719 in 1940. So a major component of the northward-advancing industrial frontiers gradually surmounted the challenges of the difficult thirties to join in the next lunge northward of the forest industries after 1945.

III

Development of electric power was a major force behind expansion in the Subarctic forest zone, the potential waterpower resources of which were brought within the range of practicable exploitation by the advance of the forestry and mineral industries into the region and by the growing need of the southern Canadian manufacturing complex for additional energy supplies. Hydro-electric power was tremendously important for Canada, a country whose coal supplies, while huge in total, are far distant from the industrialized but energy-deficient areas. Fortunately, rich sources of hydro-electric power for the centres most in need of large supplies of energy were available in the Great Lakes and St. Lawrence basins extending onto the southern margins of the Canadian Shield. The new forestry plants and mines being opened in the Subarctic near potential power sites provided large local markets, and governments gave them incentives to develop those sites by awarding them along with their forest land concessions.

The availability of cheap electrical energy attracted many industries that rapidly enlarged the nation's manufacturing sector. During the 1920s electricity was also displacing other forms of energy and finding new uses in industry, on farms, and in everyday living. Under the impetus of the increasing demand the more accessible sites in the South were soon developed, and planners were forced to look farther north for new sources. At first the high losses in transmitting energy over appreciable distances restricted development to sites adjacent to the new industrial plants and settlements in the Middle North. Through experimentation with high voltage lines and transmission arrangements, however, it became feasible to transmit power over considerable distances, and by 1930 major markets in the Toronto area were about to receive power from the heart of the Shield in Northern Ontario. It was also becoming easier to build power stations in remote places, thanks to the availability of aircraft for surveying and transporting key personnel and supplies; railways and highways too had been brought closer to the sites. By the 1930s tractor trains could haul heavy loads of supplies across lakes, rivers, and muskegs in the dead of winter to the construction locales. Thus the expansion of hydro-electric power development to northern sites was able to feed the energy-hunger of the industrial complex.

Building these very expensive plants required the raising and spending of enormous amounts of capital before any revenues could be earned. When the installation was functioning, however, it incurred few operating costs except for limited supervision and maintenance, so that the bulk of the income could be applied toward repaying the multi-million-dollar investments. The large sums involved, the long investment periods, and the high degree of security led almost always to the financing of hydro installations by bond issues. These characteristics made the plants appropriate investments for governments, which besides could build installations more cheaply because they could borrow at lower rates of interest than private developers. All this, and the obvious benefits of a utility operating in the interest of the public, made it desirable that governments themselves build and operate the installations. Yet this was the exception rather than the rule. During the interwar period most plants were built and operated by private owners for their own benefit.

Thanks to their efforts, the capacity of Canada's hydro-electric power installations was more than doubled – from 2,515,559 horsepower to 6,125,021 horsepower – during the 1920s, and despite the economic slowdown a further 2.5 million horsepower was added to that total during the thirties. Indeed, the new capacity brought into operation in 1930, 1931, and 1932 was as large as or larger than that in 1929, 1931 being the peak year. This growth resulted mainly from projects that had been started during the 1920s when the pulp and paper and mining industries were providing strong incentives for power-site development and capital was easy to raise. Quebec emerged as the leading province during the twenties, with rated capacity of 2,718,130 horsepower in 1930 against 2,088,055 for Ontario, which had led slightly in 1920. In fact, more than one million horsepower was added to Quebec's capacity in the half decade 1925–1930. Quebec increased its lead during the 1930s, for over 60 per cent of the new Canadian capacity was installed there. All the hydro power generated in Quebec was privately owned, and its main users were pulp and paper, mining, aluminum refining, and other resource industries. Another 20 per cent was exported to Ontario or the United States, and only a very small fraction of the total output went to individual customers in cities, towns, and farms.

Expansion of the industry during the interwar years owed a great deal to the easygoing policies of the provincial governments, which granted hydro concessions as almost incidental to their forestry programs. Valuable sites went for long periods at relatively low prices and royalties on production. The Quebec Streams Commission even relieved developers of large parts of their costs by building the very expensive large-scale headwater storage works required to develop the full potential of the sites and then charging them only what was needed to recoup the investments. Following its earlier actions in the St Maurice and Saguenay basins, the commission financed the Mercier Dam to improve the generating capacity of the Gatineau River plants for the benefit of the Canadian International Paper Company. The government did defer to protectionist sentiment by charging a royalty on power exported outside Quebec, but in 1926 when Premier Ferguson approached Premier Taschereau with a proposal for Ontario Hydro to purchase large quantities of power from Quebec plants, the sale was allowed and the royalty was waived. The protectionists could not be ignored, however, even by the Taschereau government. They attacked the reported sale of the Quinze site on the upper Ottawa to a Toronto group as the surrender of a provincial resource that would encourage the industrial development of Northern Ontario at the expense of Quebec and cause settlers to desert their native province for the enhanced employment opportunities in Ontario. Learning from this situation, the two provinces agreed to divide power generated from interprovincial sections of the Ottawa equally between them. In 1929, when Ontario Hydro undertook to develop the 224,000 horsepower at Chats Falls, it was done as a joint venture, with a Quebec firm as partner.

Although most power plants were built by and for private owners, an increasing fraction were being developed by public agencies. The privately owned hydro-electric power projects of the period were usually parts of larger resource-utilizing enterprises, such as the base-metal mine at Flin Flon or the pulp and paper plants at Iroquois Falls, Kapuskasing, Baie Comeau, and Marathon. Their power was developed primarily to supply the operators' main industrial activities; surpluses were sold in the most convenient markets. Less often, sites were developed by power companies engaged in producing and marketing the electric power themselves, such as the Winnipeg Electric Company, or especially the Shawinigan Water and Power Company in Quebec.

Quebec's spectacular expansion occurred in the St Maurice, Ottawa, and Saguenay–Lac St Jean watersheds, the largest being in the Saguenay district, beginning with the Quebec Development Company. In 1920, J.B. Duke, an American self-made tobacco millionaire, became an investor and partner in the corporation, along with Sir

William Price and J.E.A. Dubuc, the original principals. During the industrial recession of the early 1920s the public grew restless over the lack of progress, and as a result of protests Sir William Price was given permission to dam the outlet of Lac St Jean – the Grande and Petite Décharges, which enclose the island of Alma – with authority to raise the level of the lake to the peak springtime level. Price and Duke formed the Saguenay Power Company and began building the great Ile Maligne plant at the Grande Décharge in association with A.V. Davis of the Aluminum Company of America. Before that project was completed in 1926 Price had been drowned (1924) while investigating the damage from flooding at his paper mill at Kénogami, and Duke had died in 1925. The Aluminium Company of Canada (a subsidiary incorporated in 1925) had begun building an aluminum refinery and townsite at Arvida. The company also became the major participant, with the Duke-Price Power Company, in the still larger (600,000 horsepower) Chute à Caron enterprise, completed in 1928. Before long the Aluminium Company acquired the Duke-Price share as well, to become 80-per-cent owner of the development, with Shawinigan Power holding the remaining 20 per cent. When these enterprises were completed the Aluminium Company's investment had grown to $100 million and was then the largest in Quebec's history. As early as 1926 the company was producing 30,000 tons of aluminum ingots a year and planned to increase that output tenfold. Thanks to its rich power resources, the Saguenay was becoming a major industrial region, supplementing its forestry and agricultural industries with manufacturing based on the ample stores of cheap electric power.

In the St Maurice, Shawinigan by 1920 enjoyed a virtual monopoly of electric power developed for sale, which it secured from its own stations or through partnership arrangements with pulp and paper concerns. During the 1920s new turbines were installed at existing plants, and additional sites were developed, notably at La Gabelle, a 50-per-cent interest at La Tuque, and Rapide Blanc, completed in partnership with the Brown Corporation. Shawinigan also expanded into the Saguenay basin by acquiring 100,000 horsepower from the Ile Maligne project. At the same time the company continued absorbing smaller power concerns together with their markets and found new outlets for the power, notably with pulp and paper mills, which accounted for 44 per cent of its revenues by 1929. By then the company had trebled its power output to 600,000 horsepower from 225,000 horsepower in 1921. During the thirties, once again finding itself with surplus power, it offered very low rates to large industrial users within its market area, and, encouraged by a provincial act authorizing municipalities to pay up to half the cost of installations, it even made a beginning at rural electrification. Thus Shawinigan Power expanded and enhanced its competitive position in Quebec.

In the Ottawa basin the trend was for consolidation of small firms into larger ones for efficiency and insurance against interruptions of service. The Gatineau Power Company, a subsidiary of Canadian International Paper, set up small plants and proceeded to develop three large sites along a sixty-two-mile stretch of the Gatineau River on the strength of a large block sale (250,000 horsepower at $15 a horsepower-year) to the Hydro-Electric Power Commission of Ontario. When these plants were completed in 1931, a total of 572,000 horsepower was being generated. The MacLaren Quebec Power Company, a subsidiary of the MacLaren Paper Company, which controlled the Lièvre River, made a similar contract with Ontario Hydro and built its 136,000-horsepower installation at Masson. On the Ottawa itself other interests completed a 75,000 horsepower plant at Bryson and others higher up the Ottawa in its interprovincial section and above Lac Témiscamingue in Northern Quebec.

The system of leaving private corporations to develop the power sites of Quebec remained unchallenged almost to the end of the 1930s, when long-standing complaints forced the provincial governments to take tentative steps toward the nationalization that lay some twenty-five years in the future. The privately owned utilities, while offering cheap power in large blocks to major customers, charged small everyday users very high rates. The commercial rate at Trois-Rivières in 1932, for instance, was four times as high as at Hamilton, similarly situated near a large hydro-power supply source but served by the publicly owned Ontario Hydro system. Critics complained that the system exploited the public, slowed the full adoption of electricity, and distorted the industrial development of the province. The Union Nationale government of Maurice Duplessis made a gesture in the direction of nationalization with the creation of Syndicat National d'Electricité in 1937 with a $10-million fund to purchase or build power plants, transmission lines, or other works, and the Régie Provinciale to supervise rates and services in the public interest. That was all, even though the generating capacity under public ownership remained a minuscule 30,700 horsepower up to 1939. The successor Godbout Liberal government abolished the Syndicat in 1940, handed its few properties over to the Quebec Streams Commission to manage, and in place of the Régie Provinciale set up a Régie des Services Publics that besides regulating rates and services extended loans and subsidies for badly needed, long-overdue rural electrification.

In Northern Ontario too, private interests built numerous hydro installations, taking advantage of the capital so readily available to finance such enterprises. In the Rainy River country the Backus-Brooks Company installed a plant at the Norman Dam and purchased the Kenora municipal power plant at the eastern outlet of Lake of the Woods. This company also built three small plants on the Seine River system, mainly to supply their Great Lakes Paper Company plant at Fort William, and the Dryden Paper Company built a small plant on the Eagle River. Farther east, the Spruce Falls Power and Paper Company built its second, larger plant at Smoky Falls on the Mattagami River, while Abitibi Power and Paper developed three plants on the Abitibi River – at its mill town of Iroquois Falls, at Twin Falls, and farther down the river at Island Falls. Still lower down the Abitibi, at Abitibi Canyon, the Ontario Power Service Corporation, a subsidiary, was in the process of building a great 330,000-horsepower plant to supply markets to the south, especially the mining centres of Sudbury and Timmins, where development of local power sites was virtually complete by 1929.

In the western provinces hydro-electric power development was geared mainly to the big city markets, and the demand could still be met from sources relatively close at hand or from plentiful local coal and natural gas supplies. Only a few of the many larger northern sites on the Shield or Cordillera were developed during the interwar period to serve local uses. In connection with gold-mining operations in the thirties, Consolidated Mining and Smelting built two small hydro-electric power stations, the first in the Athabasca-Mackenzie basin. So did pulp and paper concerns at Powell River and Ocean Falls on the British Columbia coast and the Northern British Columbia Power Company at Prince Rupert. The first effort to harness the waters of the great Nelson and Churchill river systems was undertaken to enable a mining enterprise at Flin Flon to smelt its ore at its camp. The Hudson Bay Mining and Smelting Company rejected a large site on the Nelson and selected the Island Falls site on the Churchill River, across the border in Northern Saskatchewan. Its 42,000-horsepower plant, with capacity in reserve for a second generating unit, and the sixty-five-mile transmission line went into service in June 1930, allowing the mining concern to go into operation. The unseemly competition between Saskatchewan and Manitoba to secure this power development led the three Prairie Provinces to agree (October 1930) to refer any future questions regarding their joint waterways to a board of arbitration and reference.

Competition was acute in Manitoba between the city of Winnipeg and the privately owned Manitoba Power Company to develop the large sites along the Winnipeg River. The city brought a 30,000-horsepower plant at Pointe du Bois into operation by 1921 and enlarged it in stages to 109,000 horsepower by installing additional turbines; the Manitoba Power Company developed a site at Great Falls by bringing successive additional turbines into operation to generate 168,000 horsepower by 1928. (Many a hydro plant was put into operation in stages; the dam was built to exploit the full potential of the site, but only part of the turbines were installed, fuller development being carried out as markets warranted.) Electric power from these two companies helped sustain Winnipeg's position as Canada's fourth-largest manufacturing city. Both were eager by the late 1920s to develop additional sites on the Winnipeg, particularly the large Seven Sisters site. Public power advocates pressed the provincial government to undertake the development, but after a study commissioned by the Bracken government advised against public development the provincial government in September 1928 authorized the Manitoba Power Company to proceed. The company constructed the 225,000-horsepower project, incidentally wiping out a twenty-five-year-old plant on the Pinewa Channel by diverting the flow into the main river. The province maintained the mixed pattern of public and private development, however, by awarding a 96,000-horsepower site, Slave Falls, to the city of Winnipeg.

A similar mix of public and private enterprise was followed in Northern Ontario, where even in the 1920s the provincial government seemed reluctant to interfere with private development by, or on behalf of, the region's mining and forestry concerns. Nevertheless, the largely autonomous Ontario Hydro had gained a foothold there in 1909 by contracting to supply Port Arthur for a ten-year period, which it did by buying power from private companies operating in the district. By 1919, the city's industrial growth (factories started during the war and pulp and paper mills not long afterwards) greatly increased its foreseeable power needs. The commission, confident of public support and with the endorsement of the Hearst government, in 1919 decided to install its own power station on the Nipigon River to serve the region and thereby took an important step towards extending its developmental operations in Northern Ontario. The first site at Cameron Falls was delivering power in 1921 to the growing Lakehead cities. So rapidly did the market increase that it became necessary to build a second plant, the Alexander power development a mile and a half downstream from Cameron Falls, which was put in service in the fall of 1930.

Ontario Hydro also completed the first station in the District of Patricia in 1930 at Ear Falls on the English River to supply power to operate the Howay gold mine, some twenty miles distant. Construction had been delayed by a long-standing jurisdictional dispute over control of the river initiated in 1921 when the Meighen government moved to extend the authority of the federal Lake of the Woods Control Board to include the headwaters of the Winnipeg and English rivers, which originate in Ontario and flow far from the international boundary as they proceed westward into Manitoba. When Ontario refused to accept this action, the federal government simply proclaimed that all works along the headwaters of the Winnipeg River were "of general advantage to Canada" and hence under federal jurisdiction. There the matter rested for more than six years until in January 1928 an agreement was reached whereby the federally controlled board's authority over the waterways was upheld but Ontario was authorized to construct the control dam at the outlet of Lac Seul, a source of the English River. Work was begun in 1929, the dam was built, and a plant was installed to generate power for the Red Lake gold-mining camp and settlements. Delivery of power to the Howay mine began early in 1930, followed by power from a second unit in 1937 and a third in 1940. Later in the 1930s Ontario Hydro also began redirecting the northward flow of rivers in the James Bay drainage basin toward the Great Lakes to supply additional power to regional and distant customers. In 1938 the northward flow from Long Lake to the Albany was diverted southward via the Aguasabon River to Terrace Bay on Lake Superior, the 1,800-foot drop generating a large amount of electric power, as well as additional water to increase the potential of the plants at Niagara Falls.

Noteworthy also were Ontario Hydro's efforts to extend its markets to the industries and communities of northeastern Ontario. In 1929 it began purchasing privately owned companies in the region and then, using its authority under the Northern Ontario Properties Agreement Act of 1930, bought the Wahnapitae Power Company (from INCO) and the Crystal Falls station on the Sturgeon River (from Abitibi) to supply the Sudbury district. For the mining complexes at Sudbury and Porcupine it contracted for much of the output of the Abitibi Canyon station of the Ontario Power Service Corporation. When that corporation defaulted on its $20-million bond debts, Ontario Hydro took over the assets, completed the project, built a 189-mile 110,000-volt line from Hunta to Sudbury, and as the power became available fed it into the northeastern Ontario network. By 1934 its regional operations, still known as the Northern Ontario Properties, served the wide area from Abitibi Canyon to Copper Cliff near Sudbury. By the end of the 1930s Ontario Hydro had become the major supplier of power in Northern as well as Southern Ontario, generating 1,724,395 horsepower from seventy-four plants, whereas the sixty-four privately owned plants were producing only 529,940 horsepower.

The advance of Ontario Hydro to this preponderant position was not altogether a result of deliberate planning by government and did not go unchallenged even in Ontario, for during the 1930s it was attacked on the grounds of political interference by the Liberal opposition. Hepburn charged that the power purchases from the Quebec companies in 1927–28 were needlessly improvident and alleged that Hydro's purchase of the Abitibi Canyon project had been inspired by the financial involvement of Premier Henry and Senator Arthur Meighen in that enterprise. In office, the Hepburn government quickly repudiated the Quebec contracts, though it soon renegotiated the agreements with the Gatineau and MacLaren companies at a somewhat lower rate. The management of the Ontario Hydro Commission also was investigated, but the government contented itself with replacing it by one that was more amenable to the government's wishes. Ontario Hydro survived in its full role as a Crown corporation and public utility, becoming a model for the industry and an example for Canada by providing an important, valuable service to the public, trying to equalize charges to customers regardless of distance from source of supply, serving a wide segment of the population irrespective of the size of the communities in which they lived, and rationalizing production and consumption of electric power by co-ordinating the transmission of power to places where it was most needed.

IV

The forestry and hydro-electric power industries were important contributors to Canada's economic and social development and its frontier expansion during the interwar decades. They were major sources of employment in the frontier districts of Central Canada, notably in the winters when thousands of men left farms and cities to find work in the forests preparing sawlogs, pulpwood, and cordwood. A large pulp and paper or lumber company employed 2,000 to 4,000 men in the woods each winter; logging operations along the lower St. Lawrence engaged another 5,000 men preparing logs to be shipped in the coming summer as far west as Lake Superior. Other hundreds of men did winter work on the timber limits at points on the National Transcontinental such as Parent, Senneterre, La Sarre, and Cochrane. In Quebec alone during the winter of 1927–28, 44,764 men were reported at work in 3,121 camps, and as late as 1940 an estimated floating population of 35,000 *bûcherons* could still be found on the forest lands of that province. Most of Canada's sawmill workers, whose numbers ranged from 28,000 in 1921 to 44,500 in 1929, also were employed seasonally, mainly in the summers. The large permanent lumber mills and the rapidly expanding pulp and paper plants employed 24,600 workers in 1921 and 34,202 in 1929 on a year-round basis. Thus the three main forestry industries absorbed a considerable portion of the manpower in the relatively unsettled wooded sections adjoining or beyond the agricultural frontiers. In Quebec alone, the employment attributed to these three industries in 1931, given as man-years, was as follows: work in the woods, 16,846, sawmilling, 10,067, and pulp and paper, 16,538, or a total of 43,451 man-years involving perhaps 80,000 persons in all, a large fraction of them heads of families.

The forest industries also afforded additional employment for men engaged in other occupations, particularly farming and construction. A high percentage of Quebec's farmers, as many as 75 per cent in all and unquestionably the overwhelming majority in the frontier districts, derived some income from forest products, chiefly from timber sold from their own lots. In eastern Abitibi most of the logs required by the large companies were supplied by farmers or by licensed cutters. During the Depression, in fact, lumbermen petitioned the Quebec government to discourage the clearing of land in order to prevent a larger glut of sawlogs and cordwood on the overcrowded market. In Ontario, prompted by the provincial government, the mills bought as much pulpwood as settlers could supply. In addition, the camps, plants, and communities exploiting the forests furnished important markets for frontier farmers' vegetables, grain, meat, eggs, dairy products, hay and feed, and horses. Thus forestry was an important aid to frontier farmers developing their farms into successful operations.

The rapid advances of the forestry and hydro industries also created considerable construction activity in the Middle North during the 1920s and 1930s. Building the scores of pulp and paper mills, the roads and private logging railways, housing, and above all the power dams, generating stations, and transmission lines involved the labour of thousands of workmen. Constructing the relatively minor (20,000-horsepower) plant at Island Falls on the Abitibi River, for example, made work for a thousand men. Construction activities afforded extended periods of employment to thousands of casual labourers from the surrounding districts and farther afield as well as to the specialist tradesmen the contractors and subcontractors imported from the cities, some of whom settled in the communities they had helped to build.

In addition, building the hydro-electric generating stations required bringing in large tonnages of building materials and machinery, and, unlike the pulp and paper mills, these stations often were located far beyond the existing roads and railways. Constructing them, therefore, entailed improving the transportation facilities. Building Ontario

Hydro's plants in the Lake Superior district, for example, opened roads into the Nipigon River area, while the Abitibi Canyon power station was a major influence behind the resumption of construction on the Temiskaming and Northern Ontario (T&NO) Railway from Cochrane north toward James Bay. In even more remote districts, building the plants required the use of tractor trains and construction of hundreds of miles of winter roads. Nor was the more normal relationship between forestry and transportation unimportant. The tonnages of logs transported to the mills and plants, and the shipment of manu-factured lumber, woodpulp, and newsprint paper to their markets, were major sources of traffic and revenue for Canada's railways and truckers, particularly for the under-used northerly parts of the railway networks.

The products of the forestry and hydro industries found important uses in developing the mines and communities of the North, and some-times were a basis for secondary woodworking plants. The vast amounts of hydro-electric power generated in the region were mainly transmitted to the industrialized South, but much was used on the fron-tiers as well. Electric power enabled new industries and communities to come into being and to flourish. The electricity that Ontario Hydro supplied to the Lakehead cities stimulated an industrial boom that included large pulp and paper mills, a car and foundry plant, a ship-building firm, several large government and private grain terminal ele-vators, and an extensive street railway system. Hydro's northeastern Ontario operations by 1939 supplied the needs of more than three dozen mining developments, two cities, numerous smaller commu-nities and rural areas, and maintained enough reserve capacity to help other industries of the region develop and grow.

The outstanding case of development based on hydro-electric power, however, was in the Saguenay–Lac St Jean district. On the strength of it, the Aluminium Company of Canada built an enormous plant and a small city, Arvida (named for its president, Arthur Vining Davis), for its workforce; it developed Port Alfred into a leading ship-ping centre that received cargoes of bauxite, cryolite, and other mate-rials from many parts of the world and exported large quantities of aluminum ingots in addition to the paper and wood products of the district. Little of this would have occurred in the region without the huge amounts of cheap electric power available for development there – any more than the mining industries and settlements at Flin Flon, Red Lake, Yellowknife, or other places could have been developed without hydro-electric power to supply their plants and homes.

A sizeable resident white population gathered in the frontier region to serve the forestry and hydro-electric power industries. These ranged from small groups of workers and their families living at the isolated generating stations, to employees of the sawmills strung along the northern railways, to the settlers at the logging and shipping villages of the lower St. Lawrence, to the residents of the new industrial towns – Arvida, Iroquois Falls, Kapuskasing, Pine Falls – dotting the frontier from Corner Brook to Ocean Falls. The frontier communities, as well as the transitory logging camps and portable sawmills, generated a remarkable variety of societies: the all-male *Canadien* logging camps, polyglot construction gangs, and the pulp and paper towns – normal, stable, modern communities with most of the amenities of small towns in other parts of the country, contrasting sharply with the usually less stable, more rudimentary mining towns of their region. Even the pulp and paper towns varied among themselves according to the type of product made, the geographical setting, and the demographic structure. A more complete contrast could scarcely be imagined, for instance, than that between such conventional towns as Riverbend or Kapuskasing and the Pacific Mills plant and town of Ocean Falls perched on the side of a remote inlet along the rough, mountainous British Columbia coast, employing mainly Japanese, Chinese, and South Asian workmen who lived in segregated bunkhouses and suburbs, one of which, "Japtown," was torn down after Pearl Harbor.

Since large full-time industrial workforces required highly trained professional and administrative personnel as well as skilled workmen, the owning companies provided their towns with the amenities and services associated with permanent communities. Hence forestry towns, unlike the communities generated by agriculture, sprang into being with their facilities in place, reflecting the current level of interest in town planning and proper landscaping. They were provided with good-to-excellent subsidized housing, water, sewers, electricity, and roads; schools, public buildings, parks, and churches; and a fair range of commercial and professional services. Although many isolated one-industry communities later experienced economic and social difficulties, during the twenties they were centres of hope and prosperity as young people settled, raised families, and worked to build homes and turn their towns into hoped-for future cities.

The Depression years bore down heavily on many of these new industrial communities. Some of the plants were closed for a year or more as the towns faced permanent shutdowns of the industries on which they depended. Even plants that seemed immune to the Depression were forced to put their men on short time during the worst years and reduced the hourly wage rates. The slackening of production from 1929 to 1935 affected the trade in pulpwood from farms and sharply reduced the logging operations by, or on behalf of, the pulp and paper companies. So many loggers were without work that the provincial employment services had to set up temporary offices and try to find jobs for some of them in the provincial highway construction programs. The loggers who did find work during these years often had to endure deplorable conditions aggravated by the hard times.

A marked deterioration in the living conditions in the forestry camps had, in fact, been observable in the late twenties as companies relied increasingly on large pulpwood contractors, who brought a far less personal, responsible character to the woods operation. With the Depression raging, jobbers and contractors under financial pressures provided the cheapest, roughest food and lodging, overworked their men and ground down their wages, and sometimes swindled them out of their meagre earnings. These abuses, along with the activities of the Communist-led Lumber Workers Industrial Union, brought many strikes in the logging industry in 1933–34. A strike at Témiscamingue resulted in a clash between lumberjacks and provincial policemen, many arrests, and thirteen men sent to prison. The official investigation uncovered widespread abuses and exploitation that could only be remedied by the companies' taking responsibility for and operating their own camps. But although it conceded that the men had been mistreated, it blamed the clash on Communist agitators. That winter there were sixteen logging strikes involving 6,107 men across Northern Ontario from Abitibi to Fort Frances. Most were in protest against wage cuts and poor camp living and working conditions; some were undertaken to win the rights to organize, hold meetings, and have camp committees recognized as bargaining agents. Strikes against Abitibi Power and Paper at Iroquois Falls and Smooth Rock Falls were halted only after personal intervention by the Ontario Minister of Lands and Forests.

In 1934 the newly elected Hepburn government passed the Woodmen Employment Act, which provided for inspectors to examine working conditions and contracts at the camps and made the companies responsible for conditions in their logging operations. In return for reduced taxes and other concessions, the government made the operators undertake "to pay fair wages, make reasonable charges for van goods, other supplies and equipment and to comply fully with the regulations of the Department of Health."[4] Thanks to such measures, conditions in the Ontario camps improved greatly in succeeding years. So also did they in Quebec, partly because of government inspectors, partly because of the growth of community logging co-operatives. As for the LWIU, after it failed to organize a general strike across Northern Ontario in 1935 it quickly disappeared. Workers turned, instead, to the United Brotherhood of Carpenters and Joiners of America (AFL) for affiliation.

Organizing pulp and paper mill workers would seem to be a less difficult task than unionizing men scattered in hundreds of logging camps, but union activity in the milltowns had to overcome both company threats and blacklists and a strong sense of community of interest between workers and the companies, coupled with distrust of outside forces. Organizers also faced powerful opposition from the Ontario and Quebec governments, both of which sided with the employers and opposed unionization to the utmost. The Duplessis government objected to the inroads of unions from outside on alleged national grounds and encouraged the growth of Catholic unions to prevent American-affiliated organizations from establishing themselves. It intervened in a strike to defeat one such union's effort to set up a closed shop at the Wayagamack Paper Company plant as a means to forestall the Catholic union entering the mills and saw to it that the Catholic union was able to proceed with its organization effort. Elsewhere, however, unions seem to have been accepted during the late 1930s without incident, as at Ocean Falls, where a local of the International Brotherhood of Pulp, Sulphite and Paper Mill Workers was organized in June 1938.

CHAPTER 4

Uncovering the Hidden Treasures of the Subarctic

Metal mining enjoyed rapid growth during the interwar decades. In the prosperous twenties markets expanded for copper, lead, zinc, nickel, cobalt, iron, and aluminum in construction, manufacturing, and the automotive and electrical machinery and appliance industries; in the thirties the arms race created new demands. Gold mining remained important throughout but especially during the thirties, when that metal became the mainstay of Canada's trading economy. The quantities of metals produced annually over the two decades doubled, trebled, and in some cases increased by factors of five, seven, even ten. Stimulated by good markets and prices, owners expanded the outputs of existing mines to their limits while active prospecting and plentiful financing brought many new mines into being.

Most of these metals were secured from the Canadian Shield and the Cordillera in the hinterlands of the newer transcontinental railways, the only significant source outside the Subarctic being in southeastern British Columbia. The growth of metal mining during these years thus represented a large-scale northward movement of prospecting, claim development, and camp and mine construction that altered the character of already settled districts like Abitibi and northeastern Ontario, introduced modern industry to new sectors of Northern Manitoba and Northern British Columbia, and aided by aviation established bridgeheads in the Arctic of northwestern Ontario and the Northwest Territories.

I

The remarkable expansion of mining reflected the fact that while Canada's agricultural and forestry frontiers are ultimately limited by soil, climate, and biotal conditions, the mineral resources are co-extensive with its limits, and exploitable deposits may be found in any part of its lands and seabeds. But though showings of mineralization are extremely numerous, deposits of metals that can be successfully mined are rare indeed. They must be large enough and of high enough grade to permit profitable mining, concentration, refining, and marketing of the metals under prevailing technological and economic conditions. Bringing a mine into production has analogies with a poker game in that the earliest stages, like the first cards, come comparatively cheaply, while the later stages require progressively higher stakes, and full development of the operation to fill out the entrepreneur's hand may cost several million dollars. Even that investment, like the poker player's stake, can still be lost through miscalculation of the qualities and quantities of the ore and the costs of the operation or unfavourable changes external to the mine in the markets and prices for the products or in the competitive situation in the industry. As an inquiry commission reported in 1955, even in the proven rich gold fields of Ontario the odds against success are inordinately high:

> It is probable that more has been spent trying to find and develop gold mines in Ontario than shareholders have had in dividends from producers. No one will deny that, by any measure, a few mines have been very profitable. But, for each success, there have been many failures. About 4,000 companies have been incorporated in Ontario to mine gold; 200 of them have produced gold; only 73 have made enough profit to pay mining tax; 51 have paid dividends; possibly 35 have paid as much in dividends as has been spent to bring them into production.[1]

The process of ore discovery and mine development began with the prospector, who toiled over the rocks and insect-infested muskegs, through the woods and waterways of the Canadian Shield, or along the mountainsides and valleys of the Cordillera, searching for and staking promising mineral occurrences that might eventuate in mines. By 1914 the geology of the northern parts of the provinces, of the Yukon Territory, and of the western parts of the Northwest Territories had become known in a general way, thanks to geologists' and prospectors' efforts. The Pacific Slope had been prospected quite extensively during sixty years of searches for placer gold – a form of mining that an individual could successfully carry to production without much initial capital investment. Considerable prospecting had also been done near the railways, notably in Northern Ontario, since transportation improved the odds for speedy production from suitable mineral deposits. As a result of these efforts, large and important nickel, gold, silver, and base metal mines were already in operation by 1914 in Northern Ontario, along the Pacific Coast, and in interior British Columbia, and preliminary efforts were being made to develop the oil and natural gas resources of the Athabasca and Peace River districts. Many other large potential mineral deposits in more remote regions had also been recorded, thanks to surface indications observed by travellers and government scientists. Among these were the vast iron deposits of interior Labrador and in the Northwest Territories the lead-zinc occurrence at Pine Point, the oilfield at Norman Wells, and the copper-bearing rocks of the Coppermine district.

After the war, governments stepped up their surveying operations and trained war veterans to become prospectors, geologists, and mine operators. Increasing demand for and prices of many of Canada's mineral products during the 1920s caused heightened interest in prospecting. It was in vogue also because so many large tracts of mineral-rich country had only recently been brought within the range of possible mine development by the pre-war round of railway building across the Shield and Cordillera. By the twenties the automobile, motorboat, radio, and especially the airplane made it possible to extend the prospector's range even to remote northern territories. The possibilities seemed endless, for innumerable districts of promise awaited the prospectors since even the established mining districts of northeastern Ontario still had not been adequately investigated.

Prospectors were assisted in their work by the continuing output of topographical and geological reports and maps from appropriate federal and provincial agencies. The Geological Survey of Canada, for instance, regularly sent field parties to examine and report on areas of the Shield from Labrador to Great Bear Lake and along the Cordillera from Vancouver Island to the Yukon. Provincial agencies, notably Ontario's Bureau of Mines, conducted useful mapping while increasing numbers of university scientists prepared detailed studies of complex geological formations found in major mining districts. The resulting maps and reports were especially helpful in determining fields of activity for prospectors.

Material incentives also were held out to them in the systems for staking mining claims instituted by the several jurisdictions. In return for a small licence fee, the prospector was entitled to stake three personal claims in any given mining division and another six on behalf of two other licence-holders who had given him their proxies (in the Northwest Territories these numbers were doubled). Claims were usually fifty-acre rectangular lots, generally aligned in the primary directions, and clearly staked and recorded according to specified conditions. The mining claim was granted on a yearly basis, the holder being required to perform a given amount of representation work each year. Following the work, plus proof of a discovery, the claimholder could purchase the surface land required for mining and related purposes. The regulations usually included a royalty on production and graduated taxes on profits. Comparable regulations governed prospecting and mining placer gold, coal, petroleum, and natural gas. Every jurisdiction set up mining districts, which they provided with inspecting, professional, and regulating officials and machinery for settling disputes over claims.

Prospecting was a familiar activity in many communities. Local men and men from outside set forth from them in canoes with a season's gear for districts reported to contain promising mineral showings to investigate and trace the rock outcrops observable from the shores of rivers and lakes. The majority of mining claims, however, were staked when a reported strike brought a rush to the vicinity and were of the sympathetic variety. Prospectors scrambled to stake claims on the adjoining ground for themselves and their proxies, hoping that their claims would be close enough to the original find, or to a subsequent discovery, to win favourable attention from mine developers or company promoters. Massive staking rushes to The Pas, Red Lake, Lake Athabasca, or other districts accompanied every reported find. Rumours of a rich gold creek in the remote Cassiar drew over one hundred prospectors to the Dease Lake district during the spring of 1925; the creek afforded adequate returns for only three or four men and was too small even to warrant installing a hydraulic plant.

Few prospectors could support themselves while in the field or wait until they disposed of their claims. Fewer still could hold out until they received income from mines developed from claims they had staked. Some part-time prospectors hunted and trapped, living off the land they examined, while others were off-season farmers, workers, or businessmen residing near promising mineralized areas. Most required financial backing to carry on their work. Serious full-time prospectors might get support from their fellows on a share basis, from merchant outfitters, or from stockbrokers who specialized in organizing mining companies. Their prospecting expeditions were usually partnerships or syndicates with definite commitments of capital or services defining the percentages into which the proceeds of the enterprise were to be divided. Another practice that grew increasingly common in the interwar period was the employment of prospectors by established mining or mining development companies; they worked on salary, retainer, or other manner of recompense.

The scale and scope of prospecting were revolutionized during the 1920s by the increased use of greatly improved aircraft for transporting men and supplies to remote sites and as a tool for examining the ground below. As early as 1921 the value of aircraft for prospecting operations was demonstrated when E.L. Bruce, a geologist and university teacher, was carried to Lake St. Joseph in one hour's flight from Sioux Lookout, a four-day canoe journey for his party the previous summer. Bruce noted innumerable small lakes as well as several large ones he had overlooked on the earlier occasion; he also saw that a band of granite he had mapped at two separate points was one continuous unit that extended six to eight miles farther across country he had been unable to visit. He concluded his report with this prescient observation:

> It seems evident that the use of sea-planes would relieve the geologist of a vast amount of work and would save a large part of his time. . . . There will still remain a large part of the geological work that must be done by the old methods of canoe travel and traverses on foot; but it might be possible to so arrange field parties that several geological parties could each have the advantage of a sea-plane from a central station for a short time, and in this way the work of all would be facilitated.[2]

The airplane was especially helpful for studying geological features from a distance, and aerial photography vastly speeded the mapping of potentially valuable districts – for example, good exposures of Precambrian formations. By the mid-twenties improved models of aircraft were available, some, such as the Vickers Vidette and Noorduyn Norseman, adapted for service in frontier areas. By 1931 a first flying boxcar – a German-built Junkers monoplane capable of hauling loads of nearly four tons, or of making thousand-mile non-stop flights with two-ton loads – was available for transport work. Flying was improved, besides, by better ski and pontoon landing equipment, with wider experience in landing and takeoff operations, in making airframe and engine repairs under primitive conditions, and in protecting machines and men against the cold. Greater knowledge of weather conditions, improved weather reporting, and the adaptation of wireless reception to flying aircraft also were very helpful.

The period down to 1939 was the heyday of the bush pilot. Many of these men had trained with the Royal Flying Corps during the Great War and the surplus military aircraft now available enabled them to practise their trade under peacetime conditions. They were joined over the years by younger men trained at the many flying clubs. Driven by love of adventure and the desire for self-fulfilment, they found northern flying the perfect test of their skill, judgement, ingenuity, and initiative. The press acclaimed every kind of record flight and dramatized the many mercy flights, the searches for downed planes (unfortunately too frequent), and the unhappy deaths of some of the flyers. The public, witnessing, reading, or hearing of their exploits with float- or ski-equipped planes, regarded the bush pilots as authentic peacetime Canadian heroes.

Their flying operations at first were largely unregulated as they picked their way from settlement to settlement and between the lakes and rivers that served as their landing sites. But gradually airfields were designated and supervised, and following the advent of radio communications, flights were better controlled. From the mid-twenties airmail delivery contracts forced operators to conform to schedules and to the service and safety standards set by the Department of National Defence's Civil Aviation Branch. Finally, in the late thirties the awarding of exclusive licences to most air routes channelled air service along set lines and encouraged the formation of large, powerful companies. Bush pilots who flew as independents or as members of locally based firms later became officers of larger regional airlines and finally employees or executives of nationwide systems such as Canadian Airways, Trans-Canada Air Lines, and (from 1941) Canadian Pacific Air Lines. A vanishing band of heroes, their story is one of Canada's great modern-day adventures.

The main benefit of aircraft for prospecting in remote northern areas was that they made it possible to investigate places otherwise too difficult of access. Previously, most of an open-water season would have been devoted to reaching the site, leaving little time for fieldwork or the return voyage before the onset of winter. Now prospectors could be flown to these locations, left there for a set time, and resupplied or transferred to other locations by other planes. Thus a party could work the entire season in several promising locations, and – as Bruce had foreseen – a single plane could supply many parties strewn over a district that had previously been almost completely closed to prospecting.

In this fashion a Vickers Viking flying boat from Prince Rupert assisted prospectors in the Dease-Liard basin in 1925 and north of Lake Athabasca in 1926. By 1928 there was a group of well-financed aviation companies associated with major mining interests organized to conduct large-scale aerial prospecting operations in northern parts of the Shield and Cordillera. Dominion Explorers (Domex) was organized by Col. C.D.H. MacAlpine in conjunction with Ventures, Limited, the mining firm of Thayer and Halstead Lindsley, and Northern Aerial Mineral Exploration (NAME) was set up by J.E. Hammell, a Toronto mining developer playing a key part at Red Lake and Flin Flon. A smaller concern was the Cyril Knight Prospecting Company, directed by a famous Ontario geologist. In addition, established mining companies such as Consolidated Mining and Smelting, Dome, McIntyre, and Mining Corporation of Canada flew their own aircraft in connection with their prospecting operations.

These aerial prospecting organizations operated from bases that were accessible to water transport and equipped with radio stations, such as Stony Rapids. From these they established gasoline caches at advance locations, then stationed pairs of prospectors at strategic lakes to examine the adjoining country. The prospectors were kept supplied, geologists and company officials were brought in to evaluate their progress, and men were shifted to more promising locations as developments warranted. In this fashion, prospecting teams backed by air support proceeded across Canada from Nouveau-Québec – where the iron beds and the base metal and gold prospects of the Chibougamau, Matagami, and Nottaway river basins were examined – to Northern British Columbia, where planes based in Prince George and Stewart ranged across the north-central and northwestern parts of the province.

Airplanes also carried prospectors and mining engineers, supplies and essential drilling equipment to new centres of mining interest just beyond the range of existing land transportation facilities. In 1924, for instance, Laurentide Air Service ferried passengers and freight from the older centres of Larder Lake and Haileybury to the new mining camp at Rouyn, Quebec, and by 1926 J.V. Elliott Air Service and Patricia Airways were flying passengers, freight, and mail from the railway stations of Sioux Lookout or Minaki to the Red Lake camp. Other regional air services were available through Commercial Airways of Edmonton (for Northern Alberta and the District of Mackenzie) and Yukon Airways, based at Whitehorse. Every mining strike from 1926 onward brought numbers of chartered aircraft loaded with prospectors, mining engineers, promoters, and essential supplies to speed the development of new camps.

The advent of the Depression brought this activity to an end. The high costs – $6,000 to $10,000 to keep a pair of prospectors at work in the Territories – made the work too expensive, especially as the chances of bringing finds into production in the foreseeable future seemed remote. Most of the companies ceased operations and were absorbed into the well-financed, nation-wide Canadian Airways firm. NAME, for instance, sold its equipment to Canadian Airways in February 1932 and closed its business in the fall of 1935. During four active seasons its pilots, geologists, and prospectors had flown two million miles and uncovered more mining prospects than could possibly be developed for years to come.

Ironically, a renewed wave of air-supported prospecting was about to begin that would put the efforts of the late twenties far in the shade. Between 1931 and 1935, in a time of sharply declining costs, the official price of gold was almost doubled, sending a vast wave of prospectors far and wide in a frenzied quest for developable gold deposits. By the mid-thirties companies and independent bush pilots were picking up prospectors at northern railway points across Canada, at St. Félicien, Oskélanéo, Amos, and Rouyn in Quebec, at Armstrong and Hudson in Ontario, at Lac du Bonnet, Prince Albert, Edmonton, and Waterways in the Prairie Provinces, and at Prince George, Atlin, and Whitehorse for the Cordilleran and Pacific Slope districts. Canadian Airways operated planes in six divisions that spanned Canada, while Edmonton businessmen and local flyers developed two important systems, Mackenzie Air Services for operations based on the Mackenzie waterway, and United Air Transport for the area northwest from Edmonton to Dawson. Domex and NAME were succeeded by such firms as Prospectors Airways and Territories Exploration; Consolidated Mining and other companies kept their private fleets of aircraft busy with prospecting and mining activities. Prospectors were flown to secret destinations to begin testing and proving up claims, to be followed by larger cargoes of drilling and other supplies, and eventually the full range of requirements for a mine in progress and for a growing mining camp and settlement. Thus by the end of the thirties the mining and aviation industries had thrown the northern frontier of Canada wide open.

II

The process of developing the many thousands of mining claims into mines was protracted and expensive. In general, little work was done before the claims were recorded, for the regulations permitted staking merely on presumption of developable mineral deposits. Most claims were abandoned when little or no work had ever been done on them. On those that were kept in good standing, a great deal of stripping and trenching was done to prove whether the showings were extensive or existed in any depth, followed by diamond drilling to get some idea of the extent of the mineralized body and its composition and grade. By the 1930s, compact, lightweight, portable diamond drilling equipment eased the work of testing prospects and outlining potential orebodies. In 1929 Boyles Brothers developed a 1,400-pound unit capable of boring a 1½-inch core to a depth of 1,500 feet and powered by a Model-T Ford engine that could be hauled over frozen muskegs. The future workhorses for exploratory drilling made their appearance soon afterwards – 550-pound skid-mounted machines with Ford engines, capable of punching a one-inch hole to a 650-foot depth. A further improvement was a much cheaper and easier to replace cast set bit costing as little as thirty-five dollars. The Boyles Brothers and Connors Drilling companies, which opened branches at Vancouver, Kirkland Lake, and Port Arthur, undertook a variety of activities in underground mining and construction besides prospecting operations.

After these tests only a few properties would still command further investment. On those, diamond drilling would be used to outline the deposits to secure more reliable estimates of the tonnages of ore and how they might be mined. Shafts and levels would be built to trace the vein or orebody, becoming part of the workings if and when the deposit was mined. Hand-picked ore was sometimes sold to help with the expenses, sales that enhanced the reputation of the mine and might attract new parties to invest or buy out the owners. Adjacent claims were examined to see whether they could be incorporated in the mine and might be acquired. All the while samples of the ore were being analysed for composition and grade, and appropriate mechanical and metallurgical processes for mining, concentrating, and processing were being worked out. The shafts and levels were enlarged and extended, and the necessary transport systems, concentrating mills, separation units, smelting and converting plants appropriate to the operation were designed, tested, built, and installed.

A further set of considerations related to the locations of the mines, most of them in isolated, unsettled districts. The principals had to grapple with arrangements for transportation facilities, power to operate the mills and mines, and housing and other amenities to sustain the workforce. The costs of these varied markedly from region to region. Many mines in Northern Ontario enjoyed relatively good railway and road access; hydro-electric power was available from existing stations or Ontario Hydro might build new stations for their benefit. Nearby settlements offered accessible pools of labour, community facilities, and amenities. But as none of these infrastructures were available for mines located in the Northwest Territories or the extreme norths of most provinces, the added costs had to be taken into account. The effect was to inhibit the opening of mines in remote areas unless the mineral deposits were exceptionally rich, large, or easily worked.

The ore being mined was a similar consideration. Gold quartz, for instance, required comparatively straightforward, unsophisticated treatment and made relatively modest demands on transportation facilities. Such mines could be operated in quite remote, isolated locations. Base metal mines, on the other hand, needed both very cheap transportation to move their low-value products and fairly complex

and expensive ore treatment facilities. If the ores had to be fully processed at the site, the needed engineering and mineralogical facilities
were complicated and expensive, as was the large, full-time workforce
for whom a complete town would have to be built. Hence during the
interwar years gold mines proliferated across Subarctic Canada, but
the only complete base metal complexes operated in the Middle North
were located on the Pacific Coast (Anyox, B.C.) or near existing
or soon-to-be-built railway lines in Northern Manitoba (Flin Flon),
Ontario (Sudbury), and Quebec (Noranda).

The evolution of the base metal mine at Flin Flon that went into
operation in the autumn of 1929 provides an excellent illustration of
the prolonged, complicated, and costly efforts required to bring a large
mineral deposit in a fairly remote district into full operation. The area
had been surveyed by the Geological Survey in the 1890s; the promising mineral occurrence was discovered by Tom Creighton, a local
prospector and trapper, during the winter of 1914–15 and was staked
in the summer of 1915 by a prospecting party. The twelve mining
claims were optioned to a Toronto-based syndicate of mine financiers
including J.E. Hammell, who was to be the main driving force carrying
the mine to production. Hammell optioned the claims to Hayden,
Stone and Company of New York, who conducted enough diamond
drilling to locate a large orebody with a zinc content that posed a formidable metallurgical problem. When Haydon, Stone gave up their
option, Hammell approached a group of Haileybury businessmen who
undertook further diamond drilling in 1917–18, then withdrew, discouraged, after having spent several hundred thousand dollars. Next
the Cobalt-based Mining Corporation of Canada agreed to undertake
development of the mine in association with W.B. Thompson of New
York. They spent a further $300,000 sinking two shafts, proving the
reserves by finding over 16 million tons of copper-zinc sulphides. After
the Thompson interest withdrew, Mining Corporation carried on
alone, spending another $600,000 to acquire full ownership of the
property.

Finally, in 1925 Mining Corporation sold an option to the New York
financier, mine developer, and Arctic hunter Harry Payne Whitney for
a large but undisclosed amount of cash and a 15-per-cent interest in
any company formed to exploit the deposit. The Whitney interests
spent $750,000 to develop a suitable process (including contracting
out research on flotation and separation processes to the Colorado
School of Mines and the Mineral Separation Company) and build a
small pilot plant at the site. Then they decided to exercise their option
and took over the ownership. The Hudson Bay Mining and Smelting
Company, and Flin Flon Mines Company to operate the mine, were

incorporated at the end of 1927; a little later, the Churchill River Power Company was set up to build and operate the hydro-electric power development at Island Falls, Saskatchewan. When completed, the mine included a 3,000-ton-per-day concentrating plant, an 800-ton copper smelter, a 75-ton zinc plant, a power plant, a townsite, and a railway branch from The Pas, built by the CNR, representing a $25-million investment in all. Even then the operation was not quite self-contained, for the processed copper still had to be shipped to Montreal for refining.

Base metal mines had particular significance because their large investments, construction, facilities, and workforces had wide ramifications for industrial development in their regions and in Canada as a whole. Canadian base metal resources attracted widespread attention because of the rapid growth, especially in the United States, of manufacturing industries requiring huge quantities of those metals. Expansion of the resource industries, besides, was greatly assisted by the development of new oil flotation techniques that improved the recovery rate, and thus reduced the cost of concentrating the metallic components of complex base metal and silver ores. The large copper-silver-gold operation of Granby Consolidated, developed as a copper producer during the Great War, expanded in 1919 by acquiring a coal mine at Nanaimo and installing a smelter plant at Anyox. Unfortunately, the sharp fall in the price of copper at the end of 1920 forced Granby to discontinue underground development work even though its workers took a voluntary reduction in pay. Granby continued, however, to treat over a million tons of ore a year, employ 1,100 men, and sustain a town of 3,000. But the ore was becoming poorer and costs were rising. When the price of copper fell once again during the Depression, the company was forced into liquidation in 1935, effectively closing the town and several mines that had shipped ore to Anyox for processing.

The elaborate Hudson Bay Mining and Smelting operation at Flin Flon suffered, too, in the Depression, which coincided with the opening of the mine. The nearly 1.1 million tons of ore mined in 1931 yielded 3.82 per cent zinc and 1.94 per cent copper – not enough to pay the operating costs – but also 1.09 ounces of silver and .089 ounces of gold per ton. It was largely these precious metals that kept the mine and the community afloat during the Depression. Sherritt-Gordon Mines brought a second mine into operation in April 1931 at Sherridon, forty-five miles north of Flin Flon and linked to it by a line from the Flin Flon branch of the CNR. By purchasing its power from Hudson Bay's hydro plant and sending its concentrate to Flin Flon's smelter, the company greatly reduced the investment required. But since its ore was not as rich in the precious metals as Flin Flon's, the mine remained closed for most of the thirties. The Sherritt-Gordon project graphically illustrates the spin-off effects that a pioneer enterprise gives to further development of a district through the facilities it has introduced.

Greater success was achieved by the other new base metal mining operation of the period, Noranda Mines, which was fortunate enough to begin producing at the crest of the boom of the 1920s. The find that was to become the Noranda Mine was made by E.H. Horne, an Ontario prospector, in Rouyn Township in Quebec, due east of Kirkland Lake. Unlike the case of Flin Flon, the original staking syndicate sold out to an American group who quickly incorporated the company and undertook all the expenses of developing the mine and building the smelter during the years 1923–26. A forty-four-mile railway branch was built south from Taschereau on the former National Transcontinental, and electric power was supplied in 1926 from a new hydro plant on the upper Ottawa at Rivière des Quinze.

Production began in 1927 while the operation continued to be improved. By 1930 some 734,000 tons of ore had been raised, and the 37,754 tons of copper, 117,400 ounces of gold, and 692,000 ounces of silver made Quebec for the first time in sixty years a significant producer of both gold and copper. The coming of the Depression and the fall in the price of copper led Noranda to concentrate on those parts of its orebody that carried the richest gold values, so that in 1930 the mine produced less copper but twice as much gold as it had in 1929. By 1931 the company's 253,363 ounces of gold made it Canada's third-largest gold producer, while its 35,000 tons of copper accounted for 90 per cent of Quebec's copper output. The company added a 500-ton cyanide mill in 1935 to treat the tailings from the flotation plant, recovering still more gold. Thanks to its income from these two main metals, Noranda prospered throughout the 1930s and by 1936 was once again benefiting from the improving market for copper caused by world rearmament.

The stormy international situation assisted all the mining industry. Sherritt-Gordon reopened in 1937, and a new round of prospecting for and development of base metal occurrences began in Northern British Columbia (especially the Omineca district) and in Quebec (the Chibougamau district). Noranda increased its own copper-gold production and began treating large tonnages of copper-zinc-gold ores from other mines of the region. By 1939 Canada's copper output, most of it from Sudbury and Noranda, was almost triple that of a decade earlier, while zinc production (in which Manitoba and Quebec mines figured) doubled over the same period. Unfortunately, however, the prices of metals – except for gold and nickel – remained far below those of the twenties, mainly because of competition from mines in Africa and Latin America. The aluminum refining industry also recovered from its low level in 1932, when the Aluminium Company of Canada closed its older Shawinigan Falls plant, reduced production at Arvida to 10,000 tons (barely a third of the 1927 output), and used less than half its installed hydro-electric power capacity. With the improvement of markets after 1935, the company introduced a better extraction process and rapidly raised its production to 100,000 tons in 1939, of which half was exported to the United Kingdom and a quarter to Japan, no doubt for use in military aviation industries.

The search for domestic supplies of fossil fuels, which had been almost at a standstill in Northern Alberta since the short-lived flurry following the extension of railways to the Peace River and Fort McMurray districts, also revived after 1935. A more vigorous attempt to develop the oil sands deposits along the Athabasca River was begun by Abasand Oil Company, a newcomer, in the late 1930s while prospecting for oil and gas was stepped up in the Peace River district, including a British Columbia government prospecting and well-drilling program of 1939 instigated by the North-minded premier, T.D. Pattullo.

Gold, however, was the real incentive prodding mine finders and developers to expand Canada's mining frontiers throughout the inter-war period, thanks to the popularity and good price of the metal and the relative ease of establishing and operating gold mines in remote, isolated locations. During the 1914–18 war, mine development had been arrested, but after the Armistice investment capital became available to develop certain gold-mining properties. At Kirkland Lake, for example, extensive diamond drilling disclosed rich new ore reserves, improving the prospects of Teck-Hughes and Lake Shore mines and adding the Kirkland Lake and Wright-Hargreaves mines to the list of producers. At Salmon River, B.C., near Stewart on the Portland Canal, underground work on the Premier Gold mining property located high-grade ore and large tonnages of lower-grade reserves, making it possible for that gold mine, beginning production in July 1921, to become one of the greatest in the province. Most of the investment was speedily recovered from the profits of direct-shipped ore; thereafter, the company installed a 400-ton concentrating mill and had paid $14.2 million in dividends by 1929.

Elsewhere during the twenties there were gold finds at Wawa near Michipicoten and Red Lake in northwestern Ontario, at Rice Lake and Lac du Bonnet in Eastern Manitoba, and in northwestern Quebec, where developers hoped to repeat the successes of northeastern Ontario. Gold mines were discovered and were being readied for production by the end of the 1920s at Lake Osisko (where Noranda had been developed), at Granada, south of Rouyn, at O'Brien and Siscoe, southwest and south of Amos on the Harricana River, and at Beattie, south of La Sarre, the deposits outlining the future Gold Belt of Quebec south of, and parallel to, the National Transcontinental. The main gold rush of the twenties was to Red Lake, 130 miles northwest of Hudson in northwestern Ontario, where news of promising finds by the Howay brothers of Haileybury touched off both the first rush to involve extensive use of airplanes and frenzied activity on the Toronto Standard Stock and Mining Exchange. The one mine to emerge from the thousands of staked claims was based on the original discoveries, and it succeeded because of the persistent faith of J.E. Hammell, who raised enough capital from stock sales to complete the mine after Dome Mines had dropped its option on the property following some trenching and diamond drilling. Ontario Hydro's Ear Falls plant provided electric power and made it possible for production to begin in 1930.

During the later twenties gold mine development was hampered by the fixed price for gold (approximately $20.00 an ounce) in a time of rising costs. The onset of the Depression reversed this situation; the real value of gold increased relative to that of other commodities, and the spread between the gold miner's costs and his revenues widened. The situation improved still further when several countries went off the gold standard in September 1931, and especially at the end of January 1934 when the U.S. Treasury Department began buying gold at the fixed price of $35.00 an ounce in U.S. funds. After Canada devalued its dollar to ninety cents U.S. in September 1939 as a war measure, the industry was earning $38.50 an ounce, almost double the pre-1931 price. No wonder gold mining underwent remarkable expansion and its production reached a maximum 5,345,000 ounces, worth $205.8 million, in 1941.

Prospectors were attracted to the established districts. At Porcupine, Ontario, nine of the fourteen mines producing in 1954 had been developed since 1934. Two important newcomers, Pamour and Hallnor gold mines, financed by Noranda and Timmins interests, went into production in 1936 and 1938 respectively. But of the older large producers, the most successful was Kerr-Addison at Larder Lake, which had earlier been abandoned because its ores were too scattered. Following extensive prospecting and development work, the mine was brought back into production in 1938, mill capacity was increased from a daily 500 tons to 1,200 tons by 1939, then to 4,000 tons to make it Canada's largest gold producer after 1945.

Nonetheless, most prospecting took place in new districts, publicized by staking rushes and chartering of new companies. In the Long-lac district north of Lake Superior, several mines placed in production around the new town of Geraldton yielded gold worth over $100 mil-lion by 1955. There was also much activity in the Red Lake district, where the Howay mine, with the lowest operating costs of any gold mine in Canada, successfully mined its very low-grade deposit ($2.55 of gold per ton of ore). During eleven years of production before the ore was exhausted in late 1941, the mine yielded gold worth $13.1 million from 5,158,000 tons of ore and actually paid $1,950,000 in dividends. New mines opened in this area in and after 1935 also produced gratifying dividends for their shareholders. Farther afield in the District of Patricia, another group of gold mines was opened, not-able among them being Pickle Crow (another Hammell enterprise) and Central Patricia, and even on remote Favourable Lake, a source of the Severn River. The developers had to haul their equipment 170 miles or more over muskegs and through bush from Hudson or Winnipeg. Central Patricia, in addition, developed its own hydro-power source at a plant on the Albany River, twenty-six miles distant.

Farther west, in Manitoba the San Antonio Mine went into operation in 1932 along with other mines on God's Lake, Island Lake, and else-where in the province. The search for gold extended to Northern Saskatchewan, where Lake Athabasca captured attention after gold, pitchblende, and nickel-copper were discovered in 1934. Consoli-dated Mining and Smelting decided to develop a gold mine, mill, and 3,300-horsepower hydro-electric plant to exploit the claims at Gold-fields, an unusual formation in which the gold did not occur in veins or shoots but was finely mixed throughout a granitic mass. A $3- to $4-million outlay was wasted developing the large-volume, low-cost Box Mine before it was found that the grade of the ore was as low as $1.68 gold a ton. The mine was put in operation, but the Second World War mercifully brought the unlucky venture to an end. Fortunately for Con-solidated, simultaneous gold finds at Yellowknife on Great Slave Lake more than offset the disappointing result at Goldfields. In British Columbia, widespread searches for gold extending from Zeballos, on northwest Vancouver Island, to Taku, near the Yukon boundary, met little success, although a discovery in the Cariboo in 1932 did result in establishment of two producing mines and the town of Wells. In the Lillooet district, too, Bralorne Mines developed one of the province's most successful gold mines.

Northern Quebec proved the main area of gold mine development. Development proceeded from Rouyn southeastward to a new centre where the town of Val d'Or was founded in 1934, then to the Lamaque and Malartic districts, and finally northeastward toward Lake Chibougamau and the headwaters of the Rupert River. In the Val d'Or area the Siscoe Mine, under development since 1923, came into production in 1930 and before the deposit was exhausted in 1949 produced $40 million worth of gold, paying dividends from 1932. The Lamaque Mine, a subsidiary of Teck-Hughes, opened a 500-ton mill in 1935 and eventually enlarged it to 2,000 tons to become Quebec's largest gold mine. In the same district, Beattie Gold Mines, a subsidiary of Ventures and of Nipissing Mining, beginning in 1933 yielded more than $28.5 million worth of gold from 7.1 million tons of ore mined to the end of 1949. All told, in 1939 Quebec had twenty-five auriferous quartz mines in operation as a result of the gold boom. Their production of 953,377 ounces made gold far and away the leading mineral product of Quebec in that year.

In northeastern Ontario, the older gold-mining camps prospered throughout the interwar period. By 1914 several mines had gone into full operation at Porcupine, though those at Kirkland Lake were still in the developmental stage. After the war these mines suffered from occasional power and labour shortages and industrial strife that became acute when companies' efforts to pare down wages in a time of swelling profits brought prolonged strikes, notably one of four months' duration at Kirkland Lake in 1920. During the 1920s, the Kirkland Lake mines were developed into important producers, and at both camps the successful companies invested heavily in blocking out ore reserves, extensive shaft and level development, underground crushing plants, conveyor systems, improved concentration and extraction processes and plants – all to help offset the inevitable fall in ore grades. For instance, at Timmins, Hollinger Consolidated built a hydro plant to reduce its fuel costs, equipped its mine to treat 8,000 tons of ore daily, and installed a 3 ½ -mile aerial tramway to deliver tons of sand for backfilling the mined sections. The company won $169.2 million worth of gold from ores containing as little as three-tenths of an ounce of gold per ton and paid out $58.2 million in dividends and bonuses between 1910 and 1931. At Kirkland Lake the ores were richer than those of Porcupine, but the deposits were smaller and more expensive to mine. The mines – mainly Lake Shore, Teck-Hughes, and Wright-Hargreaves – began their expansion during the twenties and passed Porcupine in total production after 1931, when Lake Shore overtook Hollinger and went on to become one of the world's half-dozen largest gold producers before the decade ended.

On the other hand, the inevitable depletion of ore and depressed economic conditions in the early twenties and throughout the thirties virtually ended mining of the silver of Cobalt. Despite more efficient processes and cost-reducing company consolidations, the camp, plagued since 1914 by exhaustion of the silver ores and after 1920 by low prices for silver, continued in decline. Six mines closed between 1918 and 1921, leaving but a single mine in operation by 1922. Most of the successful corporations, particularly Mining Corporation of Canada, Nipissing Mines, Anglo-Huronian, and M.J. O'Brien, became holding companies that put their earnings to work in mining ventures elsewhere in Canada and continued to promote mining development in Canada.

It was economic conditions rather than depletion that slowed down iron mining in Northern Ontario. After its wartime markets were lost, Algoma Steel became simply a plant handicapped by its remoteness from the manufacturing and financial centres of Canada and entered on years of reduced production culminating in final collapse during the Depression. Iron mining, which with the aid of subsidies had sustained a 700,000-ton-per-annum production level through the war and post-war years, was hurt by the economic slowdown and by competition from cheaper, higher-grade ores from the adjacent Lake Superior region of the United States. Canadian steelmakers found it more economical to import American ore, and iron mining in Ontario, particularly at Michipicoten, virtually ceased. But when in 1937 the Canadian capitalist Sir James Dunn took control of the enterprise, he reorganized the plants and secured a greatly increased bounty from the Hepburn government for iron mined in Ontario. As a result the first local ore since 1923 began to arrive at Algoma's blast furnaces from the company's New Helen Mine near Wawa. Revived prospecting for iron occurrences led to the discovery in 1939 of a high-grade hematite (iron oxide) bed beside, and mostly beneath, Steep Rock Lake in the Rainy Lake district, which Steep Rock Iron Mines speedily developed into a producing mine. Thus the industry was ready when war once more engulfed Canada.

Sudbury, thanks to its important place in the small global circle of nickel producers, was able to benefit both from military markets in times of rearmament and war and from increased peacetime uses for the metal. Faced with loss of lucrative markets after 1918, International Nickel developed Monel Metal (named after Ambrose Monell, its president), a copper-nickel alloy that required little processing beyond removing the sulphur from the matte as received from the roaster. Monel Metal, being strong and resistant to corrosion and high temperatures, quickly won new uses in peacetime construction and hardware industries. After a slow period in 1919, INCO speedily regained, then exceeded its wartime production levels. The post-war depression, in fact, redounded to its advantage by causing the rival British-American Nickel Company to collapse after a brief period of operation in 1920. Production achieved new records as nickel became more widely used in coinage and, alloyed with steel, in high-speed machinery, automobiles (which used 36 per cent of the total production by 1926), and electrical appliances.

INCO achieved near-monopoly status in 1924 by taking over British-American's properties and processes. Then, in 1928, it merged with its formidable British rival, Mond Nickel Company. The merger improved the mining operation at Sudbury (particularly the Frood Mine), and bestowed large profits on the original shareholders and insiders of the two companies. The united company was better able to control the world market for nickel in spite of the appearance in 1929–30 of a small new rival, Falconbridge Nickel Company, which installed a 1,600-ton-per-day smelting plant at Sudbury and shipped its matte to a refinery in northern Norway. By 1929 INCO was mining nearly 2 million tons of ore at Sudbury, and Canada registered a record 55,000 tons of nickel production for the year. Its controlling position enabled INCO to regulate the nickel supply in relation to world consumption during the Depression to maintain an almost constant price (24.6¢ a pound in 1929, 22.5¢ in 1939) while production was declining to a low of 15,000 tons (1932), then soaring to 112,000 tons in 1937 and 113,000 tons in 1939, far beyond any previous records. Since copper was a main component of the complex Sudbury ore, the area was Canada's largest source for that metal. It was almost the sole Canadian source for platinum, recorded production of which jumped from 29,000 to 284,000 ounces between 1929 and 1939, also of many still rarer metals. Canada's metal mining and processing industries new and old came through the Depression enormously strengthened, ready for the loads they would be required to shoulder during the Second World War.

III

The metallic mineral resources, gold deposits in particular, extended Canada's horizons far beyond the limits of the farming and forestry frontiers. Even the Arctic was included, despite the heavy burdens of distance, climate, and higher operating costs. Mines engendered new centres in otherwise empty regions – Premier, Yellowknife, Flin Flon, Red Lake, Rouyn, and Val d'Or – for new regional economies and societies. Gold camps attracted hundreds of unemployed workers from distant cities and farms, and the expanding gold mining and reviving metal mining centres after 1935 greatly improved the employment situation in established districts. Mining helped diversify regional economies, producing better-rounded, more prosperous, securer settlements and societies.

Mining and forestry together, it was estimated in 1937, directly supported about a third of the Abitibi region's 60,000 inhabitants. The opening of the gold and base metal mines along the mineralized belt about forty miles south of the National Transcontinental route had spawned a series of new communities. The earliest, Rouyn, the locale of the Noranda mine, had been incorporated as a town in 1927 and reached a population of 8,800 in 1941. Val d'Or, the first of the new gold centres, was founded in 1934 to serve five new mines; by 1937 it boasted 7,000 inhabitants. By then another village, Bourlamaque, was growing up to serve the Lamaque and Sigma mines, and a year or two after that still another "city," Malartic, took shape for the mines in its vicinity and others undergoing development. Soon the area was linked with the other centres of Abitibi farther north by a highway, by a railway line with Senneterre, and by direct highway with Montreal.

Expansion of mining brought together workers with many differing backgrounds. In the remote camps city dwellers rubbed shoulders with natives, trappers, lumbermen, and European immigrants gaining their first introduction to Canada. English Canadians invaded Abitibi, a bastion of French-Canadian society, while French-Canadian Quebeckers worked in mining camps and processing plants across the country. The managerial and professional elements of the camps and mining towns usually were English Canadians, and the workmen were French Canadians, Finns or Swedes, Ukrainians or Poles, or Italians, according to the hiring and employment practices of individual mines. The combination in Quebec was likely to be one of English-Canadian or American managerial staffs and French-Canadian miners; business and professional settlers in the communities usually were recruited from adjacent areas. Indeed, the participation of Toronto businessmen in the mining and hydro development activities of Abitibi with the related influx of English-speaking settlers was on a scale to create some disquiet among politicians and public in Quebec.

Although the prospecting and development stages of mining scattered thousands of workers for only brief seasons across the reaches of Northern Canada, the process of establishing mines generally entailed forming relatively permanent communities. Many were little more than bunkhouses and messhalls adjacent to the mines and surrounded by bush; the nearest, most convenient village or city was the source for necessary services and recreation. In some areas the opening of a number of mines led to the creation of central communities with stores, hotels, postal and telephone communications, a few pioneer businessmen (storekeepers and agents of mining brokers) and professional men. There were also schools and churches if enough families arrived. Many of these centres evolved from an initial phase of gambling parlours, dance halls, and red light districts to a time when family groups and the sorts of institutions they favoured prevailed and the activities of the male-dominated societies were gradually expelled or driven underground. That trend could be traced in the new camps of northwestern Ontario (Red Lake, Central Patricia) and of Eastern Manitoba, still more in the remoter settlements of Goldfields and Yellowknife. Yet no matter how large and well-developed the mining town became, it always retained a certain air of impermanence, reflecting the fact that the industry on which it depended had a limited lifespan and the community would one day probably become a ghost town.

In their publicity releases mining companies boasted of their concern for the health of their workers, and in truth, being vitally concerned to keep their workforces, they employed monetary and other inducements to hold them. Underground workers received bonuses based on production, and bonuses based on years of seniority helped retain desirable workers. Athletic facilities, company housing, and other amenities were supplied for the same purpose, especially in remote areas where rapid turnover of staff was a constant problem and source of heavy expense. At Premier, a truly isolated camp town, the company gradually improved the standards of comfort and made possible family living. The original bunkhouses were remodelled, a nine-storey, 117-room apartment building equipped with steam heating and electricity, showers, and washrooms was provided for the single men, and another apartment building with six three-room suites for young married couples was built. A community hall offered clubrooms for concerts, dances, and meetings, a reading room and library, and in winter a basketball court – even a tennis court on a foundation of two-by-fours was installed on the side of the hill. Better steamship service from Vancouver and Prince Rupert reduced isolation, and the building of roads up the river valleys facilitated recreational travel around the district. By such means mining companies strove to accommodate their several classes of employees and keep the turnover rate as low as possible.

Well-established, permanent mining concerns did not have the same problems in attracting and holding workers. They generated large enough communities in themselves to support a full array of private and public facilities and services, and in time they secured good enough transportation services to reduce feelings of isolation among their settlers. They led the way in providing good health services, primarily for their own employees and their families, that redounded to the benefit of the whole community. The major mines employed doctors to examine miners before they were hired and periodically afterwards to ensure they were still fit for the work. They provided excellent changing and showering facilities, including brief exposure to ultraviolet rays. Full-time safety engineers working in the mines made efforts to eliminate hazardous conditions. At McIntyre-Porcupine, a group insurance policy covered the employees for disability and provided death benefits in the event of the fatal accidents that seemed unavoidable features of hard-rock mining operations.

There were limits to what even enlightened private enterprise would do, however, and recurring mine accidents brought appeals for government regulations to improve working conditions and to provide better safety and inspection services and contributory workmen's compensation systems. Concern grew over the ravages of newly recognized diseases such as silicosis, which could completely destroy the worker's health and livelihood. The notion spread that victims deserved pensions rather than abandonment to public or private charity. A new concern for the physical environment led INCO to buy farms ruined by poisonous fumes and to consider reducing future contamination by building very high smokestacks at new plants to permit the prevailing winds to disperse effluent gases.

The highly diversified permanent communities arising from the long-term mining operations offered amenities comparable to those in cities of similar size in more settled parts of Canada. Timmins, the gold-mining capital, swelled from a town of 3,800 in 1921 and of 14,200 in 1931 to a city of 28,500 in 1941; Kirkland Lake grew from 1,170 to 9,915 in the decade 1931–41. The mature Sudbury camp included eight or nine separate communities as well as the city, some of them rough shacktowns adjoining the mines, others well-built, well-equipped small towns for management and professional staffs of the companies, with Sudbury, a city of 32,000 in 1941, supplying commercial and service needs for the entire district.

The great mines were leading employers in their communities, employing about 10,000 wage earners at Sudbury in 1929, and 8,511 persons at the Porcupine camp. On the other hand, production cuts during the early thirties created widespread unemployment at Sudbury and at the processing plants at Sault Ste Marie and Arvida. There were violent hunger marches. Sudbury, among others, defaulted on its bonds and remained under the management of a provincially appointed administrator until 1940. The gold-mining centres experienced no such difficulties, as the doubling of population at Timmins during the decade indicated. The base metal and nickel-mining communities also gradually recovered as their industries revived in the later thirties.

The mines and their workmen furnished important markets for local farm products and game, lumber, transportation facilities, hydro-electric power, and the like. Salaries and wages amounted to 60 per cent or more of the operating costs of most mines and were very important even to well-established districts, since the men's pay was largely spent on food, clothing, lodging, and other local goods and services. Local businesses were the beneficiaries of spending on timber and lumber, freight and express, electric power, fuel and lubricants, and other commodities by the mining companies. Major mining centres supported large construction activities and many service personnel that consumed much local produce, forest products, and a full range of manufactured goods. The mines imported tools, machinery, vehicles, metal pipe, construction materials, and chemicals that sustained commercial and metropolitan centres, and the explosives, drilling equipment, boilers, milling plants, crushing materials, chemical reagents, and transportation equipment that the mining industries needed made them important contributors to Canada's engineering, industrial, and chemical manufacturing sectors.

The mining industries, as we have seen, helped bring hydro-electric power and improved communications to their districts. In remote areas companies often provided for their own energy needs by importing wood-burning or oil-fueled generating plants or developing local waterpower sites; some encouraged electric companies to build new hydro installations to serve them. Cheap hydro-electric power made it practicable for mining companies to install the facilities to process their ores fully in their own plants and also to process ores sent from other mines too small to warrant such expensive equipment. Larger mines built refineries to recover minor but valuable byproducts such as gold from their complex ores. The percentage of copper exported from Canada in half-processed "blister copper" form fell from 67.5 per cent in 1929–30 to below 3 per cent a decade later because of the refining done at Sudbury and at Montreal East, while the percentage of refined silver exported as bullion rose from 70 per cent to 86 per cent over the same period. Thus the mining industry with the aid of cheap electric power reached higher levels of ore processing and refining that brought greater benefits to Canadians and to Canada from its plentiful mineral resources, and the two resource industries in concert helped build better-rounded, more stable, more successful economies and societies in the Middle North.

The transportation facilities provided for or by the mining industry similarly promoted the growth of the districts and fuller utilization of local resource bases. During the prospecting and early development stages trails were broken through wilderness country, motorboats and launches were introduced on navigable waterways, and occasionally tractor roads were built to deliver urgently needed construction materials, machinery, and supplies. Governments assisted the companies with grants-in-aid, and during the later thirties a full-blown federal-provincial program for building mining roads on a shared-cost basis was begun. One mining company established, primarily for its own freight, what was to become the main public shipping concern on the navigable waterways below Fort McMurray, Northern Transportation Company. Provincial governments routinely built roads to established mining centres, such as Red Lake, as a normal service to their citizens. Quebec improved the northern regional roads, building connecting roads to Kirkland Lake on the west and south from Val d'Or across the Shield to Maniwaki, from which the Gatineau highway to the Hull-Montreal trunk road gave the Abitibi region its first direct outlet to the provincial metropolis in 1939.

One of the lasting benefits of the mining industry was the impetus it gave to Canada's youthful aviation industry. Prospectors and mine developers were the chief patrons of the chartered services offered by bush pilots at almost every strategic centre, and airlines carried the fairly large (for those times) amounts of supplies aggregating 100 tons and more that were sometimes required to convert prospects into mines. In 1934, they hauled freight and express totalling over 14 million pounds and many times more than that before the decade closed. Indeed, the isolated mining communities required scheduled freight, passenger, and mail service on such a scale as to make Canada one of the world's leading users of airmail delivery in the thirties.

The heavy transportation needs of the mining industry were a stimulant to Canada's overbuilt railway system and even encouraged the building of new branch lines. A good example was the arrangement between Hudson Bay Mining and Smelting and the CNR for a branch to the mining camp of Flin Flon. The railway was guaranteed specified tonnages at rates allowing recovery of its investment; the mine was assured of relatively cheap, dependable, year-round transport and spared the heavy burden of providing that service for itself. In the Abitibi district, the requirements of forty mines in operation or under development led the CNR to build a branch line through the Gold Belt from Senneterre to Taschereau via Val d'Or and Rouyn. As for Ontario's provincially owned T&NO Railway, the growing mining industry freight enabled the line to report a net profit of $792,012 for 1935–36, when a record 1.3 million tons of freight were hauled. Under-used, unprofitable sections of the former Canadian Northern between Long-lac and Winnipeg gained new purpose with the start of gold mining around Geraldton and revival of iron-mining activity west of Lake

Superior. Even British Columbia's PGE Railway secured unexpected traffic and its first taste of prosperity through the revival of gold-mining activity around Lillooet and in the Cariboo district. Thus the northward advance of the mining and forestry industries during the thirties increased the usefulness and helped improve the solvency of parts of the latest-built pre-war railway network that had been left in the shade by the post-war railway consolidation.

Canadian governments in various ways demonstrated their readiness to assist the mining industries, which they regarded as builders of the economy of their regions and contributors to the prosperity of their major manufacturing and financial centres. They instituted favourable mining regulations, carried out surveying and research activities, and set up mining schools, prospecting courses, and apprenticeship programs for mining technicians and workmen in addition to their spending on transportation facilities or social programs. Provincial governments fought federal government policies they regarded as harmful to mining, such as special taxes on corporate profits or import duties on essential equipment.

During the troubled thirties, Premiers Hepburn and Duplessis helped mine owners resist the unionization of their mining camps and plants. Ontario created conciliation agencies and established arbitration procedures in an effort to head off potential strikes so that the industry weathered the Depression with no more than a few brief sit-down strikes. A very intimate alliance was forged between the industry and Hepburn, who was strongly influenced by personal friendship with C.G. McCullagh, who had made a fortune in the mine brokerage business and from time to time let Hepburn in on ''good things'' in mining investments. McCullagh, in turn, influenced the aged W.H. Wright, a successful, wealthy gold-mining executive, to buy the *Globe* and the *Mail and Empire* newspapers in Toronto and merge them into the present *Globe and Mail* in October 1936. As Wright candidly admitted, his reason was ''mainly . . . my interest in mining. . . . I thought I could do something for the country by making our mining industries better known. Anything that is of advantage to mining is of advantage to the country as a whole.''[3] Now the mining industry had an important mouthpiece for directing Toronto opinion and influencing governments.

The time was opportune, for Toronto was rapidly emerging as the unquestioned financial and supply centre of the mining camps of Northern Ontario, and as the source for much of the capital and personnel developing mines throughout the Canadian Shield during the gold boom of the thirties. Toronto's mining hinterland extended from Northern Ontario into Northern Quebec and westward even into the

Northwest Territories. Brokers, lawyers, and mining executives based themselves in Toronto, where the mining and stock exchanges afforded an excellent locale for organizing and financing mining companies. The city's newspapers and business and mining press gathered and organized information on mining in Canada, attracted attention to projects, and encouraged investment in Canadian mining companies. Consulting geologists, mining supply firms, and air transport organizations serving the industry worked out of, or through, Toronto. As a result, Toronto's business community and public were kept in close touch with developments at Kirkland Lake, Pickle Crow, Val d'Or, or Yellowknife.

The corresponding interest groups were fewer in Montreal, and their activities were confined mostly to Quebec. In the West, Winnipeg and Edmonton secured much of the trade emanating from mining camps in their hinterland, though they could not challenge Toronto's controlling interest over working mines and mining developments. Expansion of mining activity in the Northwest Territories whetted the metropolitan ambitions of the western cities and led pressure groups such as the Edmonton and Northern Alberta Chamber of Mines to lobby provincial and federal politicians, pleading the interests of their members and pressing for the opening of the North generally. Their agitation for improved linkages with the North was an adjunct to suggestions from the provinces that their boundaries be extended northward to bring the new-found riches of the North within their jurisdictions. Premier T.D. Pattullo frequently expressed a wish to incorporate the Yukon into British Columbia, a dream that reflected his having gone to the Klondike as a young federal civil servant and his subsequent years as a lawyer and politician in Prince Rupert.

Of course, large sections of the mining industry were owned and controlled, not in Toronto or Montreal, but outside Canada altogether. A detailed study in 1933 concluded that about 39 per cent of the industry, including forty-nine major companies, was controlled by U.S. investors. This old story had continued in the 1920s with the establishment of Noranda, Hudson Bay Mining and Smelting, Falconbridge, and Sherritt-Gordon. The last two were developed and operated by the Harvard-educated American brothers Lindsley, one an outstanding geologist, the other a widely experienced mining engineer and engineering consultant. In concert with the Canadian mining executives Joseph Errington, Gen. D.M. Hogarth, and Col. C.D.H. MacAlpine, the Lindsleys organized Ventures, Limited, in 1928 as a holding company for properties that included Dominion Explorers, the two aforementioned future mines, and various other mining properties. In 1940 they organized Frobisher, Limited, as a new holding company that eventually owned mines and mining properties on five continents. In Northern Canada these included United Keno Hill (silver and lead) in the Yukon, Giant Yellowknife (gold) in the District of Mackenzie, and Opemiska (copper and gold) in Northern Quebec. When Thayer Lindsley retired from the presidency of Ventures at the age of seventy-two in 1955, his enterprises constituted a "world mining empire," the Ventures section of which was conservatively valued at $250 million.[4] McIntyre-Porcupine Mines in 1960 gained control of the Frobisher-Ventures holdings in Canada and in certain other lands, particularly Latin America. Canadian mining was also subject to some British controlling interest in the 1920s, notably Mond Nickel of Sudbury and the Central Manitoba Gold Mines. In the main, however, British (and some Canadian) mining investment was directed toward more lucrative mining prospects in African and Australian parts of the Commonwealth. A reversal of this relationship was the appearance in the later thirties at Vancouver of Placer Development, an Australian mining company extending its activities to North America and Canada.

The high degree of foreign control undoubtedly reflected the earlier coming of age of the economy and industry in the United States. It had more highly developed institutions for mobilizing and directing capital into mining and more experienced, skilled, wealthy, well-connected, and confident entrepreneurs than Canada. Certain of its large manufacturing industries, besides, could obtain a secure source of vital minerals and earn profits, too, by participating in Canadian mine development. Canada, on the other hand, seemed to lack a reliable system for mobilizing and directing investment toward risky mining ventures. Ironically, quite large amounts of Canadian capital were invested instead in "safe" established mining operations such as Noranda, Dome Mines, Hollinger, Kerr-Addison, and especially INCO, 21 per cent of whose capital investment (to the tune of some $200 million) was said to be Canadian. This pattern had something to do with how Canadian banks, insurance companies, and other institutions obtained and invested their funds.

Although Canadian mining entrepreneurs seemed still in the apprenticeship stage as compared with the Americans, involvement with the financing, developing, and operating of mines in the Sudbury, Cobalt, Porcupine, and other camps was giving them the skill and confidence to recognize and promote new finds elsewhere. Moreover, companies such as Mining Corporation of Canada and members of mining dynasties like the Timmins and O'Brien families were accumulating capital from the profits of earlier successes. Such groups had the expertise, specialized staffs, and equipment to bring new ventures into being and sufficient means to invest in several projects to spread the risks and ensure ultimate success. Canadian investors of this sort figured in the developmental stages at Flin Flon and at many of the gold mines of the thirties.

But true venture capital had to come from a different source – from members of the public more ready to gamble on rises in the market value of shares than on mines eventually going into production, who eagerly bought penny shares of innumerable companies incorporated to develop claims into mines. Gold mine shares were particularly attractive to these investors not only because gold had an intrinsic lure and was saleable on the open market but also because of the improved prospects of such shares for rapid price appreciation. As such share-holders left development operations to the promoters and developers, the direction of most of the new gold mines fell into the hands of Toronto-based Canadian mining men who managed the capital raised from the proceeds of stock sales. By the late twenties Howay Gold was only ''one of several mines'' that had been ''brought to the producing stage through public financing rather than by reliance on large mining companies.''[5] Promoters and developers new and old strove to raise money for mining operations by floating new companies: veterans from the 1920s like J.E. Hammell or C.D.H. MacAlpine, and newcomers in the thirties in major cities across Canada and in local mining centres such as Haileybury and Rouyn.

Marketing mining shares was an occupation in itself, a business that failed to overcome well-merited distrust in the public and the concern of state authorities during the interwar period and long afterwards. There were few restrictions upon incorporation of mining companies during the 1920s so that would-be developers found it easy to obtain mining claims in popular districts, then charter companies to raise funds ostensibly to develop the properties. Boom speculating conditions such as prevailed during the late twenties afforded unscrupulous promoters unparalleled opportunities to exploit the gullibility of the public. Cases of grave misconduct such as falsified drilling results and wash trading came to light to hurt the reputations of individuals and districts and revealed the inadequacies of the existing regulations. When the bubble burst in the autumn of 1929, Canadian mining brokers were prosecuted in several provinces, a number were convicted and sent to prison, their companies collapsed, and millions of shares became valueless. Stricter regulatory legislation was passed to make the ''intentional omission of material facts, outlandish promises, fictitious trades, the gaining of unconscionable commissions''[6] offences punishable by fine or imprisonment, and stock exchange practices were tightened. In 1934 the Standard Stock and Mining Exchange of Toronto was merged with the more reputable Toronto Stock

Exchange, which had come through the crisis without a single member becoming insolvent.

The U.S. Congress instituted far more stringent controls in 1933–34, and the Securities and Exchange Commission was set up to make it harder to take advantage of investors in that country. Canadian firms soliciting business in the United States had to conform to the commission's standards on penalty of being blacklisted and denied the use of the U.S. mails, and individuals charged with fraud under the regulations might be extradited for trial in the United States or indicted if they ventured into that country. Even so, free-wheeling promotions by mining brokers, mainly in Toronto, increased during the gold boom of the thirties. Dubious mining stocks were pushed by advertisement, word of mouth, and frequently by telephone calls to potential customers, many in the United States. The telephone proved a useful means for spreading exaggerated claims that could not be effectively policed. Abuses continued, among them the distribution of inordinately large fractions of the capital shares of companies to vending syndicates and brokers along with potentially lucrative options to purchase many of the remaining shares should the price improve, the issuing of misleading or false reports to snare unwary investors, and the timing of news releases so that insiders could realize large profits from their holdings. Harnessing the greed of individual speculators and stock salesmen was an uncertain and less than satisfactory way to finance development of Canadian mineral resources.

The remarkable growth of metallic mining, particularly in the thirties, contrasted sharply with the impact of the Depression on the other primary industries. Mining of gold and metallic minerals, mainly in the northern sections of the provinces and in the Territories, expanded dramatically, whereas that of non-metallic industrial minerals and fuels, mined chiefly in southern parts of the country, fell sharply. The output of gold – the product *par excellence* of the new mining frontiers – soared during the thirties from 12.8 per cent to an amazing 38.8 per cent (by value) of Canada's entire mineral production. Gold mining emerged as a key element in Canada's economy, its rising production contrasting sharply with the floundering agricultural industries on which Canada's prosperity since the start of the twentieth century had been based. The value of gold production increased by 361.6 per cent between 1929 and 1939, whereas the value of agricultural production in 1939 was actually 18.8 per cent below its 1929 figure. The rapid expansion of gold mining tended to reinforce the dominant economic position of the two central provinces in which the industry was mainly located, and to make mining an increasingly important part of those provinces' economies. Metal mining doubled its share of Quebec's total production from 4.6 per cent in 1932 to 9.8 per cent in 1939 and Ontario's from 7 per cent in 1929 to 14 per cent a decade later. Since gold mining formed an increasing share of these production figures, its phenomenal growth in the thirties greatly increased the significance of the sparsely inhabited frontierlands of the Shield and Cordillera relative to the older, settled parts of the provinces and brought the new regions more directly into the economic mainstream of Canada.

Besides contributing so handsomely to Canada's economic recovery, metal mining did much to improve the nation's external trading position. By the end of the thirties, gold bullion was second only to newsprint – another product of the northern frontiers – among Canada's commodity exports. The value of non-ferrous metal exports represented 32.1 per cent of Canada's total by 1938–39, and alone practically equalled in value the full range of agricultural products exported. (In 1927 the value of exported vegetable and animal products had been more than nine times as great as that of the non-ferrous metals.) The total exports of metal also passed those of forest products during the later thirties. This meant that agricultural exports represented only 34.7 per cent of the trade figure in 1938–39 whereas non-ferrous metals and forest products amounted to 51 per cent of the total. The new industrial frontiers of the Shield and Cordillera had quite eclipsed western farming as the mainstay of Canada's foreign trade.

The traditional trading pattern, in which western farm produce earned surpluses that offset Canada's imports and costs of servicing the national debt, had been supplanted by one in which products from the forests and rocks of the Middle North played a leading part. Indeed, by 1939–40 wheat ranked no higher than third in dollar terms among Canada's exports, behind newsprint and gold bullion. After wheat came nickel in fourth place, copper in fifth, lumber in sixth, woodpulp in seventh, and aluminum bars in tenth place. Thus seven of the ten leading exports in 1939 were products characteristic of the northern industrial frontiers. The new staples also reoriented the national triangular trading pattern with Britain and Europe and the United States into a more bilateral, continentalist alignment. Canada was becoming ever more closely integrated with the United States, to which its exports were mainly forest and mineral products (74 per cent of that country's imports from Canada in 1939), and less a trading partner with the United Kingdom, which still drew mainly on Canada's agricultural products.

Mining development during the interwar decades extended Canadians' horizons even farther northward than had development of the

Subarctic forests, waterpowers, and arable soils and did more to integrate the North into the national economic structure. It helped diversify the economies of provinces and northern regions, enabling them to establish more advanced, better-rounded societies than could have been formed by the other resources alone. Moreover, in the empty regions of the Shield it generated centres of settlement and development, such as Yellowknife, that might become the basis of future regional economies and societies, as Noranda or Flin Flon had been during the twenties.

The new mining frontiers performed a still more general service during the grim years of the Depression: they ameliorated Canada's economic position and revived the people's confidence. Establishment of large gold-mining camps in remote centres demonstrated that the isolation of the North could be overcome and its natural wealth used to promote future settlements. Canadians came to regard the mineral-rich lands of the expanding North as an alternative basis for national prosperity, in place of or as a supplement to the currently depressed agriculture. Thousands looked north to the mining camps for employment. The mining industry of the North in the thirties helped relieve the national gloom a little, breathing some hope into an otherwise dejected people, and renewed their faith in Canada as a land of the future.

CHAPTER 5

The Wildlife Industries in Retreat, 1914–1967

The wildlife of Canada resembles its mineral resources in being diffused over the entire country. But whereas mines can be developed at only a few sites where favourable conjunctions of resources and economic factors occur, the wildlife resource can be, and has been, exploited everywhere, for "90 per cent of the area of Canada supports wild life and two-thirds of it will yield no other permanent crop."[1] Much of the history of Canada lies in the arrival of white men with their wide range of industries and occupations in territories occupied by small, scattered, nomadic bands of hunters living off the diverse wildlife of their homelands. As the agricultural, forestry, hydro, and mining frontiers after 1914 penetrated ever deeper into the remaining hunting and trapping areas of Subarctic Canada, the wildlife and the natives that depended on it were driven into ever more remote districts where the fur trade still held sway. Even in these places they were now challenged by white competitors who extended their activities throughout most of the forested Middle North and beyond onto the Arctic tundra. The newcomers consumed some of the game, but their main quarries were the wildlife species that supplied the lustrous, expensive furs so avidly desired by the wealthy of Europe and America.

I

Large numbers of white men had gone into trapping, encouraged by the rise in prices for furs and the changes in fur-trading operations that started in the middle of the Great War and picked up speed in the post-war period until the general economic collapse of 1920–21. The bottom suddenly dropped out of the fur market in April 1920, but the frenzied scramble for fur continued unabated wherever traders were beyond the range of telegraph or radio contact. As a fur-trade inspector in the Mackenzie district reported:

. . . fur which had continued to pyramid in values since the days of the war panic had suddenly crashed to almost nothing, yet, owing to the lack of communication in the North, we were the first ones to bring along the news, and it was with wry faces that the traders learned that the marten skins for which they had paid a hundred dollars just the day before were now worth only ten and that muskrats had dropped in value from four dollars to seventy-five cents apiece. . . .

We proceeded to inspect the posts and learn the worst about the past outfit's trade. . . . The losses at every one of the trading posts were enormous, while, jointly, the traders owed the trappers and Indians nearly fifty thousand dollars for furs worth perhaps a fifth of the price, and the white men wanted cash.[2]

Despite its own losses, the Hudson's Bay Company could regard the situation with equanimity. "While this naturally presents difficulties," Lord Kindersley told his shareholders on July 30, 1920, "it has the advantage of eliminating a great deal of unhealthy and undesirable competition by small and unscrupulous traders."[3] And no wonder! The company's fur-trading operations returned good profits in both 1919 and 1920, whereas the price collapse before long bankrupted the Lamson-Hubbard concern and forced the Northern Trading Company through a drastic reorganization.

Following the abrupt collapse and a few years of uneven, fluctuating fur prices, a rapid rise set in after 1924 that reached very high levels during the last three years of the twenties. Again many adventurous white men began trapping for fur to take advantage of the excellent prices and markets. As R.M. Anderson, then head of the Natural History Section of the Geological Survey, observed:

The demands of fashion for every kind of fur or near-fur have during the past few years raised prices to such a height as to induce the trapper and the fur-buyer to penetrate the most remote parts of the country, and nearer at home set many a homesteader and farmer's boy to running traplines. The common-sense conservation policies followed under the guidance of the old-time trading companies have been largely weakened by the enormous increase of cut-throat competition, and the virtual bounties which are now on the lives of many of our most valuable fur-bearers in the shape of excessive prices for their pelts.[4]

White men moved into the forests to trap fur as a part-time activity, or full time for a few years to gather stakes for future careers in other places, or even in order to savour the experience and satisfy a craving for the "natural" outdoor life. The northern parts of the provinces attracted the bulk of these trappers; Saskatchewan, for instance, issued no fewer than 7,500 trappers' licences to residents in 1924. The drastic price declines in the thirties probably encouraged rather than discouraged the expansion of trapping by whites. Many persons, particularly in hard-pressed pioneering farming areas like the Peace River district, departed every autumn from their homesteads to scatter their traps about the surrounding country. Expansion of trapping was assisted by the access to relatively undepleted trapping districts offered by the railway branches built before and during the Great War and during the twenties and by improved transportation on the Mackenzie waterway and along the Arctic coasts of mainland Canada. Furthermore, the white trapper no longer had to dispose of his furs to established companies. Fur auction houses had sprung up in Montreal, Winnipeg, Vancouver (and later Edmonton), and at St. Louis and New York in the United States to which a trapper could consign his furs and obtain more favourable prices than those prevailing at the local trading posts.

Policemen and others who witnessed the increasing numbers of the new trappers and the enormous spread of their activities worried about possible clashes with Indians and the effects on the natives' livelihood. The Saskatchewan constable at Fond du Lac observed that seventy-two white and Métis trappers had made that remote post their base of operations in 1924, while in the even more remote district east of Great Slave Lake eight to ten white trappers and wolfers were operating from the post at Snowdrift. L.T. Burwash noted a dozen white trappers along the Arctic coast near the Baillie Islands in 1925 and reported that the De Steffany brothers had taken 2,000 white foxes trapping and trading south of Queen Maud Gulf even farther east. It was the same in the mountainous northern Cordillera. White trappers encroaching on the hunting grounds of the Indians in the northern part of the Rocky Mountain Trench were cited as a reason for the setting up of an RCMP post at Fort Grahame. Even the still mysterious upper Liard–South Nahanni country received its quota of newcomers who combined the trapper's life with prospecting for minerals and panning for gold. The police found their work of checking and enforcing the game laws and trapping regulations much heavier than before, and they had the added task of making sure that the newcomers did not come to harm. Some, indeed, lost their lives through scurvy, ptomaine poisoning, freezing, starvation, or drowning; others were severely wounded by falls, axe-cuts, or attacks by bears or suffered mental breakdowns that sometimes culminated in murders and suicides. These were some of the casualties of this advancing individualistic frontier.

The impact on the wildlife of so many transient hunters caused great concern, for the white trapper, unlike his native counterpart, was unencumbered by family ties, had no permanent stake in the district in which he operated, and aimed only at securing as much fur as he could: "An influx of white trappers into regions normally visited only occasionally by wandering Indians or Eskimos means an immediate decimation of the game and fur resources, for the free-born trapper and hunter assumes a vested right to live as largely as possible 'on the country,' and this pioneering in many cases means ruthless exploitation and the leaving of a stripped and denuded region for the permanent residents who may follow."[5] The unskilled, part-time trapper was a particular problem because he frequently used homemade wire snares, which might never be picked up, wasting much fur and bringing "alarming numbers of fur and game animals" to "the inevitable fate of starving to death."[6] At the other end of the scale was the well-organized, well-financed trapper who brought in his own supplies, even staple food, which he distributed among the cabins he had erected "a sleep apart" along his trapline. These trappers used ten or twenty times the sixty traps the average native family set, and took that many times more fur than they did. Moreover, they selected for attention areas that were richest in whatever furs were currently most valuable. When prices for fine furs were high, they pushed into the mountainous country west of the Mackenzie River, and when the price of muskrat became favourable, they hurried to establish themselves in the muskrat-rich deltas of the Mackenzie and other northern rivers.

The professional trappers posed an even greater threat to the native people after aircraft became available to them. They could afford to charter planes to reach the rich, remote trapping grounds where they might clean out the best furs before the Indian families could reach their traditional trapping grounds. In the same way that they were used in prospecting, planes could place several trappers in good locations and return periodically to bring supplies and remove the accumulated furs. Moreover, when flown by the trappers themselves – and at least one trapper had his own plane in the thirties – they might even be used to poach in unpoliced places, evade closed seasons, or smuggle furs beyond the reach of the authorities. Consequently, very strict regulations and punishments were instituted to prevent establishment of such practices in the northern districts.

The threat of exhaustion was not confined to the fur-bearing animals. Most white trappers lived as much as they could off game, and the employees of the other new industries situated on the frontiers did a great deal of hunting, seriously depleting the game animals near their camps and the agricultural fringe. Automobiles and improved roads brought town and city dwellers and farmers to the wilderness each year to hunt deer, moose, or bear. The mining camps were unofficial markets for game and offered trappers employment as guides or woodsmen or opportunities to earn additional income staking mineral claims for resale.

By the thirties, the authorities were becoming painfully aware of the serious depletion of the fish, game, marine animals, game birds, and fur-bearing species. Studies by wildlife experts reinforced their concern. That certain natural conditions – too heavy or too light snows, droughts that affected water levels or increased the frequency of forest fires – should reduce the number of game and fur animals was well known. So too were the natural cyclical variations that made it difficult to assess the actual condition of many species. But a careful study of the fur-trade trends in the Northwest Territories from 1920 to 1943 made it clear that beaver showed "a tendency towards depletion," and that the peak yield of mink in 1923–24 (21,000 skins) was higher than the succeeding peaks in 1932–33 (18,000) and 1940–41 (15,000). As for the important white fox, the "definite short-period cyclical variation in numbers" created "real instability" in the economy of the Inuit. On the basis of the returns from particular districts, the study concluded that "the variation [for white fox] is one of abundance every four years, with a particularly low year occurring between the peaks."[7]

From policemen, Indian agents, missionaries, and scientists came reports of extreme hardship among those who depended on the wildlife for their sustenance. The Department of Indian Affairs reported that depletion was very serious in the "intermediate territory between civilization and the wilds,"[8] while from the relatively remote District of Mackenzie came impassioned pleas from Bishop Gabriel Breynat on behalf of the destitute natives of that region. In frequent representations to officials and in an unprecedented series of popular articles he appealed for assistance for "nearly 4,000 of the unhealthiest people in Canada,"[9] whose per capita cash income in 1935–36 was only $110. The former fur trader P.H. Godsell in articles and books championed the view that the wildlife of the northern districts had been drastically reduced under the conditions that had prevailed since 1900 until the natives faced an unrelenting possibility of starvation. The difficult situation of the Inuit raised fears that overhunting might reduce seals and other marine mammals to the condition of the great whales, which had been brought to the verge of extinction by the predations of the pre-1914 whaling industry.

For the fur trade also, the decades of the twenties and thirties began and ended in a state of crisis. The Great War, as we have seen, had disrupted the traditional trade of the Hudson's Bay and Revillon Frères firms and inspired many "free traders" to establish posts and introduce new transportation facilities, mainly in the norths of the western provinces and the District of Mackenzie beyond. The concurrent opening of the Arctic coastlines of Canada and final collapse of the whaling industry also paved the way for the fur trade to expand into the Inuit country. During the 1920s, trading posts were opened on the southern and western margins of the Barren Lands of Keewatin, the long east coast of Baffin Island, along the north coast between Alaska and the Boothia Peninsula, and in other previously neglected areas in the interior. By the mid-twenties, the Hudson's Bay Company was operating posts in some 250 centres in Subarctic and Arctic Canada, competing with several regionally important chains, each possessing four to forty posts, and hundreds of independent traders, most of whom operated a single post. During these boom years every important location had three to five trading posts competing for furs from native and white trappers.

In addition to these established traders, varying numbers of itinerant fur buyers visited trappers' camps and Indian settlements. Such persons, unhampered by the expense of maintaining posts that advanced credit, sometimes were able to skim the best furs from the trappers and move on before the value or quality of the goods they gave in exchange could be checked, leaving the local trader and sometimes the trapper the losers. As Inspector T.B. Caulkin of the RCMP reported, ". . . I do think a little more protection could be afforded the established trader, against the tactics of the transient non-resident trader. . . . The transient traders generally land down river a week before the established trader's vessel, and bring inferior goods, when the established trader's stock in hand is at low ebb, and they take considerable fur from natives which rightly belongs to the established trader, who in all probability has advanced credit in lean times to some of them."[10] Established traders, understandably, denounced the practice, and some jurisdictions took steps to prohibit it by law.

Trappers sometimes disposed of furs to merchants in nearby towns such as Prince George or Fort McMurray, and many newcomers consigned their furs to the fur auction houses or disposed of them during resupply and pleasure trips to outside cities. Finally, a certain number of furs were given by trappers in payment for service to doctors, hospitals, hotels, and the like or were donated to the missions to support their work. Usually these furs were turned over to the local trading post to apply against the recipients' accounts.

The Hudson's Bay Company responded to the generally optimistic situation by expanding its trading and transportation operations and even extending them for a time (1917–24) to eastern Siberia. It also attempted to branch out in related fields, such as fishing for Atlantic salmon and beluga, and collaborated with Stefansson's abortive Wrangel Island plan and his unsuccessful reindeer-herding enterprise. The Hudson's Bay Reindeer Company, the subsidiary organized to operate a grazing industry on the 113,900 square miles of southern and western Baffin Island leased to Stefansson in 1920, faced organizational difficulty almost at once. Storker Storkerson, Stefansson's nominee as manager, speedily resigned, and the HBC representative hired Lapp herders and purchased 687 reindeer in Norway, 550 of which lived to reach the island. Landed there, the herd was immediately dispersed by a storm, and only 210 animals were recovered by the following spring. The vegetation was sparse and largely of an unsuitable type, the climate was more severe than had been anticipated, and the Lapp herders were unfamiliar with working in a treeless Arctic environment. They returned to Norway in 1923, leaving the HBC post manager to look after the surviving deer with the help of local Inuit. Having lost its $200,000 investment, the Hudson's Bay Company did not attempt to fulfil the contract terms (a herd of 4,000 head in 1924, 10,000 head in 1932) but wound up the company. Despite Stefansson's complaints that company delays and parsimony had destroyed the project, the real causes were that it had been badly conceived, was based on little research and no advance preparations, and was mainly the product of Stefansson's fertile imagination and visionary optimism.

Always ready to take advantage of the financial embarrassments or simple weariness of its competitors, the Hudson's Bay Company used its strong position to absorb rivals whenever opportunity permitted. Thus it eliminated its Baffin Island opposition (Robert Kinnes and the Arctic Gold Exploration Syndicate) in 1923, the Alberta and Arctic Transportation operation along the Mackenzie waterway in 1924, and the Labrador fur trade of the Moravian Missionary Society in 1925. The difficult thirties enabled it to buy out the large Revillon concern, "the French Company" operating in the Hudson Bay, Keewatin, and Eastern Arctic sectors, in stages during the decade ending in 1939. In 1938 it bought out its chief competitor on the Arctic coast, Canalaska Trading Company, and Northern Traders, its main rival in the District of Mackenzie in 1939. By the end of the 1930s the Hudson's Bay Company overwhelmingly dominated the Canadian fur trade, opposed only by individual traders and by the fur auction houses. It was, however, facing a new challenge that also threatened the trapper – the fur-farming industry, which accounted for 40 per cent of Canada's total fur production in 1940, including 50 per cent of the mink and practically the entire silver fox fur output. At the same time experiments were proceeding with breeding fisher, marten, and lynx, other species that figured in a major way in northern trappers' catches.

The company did not escape entirely unscathed. Heavy losses were experienced in 1930, 1931, and 1932 before the corner was turned in 1933 and profit resumed. Charles Sale was replaced as governor in 1931 by P. Ashley Cooper, and C.H. French as Fur Trade Commissioner by the efficient Ralph Parsons, district manager in the St. Lawrence and Labrador regions. By taking advantage of radio communication and air transport the company was able to consolidate several districts and dispense with the redundant inspecting officers. With closure of unprofitable posts the 1931 total of 334 had been reduced to 230 in 1937. Among those remaining were a few posts in previously neglected areas such as Port Simpson, B.C., and Frances Lake, Yukon Territory, and recently opened stores in new mining centres of the Subarctic such as Goldfields, Yellowknife, and Manson Creek and Finlay Forks in British Columbia.

In the Arctic the company strove to complete its chain of posts from the Atlantic to Alaska. The task had been begun in the twenties, and the Canadian government had aided the effort by enforcing the customs regulations against competitors who drew their supplies from U.S. points (notably the Canalaska Trading Company, headed by C.T. Pedersen, and the pioneer trader-settler Charles Klengenberg). The Northwest Territories administration gave invaluable support by granting the company licences to operate posts in the Arctic Islands Game Preserve. By the close of the decade the company was represented by a string of posts east from the Mackenzie delta to Gjoa Haven on King William Island. During the thirties it succeeded in opening Fort Ross on Bellot Strait, in the gap between its westernmost Baffin Island post of Arctic Bay and Gjoa Haven, but the post had to be closed after a few years because of supply difficulties. For a time (1934–36) the company also operated a post at Dundas Harbour in the Queen Elizabeth Islands, having induced fifty-two Inuit from Baffin Island to establish themselves on Devon Island; when that experiment failed, the company returned most of the natives to their Baffin Island homes and some to the newly opened Fort Ross.

Suitable transportation facilities, necessary for successful conduct of the fur trade in the remote districts, had to be developed by the traders themselves for their own needs and to capture whatever commercial freight might offer itself. The principal freighting services in Hudson Bay and the Eastern Arctic during the twenties were those of Revillon Frères (the ship *Albert Revillon*) and the Hudson's Bay Company. The latter's ship *Nascopie* was supplemented by several motor schooners that worked around the inlets and about the company's posts. Trav-

ellers along the waterways between Fort McMurray and the Mackenzie
delta could use three different traders' systems in the early 1920s,
those of the Hudson's Bay Company, the Lamson-Hubbard Company,
and the Northern Trading Company. These were reduced to two after
the HBC took over Lamson-Hubbard's equipment and merged their
Alberta and Arctic Transportation with its own Mackenzie River Transport service.

To supply its Western Arctic trade from Vancouver the company
built the ship *Lady Kindersley* in 1920, and after she was sunk in 1924
replaced her with the *Baychimo*, only to lose her in similar fashion in
the polar ice pack in 1931. These ships sailed as far east as ice conditions allowed, then transferred the cargoes for more easterly stations
to smaller company vessels (including Amundsen's historic *Maud*,
which was purchased in 1926 and renamed *Baymaud*), or, in at least
one emergency, to the RCMP schooner *St. Roch*. After trying a chartered
ship for two seasons the company decided to supply the Arctic stations
via the Mackenzie route and developed a new base, Tuktoyaktuk, as
the transfer point on the coast. *Distributor III* being unable to proceed
safely from the river to the ocean, she discharged her cargoes at Kittigazuit at one mouth of the delta, whence smaller motor schooners
carried the freight to Tuktoyaktuk for distribution along the coasts.
Motorized vehicles travelling overland from the posts on Foxe Basin
or Hudson Bay were also tried for supplying the least accessible posts
in the Central Arctic but proved impractical.

Other users might take advantage of the fur traders' facilities, but
they had to accommodate themselves to the needs of the trade. On the
Mackenzie system, for example, delays occurred at every settlement
while goods and supplies were unloaded, cargoes of furs came aboard,
and inspecting officers transacted business. As speed was of little consequence and the trade's needs were small, the companies stuck to
low-powered, slow vessels. The old wood-burning ships were kept in
service as long as possible, the frequent halts for wood creating further
delays. Still, as the volume of freight soared from the 400-ton level in
1920 to several thousand tons by the end of the decade, the boats' carrying capacities were increased by the use of pushed or towed barges.
In the thirties the company introduced diesel-powered tugs to handle
its own freight and bid for the increasing commercial freight on the
waterway. The large, comfortable, wood-burning paddlewheelers
were used mainly for tourist and other passenger traffic as long as that
market persisted.

The fur trade was the principal *raison d'être* of scores of small
centres where the predominantly native clientele was served and
to which they came for other services. It accounted for the presence
of an HBC post and often one or more competing stores with their

warehouses, storage sheds, traders' homes, and boathouses. Traders, clerks, accountants, and labourers comprised the basic element of a post's permanent population. The life of the settlements followed a regular annual rhythm. In winter, during the trapping season, business was almost at a standstill, though individual trappers came and went and traders visited neighbouring camps. The spring brought activity, getting ready for the shipping and trading season. Then came the summer, the long days filled with the comings and goings of boats, loading and unloading supplies, and the arrival of scores of Indians to trade furs, collect treaty payments and rations, and get medical attention. Dozens of tents would mushroom overnight along the fringe of the settlement, empty cabins would suddenly swarm with native families, and the shore would be lined with their boats while the air resounded with the howls of hundreds of tethered dogs. With the autumn the last ship of the season would depart, local boats would be hauled ashore out of reach of the ice, and the piles of firewood and stages of drying fish would grow in size. Then suddenly the native families were gone to their remote hunting and trapping grounds, and quiet would descend on the settlement.

This routine was enlivened by fires, floods, epidemics, even an occasional robbery. Between 1930 and 1935, a slowdown gripped HBC building activities, after which construction of new stores, warehouses, and homes resumed. Supply systems were improved by the use of the expanded railway and road network and shipping systems and greatly improved radio communications. Many HBC personnel were trained as wireless operators, and no fewer than fifty-four of the posts were equipped with transmitters by 1946. Radio reports supplied traders with new instructions; company aircraft were available to inspect posts and ship furs to market without delay. The growing complexity of governmental regulations meant far more paperwork and inspections by a variety of public agents. Above all, the pattern of trade changed in many places as cash was increasingly available to purchase goods and larger numbers of whites and more acculturated natives demanded a variety of goods more like those offered in general stores outside. Indeed, while their purchases of fur were declining, the HBC posts were selling more merchandise than ever, perceptibly approaching their future role of a general-merchandising chain-store system.

II

The scale and effectiveness of governmental regulation of the wildlife resource and of the industries based on it were so much increased during the interwar period that the traditionally free, unfettered life of the trapper was brought within fairly restrictive confines. Restrictions were encouraged by the rapidly accelerating "race to destruction" of some important fur-bearing and meat-producing species; the rise of a scientific approach to wildlife and a conservationist outlook, particularly among those administering the resource; the increased concern over the deteriorating condition of the native groups that depended on wildlife for most of their sustenance; and the improving ability of governments to implement their management programs. The approaches of the federal and provincial governments, however, were affected by their differing constitutional responsibilities and political interests.

The essential difference was that the provinces largely controlled the wildlife resource whereas the federal government was officially responsible for the Indians and Inuit who were most directly interested in the wildlife and were its principal users. The demarcation was not clear cut, however, because the federal government had some control over wildlife within the provinces by virtue of its authority over national parks, commercial fisheries, and, thanks to international treaty, migratory game birds. The provinces, for their part, were directly responsible for Métis, non-status Indian, and white groups who harvested wildlife and were concerned for the welfare of the Indian bands residing within their boundaries. They were also responsible to white electorates (few status Indians enjoyed the franchise at this time), which had an effect on their management of this resource, whereas the federal government was politically better able to pursue policies more closely attuned to the needs of the wildlife and the Indians.

Administrators at both levels of government, however, followed the same approach – strongly influenced by the Commission of Conservation – of regulating hunting and trapping activities so as to conserve wildlife against irreversible depletion. They were interested also in the newest techniques, and the governments readily co-operated in instituting and enforcing complementary regulations on seasons, quotas, royalties and taxes, and conservation measures. Increasingly these were based on careful scientific field investigations and research into the population dynamics of the various species, a prime example being C. Elton's study, *Voles, Mice and Lemmings: Problems in Population Dynamics* (1942), which utilized the annual returns from the Canadian snowshoe rabbit inquiries (started in 1924). Studies in the biological sciences during the thirties brought far better understanding of wildlife cycles and laid a basis for even greater research and management efforts after 1945 by the Canadian Wildlife Service.

In administering wildlife the provinces had more than those dependent on hunting and trapping in mind. While they guarded against undue depletion by banning the kind of market-hunting that had almost exterminated the bison, they did remember the thousands of citizens who hunted or fished for sport. For these they devised licensing systems that permitted every holder to take annually a set number of game birds as they passed along the flyways between the Northwest Territories and the Gulf of Mexico, a set number of fishes, and one or two moose, deer, caribou, elk, or bear. The provinces also were concerned to stimulate hunting by tourists, who were allowed to hunt certain protected species of wildlife under permit (and to ship home the trophies), such as grizzly or polar bears, varieties of mountain sheep, even muskoxen and wood buffalo. This action, they hoped, would encourage sportsmen to visit remote northern or eastern regions and boost their economies by employing residents as guides and outfitters on their hunts.

British Columbia, which could offer excellent scenery as well as an interesting assortment of wildlife, nurtured this industry by allowing fairly generous bag limits, licensing guides, supervising the quality of lodgings and other facilities, and carefully recording the results of the hunts. Although the passion for collecting and displaying mounted animal heads was not what it had been before 1914, some centres, among them Jasper, Fort St. John, Telegraph Creek, and Whitehorse, continued to earn thousands of dollars from the parties that hunted their districts and employed their residents as guides and outfitters. Often the income from a single large party was enough to support an outfitter for a year when combined with his regular ranching, farming, and hunting activities, and the limited number of animals that fell to the huntsmen was considered a very small price for the profits that resulted.

For the activities of full-time, non-native hunters, trappers, and traders, the authorities enacted regulations in the interests of both the animals and the natives who depended on that resource. By 1921 trappers other than natives were required in most jurisdictions to purchase annual licences that usually were cheap for residents but quite expensive for foreigners. Licensing of traders, instituted about 1913 in most jurisdictions, in like manner differentiated between resident, non-resident British, and foreign applicants. The itinerant trader was restrained, in the case of the Northwest Territories, by measures requiring every trading post to be licensed (1926), to be situated at a specified location (1927), and to be kept open for a stated period each year (1929).

Between 1916 and 1929 most jurisdictions began to levy royalties on furs. These were usually paid by the trader or the trapper who exported his furs outside the province or territory in which they had been trapped and were a means of raising revenue to help offset the costs of regulation and conservation. The tax compelled traders to obtain export permits for furs and keep full records of all their transactions for examination by authorized persons such as game wardens, police officers, and Indian agents. Shipments of furs from the Northwest Territories had to be properly baled, sealed, and certified; public carriers were required to maintain accurate records of all shipments and permit them to be examined on request. Wardens and policemen were even given open warrants to search vehicles, boats, tents, or baggage on mere suspicion that furs were being unlawfully transported from the Territories. These regulations, while aimed at protecting the native hunter and trapper against competition and exploitation, actually reduced his already inadequate income because he ultimately paid the royalties.

Another group of regulations endeavoured to conserve wildlife to give hunters the maximum return and, to a smaller degree, to spare the hunted animals needless suffering. Considered to be enacted in the best interests of all concerned, they applied to native as well as non-native hunters and trappers, but enforcement was less stringent against resident Indians, about whose legal position under provincial regulations some question existed. Hunting with dogs, shooting game from moving vehicles, using machine guns, spring guns, poison bait, and wire snares, spearing fish, and shooting marine mammals without some previous arrangement for retrieving the quarry were prohibited. Seasons for hunting and trapping were selected to give the hunter the best pelts or meat while interfering as little as possible with the normal life cycles of the various species. They might be adjusted according to climatic conditions or observed changes in numbers of animals or even closed for a period of years to give a species time to recover (as with beaver in most provinces during the interwar period). Some species or goods were put on the prohibited list (muskoxen, wood buffalo, caribou skins). At the other extreme, control of predators such as wolves was assisted by offering bounties for pelts or even hiring hunters to concentrate on this quarry. (By the thirties, informed opinion was questioning the efficacy or the desirability of such programs, although supporters urged the income benefits to the hunters.) Successful enforcement of all these regulations entailed close co-operation among the different agencies in setting uniform conditions, rates, and seasons and in co-ordinating enforcement on their sides of shared borders. Protective activities by game wardens and police in remote, out-of-the-way areas were greatly stepped up during the interwar period, particularly after aircraft became available for such work.

A widely applied method of controlling depletion of wildlife was to give the non-native hunters and trappers a vested interest in following sound conservation practices. In the Northwest Territories, where there were no voters to worry about and where the native element was in a large majority, the administration kept down the numbers of non-native hunters and trappers by licences and by instituting a so-called grandfather clause ending the issuance of licences to newcomers to the Northwest Territories in 1938. More significantly, about half the total area of the Northwest Territories (some 670,000 square miles in all) was set aside in the twenties as game preserves in which only members of the native bands that customarily used the regions and the few whites who had operated in them before the preserves were proclaimed were allowed to hunt and trap. These regions thus were closed to future waves of trappers, such as those who sought entry in the 1930s, and were reserved to natives alone, who, it was hoped, would be able to regulate their catches and manage the game in the traditional fashion when freed from white competition.

There even was discussion in 1932 of making the entire Northwest Territories a game preserve, and the federal Advisory Board on Wildlife Protection recommended that the northern parts of the provinces should also be included. Quebec declared the whole of Nouveau-Québec a game preserve in 1932, Ontario followed suit by greatly enlarging the game preserves in its northern areas, and Alberta closed the district centring on Fort Chipewyan to non-resident trappers. Numerous smaller game reserves already existed in the provinces, mainly in the forest reserves, in which regulated hunting and trapping were usually permitted, and in federal or provincial parks, where they were sometimes allowed.

The Northwest Territories contained in addition two large special game preserves: Wood Buffalo Park, established athwart the Alberta–Northwest Territories border in 1922 and extended to 17,300 square miles in 1926, and the Thelon Game Sanctuary instituted in 1927. Their primary purpose was to assist in protecting several endangered species, the first the wood buffalo, a hardier, darker, larger animal than his prairie cousin, and the second the muskox and migratory caribou herds. The rationale for Wood Buffalo Park was quickly lost in an emotional desire to rehabilitate the prairie bison, which had been so nearly exterminated during the nineteenth century. A total of 6,673 bison were shipped from central Alberta to the park between 1924 and 1927, to be turned loose to graze and perhaps interbreed with the indigenous subspecies. Natives who had hunted and trapped before the park was established were allowed to continue these activities but were never to hunt bison on penalty of fine, imprisonment, or banishment from the park. A few natives convicted of this crime lost their hunting rights in their ancestral tribal area – a fate the region's natives strongly resented as a violation of their treaty rights.

The 15,000-square-mile Thelon Game Sanctuary was set up in the region east of Great Slave Lake in which virtually no hunting or trapping had been done prior to the arrival of white trappers. This preserve was closed to regular hunting, trapping, and prospecting activities from its inception. The main objective was to protect the migratory caribou over a large part of their thousand-mile migration route, at either end of which they were sedulously hunted, in the north by coastal Inuit, in the south by inhabitants of Northern Saskatchewan and Manitoba. The presence of muskoxen, first reported by John Hornby and Captain J.C. Critchell-Bullock, who traversed the region in 1924–25, gave added point to creating the sanctuary, as perhaps did the tragic fate of Hornby's subsequent three-man expedition to the area in 1926–27.

The province of British Columbia (followed by Ontario in 1935 and by other provinces after 1945) inaugurated a somewhat comparable program in 1922 to protect the established hunter and trapper and encourage him to conserve wildlife by giving him a vested interest in behaving responsibly. This was a system of registered individual traplines, awarded for five-year periods and renewable but subject to cancellation if the holder violated the regulations or failed to operate his trapline. The process of investigating, checking, and reconciling claims, mapping the holdings, and issuing patents took many years. At first Indians were unwilling to apply for registration and sometimes were victimized as a result. Nonetheless, by 1936 the registration in Division G (north of the CNR branch to Prince Rupert) listed 2,228 whites, 1,322 Indians, and another 214 persons participating in group licences. The proportion of Indian registrants increased because the Indian Affairs Branch set about picking up any lapsed patents for the benefit of their Indian applicants. The success of the system was quickly recognized, according to its originator and director, Game Commissioner A. Bryan Williams:

We feel quite safe in saying that the steady improvement in the stand of our valuable fur-bearing animals is mostly due to the regulation covering the registration of trap-lines.

Years ago, or at least prior to 1925, trappers had no assurance that the trapping territory held by them in any year would be theirs to trap the following year. This state of affairs led the trapper, once he was on a trap-line, to take as many animals as possible. Under the present system, however, this condition does not exist any longer, as a trapper now has the assurance that he will have the same trapping territory from year to year, providing he abides by

Family of trader Charles Klengenberg at Victoria Island, c. 1925.
L to *r*: Jorgon, Andy, and Lina Klengenberg, Mrs. Charles Klengenberg ,
Edna Klengenberg-Bolt, Ikey Bolt, and their daughter Kinnawear.
(Public Archives Canada, PA – 164642)

Eskimo schooners from Mackenzie delta visiting Herschel Island to trade,
c. 1928. (PA – 164641)

ss *Distributor* at Good Hope ramparts on the Mackenzie, c. 1928;
an A.E. Porsild photograph. (PA – 101042)

A pontoon bridge serves while the more permanent structure is built on the
Alaska Highway, 1942. (PA – 130459)

American soldiers unloading equipment for construction of the Alaska Highway at Dawson Creek, B.C., 1942. (PA – 113193)

American black troops unloading pipe for the Canol Project, Fort Smith, N.W.T., 1942. (PA – 101813)

Yellowknife in 1947, from Latham Island. (PA – 116541)

Eldorado Campsite on Great Bear Lake, c. 1937. (PA – 14821)

The terminal of the White Pass Railroad at Whitehorse, Y.T., with docks and
warehouse, in the 1920s. (PA – 48318)

Building the Northwest Territories Administration Building at Fort Smith,
1921. (PA – 96540)

O.S. Finnie and L.T. Burwash (*left*) outside their "office" at Fort Smith, 1921, photographed by D.L. McKeand. (PA – 102635)

The Roman Catholic Mission at Fort Resolution in 1941: church, residence, school, and hospital. (PA – 101853)

The RCMP station at Craig Harbour on Ellesmere Island, 1925. (PA – 100771)

RCMP patrol ship *St. Roch*, icebound for the winter, probably 1930s.
(PA – 121418)

A Northern Transportation Company convoy of steel barges at Bell Rock,
N.W.T., with supplies for northern settlements; the tug *Radium King* drove
them on the first leg of the voyage to Fort McPherson and Inuvik, 1958.
(The author)

New settlers in the Abitibi district of Quebec join in a digging bee, 1934.
(PA – 27507)

Farm families trekking north on the "Overland Trail" from the dry belt to the Meadow Lake district, Saskatchewan, 1930. (PA – 44575)

Lumberjacks at work on a log drive on a northern Quebec river, 1927. (C – 10226)

The Premier gold mine and mill at Premier, B.C., 1937. (PA – 14991)

Flin Flon, Man., in the late 1920s, with Hudson Bay Mining and Smelting Company buildings in foreground. (PA – 47935)

The new Ile Maligne development of the Duke-Price Power Company on the Saguenay River, 1927. (PA – 44112)

The Pointe du Bois dam and power station on the Winnipeg River, c. 1930. (PA – 41499)

(ABOVE) Indian school children and teachers at the Anglican Mission, Hay River, N.W.T., 1925. (PA – 20022) (BELOW) Montagnais Indian summer encampment at North West River, Labrador, from a watercolour by Stephen Hamilton, probably of 1950s. (Stephen Hamilton) (OPPOSITE TOP) Inuit trader Angulalik shows the results of his trading at his Perry River post, probably 1950s. (PA – 102701) (OPPOSITE BOTTOM) Inuit mother signing for Family Allowance at RCMP post, Coppermine, N.W.T., probably in 1950s. (PA – 129879)

Inuit artists Iyola and Eejyvudluk at work on a stone block at the Cape Dorset Art Centre, 1961. (PA – 145607)

A main station, "Dye," of the Distant Early Warning (DEW) Line system above Davis Strait at Cape Dyer, N.W.T. (National Defence Canada)

the game laws and regulations and does not overtrap. In other words, a registered trapper is now a "fur farmer" and is only taking off a limited number of animals from his trap-line each year, leaving plenty of animals for breeding purposes.[11]

Though the system brought stability to the industry and conserved the resource for the long-term benefit of all, it created a sort of proprietary right that enabled a holder to profiteer by subletting his trapline. More seriously, on the one hand it interfered radically with the traditional wide-ranging cyclical hunting routines of resident Indians, and on the other the proprietary aspect challenged the Indians' feeling that theirs was the higher right to use the wildlife resources of their home territories.

Prevention of excessive destruction of wildlife did not represent the entire scope of administrative conservationist activities. There were other options based on improvement of the environment so as to increase its carrying capacity. One of these was the introduction of new species, as was attempted in transplanting the plains bison to Wood Buffalo Park. Another was the often tried project of introducing domesticated reindeer to regions denuded of caribou through overhunting. Stefansson had proposed in December 1920 that a herd of Alaska's reindeer might be established in the Mackenzie delta region on territory leased from the Crown as had been done on Baffin Island.

In 1926, the Northwest Territories administration engaged the Greenland botanist brothers, A.E. and R.T. Porsild, to study prospective herding locations in the Arctic parts of mainland Canada. Three thousand reindeer were purchased from the Alaska firm of Lomen Brothers in 1929, and the company was to deliver the herd to the selected site east of the Mackenzie delta. The drive took an arduous five years before a total of 2,370 reindeer was delivered to Kittigazuit in March 1935, and there were fewer than 700 in the herd of the original 3,400 animals that had left Nome in late 1929. A grazing preserve was set up for the reindeer, selected Inuit were trained as apprentice herders, and from 1935 meat from slaughtered animals was distributed to mission schools and hospitals, and the hides were given to the natives for clothing. In 1938 and 1940 another two herds of 800 animals each were started by Inuit herders in the Anderson and Horton rivers districts farther east, and the industry seemed on the way to adding a valuable new wildlife resource and a successful industry to the Arctic economy.

There were in addition projects to improve the supplies of beaver and muskrat during the interwar period. The leading force in rehabilitating the beaver was James Watt, an HBC trader in the James Bay district of Quebec. He became interested in rebuilding the beaver population in an area where it had been almost exterminated by 250 years of unregulated trapping, and he persuaded the Indians to stop this trapping to give the beaver a chance to recover. Quebec co-operated with the plan by establishing a beaver sanctuary in the Rupert River area in 1932. The 254 pairs of beaver located on the preserve in 1935 increased to 13,370 pairs by 1942, enough for a harvest of 5,000 pelts, and an annual quota of 15,000 was envisaged within a few years – as much as the area had yielded in the most successful years of the fur trade centuries before. Leases to similar beaver sanctuaries were granted by Quebec, by the Northwest Territories (for islands in James Bay), and by Ontario to the Indian Affairs Branch and the Hudson's Bay Company during the late thirties. By then the cause of the beaver, and of wildlife conservation generally, was being powerfully and effectively aided by the writings and lectures of the remarkable Englishman-turned-Indian Archie Belaney, alias Grey Owl.

An even more successful experiment was undertaken in the vicinity of the Saskatchewan River estuary, where the once prolific muskrat population had been reduced almost to nothing by overhunting and lack of proper control of the water levels. During 1936 and 1937, aided by a $107,000 grant, some one hundred Indians and Métis built dams, dikes, ditches, and canals to regulate the water levels so as to provide an ideal environment for the muskrat. The 5,000 pairs of 1936 increased to 200,000 by 1940, when 122,000 skins valued at $161,000 were harvested, with even larger yields anticipated in future years. The success of this Summerberry project suggested similar ones in the marshy lower Saskatchewan River district of Manitoba and Saskatchewan. These few efforts demonstrated the remarkable recuperative power of certain wildlife species under proper management and indicated the important role a managed resource could play in providing a healthy economy for native people whose livelihood was based on the animals of their homelands.

III

In the period after 1945, utilization of the wildlife resources of Canada became altered almost out of recognition. Government controls were intensified, hunters and trappers were subjected to more stringent licensing conditions, and sale, export, or processing of unregistered, untaxed furs became strictly prohibited. Enforcement of these and other regulations was greatly improved when much larger forestry, game, and park warden staffs were employed, backed by northern detachments of the RCMP or provincial police forces. The basis for regulations governing the harvesting of all forms of wildlife was more often the findings of wildlife experts, and new programs to conserve the numbers of certain threatened species were instituted and earlier ones expanded.

A disturbing aspect of the post-war situation was the widespread destruction of many wildlife habitats when industrial activities expanded into districts previously left to the hunter and trapper. Farming was the culprit in a few areas, but a greater villain was the enormous increase in logging operations, especially the practice of clear-cutting. The widest impact came from prospecting for minerals and oil and natural gas, extending even to the Arctic islands. The establishment of industrial plants throughout the Subarctic – mines, lumber mills, pulp and paper plants, and hydro-electric power stations – radically altered the environments of wide surrounding areas, especially as procedures adopted for the best economic interests of the companies ignored environmental considerations. Vast stretches of land and water were degraded through the widespread use of mercury as a reagent by pulp and paper mills, the discharge of poisonous chemicals in mine tailings, and the noxious fumes discharged from smelting plants, as through Sudbury's smokestacks. Before 1967, however, these depredations still aroused little attention or controversy, for the environmentalist cause only began achieving importance in Canada after that date.

Notwithstanding these difficulties, thousands of natives and some white residents of the northern regions continued to hunt and trap as best they could. To protect them against interlopers the systems of registered traplines, group conservation blocks, and wildlife preserves inaugurated during the interwar years were extended, while newcomers were discouraged or prohibited entirely from participating in the industry. As before, administrations regulated hunting and trapping of individual species by adjusting or closing seasons or establishing quotas for catches. The programs to re-establish a number of threatened species, notably beaver and marten, were continued, and muskrat yields were greatly increased by improving their habitats. But although the programs generally succeeded in producing greater numbers of animals, they were not the earlier anticipated panacea because there were failures to maintain necessary works or harvest the fur crops conscientiously.

In developing these programs the governments were assisted by better statistics than formerly and by the continuing researches of the Canadian Wildlife Service, the Fisheries Research Board of Canada, and other wildlife biologists. It was possible to report, for instance, that "Great Slave Lake is the only major fishery in the world that was organized on the basis of research information, and it has been continually monitored."[12] There were complaints, in fact, that some of the regulations conceived by these scientists were too narrowly concerned with the interests of the wildlife and overlooked the economic and socio-cultural needs or abilities of the hunters and trappers who depended on it.

Indeed, in spite of all these efforts, only a diminishing number of persons was able to secure adequate livelihoods purely from hunting, fishing, and trapping. Fur prices continued poor throughout most of the 1945–67 period, and native trappers found themselves steadily less able to earn enough from trapping to offset rising expenses and meet the costs of supplies and equipment required for the work. Those who were able to obtain regular employment gladly abandoned the hard, uncertain life on the land for the more secure, comfortable life of the wage-earning settler. But natives who continued to carry on the traditional life were compelled to look for alternative incomes from seasonal work, the broadened range of government pensions and allowances, and increasing welfare assistance. The whites who held provincial licences and had acquired registered traplines (who were said to number 75,000 in 1975) concentrated on securing the maximum number of high-value fine furs from their traplines and used them mainly as income supplements that yielded rich returns from short, efficient wintertime forays. They disposed of their furs mainly by shipping them on consignment to the growing number of fur auction centres, notably to the large co-operative one established at North Bay after the war. Native hunters, as before, continued on the whole to exchange their furs at local trading posts, though some effort was made to direct them to the co-operative societies (where they existed) or to government-supported fur-marketing systems.

The Hudson's Bay Company faced less direct competition after the war in most localities because of restrictions aimed against newcomers to the trade, in contrast to the encouragement and support the administrators directed at the rare native entrepreneur, like Angulalik of Perry River. The very difficult economic position in which the company's native trapper clients found themselves greatly increased their need for advances and outfits to carry on but simultaneously reduced their ability to pay debts. More of them, besides, were choosing, or being compelled, to market their furs elsewhere and were not such dependable suppliers as heretofore. Company traders therefore tightened credit to trappers, and the fur trade became a doubtful proposition. In any case, the company was no longer the lender of last resort; government agencies had assumed that responsibility, and the special relationship between company and native trappers was gradually replaced by a strictly commercial one.

In addition, the nature of the trade was rapidly changing, and the Hudson's Bay Company adjusted to the situation by using its financial power to compete effectively with, or drive out, private competition. Trapping now formed only a part of the income of many natives, along with wage earnings, family allowances and pensions, and relief vouchers; on the other hand, the store goods they demanded (mainly foodstuffs and clothing) increasingly resembled those sold in southern Canada. The company responded by reducing store overheads and the costs of importing trade goods until its stores could undercut the prices of their competitors. Then, even if a competitor outbid the company for some of the furs, the trappers were still likely to find it advantageous to spend their proceeds on the merchandise offered at the HBC store. As part of the altered situation the company also dropped most of its public transport functions after the war in favour of other commercial operators except in districts where no commercial carrier service operated.

Recreational hunting also underwent modernization as bon-vivant aristocratic sportsmen were succeeded by sophisticated city-dwelling men of wealth who were far less interested in living close to nature and in any event could spare only hurried vacations away from their heavy business commitments. Sport fishing and game-bird hunting at fly-in camps were far more likely to appeal to such hunters. Governments assisted the sportsmen's visits in every way because they were viewed as generating employment and local business that far exceeded any damage they could inflict by destroying a small, carefully counted number of animals. "Care to harpoon a 1,000 pound white whale from the deck of a Peterhead boat, or ride the tall grass prairies of the Slave River flats in search of wild buffalo?"[13] beckoned *Travel North*, a booklet the Northwest Territories Tourist Office published in 1962.

Far more harm was inflicted on the game resources, and indirectly on the fur-bearing species, by the great numbers of working Canadians who found the wildlife of the northlands increasingly accessible thanks to the highways, roads, and trails opened to vehicular traffic since the war. Such persons regarded hunting and fishing trips to the northern wilderness just off the roads as enjoyable, healthful, cheap, potentially profitable vacations. They brought in as much of their food, shelter, supplies, and equipment as they could carry and took out as much meat or fish as their licences allowed. The inexpert, careless, ignorant, or wilful conduct of a small fraction of these campers and their disregard for animals or property disrupted the orderly management of the wildlife resource and did wide damage to the environment. A few administrators, those of Northern Saskatchewan and the Territories for instance, did what they could to sustain the policy that "the wildlife resources are first for the people who live there. Out-

siders are only allowed to hunt when there is a surplus the local inhabitants do not require or take."[14] For the most part, however, the
hunting lobby was powerful enough to introduce changes to the regulatory systems that encouraged and supported their kind of hunters
and fishermen. In the Yukon, for instance, the system designed for the
pre-war residents was overthrown by newcomers to the territory in
favour of one more attuned to the interests of working-class residents
and visitors.

Other interest groups were also emerging in the 1950s whose needs
called for different sorts of regulations to control the activities of hunters and trappers: recreational groups such as operators of tourist facilities and their staffs and especially the growing numbers of field
naturalists, bird watchers, and wildlife photographers. As early as
1959 a multiple-use approach to wildlife was being enunciated as a
goal for the Canadian Wildlife Service:

> Canada is emerging from the era of exploitive use of the wildlife
> resources, which was an essential part of the opening up of the
> country. There will always be some reliance on wildlife for food in
> remote areas, nevertheless, the major wildlife use will be recreation
> and that use will increase in importance and its contribution to the
> economy of the country. The increasing demand for wildlife for
> recreational use can be met only by wildlife management closely
> co-ordinated with the other land uses and steadily improved in
> quality and increased in quantity.[15]

Administrators, conscious of the growing numbers who were flocking
to the public parks or wildernesses to observe, photograph, and enjoy
the scenery and wildlife, enunciated the general policy that "all users
of public lands should be required to take wildlife and recreational
values effectively into account."[16]

For its part, a segment of the increasingly urbanized population was
coming to view wildlife as a significant facet of their environmentalist
creed and its preservation as a vital cause for which they should work.
Humanitarians, indignant about existing trapping methods, began to
demand an end to trapping animals for their pelts or slaughtering wildlife for sport. Many members of wildlife protection organizations,
impelled by sentimental concern for all forms of life, pressed administrations to discard scientific conservation policies and replace their
wildlife management programs with policies oriented to their own
more emotional opinions. As politicians appear more likely to bend to
these powerful pressures from interest groups based in Heartland Canada, the very foundations of wildlife resource development, perhaps
even the continuing survival of the historic wildlife industries in
Hinterland Canada, are at the time of writing being challenged as never
before.

CHAPTER 6

Under Trusteeship: The Native Peoples of the North, 1914–1940

I

The steady advance of the agricultural frontier into the forests of the Middle North in Central Canada and north of the prairies left many Indian reserves standing like islands in the midst of occupied farmlands, or, in a few cases, led to their sale and the eventual granting of new reserves in more distant, less threatened areas. The adverse effects of nearby settlements on the Indians' traditional livelihood, coupled with strong demands for good farmland, led to the subdivision of some reserves in the Peace River and Rainy River districts during the 1920s. Métis, not tied to reserves and free to pull up stakes, also withdrew northward from the threatened sectors. Dr. Mary Jackson reported from the northern Peace River district, in words reminiscent of those of Bishop Bompas in the 1880s:

> At present practically the whole population north of the Battle River Prairie is breed, and Cree, Beaver and Slavee Indian right up to the N.W.T. They have been driven steadily northwards during the last 50 years, and the movement is still going on.
>
> Several half-breeds at Notikewin have sold out in the last few weeks; they will move north to where moose and deer and furs are still plentiful. They are not made for farming.[1]

Elsewhere in the Middle North, forestry, hydro, and mining operations impinged even more widely, though not so completely, on the native peoples' traditional life. More threatening because of the direct challenge to their livelihood was the extension northward of commercial trapping and fishing activities of white men. Except where restricted by government regulation, these trapping and fur-trading activities spread throughout the Subarctic forests; pioneers reached the Arctic and the mountains and valleys of the northern Cordillera to

151

the Alaskan border. Commercial fishing (which was undertaken even at Lake Athabasca in 1920–21 and after 1926) was particularly serious because many of the Indian reserves and settlements had been selected with the reliable fish resource in mind.

During the prosperous middle and late twenties, contacts between whites and natives seemed relatively beneficial. Even very isolated groups, such as the Inuit of the Central Arctic, began visiting the recently opened trading posts on King William Island. In 1928, "they arrived in some numbers and appeared to take the credit for granted and to consider commodities, of which four years before they had no knowledge, as essential to their well-being."[2] Farther south some more advanced native groups took advantage of the prevailing good prices for produce to expand their commercial fishing activities; others found employment in fish canning, lumbering, and transport work or in the manufacture of increasingly popular handicrafts: baskets, lacrosse sticks, snowshoes and toboggans, moccasins and gloves, decorated blankets, and objets d'art in wood, bone, argillite, and silver.

The improved material conditions of many natives (and their growing adaptation to white modes of living) were reflected in increasing purchases of processed tinned foods, factory-made clothing, household appliances, gramophones, gasoline motors ("few self-respecting Indians paddle a canoe in these days"[3]), and automobiles. The transformation of the trading and trapping Inuit of the Western Arctic was particularly notable:

> No longer are they ignorant savages dwelling in snow igloos in winter and forced to eke out a pitiful existence in a terrific struggle against all the forces of nature. The igloos have given place to comfortable winter dwellings of logs or rough lumber, in many cases finished with wallboard and dressed lumber.
>
> White flour, sugar, butter, jam, canned fruit and other luxuries are included now in their diet. Long winter evenings are passed pleasantly listening to good music provided by expensive gramophones and radio sets. Brass and iron spring beds take the place of the old family couch of skins. Up-to-date sewing machines make the lot of the women easier.
>
> Highly powered motor schooners, costing from $3,000 to $7,000 each, provide floating summer homes as the people move about the delta or along the sea coast in search of sea animals or to visit the trading posts. Cameras, watches, thermos bottles, safety razors, high-powered rifles and many other products of modern civilization are in general use. Practically all these Eskimos can read and write in their own tongue and most of them have a fair grasp of English.[4]

Unfortunately, the widespread adoption of white men's foods, clothing, and wooden housing by previously nomadic groups proved harmful to their health, for they were often quite ignorant of the sanitary practices or good nutrition required for safe living in the new environments, although they had dealt satisfactorily enough with these matters in earlier times. Cooped up in tiny cabins, they were sometimes stricken with typhoid fever from contaminated water supplies, or more frequently with tuberculosis from being at close quarters with sufferers. Store foods were far less healthful than the meat, fish, and berry diet of former days, and signs of malnutrition became more noticeable. W.A. Price, an American dentist who visited several reserves in 1933, concluded that Indians who changed from an all-meat to a store-food diet became about one hundred times more susceptible to tooth decay and were more prone besides to suffer from arthritis and tuberculosis. A specialist employed by the Department of Indian Affairs, Dr. J.J. Wall, discovered that over a quarter of the Indians he examined, up to 7,000 persons, had trachoma, a little-known, highly infectious eye disease that could attack the corneas of its victims and resulted in impaired sight, even blindness, if unchecked. Tuberculosis reached a mortality rate among Indians in 1931 of 670 per 100,000, over ten times the national average. And the deterioration of the native economy in the 1930s would further hasten the decline of native health.

New perils for native health accompanied the increasing contacts between whites and northern Indians that attended the prosperity of the twenties, notably during the habitual gatherings in connection with the fur trade, treaty payments, and ship arrivals. The northern native peoples had little resistance to many epidemic diseases or experience in how to cope with them: "When Indians become sick they huddle together in their little huts. Communicable diseases – measles, typhoid, whooping cough, influenza and worse – assume epidemic proportions whenever they appear."[5] Diseases carried into remote areas could rage unchecked for weeks, killing entire families before news could reach the outside world and help arrive. The worst single epidemic of the twenties came in 1928, when influenza was unwittingly carried the length of the Mackenzie River by the first ship of the season, *Distributor III*. The disease broke out at every settlement where the ship had docked to transact business. Despite heroic efforts by resident whites, scores and hundreds of Indians speedily succumbed in the settlements, and in the coming weeks and months further outbreaks followed at Indian encampments remote from the river posts.

The interwar years saw the legal relationship of the Department of Indian Affairs with its client peoples increasingly formalized and extended toward the farthest limits of Indian settlement in Subarctic Canada. Treaty No. 11, as we have seen, brought the Indians of the Mackenzie basin north of Treaty No. 8 into a formal treaty relationship, and between 1926 and 1930 the terms of Treaty No. 9 (Northern Ontario, 1905–6) were extended to the Indian population of the District of Patricia. New reserves were created for bands living north of Fort McMurray along the Athabasca River, at Fort Chipewyan, in the Rocky Mountain Trench region, and in southern Yukon that desired them. In British Columbia, since 1912 a redefinition and resurvey of reserves had been proceeding that involved many exchanges of land and eventual transfer of the adjudicated lands to the federal government in 1938.

The Indian agencies, the units of regional administration, were increased to 115 by splitting larger ones (for instance, Mackenzie River) into more manageable sizes, and new agencies were opened in such localities as Fort Good Hope (1930), Churchill (1934), Fort St. John (1937), Sioux Lookout (1938), and Abitibi (1939). The department tended to align administrative districts with provincial boundaries. By 1924 nine of the fourteen inspectorates were within provinces; another three dealt with the northerly areas covered by Treaties 8, 9, and 11, and the remaining two were devoted to the Ile à la Crosse district and Yukon Territory. The principal change within the agencies, for reasons of economy and efficiency, was the appointment of a number of doctors as both Indian agents and physicians. That the combination was not altogether satisfactory may be judged from a complaint by a harassed Dr. C. Bourget of Fort Resolution, "Après tout il est difficile d'être juge de paix, médecin, agent, inspecteur d'écoles, médecin du Bureau de santé, coroner, officier du ministère de la marine, gardien du quai, maître de poste, et, en plus, père de famille, sans committer une erreur par-ci par-là."[6]

A major element of the government's trusteeship over the native peoples was its police force, the Royal Canadian Mounted Police, whose jurisdiction from February 1920, like its new name, was co-extensive with Canada. Four divisions were added to the existing seven to reflect its expansion into Central and Atlantic Canada. The 1,680-man force was purely a federal agency at this time, the provinces that had used the RNWMP having established their own police forces in 1917 at the request of the federal government. Under the Liberal government of 1921–26, the RCMP gradually declined to a low of 963 men in 1926, and subsequent increases were largely a reflection of reabsorption of the police forces of the Prairie and Maritime provinces. Significantly, during the twenties a growing number and fraction of the RCMP's men were stationed in northern locations – as much as 16 per cent of the 1,199 enrolled in 1929, of which ninety-five manned the twenty-four Northwest Territories detachments. Most of the remainder were based farther south in the vicinities of Indian reserves or semi-nomadic bands still living by hunting, fishing, and trapping at such centres as Hazelton, Grouard, Alberta, Cumberland House, Saskatchewan, The Pas, Moose Factory, Ontario, Amos and Bersimis, Quebec.

The primary function of these representatives of the federal administration was to supervise the native inhabitants (who were the federal government's direct responsibility), and watch their relations with their white neighbours. They were supported by provincial policemen and game wardens stationed in their districts and gave reciprocal assistance to their provincial colleagues. For instance, RCMP detachments administered provincial as well as federal laws and regulations as a matter of course and sometimes undertook special tasks on behalf of the provinces. Thus Ontario licensed Inspector C.D. LaNauze as a provincial magistrate to try a case at Fort Albany (which was located on an RCMP patrol) to spare the province the costs of sending in a party or bringing out the accused for trial.

The basic RCMP activity was to patrol the enormous districts in response to reported emergencies or simply as a regular operation to gather information and "show the flag." The police officers took action on reported homicides among natives, and in crises between white and native trappers; they tried to alleviate epidemics, threatened starvation, feuds, or outbreaks of frenzy that might lead to loss of life. Sometimes a series of patrols extending over several years might be required to bring a remote section under control. The three patrols that Inspector T.V. Sandys Wunsch led into the upper Liard region are a good example. The first visit in 1924 checked on a reported murder of a boy by witchcraft-fearing Indians; five persons were arrested and brought to Vancouver for trial. The inspector returned in 1926 to investigate relations between non-treaty Indians and the whites who lived among them, during the course of which he distributed medicines and other aids and brought out an insane Indian. On the third visit, 1930–32, a police post was set up and the surrounding district was patrolled, principally to investigate the alleged murder of a trapper, enforce provincial game statutes, and provide relief to needy residents.

In upholding the law the police officer followed his discretion according to circumstances of place, time, and the type of persons with whom he was dealing. The difficulty and expense of bringing native offenders from remote areas for trial ensured that trivial charges would be ignored and only serious crimes prosecuted. With the objective of maintaining public order and tranquility, the police kept a close watch on the white inhabitants as the likeliest sources, or focuses, of possible disturbances. Besides, more was expected of whites, who could be assumed to understand the laws and be able to comply with them. Individual policemen, no doubt, differentiated between British subjects and aliens, or Anglo-Canadians and "foreigners," from the standpoint of their supposed law-abiding habits. They tended to look on Indians as not wholly responsible for their actions by reason of ignorance or social immaturity, like minors or wards in white society, and treated them accordingly. Their view of the Inuit was more ambiguous – the sense of wardship was tempered by respect for their obvious skills, intelligence, and initiative. They tended, therefore, to excuse Inuit offenders or impose inadequate penalties on them until the occurrence of several violent crimes brought a round of heavy punishments to deter such behaviour.

Another discretionary consideration was the level of development of a district, from a policing standpoint. In a district rarely or intermittently visited, officers could do little more than observe and report on conditions and alleviate distress. On the other hand, as an area became better policed and the natives grew more familiar with the laws, RCMP officers were better able to take direct action against crimes by natives, often forestalling them altogether simply by their presence. The natives, for their part, became more accustomed to the presence of the police and co-operated with them to maintain local order. Greater familiarity with the role of the police brought pronounced changes among the more backward groups, such as a marked reduction in violent actions induced by witch-fear, in cases of infanticide, and in abandonments or murders of aged persons.

The Christian missions exerted a more powerful force for acculturating the native peoples of the North. Their role was semi-official in that the government used them as its agents and gave them money grants for supplying education, health services, and welfare assistance to its native wards. The relationship, though advantageous to both sides, did not completely satisfy either party, nor did it produce the best results for the native clients. The Department of Indian Affairs felt that church-directed services were economical and likely to have very beneficial effects on the Indians, but it was concerned by the sites the missions chose for schools and hospitals and, to a degree, with the overall quality and other aspects of the services they provided. The missions, for their part, complained that the gross inadequacy of government support greatly restricted the assistance they could provide and that administrative decisions interfered with their proper work.

The situation at Aklavik, which was becoming the recognized capital of the Western Arctic and a key strategic location for activities along the Arctic coast in the twenties, affords a good illustration. Both Anglican and Roman Catholic missions established schools and hospitals at that centre, and when the Northwest Territories administration attempted to withhold grants from the unauthorized Catholic hospital, Bishop Breynat complained angrily to Commissioner W.W. Cory: "Respectueusement mais énergetiquement je proteste contre votre decision et toute tentative du réglementer notre travail missionaire."[7] In the end, thanks to the pressure the bishop could muster, the Roman Catholic hospital secured its full grant, and Aklavik had two hospitals. Duplication was perhaps more defensible in the educational field, which was the central facet of missionary work with native peoples. Four of the twenty-three Roman Catholic residential schools in the Subarctic and Arctic were located in communities that were also served in this regard by another denomination. Such duplication, dictated by the interests of the missions, naturally meant other centres went without schools.

The administration and the missions differed in several ways over educational services. The French-speaking orders of priests and nuns who supplied the Roman Catholic missionary endeavour had to defer to the administration's preference for English as the language of instruction. The administration preferred day schools wherever possible on the ground that they might spread the effects of education within the family circle and were less disruptive to family relationships than residential schools where children were separated from their families for months and years and might become helpless misfits when they finally returned to their home settlements. The missions, however, considered that residential schools afforded the best opportunity to train children in ways that promised healthier future lives, good regular habits, ethical values, and moral conduct. Bishop Breynat, in his usual positive, vigorous prose, affirmed the superiority of the residential school over its day school rival: "Bref, après une experience de 50 ans chez les Indiens, n'ayant en vue que la survivance, le bien-être et l'éducation progressive de la race, mon humble avis est que dix écoles du jour ne donneront jamais d'aussi bons resultats qu'une seule école-pensionnat."[8]

Missionary-directed education was further questioned on grounds of the scarcity of professionally trained teachers, the academic results attained, the kinds of manual and other training offered, and the strongly religious tone of the instruction. Former students later complained of the religious orientation of the schools and reported adverse psychological effects from the punishments imposed and from the confining, highly disciplined school environment. The 1947 report of the North Pacific Planning Project criticized the social effects of the mission-directed Indian schools, particularly the residential schools:

> Training in manual and domestic arts, while the aim is practical, tends to develop skills, tastes and ambitions more adapted to the white man's way of life than to the development and preservation of native culture. Long separation from the family life has its effect, and too frequently the result is an ambition to adopt the white man's manners and customs, impossible to preserve in the conditions obtaining in the native communities and which can only lead to frustrations and reversions, the results of which, culturally, is a loss of the dignity of race and the native pride on which the preservation of these human values so vitally depends.[9]

A central feature of education in the post-1945 era would be the virtual exclusion of the missions from their long-standing function of furnishing social services to native groups and the assumption of this role by the state.

By the twenties the Anglican and Roman Catholic missionary organizations were fully established across the Middle North from Labrador to the Yukon and were progressing with proselytizing the Inuit. The Roman Catholics had beaten the Anglicans in the competition for the support of the Indians and Métis, for the Oblate-directed effort recruited enough priests, lay brothers, and teaching and nursing sisters to spread their chapels, churches, residential schools, hospitals, and convents across the Middle North. Apostolic prefectures were raised to apostolic vicariates and eventually to regular dioceses, which were subdivided into smaller areas as the effort was intensified. The work also was pushed into districts that had formerly been almost monopolized by the Anglicans, for example in the James Bay district, where a number of stations were opened and the diocese of Moosonee was established (1938).

Bishop Breynat's work in the Mackenzie district from 1902 to 1943 exemplifies the practical reasons for the Roman Catholics' success, for it was a classic illustration of how to adapt a religious organization to local conditions and opportunities. Along the Mackenzie waterways he developed an integrated system of churches, schools, and hospitals, sawmills and farms, linked together by boats and aircraft into a system worthy of Sir George Simpson. His sawmills and farms supplied other stations, even in the Arctic; his series of improved boats carried his missions' freight and even earned some revenue in the process. His system, marshalling the labour of priests, lay brothers, nuns, and pupils, was largely self-sufficient, while the bishop himself was untiring in securing funds from government agencies and private sources to promote the work of his church.

The Church of England, by contrast, found its support diminishing and its establishments harder to maintain. Its one-time advantage in the Yukon was being overcome by Roman Catholic institutions established in the wake of the gold rush. It almost disappeared from the former strongholds of Fort Chipewyan and Fort Simpson, and in only a few places, such as Fort McPherson, were the Anglicans able to slow, but not arrest, the relentless drive of Roman Catholicism. During the twenties their already difficult competitive position was aggravated by the misappropriation of most of the endowments of the dioceses of Athabasca and Mackenzie and much of those of Rupert's Land by a trusted employee of the archdiocese.

Although the Anglicans enjoyed better success with the Inuit, among whom they had established several footholds before 1905, even here the Roman Catholics made some headway on the Keewatin coast. The work there was inaugurated by Father Arsène Turquetil at Chesterfield Inlet in 1912 and was extended to Eskimo Point, Southampton Island, Baker Lake, and Pond Inlet during the ensuing decades. Turquetil was elevated to bishop in charge of the Apostolic Vicariate of Hudson Bay, with its seat in the new railway centre of Churchill, in 1931. Farther west, Bishop Breynat's first mission in 1912–13 collapsed with the murders of Fathers Rouvière and LeRoux, but it was renewed in the twenties. Father Pierre Fallaise, Breynat's agent and a future bishop, began work in the Coppermine district in 1920 and opened a series of stations from Aklavik during the next two decades.

The Anglicans' work among the Inuit was extended after 1920 in the Eastern Arctic (east coast of Hudson Bay and Baffin Island) and along the Western Arctic coasts. In response to the challenge, the work among the Inuit was reorganized in 1927 under a single head, the Archdeacon of the Arctic. The appointee, the Rev. A.L. Fleming, who had had a very successful earlier missionary career at Lake Harbour, opened a number of missions in rapid succession. At first he was responsible to the bishops of four different dioceses but eventually in 1933 (following the financial collapse) he was consecrated bishop of a new diocese of the Arctic, carved from northern parts of five sees and covering the entire Arctic zone of Canada from Labrador to Alaska. Aklavik became the centre of the new diocese, the site of its pro-cathedral and main religious, educational, and health-care activities. Thereafter both Roman Catholic and Anglican work expanded rapidly from new stations at key locations such as Tuktoyaktuk, at minor sites such as Gjoa Haven, Igloolik, Payne Bay, and Spence Bay, and even at remote inland Garry Lake. By 1940 both churches were represented at Coppermine, Baker Lake, Eskimo Point, and Cape Dorset as well as the larger Arctic centres, and the competition for the souls of the native inhabitants, formerly waged along the Mackenzie for the Indians, was being renewed for the Inuit of the Arctic wastes.

II

The Department of Indian Affairs, whose origins went back more than a century, had assumed permanent form around the time of Confederation. Through the interwar decades the department grew only gradually and far less than need demanded, deploying an inadequate budget that inched to $4 million in 1927 and stood only at $5.6 million as late as 1939–40. During the thirties the department was reduced in status, finally being abolished in 1937, and the Indian Affairs Branch became simply one of the disparate units lumped together in the omnibus Department of Mines and Resources. The department/branch, presided over as deputy superintendent general until his retirement in 1932 by the poet Duncan Campbell Scott and then by Dr. H.W. McGill, was responsible for administering the Indian Act and other regulations to which the registered, or status, Indians, numbering some 118,378 in 1939, were subject. Its responsibilities did not extend to the equally large body of mixed-bloods or Métis, many of whom lived with and like Indians, nor the very much smaller category of enfranchised Indians, whose numbers were being augmented by about one hundred each year, mostly through marriages of Indian women to white men or Métis.

Nor did they include the approximately seven thousand Inuit, who were in a unique position. Like Indians, Inuit were thought to come under federal authority, but when the government in 1924 sought to regularize the situation by giving the Department of Indian Affairs formal administrative responsibility for Inuit, the legislation was vigorously protested in the House of Commons. Later, under a federal order in council of 1928, administration of Inuit affairs was transferred to the Northwest Territories Council and the Northwest Territories and Yukon Branch of the Department of the Interior. Inuit – at least in the Northwest Territories – enjoyed equal status with white and Métis populations, differing from that of the Indians. That arrangement covered the majority of Inuit except for those who resided in the provinces, particularly in Arctic Quebec, about whose status some uncertainty remained. A dispute during the thirties over which government, Quebec or Ottawa, was liable for relief expenditures for Quebec Inuit was carried to the Judicial Committee of the Privy Council, which ruled (1939) that Inuit were not a provincial but a federal responsibility the same as Indians, even though they were, and remained, under a different agency of government and outside the provisions of the Indian Act.

The department/branch, lacking any real support from its political masters, was dominated by aging, conservative-minded administrators and antiquated policies and programs, and it underwent little change, nowithstanding the serious difficulties the native peoples faced. The apparatus of the previous century remained virtually intact – the treaties, reserves, Indian agents, enfranchisement, and band funds, the social services still supplied largely by missionary organizations assisted by departmental subsidies, and relief dispensed to destitute natives when notice of the need came to the attention of the department/branch. In his report for 1927 Scott complacently reviewed the past sixty years' achievements, congratulating the Indian for having "valiantly borne the ordeal of contact with our boasted civilization," and concluding that "on the whole it may be said that the Indians have reason to be grateful to the Canadian government for the benefits and consideration that they have received, while Canada may well be proud of what has been accomplished by the members of the aboriginal race."[10] What the Indians should have been grateful for, apparently, was the fact that the familiar organization was still in place, unaffected by the pressures and challenges of the past sixty years and quite inadequate to face the strains of the coming decades.

The central goal of the Indian administration was to assimilate their native charges into the majority society, in which education and training played the largest part. As Scott reported:

> . . . the Indians of Ontario and Quebec, in the old regions of the provinces, are every day entering more and more into the general life of the country. They are farmers, clerks, artisans, teachers and lumbermen. Some few have qualified as medical doctors and surveyors; an increasing number are accepting enfranchisement and taking up the responsibilities of citizenship. Although there are reactionary elements among the best educated tribes, and stubborn paganism on the most progressive reserves, the irresistible movement is towards the goal of complete citizenship.
>
> These latter people [the "civilized tribes"] have long ago proved their worth, and only need to develop and mature under protection until they, one and all, reach their destined goal, full British citizenship.[11]

Neither Scott nor his assistant, J.D. McLean, seemed capable of considering more than minor changes to the existing systems of administration or services to Indians. When the post-war assimilationist drive slowed after a first few promising years, the only solution Scott seemed to have for the mounting problems was to strengthen and intensify the already ironclad controls from earlier days.

As parts of that drive, Indian war veterans were accorded the full benefits of the Soldier Settlement Board legislation, and enfranchisement was made easier for the individual who did not live on a reserve or follow the native way of life but satisfied the authorities ''that he [was] self-supporting and fit to be enfranchised.''[12] If the majority of the members of a band wished to become enfranchised, the reserves and other band property might be divided into individual holdings. A Criminal Code amendment forced white men to leave reserves where they were living with Indian women; this arrangement, plus the enfranchisement of Indian women who married non-Indians, brought a marked increase of enfranchisements. Scott boasted in 1921 that whereas 102 Indians had been enfranchised in the fifty-three years after Confederation, in the preceding eighteen months the total had reached 487.

Further legislation of the interwar period gave the administration ever wider discretion in directing the economic development of the reserves. Thus it could spend a band's capital against its wishes whenever it judged ''that such refusal is detrimental to the progress or welfare of the band,''[13] could lease uncultivated land or use the band funds to secure cultivation of reserve land on the Indians' behalf, could issue leases for mining purposes and fix the compensation owed the Indians. Above all, education was brought under firmer administration control: authority was given to establish schools on reserves, make agreements with other schools to accept Indian children, and apply the children's annuities or interest from the band funds to pay for such schooling. For the first time, also, it gained authority to compel Indian children to attend school between the ages of seven and fifteen (or whenever high school entrance standard was achieved) and to employ truant officers who could fine parents or guardians who failed to comply. As Scott complacently observed, ''The recent amendments give the department control and remove from the Indian parent the responsibility for the care and education of his child, and the best interests of the Indians are promoted and fully protected.''[14]

Paternalistic intervention on the Indian's ''behalf'' also extended into other areas. The curbs on the long deplored, allegedly undesirable potlatch were strengthened: organizing a potlatch was made a summary offence. Arrests and jailings ensued, including that of eight Indians as the result of a potlatch at Alert Bay. Scott's concern for the dignity of the Indians led him to support stricter enforcement of the statutes against their exploitive display at pageants, fairs, and stampedes. Aroused cultural nationalism and, to a smaller degree, concern for Indian arts were reflected in an amendment of 1927 that gave the administration greater control over native archaeological, religious, and artistic memorials in order to protect them against unauthorized removal or disfigurement.

The troubled thirties brought more amendments to the Indian Act to further strengthen the administration's power to intervene in Indians' lives. In 1930 it received powers to extend compulsory school attendance past the age of sixteen at its discretion, to seize and confiscate vehicles carrying liquor to Indians, and to bar access to a poolroom if an Indian "misspends or wastes his time or means to the detriment of himself, his family or household" through "inordinate frequenting"[15] on penalty of a fine to the owner. Indians required the written consent of Indian agents to buy or sell cattle, crops, or other commodities off reserves; the administration could regulate selling, peddling, or hawking on reserves, remove unauthorized squatters from reserves, control operations of vehicles on reserve roads and the conduct of reserve council meetings, lease reserve lands for oil and gas exploration purposes, and regulate the acquisition and disposal of furs and wild animals by or from Indians. All these amendments and regulations, of course, had the natives' well-being (as the administration saw it) as their prime consideration. But they represented ever greater intrusions into Indians' lives and brought the day closer when virtually every action would require ministerial authorization.

Imposition of these controls did not go unopposed. The Six Nations took strong exception to a new provision of the Indian Act empowering the department to commence enfranchisement proceedings against Indians. They contended that this 1920 enactment, along with others making band councils elective and extending Soldier Settlement Board regulations to farmers on the reserve, infringed on their right of self-government guaranteed by the charter under which their ancestors had settled in Canada. When individual Indians denied the jurisdiction of Canadian courts and defied Canadian laws, the response was a stronger RCMP presence on the reserve. In the meantime the Six Nations' complaints, supported by a lawyer from Rochester, N.Y., were carried first to the King in 1921, then to the League of Nations in 1923.

The Liberal government adopted a more conciliatory stance. An amendment to the Indian Act in 1922 modified the enfranchisement provision to give individuals or bands, not the department, the power to initiate proceedings. The new Minister of Indian Affairs opened negotiations with the Six Nations Council, and eventually a commission to investigate the Indians' complaints was set up. But the government set its face strongly against the moves to internationalize the campaign. Indians' efforts to raise money, or draw from their trust fund, to pursue their claims abroad were blocked. Their petition to the King for redress was returned to the Canadian government for action. The League Council refused to consider their 1923 petition for recognition as "a State within the purview or meaning of Article 17 of the Covenant,"[16] nor was any delegation willing to sponsor it. The official journal of the League of Nations did, however, publish the Canadian government's point-by-point refutation in full. After an elected council was installed on the reserve in 1924, a less hostile mood gradually prevailed. A 1927 amendment to the Indian Act created a new offence punishable by fine or imprisonment: raising money from Indians to prosecute a band claim on their behalf without having first secured the written consent of the administration. Clearly reflecting the contretemps with the Six Nations, the amendment may also have been a factor in reducing this and other agitations among native groups.

British Columbia's Indians shared the Six Nations' concern over the 1920 enfranchisement bill, to which they added complaints of their own about provincial restrictions on their trapping, hunting, and fishing activities. Their main grievance, however, was that both levels of government ignored their aboriginal land claims even while wrangling bitterly over Indian reserve lands. Argument had been going on for fifty years over the province's "reversionary right," which was British Columbia's power to reclaim the lands it had granted for reserves whenever they became surplus to a band's entitlement and were no longer needed for reserve purposes. Under the McKenna-McBride Agreement of 1912 the federal and provincial governments appointed a joint commission to make a detailed investigation of the reserves to determine what lands ought to be "cut off" or added to meet the province's criteria. When these changes had been worked out the province was to relinquish its reversionary right, and Indian reserves in British Columbia would become the same as those elsewhere – that is, they would be managed by the Indian Affairs department in trust for the bands. The report, cutting off some 47,000 acres and adding another 87,000 to the reserves, was ready by 1916; but the province refused to implement it until 1933, and the actual changes were not completed until some years later.

In the meantime, British Columbia Indians took the stand that they could not accept any land settlement that did not also consider their aboriginal claims. In 1913–14 the Nishga, a Northwest Coast people, had sought to have their claim tried by the Judicial Committee of the Privy Council, but the federal government after pledging assistance decided not to proceed with the reference. On the one side, the provincial government would not agree to a case based on aboriginal rights; on the other, the Indians would not relinquish their claims until the court had decided on the matter. The Indians' refusal to proceed on their own, in turn, was interpreted to mean that the claims no longer had to be considered. There the matter stood until the mid-twenties when the Allied Indian Tribes of British Columbia (formed in 1916) took up the cause. Indian delegations met with federal cabinet ministers in Ottawa and Vancouver and made another appeal to the Throne, and the Allied Tribes petitioned Parliament to resolve the matter.

A special joint committee of the Senate and Commons took up the question in 1927, and testimony was secured from the Indians and the department, though the province still refused to participate. The committee concluded that "the petitioners have not established any claim to the lands of British Columbia based on aboriginal or other title,"[17] but to settle the specific grievances it proposed paying the Indians an annuity comparable to those received by treaty Indians elsewhere in Canada. Unlike the usual small sums paid to individuals, however, the award took the shape of a collective $100,000 annual grant to the Indians of British Columbia to be used for such common purposes as technical education, promotion of agriculture and stock raising, irrigation works, hospitals, and medical aid. This settlement seemed to quiet the agitation for the next twenty years.

The Indian Affairs department's generally reactionary attitude was exemplified by its treatment of reformist ideas that emanated from Indian sources. A case in point was its behaviour toward the Congress of Indians of Canada League, organized in January 1919 by F.O. Loft, an Iroquois war veteran of the Deserontayo Reserve. For years Loft devoted himself to the league, addressing meetings on reserves (mostly in the Prairie Provinces) and dispatching memorials to Ottawa with suggestions that evolved as the situation changed. In 1919 he advocated halting the stepped-up enfranchisement drive, but in 1923 he proposed that Indians should be given the vote without losing their Indian status. He demanded better management and accounting for band properties and greater Indian control over them. The department's failure to stimulate the Indians' economic development, he complained, was holding them back and making them dependent on government handouts. He criticized departmental reluctance to defend the Indians' treaty rights against the provinces' efforts to regulate their fishing, hunting, and trapping activities and called for natives-only game preserves. His views on education were modernist. With the goal of raising Indian educational standards and levels of attainment, he advocated better schools operated along secular lines, compulsory attendance enforced by non-Indian truant officers, and even a non-segregated school system controlled by the provinces.

For its part, the department, instead of encouraging, supporting, and adopting these sensible, progressive proposals, eyed them with alarm and treated Loft as a person whose every movement was suspect. At one time it considered subjecting him to compulsory enfranchisement, and as a preparation for proceeding against him it collected his statements and prepared a dossier on his activities. It had the RCMP attend and report on his meetings, sometimes planted questioners in his audiences to weaken the effect of his oratory, and tried to reduce his impact by urging Indian agents to do what they could to keep their reserves from supporting his causes.

This underhand behaviour of authorities charged with directing Indians' progress to full citizenship was fortunately out of step with a marked and growing improvement in public opinion regarding Indians and their rights. The new attitude had begun during the Great War when Indians "fought side by side with white men for the glory of Canada and the integrity of the Empire."[18] There was growing appreciation of the Indian's view of nature and his ability to live in harmony with a difficult environment; there was hope that he could become a full member of the community while retaining his identity. Indian blood was even becoming less of a stigma, as witness the applause accorded such idols as the athlete Jim Thorpe, the raconteur Will Rogers, or the war hero, Western Canadian newspaperman, and Hollywood actor Long Lance. The traditional controls, programs, and institutions that regulated the Indian's conduct and seemed to hamper his adaptation to modern life began to be questioned, although the Department of Indian Affairs did not attract as much blame as it deserved. Instead, perhaps because of Scott's reputation as a poet, the department received credit for being well-intentioned but thwarted by governmental indifference and niggardliness.

Some members of the public also were taking an interest in the native peoples from anthropological and artistic standpoints. By the twenties an appreciable amount of study of Canadian Indians was being done by Canadian scholars, and their findings were having some impact on the public and even on government. Diamond Jenness followed his studies on the Central Arctic Inuit with others on the Carrier and Sekani Indian bands of British Columbia and Ojibway of Georgian Bay. In 1932 he published the first sympathetic, though pessimistic, comprehensive study of the native peoples, *The Indians of Canada*, which was well received and reprinted several times. Marius Barbeau, also of the National Museum, studied the archaeology and culture of the West Coast peoples, in particular the totem poles of the Tsimshian and other northern tribes whose tourist potential was attracting attention from governments and railway companies and inspiring efforts to preserve and restore them. British Columbia passed legislation prohibiting unauthorized removal of these important culture objects in 1925. Barbeau's efforts resulted in the restoration and re-erection of scores of poles in Kitwanga and other villages, a step that helped revive traditional native art forms and stir the people's pride in their heritage. T.F. McIlwraith's comprehensive work on the Bella Coola and similar studies, multiplied across the Subarctic, contributed to better-informed opinion with a more sympathetic appreciation for the Indians' distinctive cultures, customs, and arts. Native and northern motifs were used increasingly by Canadian artists, as in Emily Carr's dramatic portrayals of the British Columbian coastal environment and peoples; they appeared in literature in Barbeau's 1928 novel, *The Downfall of Temlaban*, and Grey Owl's popular, influential writings. Such works also revealed the public's strengthened feeling that native Canadians merited a better fate than simple assimilation and submergence within Canada's mass cultures.

III

The Depression of the thirties was particularly disastrous for the native economy and imposed heavy sufferings on the native peoples. The drastic decline in fur prices after 1929, coupled with reduced yields, created great hardships for those who relied on furs for some part of their livelihood. Increased prospecting activity and travel in the northern forests added to the problem by causing widespread bush fires that blanketed the country with smoke and wreaked havoc on the game and fur-bearing species. The depletion of meat animals imperilled the food supply that sustained thousands of native families and cast them into acute deprivation and precarious health.

At the same time, alternative work opportunities all but disappeared. Reserve-dwelling Indians saw work as guides, in lumber camps, on farms, or in commercial fisheries dwindle almost to zero, and makeshift attempts to cut timber from the reserves for sale or catch fish for local mink ranchers afforded lean substitutes. Scores of James Bay Crees, after two successive years of falling fur catches and prices, roamed about from one trading post to another looking for odd jobs to sustain themselves and their families. In British Columbia, the low price of fish was the main concern of the 10,000 Indians dependent on the commercial fishery. To combat the canning companies that set the prices, the natives joined fishermen's co-operatives. These not only offered better prices for the fish but also helped reduce members' expenses by sending depot ships to collect the catches and supplying goods at cost. Yet native fishermen lacked means or access to capital to acquire the powerful gasoline-engine boats needed to work the most lucrative fishing grounds, which had to be left to white or Japanese fishermen and the companies.

The lack of paid work threw natives in many areas back on the traditional self-sufficient life of trapping fur and feeding their families on fish, birds, moose or caribou, and hares. In remote regions not yet too badly depleted of fur and game, Indians and Inuit were able to revert to the lifestyle they had given up when the fur trade arrived in their midst. The prosperous "progressive" Inuit white fox trappers of Banks Island were forced to lay up their expensive schooners for lack of fuel and to return to securing their livelihood from the fish and game resources of the Mackenzie delta or Coronation Gulf districts. In Labrador, the Hudson's Bay Company had just transformed the Inuit from largely self-sufficient seal hunters living on the coast into widely dispersed family trapping groups living in the interior and depending on the traders for their needs and coveted luxuries. Now an about-face in company policy posed great difficulties, for Inuit tastes had changed and old skills had atrophied; even the seal nets on which they had relied had rotted, and they could not afford to replace them. Forced back to the nearly forgotten practice of spearing seals through the ice, the Inuit reverted to a style of living that preceded the coming of the whalers and Moravian missionaries to the region some two centuries earlier. The more recently contacted Inuit of the barren region around King William Island were also compelled to depend once more entirely on their seal hunts; unusually severe winters added to their difficult readjustment, and malnutrition, disease, and starvation took their toll.

The sufferings of the native peoples and their losing struggle to adapt to the changed economic situation further encouraged many individuals to leave the land. During the twenties, employment opportunities had attracted natives to centres like Norway House. Economic changes also led some bands to regroup and relocate, as on Baffin Island, where the shift from whaling to trapping caused Blacklead Island to be abandoned in favour of Pangnirtung or other new trading centres. The Depression accentuated the trend. Aggregations of cabins occupied more or less regularly by from three to fifteen families sprang up around the edges of most settlements, even such remote ones as Fort Rae and Fort Liard. The men found whatever odd jobs they could in water transport, guiding, interpreting, and trapping, but often they loitered for days waiting for such occasions to materialize.

These relocations sometimes were attended by undesirable consequences, as the case of the Salt River Settlement, twenty miles south of Fort Smith, demonstrates. Some fifteen families had derived a relatively healthful, satisfying living there from a combination of fishing, hunting, and farming, but during the thirties the families moved to Fort Smith to share the better employment opportunities in the stores and in river transport and to enjoy the services of mission and school. The unfortunate result was that the resources at Salt River were not utilized and the town-living lifestyle undermined the physical health and well-being of the people and destroyed their former self-reliant, self-confident attitudes. Observers were almost unanimous in reporting that many of the difficulties arose from the unhealthy, unpleasant environments of the towns and would not end until the Indians returned to their former life on the land. Bishop Breynat felt that even the annual treaty payment meetings were an evil because while the Indians were waiting at the posts for the arrival of the Indian agent and doctor, they spent the earnings from the previous winter's hunt and were liable to make undesirable contacts.

The Indian Affairs department/branch, with insufficient funds (and personnel, to a lesser extent) at its command, found it very difficult to deal with the widely differing needs of many scattered native groups. The most immediate need was for relief assistance, on which it spent between $800,000 and $1 million annually; about a third of all Indians by 1937 were receiving some form of relief, however small. Much of this aid was dispensed by RCMP constables in rigid, unsympathetic, grudging fashion, calculated to dispel any tendency by recipients to depend unduly on government:

> The problem of destitution in the North West Territories and the issuance of relief rations to indigent whites and natives is one with which almost all police detachments are vitally concerned. . . . To encourage natives to be thrifty and self-supporting is the aim of the detachment man, who is well aware that many natives are habitually lazy and improvident and are only too willing to be supported at Government expense for an indefinite period. Thorough investigation of the circumstances of each relief applicant is made. The policeman has wide discretionary powers, and it is with him that the final decision rests as to whether the case is one of genuine destitution. It is his duty to see that charges made for relief issues are properly allocated. . . . To determine whether an Indian is treaty or non-treaty is often no easy matter . . .[19]

The attitude of the administration was no more charitable. The department kept reminding Indian agents and traders that relief should be restricted to aged, destitute, or sick Indians and not used to outfit the healthy to pursue their hunting and trapping activities. It worried that it might be called on to take over the trader's role of advancing credit to trappers and enjoined its agents not to give any encouragement to Indians that the government might finance their trapping. Agents who nonetheless advanced such aid were instructed to have the Indian sign an agreement to turn all his furs over to the department, which would retain them until the loan was repaid in full; any Indian who violated his contract and sold any part of his furs was to be prosecuted to the limit. Traders were ordered to make no relief outlays without first securing authorization from an Indian agent, missionary, policeman, or other responsible official and to supply only such necessities as flour, pork, tea, plain work clothing, and ammunition.

The northern Indians could be best assured of achieving an adequate livelihood, the administration felt, by being kept in their traditional life. There, as T.A. Crerar, the first Minister of Mines and Resources, observed in 1936, their position was assured: "The fur trade requires thousands of operatives, and the Indians by heredity, inclination and training are naturally its most skilled workmen."[20] The trapper's life would "put the Indian in a position where he can stand upon his own feet and provide himself with the necessities of life,"[21] rather than depend on welfare dispensed by public authorities, with its demoralizing consequences. The administration did try to improve the native's situation by appealing to provincial and territorial authorities to give him a preferred position in using wildlife resources while imposing further restrictions on his white competitors. As for assisting Indians to develop other resources, it took a cautious wait-and-see position, and not until 1938–39 did it set up a revolving fund from which loans could be made for purchasing stock, equipment, or machinery, clearing land, or developing reserves in other ways.

Most economic development programs were planned and managed at the local level. A good example was the one at the McIntyre Bay Reserve (on Lake Nipigon) that made sixty-five families once more self-supporting. Working together, they cleared forty acres and planted enough vegetables for their needs, cut logs and built houses, mills, a warehouse, barn, icehouse, toolsheds, and local roads. They established a sawmill, a shingle mill, a planing and edging mill, and gained a contract to manufacture boxes for the local fishery. The experiment was largely self-financing, requiring only a small amount from the band's fund. The province of Alberta during the late thirties attempted an even larger program as a way of rehabilitating the uprooted Métis populations of its northern districts. A number of colonies were established for them on the basis of 320 acres of land to a family, and funding and advisers were provided to direct the development of these Métis Reserves. By 1949 there were seven such projects made up of 1,365 Métis settlers.

Another economic option, one initiated by a private group, was the handicrafts industry. Wilfrid Bovey, president of the Canadian Handicrafts Guild, urged in 1933 that the federal government should provide backing to develop ancestral native arts as a source of badly needed income and a lift to morale. The administration supported the program by organizing exhibitions of native art, established a warehouse and wholesale outlet in Ottawa, and arranged to expand the trade. Training classes were set up, and old arts were revived while guild and government tried to increase the number and improve the quality of the products. That the program still lacked aggressive drive can be seen from the North Pacific Planning Project's later recommendations that handicrafts production should be greatly expanded and the U.S. system of opening craft centres and selling work direct to interested visitors should be attempted.

The extremely grave situation caused by the widespread deterioration in the natives' health was coming to the notice of socially conscious organizations and persons. Traditionally the department had relied on the missionary organizations, which built and operated hospitals for their largely native followers in connection with their religious and charitable work. It assisted these hospitals sometimes by grants in aid of construction and equipment and regularly by per-diem payments on behalf of Indian patients, only rarely building and operating its own hospitals. Similarly, it relied mainly on local physicians, who were paid for services rendered or by a fixed-retainer arrangement, but sometimes it also employed its own physicians. The department in 1922 also began hiring travelling nurses to visit reserves, inspect sanitation and health conditions, and instruct the women in sanitary and dietary practices and in home making generally.

Not until 1927, however, when the department appointed a full-time medical superintendent, can it be said to have made proper provision to discharge its enormous, growing responsibility for native health. The new superintendent, Dr. E.L. Stone, who as an Indian agent at Norway House had launched a serious effort to curb the spread of tuberculosis and other diseases in his agency, speedily drew up public health regulations, set up nursing stations, ordered active cases of infection kept out of boarding schools, and stepped up the campaign against tuberculosis. Despite all his efforts, however, the per capita medical spending for natives in 1930 was below half that for the population as a whole – and this the single group of Canadians who unquestionably had greater need than any other for good medical care.

The acute northern native health problem during the thirties – indicated by the recorded decline in the Indian populations of the three
Northwest Territories agencies from 4,455 in 1916 to 3,627 in 1944
(half of it occurring during the 1930s) – was addressed by policemen
and medical personnel who visited the sick by dogteam, motorboat,
automobile, or airplane, inspected sanitary conditions in hospitals and
schools, and regularly examined the Indians at the annual treaty pay
gatherings. The northern hospitals had been planned for regular medical service and were not equipped to cope with a major disease of epidemic proportions such as tuberculosis was becoming. The campaign
against trachoma, fortunately, was easily, cheaply, and successfully
waged once the disease was recognized. Doctors, school teachers, and
others were alerted, and five years after the counterattack was
launched in 1934 the incidence of the disease had been cut by 50 per
cent. Unfortunately, the dental problems that Dr. Price and others had
reported were not easily capable of solution, and only such small
assistance as the department's limited funds could provide was
offered. Minor dental work was done on the teeth of children in
schools, but for adults the budget would allow for nothing beyond
extractions. Indians themselves were expected to pay part of the costs
of plates or other dental work.

Little treatment was available to keep tuberculosis, the principal
threat, from spreading rapidly. Scott estimated in 1931 that there were
at least 5,000 active cases whose treatment would require a yearly minimum of $1,000 per person but for which only $150,000 was available.
The appropriation did not increase appreciably in ensuing years, and
the branch, making the best of its situation, accepted as priorities "the
clearing of residential schools of active tuberculosis cases; the examination and survey of the most accessible reserves, and the isolation
and treatment of the Indians found to have active tuberculosis."[22] And
these were only the most accessible cases; more remote groups had to
suffer with little hope of relief. Only a few cases – 358 in 1938 and 512
in 1939 – were taken to special hospitals for treatment, and not until
1939 was the Indian Affairs Branch preparing to establish its own institutions and sanatoriums to cope as effectively as possible with the disease. Unquestionably it would have liked to do far more, but the health
budget put that completely out of the question.

That budget, $1.05 million in 1931–32, was actually reduced to
$793,000 in 1933–34, and by 1939–40 was still only $1.478 million,
completely inadequate even to start an effective campaign against the
now overwhelming tuberculosis problem. The thirties might have
brought more realistic understanding of native Canadians' medical and
other problems, but they provided only grossly inadequate means

with which to fight disease. A vigorous medical onslaught would not come until after 1945, when responsibility for the health – and more besides – of the native Canadian passed into the hands of a well-funded, well-staffed, specialized Department of National Health and Welfare. Armed with a new goal of extending the opportunities and responsibilities of full citizenship to native persons, federal administrators would then embark on the difficult tasks of conducting them through the uncharted shoals of Canada's post-war economy and society.

CHAPTER 7

The Northern Territories, 1921–1940: Advancing Administrative and Mining Frontiers

I

For the Yukon, the two decades between the wars were a prosaic time during which precipitate population decline and economic deterioration were finally arrested. The economic growth, however slow, accounted for a small increase in the number of white settlers from about 2,500 to a little over 3,000 and in the total population from 4,157 in 1921 to 4,914 in 1941. The main component of the Yukon economy, as in the past, was the gold-mining operation in the Klondike district, where an unrelenting struggle with the ever leaner auriferous gravels continued. Yields fell below a yearly $1 million after 1923, with annual productions of 30,000 to 45,000 ounces persisting until the mid-thirties. Then the sharp rise in the price of gold greatly improved the situation.

A new management at Yukon Consolidated Gold Corporation, which produced 85 per cent of the territory's gold, launched an ambitious modernization program by enlarging the hydro-electric power plant on the north fork of the Klondike River and acquiring new power equipment. Using larger, more powerful dredges and a workforce that reached 680 men on occasion in a lengthened operating season, the company was able to treat over 10 million cubic yards of gravel in 1939. Preparation of the gravel prior to dredging led to major savings. In the twenties the company introduced a new system of drilling holes into the gravel at seventy-five-foot intervals into which large quantities of river water were pumped to thaw the gravel in advance of the dredges. By the late thirties, other refinements were added – intensive

174

drilling to locate the best-paying gravels and stripping away the frozen overburden by hydraulic means to allow the sun's rays to soften the gravel. Gold output from the Yukon reached heights of 72,000 and 88,000 ounces in 1938 and 1939, more gold than had been recovered in any year since 1919 and in dollar terms ahead even of the value for 1907, the last year of the original mining phase of the Klondike.

A second mining industry based on rich silver-lead ores sporadically helped the economy of the Mayo district on Stewart River. The Treadwell Yukon Company, owner of the area's only concentrating plant, shipped concentrates and high-grade ores to Tacoma, Washington, for refining. Transportation limitations kept production at 10,000 tons per annum, and low prices and exhausted ore supplies even caused the mill to be closed between 1932 and 1935. Then improved prices and the discovery of additional ore reserves brought a short-term revival, but the company finally went into liquidation in 1942. A small, low-grade coalbed at Tantalus Butte, yielding less than a thousand tons of coal annually for local markets, was the one remaining mining operation of note.

For the rest, hunting and trapping by resident whites and natives, and prospecting for minerals continued; mining claims were staked, timber permits were issued, and a homestead or two was patented each year. Every spring ushered in a contingent of federal geologists and land surveyors and groups of sportsmen hunters. Above all, each summer during the twenties brought a considerable influx of tourists, mostly from the United States, to visit Alaska and the Klondike. Generally they travelled from Skagway to Whitehorse by train, transferring to steamers that carried them to Dawson and into Alaska for a connection at Fairbanks with the Alaska Railroad and a return to the ship at Anchorage. The employees of the tourist industry (including the workers on the boats) swelled the Yukon's population every summer. The territory emptied as soon as the seasonal visiting ended and workers returned outside or gathered to winter in Dawson, whose population rose slowly from 819 to 1,043 in the thirties, or Whitehorse, which increased from 541 to 754.

The Yukon had been given elective political institutions and its own civil service during the exciting, optimistic days before 1914. When the subsequent decline of the economy and population reduced the effective power of those institutions, it correspondingly enhanced federal control until it was almost as complete as it was in the Northwest Territories. The triennially elected three-member legislative council sat for a week or ten days each year in Dawson under the presidency of the controller (formerly gold commissioner) to pass and amend territorial ordinances, some of which implemented relevant federal legislation such as that for old age pensions. It managed the local revenue, oversaw the departments of the territorial civil service that regulated municipalities, hospitals, and schools, built local public works, licensed the businesses and professions, and the like. Of course, the degree of autonomy was limited in practice. The Northwest Territories and Yukon Branch of the Department of the Interior supervised the Council's legislative activities; federal grants comprised a large part of the territory's income; and federal officials controlled the all-important natural resources sectors (apart from wildlife) and performed many normally provincial functions throughout the territory. Not until the Second World War had wrought momentous changes in the Yukon did the territory resume the paths of economic, political, and social advance.

The Northwest Territories also seemed to stagnate during the twenties after the anticipated oil boom fizzled out and the two wells below Fort Norman were closed in 1925. It was true that improved access to the region and good fur prices attracted white trappers and fur traders while the increasing scale of government activity brought more policemen, administrators, medical and missionary personnel to live in the vast area. Still, the 1931 census listed only 1,007 non-native (white and Métis) residents, barely one tenth of a total population of 9,316 that included 4,615 Indians and about half of Canada's 7,100 Inuit. Except for 40 whites in the Eastern Arctic and another 25 in the Hudson Bay region, the non-native population was located mainly along the Slave-Mackenzie waterway, half the number in the vicinities of Forts Smith, Resolution, Providence, and Simpson and Aklavik. Most were single or separated males, the bulk engaged in the wildlife industries, in professional work, or in the public service.

There was a considerable growth in RCMP manpower, detachments of which had been opened by the end of the twenties in virtually every centre on the Mackenzie waterway, at Fort Liard, at major centres in the Western Arctic (where the schooner *St. Roch* was introduced in 1928 to patrol the coasts and move supplies), and in the Hudson Bay and Eastern Arctic regions. Another important group of government employees was the Royal Canadian Corps of Signals (RCCS), which built and operated wireless stations along the waterway (Fort Simpson, 1924; Fort Resolution, 1927; Fort Norman, 1930) that were linked with still others operated by the Departments of Marine and of Railways and Canals and with stations on major vessels, at trading posts, and, after 1928, at aviation companies' bases.

The process of introducing trading, transportation, and administrative activities into new districts accounted for the growth of some communities during the twenties. A striking case was Aklavik, which was first a sleep camp between Fort McPherson and Herschel Island and then a small fur-trading post. A Church of England mission arrived in 1919, then a Roman Catholic mission, then hospitals of both denominations, police post, wireless station, post office, and more trading posts. Aklavik became the terminus of the river transport (and airmail service) systems and the main departure point for the Western Arctic. The spread of similar functions during the twenties to the Inuit country accounted for the appearance of small settlements at such strategic locations as Coppermine, Cambridge Bay, Chesterfield Inlet, Lake Harbour, and Pangnirtung.

The economy and society of the Territories settlements in the 1920s, largely cut off from contact with the outside world except for an annual ship or two, revolved around the trading-post routine. Existence was largely self-sufficient; settlers hunted and fished for most of their food, cut wood for fuel, raised vegetables where arable land permitted, and travelled about by boat in summer or by dogteam in winter. They formed their own local societies and found their own entertainments among the store, government, and mission personnel and the miscellaneous trappers and prospectors who made the settlement their base. Each year would bring a considerable turnover, making the autumns a time for new arrivals to get acquainted with their neighbours and surroundings. The disruptions seriously hampered proper development of permanent communities.

The quality of life was improved during the twenties by the radio, which came into use to bring news of the outside world and fill idle hours and, assisted by wireless telegraph, permitted reports to be transmitted to the outside. The posts could offer canned and packaged foodstuffs, cosmetics, and manufactured clothing. Homes boasted hand-wound gramophones, and motion pictures made the rounds among settlements. When water travel was improved by motorboats, the more frequent calls at settlements meant much better mail service. Post offices were opened in the main centres, and by 1926, 80,000 pounds of mail were carried into the District of Mackenzie. Aklavik was then receiving up to five deliveries by the river steamers during the summers but only one or two by the winter packets, which continued to make deliveries from Fort McMurray – a gruelling 3,332-mile round trip with 150-mile stretches between settlements, in which the drivers pushed their sled-dogs over snowdrifts and piled ice and through blizzards. By the end of the 1920s, however, airplane service had made the heroic "Winter Packet" unnecessary; Aklavik received no fewer than twenty-three airmail deliveries during the winter of 1929–30.

The coming of the airplane drastically altered living and working

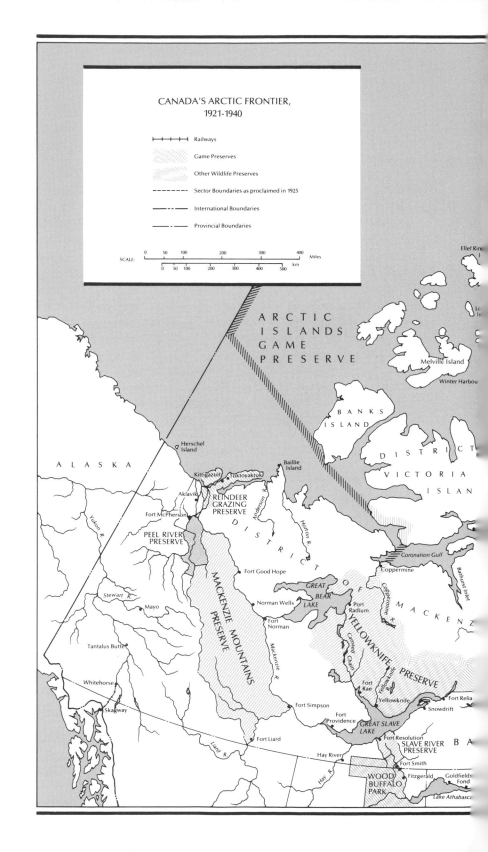

CANADA'S ARCTIC FRONTIER,
1921-1940

├┼┼┼┼┤ Railways

Game Preserves

Other Wildlife Preserves

-------- Sector Boundaries as proclaimed in 1925

—··—··— International Boundaries

—·—·— Provincial Boundaries

SCALE: 0   50 100   200   300   400 Miles
        0 50 100   200   300   400 500 km

ARCTIC
ISLANDS
GAME
PRESERVE

Ellef Rin
I

Lo
Is

Melville Island

Winter Harbou

BANKS
ISLAND

DISTRICT

VICTORIA

ISLAN

ALASKA

Herschel
Island

Baillie
Island

Kittigazuit   Tuktoyaktuk

Aklavik

REINDEER
GRAZING
PRESERVE

Fort McPherson

Anderson R.

Horton R.

DISTRICT

OF

MACKENZ

PEEL RIVER
PRESERVE

Yukon R.

Fort Good Hope

Coronation Gulf

Coppermine

Bathurst Inlet

GREAT
BEAR
LAKE

Port
Radium

Coppermine R.

Stewart R.

Mayo

MACKENZIE MOUNTAINS PRESERVE

Norman Wells

Fort
Norman

YELLOWKNIFE PRESERVE

Camsell Chain

Tantalus Butte

Mackenzie R.

Fort
Rae

Yellowknife R.

Fort Relia

Whitehorse

Yellowknife

Snowdrift

Fort Simpson

Skagway

Fort
Providence

GREAT SLAVE
LAKE

BA

Liard R.

Fort Liard

Fort Resolution

SLAVE RIVER
PRESERVE

Hay River

Fort Smith

Hay R.

WOOD
BUFFALO
PARK

Fitzgerald

Goldfields
Fond

Lake Athabasca

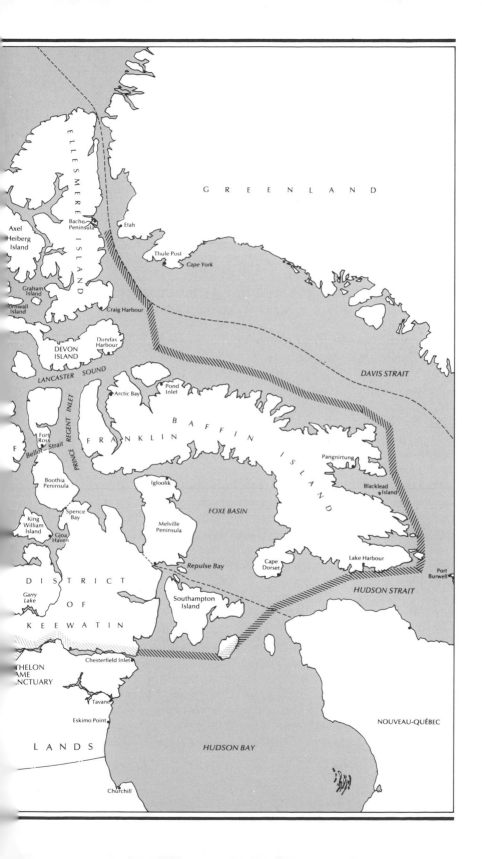

ELLESMERE ISLAND

Axel Heiberg Island

Graham Island

Cornwall Island

DEVON ISLAND

Bache Peninsula

Etah

Thule Post

Cape York

GREENLAND

Craig Harbour

Dundas Harbour

LANCASTER SOUND

DAVIS STRAIT

Fort Ross

Bellot Strait

PRINCE REGENT INLET

Arctic Bay

Pond Inlet

FRANKLIN

BAFFIN ISLAND

Pangnirtung

Blacklead Island

Boothia Peninsula

Spence Bay

King William Island

Gjoa Haven

Igloolik

Melville Peninsula

FOXE BASIN

Lake Harbour

Port Burwell

DISTRICT

OF

KEEWATIN

Garry Lake

Repulse Bay

Southampton Island

Cape Dorset

HUDSON STRAIT

THELON GAME SANCTUARY

Chesterfield Inlet

Tavane

Eskimo Point

LANDS

HUDSON BAY

NOUVEAU-QUÉBEC

Churchill

conditions, even though planes still carried small cargoes and the absence of landing fields meant they had to be equipped with floats or skis and were inoperative for a month every freeze-up and break-up season. Still, they greatly reduced the dependence on ships for annual deliveries of goods and for carrying passengers, including patients needing transportation outside for medical reasons. One of their great assets was the lift they gave the settlers' morale. As one resident of Fort Resolution reported in 1929, "The North has been brought to civilization through the aid of air mail, and the depressing isolation of our winter is soon to be forgotten."[1]

Aviation may also be credited with introducing the mining industry with its attendant effects into the Territories. There had been intermittent prospecting in the District of Mackenzie ever since Klondike-bound hopefuls had passed through the country; interest revived fitfully after 1918, though prospecting was restricted to the short open-water season and little serious work could be done except by wintering in the region. Still, the successes in Northern Ontario and at Flin Flon focused the sights of mining companies on mineral possibilities in the Shield's vast expanses in Keewatin and along its western margin intersected by the great lakes of the North. In 1927 the Nipissing Mining Company organized a traditional prospecting foray that concentrated particularly on the Tavane-Ferguson rivers district west of Hudson Bay and on the Thelon-Hanbury route from Baker Lake to Great Slave Lake. (It was prospectors from this operation that while travelling from Great Slave Lake to Baker Lake discovered the emaciated remains of the John Hornby party.)

In the meantime techniques of air-supported prospecting operations were becoming perfected in Central Canada. In 1928 a large-scale airborne onslaught was launched on the northern parts of the Shield by the newly organized Dominion Explorers (Domex) and Northern Aerial Mining Explorations (NAME), and by certain larger mining companies – Consolidated Mining and Smelting in 1928, and Dome, McIntyre, and Mining Corporation of Canada in 1929. These organizations operated from bases that were accessible by water or rail, such as Baker Lake and Fort Reliance, and the Barrens resounded with the flights. Lonely outposts of the fur trade became centres of unaccustomed activity, periodically visited by planes, officials, and prospectors.

Prospecting operations in 1928 concentrated on the region west of Hudson Bay, then in 1929 shifted to the western margin of the Shield north to the southeastern section of Great Bear Lake and to Bathurst Inlet on the Arctic coast, where the long-known copper occurrences were the subject of a late-season staking rush by several companies. Supplies were sealifted from Vancouver and the prospectors flown in from Stony Rapids and Fort Reliance. A newsworthy event of the prospecting season was the disappearance somewhere on the Barrens of a Domex plane carrying Colonel MacAlpine and several passengers, including Richard Pearce, an editor of the *Northern Miner* of Toronto, during an inspection trip between Baker Lake and Bathurst Inlet. News reports from the region were featured around the world as scores of planes scoured the area. Fortunately the MacAlpine group, unlike some other parties forced down in this period, made its way to safety on foot, arriving tired and hungry but none the worse for the ordeal at Cambridge Bay, from which the Hudson's Bay Company's wireless quickly flashed the good news to the outside world.

By then the Depression had struck, and the market for metals as well as financing for costly airborne prospecting operations rapidly dried up. Domex and NAME soon abandoned their prospecting programs in the Territories, and activity on the Coppermine front was rapidly halted. Some small interest continued in the Great Bear Lake sector, however, thanks to Gilbert LaBine, manager of the moribund Eldorado Gold Mines, Limited. While flying out of the district in the fall of 1929 LaBine had spotted the cobalt bloom on a cliffside on the east coast of Great Bear Lake that J.M. Bell had reported in the first survey of the area in 1900. LaBine returned with a partner in April 1930 and soon discovered silver-pitchblende occurrences. These were traced and staked at two sites by Eldorado agents during the summer of 1930 and the ensuing winter. After the news spread, nearly three hundred men descended on the remote location in 1932, scouring the surrounding country and the interconnected Camsell River system of lakes and rivers linking Great Bear and Great Slave lakes. In spite of the Depression, many companies were incorporated in Toronto to mine the riches of the region, inspired by reports that pitchblende samples assayed at $7,225 to $8,600 radium values per ton and by the jump in Eldorado share prices to $1.27 from $0.16.

Only five of the companies attempted to develop their claims at the southeastern corner of Great Bear Lake, and Eldorado alone was successful in establishing a mine and settlement in what was one of Canada's most remarkable mining enterprises. Without backing from financiers or the major mining companies, Gilbert and Charles LaBine built their company from the proceeds of rich silver surface ores and from minute quantities of radium contained in the pitchblende, and from unissued company shares, into a $5-million concern and retained control of it to the end. Before long Eldorado boasted a unique mine, concentrating plant, and settlement at Port Radium, a river transport system between Great Bear Lake and the railhead at Waterways (the Northern Transportation Company), and perhaps the most advanced radium extraction plant in the world at Port Hope, Ontario – an enterprise so vital to the war effort that it was expropriated in its entirety in 1942 and turned into a Crown corporation. Imperial Oil reactivated its oilwells and refinery at Norman Wells in 1932 to supply the fuel and power requirements of the new establishments. The oil, as well as all other supplies that could not be delivered by plane, had to be moved to Fort Norman on the Mackenzie during the short open-water period, then hauled up the shallow, rock-strewn Great Bear River with its miles of more or less continuous rapids, and finally shipped across the 200 miles of sometimes stormy Great Bear Lake. The process required four different boats to deal with the varied navigational conditions along the route, plus a portage road and eventually an 8½-mile oil pipeline around the rapids section.

Eldorado for a time seemed immune to the economic effects of the Depression in view of the rarity and very high price of its chief product, radium. Yet the market for radium was tiny, and the company had to compete for its share with the established Belgian monopoly. As a result, the price gradually was cut in half, and unsaleable radium and radium concentrates piled up at Port Hope alongside larger quantities of unmarketable by-product uranium salts. When the best ores were mined out, the company suspended operations at Port Radium and put the mine on caretaker status in 1939, turning the camp and settlement into a virtual ghost town.

By then, a second mining centre was rising 290 miles to the south on the North Arm of Great Slave Lake – the gold-mining camp and town of Yellowknife. Prospecting and travel to and from Great Bear Lake along the Camsell River chain led to discoveries of attractive gold showings along the shores of Yellowknife Bay at the mouth of Yellowknife River. Staking began in 1934, and the ensuing discoveries inspired great interest and incorporation of new companies on the Toronto stock exchanges (where even more excitement was aroused at first by the finds on the north shore of Lake Athabasca, on which the gold-mining camp of Goldfields was arising by 1935). The lakeshore at Yellowknife was covered by claims, and several groups were developing their holdings in 1935 while prospectors were ranging over the 50,000-square-mile Yellowknife Mining District. Additional finds attracted more prospectors, the peak year being 1938, when over thirty companies were active in the district and 3,500 claims were staked.

Soon three gold mines were in production at Yellowknife, two owned by Consolidated and one by Negus, a Toronto-financed enterprise; in the immediate area were also the Ptarmigan and Thompson-Lundmark mines, both owned by Consolidated. The Second World War brought the staking rushes and mine development to an end and also closed the five mines after 1942, in which year they produced 99,000 ounces of gold. From September 5, 1938, when the Northwest Territories' first gold brick was poured at Consolidated's Con Mine, until the closure, the Yellowknife district mines had recovered 366,000 ounces of gold. Consolidated also built and put into operation (1941) the Territories' first hydro-electric power station, a 4,700-horsepower plant on the Yellowknife River, seventeen miles north of the community. On the shores of Great Slave Lake within a five-year period a large, modern, permanent settlement had arisen that soon was transforming the economic, social, and administrative complexion of the Northwest Territories.

The main economic consequences of the advance of the mining frontier into the Territories were unquestionably in the field of transportation. The extraction industry's need to import heavy machinery and supplies and export ores and mineral concentrates, plus the requirements of a modern white society with standards like those of Canadians outside, demanded an improved river transport system, a greatly expanded air service, and the beginnings of overland transportation using trails and pipelines. River transport, still the cheapest and main means for moving freight, changed in style and in scale as the traffic doubled and redoubled, to reach 26,460 tons by 1938. The greater freight volumes, as well as the gradual loss of passengers to the airlines, led operators to replace their slow steamboats with small, powerful, manoeuvrable diesel tugs and to increase the size and number of their freight-carrying barges. Some of these were built to handle specific cargoes – bulk tankers for petroleum products (a major commodity), refrigerator barges for perishable foodstuffs, and reinforced barges to carry heavy cargoes. Equipment also was shifted from place to place to deal with frequently changing traffic needs, and there was even an encouraging increase in southbound (upstream) freight to help balance the one-sided downstream flow.

To handle the greater tonnages, the tug operations were speeded up and the seasons were extended to the limit, putting pressure on the government to reduce or eliminate the worst bottlenecks and provide better docking and harbour facilities. Northern Transportation Company, with its Sorel-built, steel diesel-powered tugs *Radium Queen* and *Radium King*, its numerous barges, and its improved portage road around the Slave River rapids above Fort Smith, challenged the Hudson's Bay Company's domination of the river transport service. That company perforce modernized its river fleet to handle its own growing traffic and compete for the now greater amount of commercial freight. Thanks to the improvements in the service and to the competition, river shipping rates to users were reduced, besides which pressure from the industry and Edmonton businessmen brought a lower freight rate over the important Edmonton-Waterways railway (NAR) portion of the route.

The new economy and society called for better air services than had previously been available in the region. Company and government officials and inspectors were using planes frequently on their business and administrative duties. Eldorado found it worthwhile to lease a plane to fly loads of radium concentrates to convenient river points or to the railhead and bring back passengers, perishable foodstuffs, or needed supplies, thereby helping to overcome their community's handicaps of short seasons and long distances. Regular air service increased the quantity of airmail carried into the District of Mackenzie between 1934 and 1938, the most active interwar period, by over 400 per cent. In fact, the few thousand settlers of this northern area accounted for an eighth of all airmail delivered in Canada in 1937 and 1938. No longer did travellers have to wait at trading centres for planes that might be flying in the desired directions: by the end of the thirties, a weekly scheduled service between Edmonton and Aklavik supplied the communities along the Mackenzie waterway, and another service linked Edmonton with Peace River, Yellowknife, and Port Radium. These contract mail services were provided by the two main companies active in the District of Mackenzie, units of the nation-wide Canadian Airways operating from the regional centres of Edmonton, Prince Albert, and Prince George, and the Edmonton-owned Mackenzie Air Services, organized in 1932. Other companies and individual bush fliers offered charter flights between northern centres and around their hinterlands. Altogether, aviation became a reliable, effective transportation medium in the District of Mackenzie during the thirties.

Even motorized overland transportation made an appearance late in the thirties in emergencies when water transport failed to complete deliveries before freeze-up, stranding supplies and halting important construction programs. There being no roads, such freight was carried by tractor trains that crossed the thick ice of quiet rivers and lakes in the dead of winter and occasionally over the frozen muskegs. Trails had first to be located and marked, then roughly prepared by clearing the brush and improving the grades at steep inclines. The tractor train consisted of one or two diesel tractors pulling as many as six heavy, freight-laden sledges, the rear unit often being a caboose with living quarters for the crew that kept the train plodding onward round the clock as long as ground conditions permitted. Even trucks could use the route until the track deteriorated with the approach of spring. This kind of transport was very expensive because of the high cost of equipment and preparation of the short-term road, to say nothing of the tractors lost through the ice of lakes and rivers. The rates were far higher than for water freight. A 300-ton load cost $150 a ton delivered from Waterways to Yellowknife in 1937–38, so that the method was truly one of last resort. Nevertheless, tractor trains were used for comparatively short overland hauls, like that from Yellowknife seventy-five miles to the mining properties under development at Gordon Lake.

As it became clear that transport was incapable of meeting all the needs of the Yellowknife mines and community, settlers began looking for a cheaper long-distance overland route from the Peace River railhead to Hay River, then along the margins of frozen Great Slave Lake to Yellowknife. That route was pioneered during the winter of 1938–39 and used again in 1939–40 to deliver equipment for the hydro-electric station on the Yellowknife River. The improvements made during the first winter survived in some land portions of the trail so that trucks could be employed on much of the route, leaving only final sections to the tractor trains. Thus the future Mackenzie Highway was gradually being brought into existence.

The mining industry introduced a new type of community completely different in character from the trading and administrative centres. It started with small temporary camps where workmen, mechanics, and tradesmen were assembled by a company striving to develop a mine, then dispersed when the project was abandoned. Tents or crude bunkhouses could suffice for these. But producing mines and oilwells required more permanent settlements that entailed building houses as well as mining plants and providing utilities, services, and amenities appropriate to the scale and prospects of the enterprise – or within the companies' means, for no assistance from the territorial administration was forthcoming. Norman Wells, for instance, operated in summer and was closed in winter until 1938, when the management decided to keep the wells producing through the year. The settlement became a permanent community as a result of local developments during the Second World War. Port Radium (previously Cameron Bay), on the other hand, started out in 1932 as a small community of 200 with a general store, a café, many tents, and a few wooden buildings. The following year the townsite was surveyed, streets were laid out, lots were leased, twenty-five buildings were erected, and a few government agencies – post office, RCMP detachment, RCCS station – made their appearance. The community speedily deteriorated, however, when prospecting and development moved elsewhere and Eldorado established separate facilities (camp buildings, houses, medical and other services) for their employees at the mine site, leaving only a handful of settlers, the HBC store, post-master, and RCMP at Port Radium, which, like the mine, was abandoned in 1939.

Yellowknife was a different matter. The future capital of the North-west Territories began to take shape in 1937 when a dozen or so settlers established themselves along the shore of Yellowknife Bay. During the summer of 1938 lots were surveyed and leased, 100 buildings were erected, and a resident population of 500 (in addition to the 500 men at work in the surrounding district) came together. The 1938 settle-ment included a bank branch, druggist, the first resident lawyer in the Territories, and a newspaper (another "first"). By 1939 the mines were employing 300 men whose sizeable payroll encouraged a whole range of new businesses and services, and there were one hundred families in residence. The settlement, having overflowed Latham Island, was moving up the shore of the bay; Jolliffe Island was the locale of the oil storage tanks, lumberyards, and other "heavy" industry. The presence of two mining operations, both close to the settlement, probably pre-vented the rise of a separate company town. Yellowknife was, in any case, the natural centre for an area with good prospects. The tie between mines and community became indissoluble in 1939 when Yellowknife was incorporated as a municipality and the Consolidated and Negus mines were included within the town limits.

The new communities, especially Yellowknife, had little contact with the native groups and the fur-trading economy that were the essence of the older trading centres; indeed, Indians from nearby Fort Rae quickly felt unwelcome in Yellowknife and avoided visiting the town. Instead, they were designed to promote and facilitate working and living in a modern industrial setting. It was intended that they establish the same sort of society in the District of Mackenzie that pre-vailed elsewhere in Canada, one that afforded maximum opportunities for advancement and self-fulfilment to their inhabitants, whose com-munal institutions could be used to further those goals.

The new society was notable for diversity. The white population of the District of Mackenzie increased during the decade 1931–41 from 782 to more than 2,400 persons (in a total Territories population of 12,028), almost all attributable to the new economy. The census for 1941 revealed large increases in the employment categories of miners, mechanics, stationary and other engineers, carpenters, clerical work-ers, and service personnel, and reductions in numbers of persons representing the old order – persons engaged in trade, policemen, and public employees (reflecting the wartime situation in 1941) – except for an increase from 105 to 143 in mission workers (reflecting the expansion of their work during the thirties). The new society was composed mainly of persons of British and diverse European extractions in the midst of the indigenous Métis or Halfbreeds (282), Inuit (5,404), and status Indians (4,052). The newcomers were predominantly male, particularly in the age groups most likely to be on the move.

Both societies, old and new, made use of the new material improvements to the quality of life in the North. Radios became generally available in the 1930s (at least to the whites) as a source of information and entertainment from afar (the Canadian Radio Broadcasting Commission's Northern Messenger Service) or near (the beginnings of broadcasting from certain RCCS stations, notably Aklavik). The improved shipping made all manner of supplies more readily available and cheaper than before, and the volume of mass-circulation magazines, mail-order catalogues, and newspapers increased. Especially important was the relatively cheap fuel oil Imperial Oil shipped by barge-loads from Norman Wells and stored locally in the bulk storage tanks that sprang up as prominent features of the settlements along the waterways. Local generating plants provided electric lighting and power to settlers at most major centres, reducing the risk of fires that previously had been only too frequent. Buildings benefited from better construction methods and insulating materials.

Interest also was expressed in curbing the effects of the ice jams and floods, erosion of waterfront properties, and deteriorating sanitary conditions that springtime brought. A survey in 1938 found that sewage disposal was a serious problem because of the haphazard, unplanned growth of settlements, the annual springtime influxes of large numbers of Indians and their dogs, and the use of water sources that tended to become contaminated. The report recommended that proper water supply and sewage disposal systems be installed in as many settlements as possible and that medical officers monitor local situations. But a sanitary control ordinance had to wait until 1941. Only in Yellowknife was significant action taken. When poor sanitary conditions during the summer of 1938 made it necessary, the water supply was chlorinated, public latrines were installed, and a water tower was built as the start of a water delivery system.

As the thirties drew to a close, Yellowknife was the one sizeable modern industrial community in the Northwest Territories that had good prospects of long-term survival and growth. Its needs indicated how far the existing administrative arrangements would have to be revised to accommodate the settlement advancing into the region. In fact, the Yellowknife community's campaign to bring about these reforms, and the changes that ensued, were important steps in both the political and the social development of the Territories. After gaining the status of an incorporated municipality the settlement could pass bylaws on local public works, fire and traffic regulation, health and sanitation, schools, and poor relief. It was empowered to levy taxes on real property, license business, and collect poll taxes. The town was administered by a board of two elected and three appointed trustees, but it was intended that the board should evolve into a fully elected body. The schools for arriving families were provided by establishing a public (and later a separate) school district, managed by elected school trustees, financed from local tax levies as well as territorial government grants, and following a southern (in this case Alberta) curriculum, teacher standards, and system of operations. In these ways the gold-mining community of Yellowknife established a pattern for future municipal evolution in the Northwest Territories.

II

The task of adapting Northwest Territories institutions to meet the needs of the new economic-social order was the responsibility of the federal government agencies charged with administering and legislating for the northern territories. Prior to the late thirties that administration was concerned mostly with protecting the region and its native majority against the effects of too rapid changes and had been content to let sleeping dogs lie. Federal control was more complete in the Northwest Territories than in the Yukon; the legislative council for the Territories was still a body of seven high-ranking federal civil servants who met informally in one-day sittings in Ottawa as business required. Between 1921 and 1928 there were but seven sessions, then five in 1929, eleven in 1930, and by the late thirties fifteen a year on the average, held typically at two- and three-week intervals during the winters and bi-monthly in the summer months, when councillors were likely to be occupied with the heavy programs of their branches or absent from Ottawa on inspection or other duties.

The membership of the council changed considerably over the two decades. Only two of the original seven members, R.A. Gibson and Charles Camsell, remained for the entire time. The deputy superintendent-general of Indian Affairs joined the council in 1928, replacing a deceased officer of the Department of the Interior, and no fewer than four commissioners of the RCMP sat successively on the council. Other changes in personnel resulted from the political changes associated with the defeat of the Liberal government in 1930 and its return to office in 1935. The amalgamations of the Departments of Mines, Interior, and Indian Affairs into the Department of Mines and Resources carried the commissionership to Camsell, the deputy minister of the new department. In 1938, the distinguished undersecretary of state for external affairs, O.D. Skelton, seconded by H.L. Keenleyside, joined the council, as had A.L. Cumming (in 1936), who had served in the District of Mackenzie as mining inspector, district agent, and superintendent. The Council of the Northwest Territories actually resembled an interdepartmental committee of civil servants from the several branches of government most directly concerned with the management of that region. The sessions allowed these leading officials to exchange reports and views, suggest actions by their respective agencies, and concert joint programs. Representatives of other departments, such as National Health, Justice, Post Office, and External Affairs (before 1938), attended whenever matters involving their departments were being discussed.

For advice, the council could often refer to reports and opinions of the many RCMP officers, Indian agents, and scientists of the Department of Mines and the National Museum on situations observed in the North. Special reports were commissioned from experts such as L.T. Burwash (described as "Exploring Engineer"), or L.A. Giroux, an Alberta lawyer who toured the Mackenzie waterway in 1929 studying the territorial game regulations. A special session was held on May 1, 1925, to question Knud Rasmussen concerning the condition of the Canadian Inuit whom he had just finished investigating. Other experts who appeared were spokesmen for the Indian Affairs Branch, government wildlife specialists, and representatives of private groups such as the Hudson's Bay Company, mining companies, and the missionary organizations, particularly the redoubtable Bishop Breynat, a frequent visitor pleading the cause of the needy Indian or seeking financial or other assistance for the work of his church.

The council also had a legislative function, the power to enact new ordinances (of which there were about a dozen during the twenties, but many more after 1936), for it was the continuation of the Legislative Council and Legislative Assembly of the original North-West Territories. In fact, it inherited the whole corpus of unrepealed ordinances from the pre-1905 entity, no matter how inadequate, inappropriate, or even dangerous they were for the new Northwest Territories. Ordinances within the competence of the council were quite easily enacted, but those that required enabling legislation from parliament, such as the Eskimo Ruins Ordinance or the Fur Export Ordinance, took years (five years in the case of the latter) to become effective. As early as 1928 the council discussed the desirability of replacing the pre-1905 ordinances with a new and more appropriate series, but action did not begin in earnest until the late thirties, when events began to force its hand. It was possible to ignore some of the original ordinances as archaic and irrelevant, but others capable of being perverted to fraudulent ends had to be repealed. There was a large group that needed to be revised or repealed because unsuited to existing conditions, among them the Mechanics Lien, Small Debts, Steam Boiler, and Workmen's Compensation ordinances. New ones were needed to regulate the trades, occupations, and professions becoming established. The beginnings of motor traffic accounted for a Highway Traffic Ordinance and a Motor Vehicles Ordinance, but a distinctive Northwest Territories automobile licence plate did not appear until 1941.

The Fur Export Ordinance, which proposed to levy a royalty on all furs exported from the Territories to be paid by the exporter, was the one measure that aroused local opposition during the twenties. Independent traders collected many signatures on a petition contending it was taxation without representation and hence unlawful. The petition, plus a suggestion from D.F. Kellner, Progressive M.P. for Edmonton East, that the Territories should be represented in the House of Commons, were the only questionings of the council's management of territorial affairs during the 1920s. By the thirties, however, other challenges appeared as business interests and settlers began complaining about the unrepresentative character of the council and its alleged antipathy toward groups that saw themselves as promoters of the advance of civilization. As early as 1932 a Fort Smith merchant organized a petition calling for a resident commissioner and council of ten members, five of whom should be elected from the district, a sentiment that the Edmonton Conservative Association echoed. The council, challenged in this fashion, had a memorandum prepared listing points in defence of the established order: its members did not have to be paid and could call on the federal civil service for free expert advice; an appointed council, removed from political interference, was better able to attend to the needs and look after the welfare of the disfranchised native majority; Ottawa was well situated for communicating with the northern and eastern parts of the Territories and with the head offices of the corporations involved with the North. On the other hand, Fort Smith (the challengers' choice for capital) was a poor location apart from offering access to the District of Mackenzie; a council that met there would be exposed to pressures from local interests and the white community and less able than the Ottawa-based council to protect the interests of the natives.

Edmonton transportation, mining, and business interests involved in the development of the Mackenzie region inspired frequent applications to the council from the Edmonton and Northern Alberta Chamber of Mines for desirable aids and actions and the stationing of an agent with authority at Fort Smith to expedite decision making. The upshot was an instruction to A.L. Cumming, the district agent, to assume more responsibility and not to refer so many matters to Ottawa. The awakened interest in northern development was reflected in 1938–39 in the renewal of the proposal, emanating mainly from Edmonton and Northern Alberta but also enjoying some support in the District of Mackenzie, to give representation to the Northwest Territories in the House of Commons. Outside, a different reaction appeared in proposals to incorporate the region into the existing provinces by extending their boundaries north to the Arctic Ocean, as Clifford Sifton had suggested in 1905. British Columbia's drive for the Yukon was accentuated by the northern expansionist visions of its premier, T.D. Pattullo, who oscillated between promoting expansion northward to annex the Yukon, or expansion north along the 120th meridian, his province's eastern boundary, to include a large part of the District of Mackenzie as well. The Alberta legislature went so far as to pass a resolution by a 50–1 vote in March 1939 calling for the attachment of practically the entire District of Mackenzie to Alberta. Nothing was done, however, and the council's sway over the Northwest Territories continued unchanged until after the Second World War.

The administrative side of the council entailed overseeing (but not controlling) increasing numbers of federal government agents, for it employed no staff of its own until it opened the liquor store in Yellowknife in 1938. In their individual capacities the councillors controlled and directed the operations of their agencies and, when agreed, arranged for them to carry out assignments on the council's behalf. The agency directly concerned with administering the territories, whose director was a key member of council, was the small Northwest Territories and Yukon Branch (after 1936, Bureau of Northwest Territories and Yukon Affairs). A reorganization in the thirties placed two regional superintendents under the director, one responsible for the District of Mackenzie and stationed at Fort Smith, the other for the Eastern Arctic stationed normally in Ottawa, whose major function included directing the annual Eastern Arctic Patrol. The establishment at Fort Smith was headed by J.A. McDougal as district agent, by Cumming from 1934 to 1936, then by three other officials in succession, two of them government physicians. The establishment at Fort Smith during the twenties was described thus:

> The local organization now consists of a District Agent whose duties include those of Mining Recorder, Dominion Lands Agent, Crown Timber Agent, Superintendent of Wood Buffalo Park and

Chief Game Warden. He is a Justice of the Peace and a Notary Public. He is also Postmaster under the Post Office Department and has charge of wharfs and aids to navigation for the Department of Marine and Fisheries. His staff consists of an assistant and two clerks, a park warden and twelve game wardens and four seasonal fire wardens for the Simpson and Liard Districts.[2]

The combining of offices in one man was applied in other centres whenever the branch felt a new function was needed and an official even remotely suitable was already on the spot. Thus Dr. J.A. Urquhart, the branch's physician at Aklavik, was made supervisor of the reindeer herd that had recently arrived in his district. At new settlements, however, the branch had to appoint its own representative. In 1933 it dispatched M. Meikle to Cameron Bay as its agent; in 1936, after the need at Port Radium had ceased, it transferred him to Fort Smith. In similar fashion in 1938 it sent J.E. Gibben, a lawyer, to Yellowknife to guide that settlement through its legal and administrative growing pains. Lastly, the branch had an inspection service, performed until 1934 by J.F. Moran, who visited the Mackenzie on its behalf almost every summer. O.S. Finnie, head of the branch from 1920 to 1931, made a similar survey in 1929 that included the first plane flight from Aklavik to Dawson to continue the Yukon leg of his inspection. The area superintendents performed the inspections after 1934, besides which officials and members of council took advantage of the improved air service to visit the region during most summers.

The RCMP was the most important single administrative agency in the North during the interwar period. From the more than thirty detachments in the Yukon and Territories its men represented the federal and territorial governments in their districts. During the 1920s the manpower and number of detachments in the Northwest Territories were increased, then during the thirties reductions and consolidations followed, as the roster declined from forty-six men (in 1930) to twenty (in 1938) in the Yukon, and from ninety-eight to eighty in the Northwest Territories. In the Mackenzie valley the staff was reduced from fifty-two to thirty-one by closing three detachments and eliminating the Fort Simpson subdivision. The reductions were typical of the current economizing mood but also reflected noteworthy improvements in operating efficiency, such as the radio, which made it possible to transfer control of whole divisions to Ottawa, and the deployment of the *St. Roch* to superintend a large section of the Arctic coast or a plane to patrol the Mackenzie valley in 1939. At the same time certain other improvements at the local level made it possible for detachments to function with two, rather than three, men. Oil heating, for example, reduced the time and effort detachments spent on getting in wood. But it was still impossible to travel in winter without sled dogs, so much time had to be spent catching fish for their feed.

The duties of a northern RCMP officer were largely administrative rather than policing, as generally understood. The officer at Dawson in charge of "B" Division (Yukon) in the 1920s was sheriff, immigration officer, fisheries inspector, inspector of weights and measures, and registrar of vital statistics for the territory, while the officer at Whitehorse was mining recorder, Crown land and timber agent, and fire inspector for his district. Commissioned officers elsewhere had similar responsibilities. Constables collected radio licence fees, enforced quarantine and other regulations, distributed liquor rations and collected the permits. They acted as guards and ceremonial officers at Indian treaty payment meetings or with judicial parties, and they escorted visiting dignitaries (Governor General Viscount Byng in 1925, for example) on their tours about the North. They were always important figures in the small communities, maintaining order and taking part in fighting forest fires and other emergencies, and even overtook departed steamers in their motor launches to put stranded tourists abroad.

During patrols they issued licences, collected income tax and sometimes customs duties, took the census, and spread information about changes in regulations and laws. They executed the estates of deceased persons on behalf of the public administrator and even acted as a banking system for the government. In 1930–31, for example, "G" Division (Mackenzie valley) collected $115,335, "practically all of which . . . [was] turned over to the departments concerned without expense to them."[3] The men often carried medicine, clothing, and food to meet emergencies along with mail addressed to persons in the field. Trappers and prospectors therefore welcomed their visits for the news they brought, the company they provided, and above all for the comforting knowledge that the police were keeping track of them to bring help or rescue if necessary. Indeed, police patrols often brought injured and insane persons to settlements for treatment, or the corpses and effects of the dead. Occasionally policemen perished in the course of their duties from fires or accidents, influenza, diphtheria, or other diseases, or from homicides. The wife of one officer died in 1924 at Chesterfield Inlet as a result of a severe mauling by savage huskies running at large.

The most serious and dangerous manhunt of all, one of Canada's very few Wild West "shoot-outs," occurred in 1931–32 during the fifty-five-day pursuit of the mysterious Albert Johnson (almost certainly a pseudonym). "Johnson" appeared at Fort McPherson in July 1931 and without any authorization built a cabin stronghold on the

Rat River southwest of that community, from which he was reported to be interfering with local traplines. The police, after trying to reason with him and being fired on for their pains, returned in force to arrest him only to find him gone. He was located after a fortnight in a thick patch of timber on high ground, but once again he fought off a party of policemen, RCCS personnel, and local trappers and resumed his flight. A week later Johnson was surprised in the open along the Rat River; refusing a demand to surrender and probably wounded, he threw himself into the deep snow, kept firing from behind his packsack, and was eventually killed. By then he had killed one RCMP constable and wounded another along with one of the RCCS volunteers. A complete mystery to the end, he had no identification but carried $2,410 in cash, a large sum for that time and place. It seems likely that Johnson was the same person (also unidentified) who had earlier intimidated trappers in Alaska, just across the Canadian border, and vanished sometime prior to Johnson's visit to Fort McPherson.

During the 1920s the Northwest Territories and Yukon Branch tended to give priority to the needs of the native majority, but its efforts were frustrated at every turn by the inadequate funds provided by a rather indifferent parliament and government. The branch, following the Indian Affairs approach, left largely to the missionary organizations the provision of social services to the non-Indian (that is, white, Métis, Inuit, or enfranchised Indian) section of the population for which it was responsible. Thus it assisted the missions with grants on behalf of pupils from these categories who attended their day and residential schools. The branch paid $0.50 a patient day for all patients in hospitals in the Territories and $1.50 additional for indigent whites, Métis, or Inuit patients (the same amount that Indian Affairs paid on behalf of status Indian patients). The two agencies collaborated in a policy of hiring two registered nurses for each hospital in the Northwest Territories. The council made grants-in-aid toward construction of new hospitals for Inuit patients, and hospitals were opened in Inuit territory at Pangnirtung (Anglican, 1929), Chesterfield Inlet (Roman Catholic, 1939), and Aklavik (both denominations, 1928–29).

The branch also paid Indian Affairs or company doctors for services to non-Indian patients and hired doctors of its own to serve on the Eastern Arctic Patrol and in Inuit districts. Dr. L.D. Livingstone, who had often served on the patrol and at Pangnirtung, was appointed head of a Northwest Territories medical service, and in 1929 two additional physicians were secured – Dr. J.A. Urquhart to supervise the two Aklavik hospitals, and Dr. R.D. Martin to open a new station at Coppermine to serve the Arctic coast. The latter project soon was cancelled, but Urquhart remained at Aklavik until 1939, when he was transferred to

Fort Smith and Livingstone replaced him at Aklavik. The administration also aided an important pioneer innovation at the Chesterfield Inlet hospital, the shelter and care of elderly or seriously crippled Inuit who were no longer able to survive in the harsh Arctic environment and would certainly have perished under traditional practices.

For most of the period the administration was only occasionally concerned with the needs of would-be developers of the mineral resources of the North and the economic, social, and political problems they brought in their wake. But as modern industry began to move into the Territories in the thirties it found itself importuned to provide financial and other assistance to facilitate developers' efforts. The pro-development side of the northern administration was quite sympathetic, but it lacked the means and the authority to meet requests for projects to dredge the Athabasca River shallows to improve the shipping route along the waterway, or to build roads to link the District of Mackenzie with road systems in the adjacent provinces. Its response generally was to examine the requests and then pass them along to appropriate departments such as Public Works, and after 1936 Transport, for action under the Mining Roads Assistance Act or other relevant legislation. By these means some improvements were made to increase the navigability of the waterway, and a survey was made of the navigable channels of the Mackenzie delta. The need to improve the portage road around the Slave River rapids that spanned the Northwest Territories–Alberta boundary led the administration to approach the Alberta government to share the cost of that work and again for the projected road link between the Peace River district and Great Slave Lake. Requests for post offices or for RCCS stations were readily met by the departments responsible for those services, as were requests for adjustments to the mining regulations such as the temporary suspension of the work provisions on mining claims during the worst days of the Depression.

In general, the administration (as represented by the council, at least) supported economic development to the small extent that its means and authority, and its generally frugal bent, permitted. Its attitude was that developers of the Territories' resources should themselves meet the social responsibilities associated with their activities such as providing accommodation, medical service, and liability insurance for their workmen. It did little to monitor compliance with these obligations, however, so that practices varied enormously from the large companies that made good provision for these needs and the numerous fly-by-night operators who did virtually nothing at all. Eventually the council found itself compelled to pass ordinances to prevent the worst abuses. The Companies and Foreign Companies ordinances were repealed, a new Mechanics' Lien Ordinance was enacted to help workers recover claims against employers, and when difficulties arose over failures of some employers to insure their workmen, a proper Workmen's Compensation Ordinance was enacted. Thus the administration reluctantly began to take a more direct hand in modernizing the Territories.

The administration was also slow to adapt territorial institutions to accommodate the wishes of white settlers until the late thirties forced action upon it. Previously it had treated them as outsiders who were expected to conform to the system already in place. As long as most white settlers were employees of large corporate organizations or independent, self-reliant fur trappers and traders, that policy sufficed. Thus the council resolutely refused to change the antiquated liquor permit system designed to keep liquor out of the hands of native persons. Under that system a qualified resident could apply for a permit to import one shipment yearly of two gallons of liquor (or corresponding amounts of beer or wine) for medicinal or religious purposes. The consignment was delivered to the local RCMP constable, who handed it to the permit-holder in person. The result was that heavy drinking bouts accompanied the annual deliveries, followed by prolonged intervals of involuntary abstinence until the cycle could be repeated. Nevertheless, the system served the intended purpose because Indians were ineligible to apply for permits (through the Indian Act) and Inuit, who might have qualified, were discouraged from applying. When the administration at last had to respond to agitation for a system of liquor control more acceptable to whites (and one that would generate badly needed revenue), the council opened and operated a liquor store in Yellowknife supplied from the Saskatchewan Liquor Commission and licensed a local hotel to operate a beer parlour. Thus it met the immediate problem by lifting the old system from one tiny corner of the Territories while preserving it intact elsewhere.

Of more consequence was the need for entirely new ordinances to meet a new set of social needs. When a group of settlers at Fort Smith met at the end of 1927 to organize a public school district and applied for the government grant of $1,800 to hire a teacher, the council first tried to satisfy them with a mission school, then delayed until enough children had been sent away to school to disqualify the application. A year or two later it responded to revived discontent over schooling at Fort Smith by advising the settlers to form a public school district. But that proved impractical because no local government existed to levy the taxes needed to support the school, which had to pay for the first year with fees, donations, and fund-raising activities. That unsatisfactory experience led to the inauguration in 1939 of a complete system of municipal institutions that included schools for the industrialized settlement of Yellowknife.

Administration of justice, in the North as elsewhere, depended in the first instance on justices of the peace, appointed from among responsible businessmen, government officials, and other residents, who dealt with minor crimes at the local level. Offences for the most part were few and of a minor sort, mainly vagrancy, drunken and disorderly behaviour, damage to property or mistreatment of animals, and also common assaults, thefts, sexual offences. Police records leave the impression that the population was orderly and law-abiding by nature and that the large police presence plus the sparsity and high visibility of the policed population served as deterrents to crime. This did not apply, however, to the Inuit of the Eastern and Central Arctic, who still had not been made aware of, or accustomed to, white man's law and standards of conduct. While the Yukon had had as many as three resident judges and still had one, the Territories were not considered to require one. Instead, travelling stipendiary magistrates, who could deal summarily with minor crimes and summarily or assisted by a six-man jury with major ones, were appointed for the District of Mackenzie and for the Eastern Arctic.

Thus in 1923 the Eastern Arctic Patrol brought a magistrate, L.A. Rivet of Quebec, with a complete court including counsel, registrar, and interpreter, to Pond Inlet to try the three Inuit accused of murdering the trader R.S. Janes. The jury was drawn from among the personnel of the *Arctic*, witnesses were brought from Arctic Bay, and after a four-day trial one man was acquitted, a second was sentenced to two years' hard labour at Pond Inlet, and the chief culprit, found guilty of manslaughter, was sentenced to ten years' imprisonment at Stony Mountain Penitentiary in Manitoba. In the West, the magistrate for Mackenzie was Lucien Dubuc, a District Court judge at Edmonton who travelled the waterway in the summers from 1921 onward, holding court at various settlements as required. In 1923 he and his judicial party proceeded to Herschel Island to try five Inuit accused of homicides during the preceding years. Two of them, found guilty of murdering an RCMP corporal, an HBC trader, and an Inuk, were eventually hanged at Herschel Island in spite of considerable outcry, the first Inuit to suffer the death penalty.

The police hoped that these extreme punishments would deter such violence and give Inuit a respect for white man's law that apparently was not engendered by the short-term, rather innocuous sentences served at Fort Resolution, Pond Inlet, or other northern centres. Indeed, fewer capital trials were required thereafter even though the police by now were able to investigate every reported homicide involving Inuit. Dubuc heard such cases at Aklavik in 1924, 1926, and 1929, as a result of which two Inuit were sentenced to a year's imprisonment at Herschel Island while a third was sentenced to five years in a penitentiary. The Arctic region was gradually being brought under effective police control and made safer for white and Inuk alike.

A main concern of the Northwest Territories and Yukon Branch and of the council was the annual Eastern Arctic Patrol, its principal means for administering that region. The patrol had been instituted in 1922 to patrol the islands of the Canadian Arctic Archipelago, reprovision the government posts, establish new posts when necessary, and particularly to transport government agents to and from their tours of duty in the area. The patrols of 1922 through 1925 were made in the antiquated, unwieldy, slow CGS *Arctic*, half of whose cargo space had to be reserved for the 500 tons of bagged coal required to fuel the archaic steam engine. The *Arctic* was succeeded during 1926 through 1930 by the chartered SS *Beothic*, a larger, more powerful, steel-hulled sealing ship capable of performing far more useful work than its predecessor. The *Arctic*, commanded by the aged but enthusiastic seadog J.E. Bernier, had been able to do little more than sail north along the Greenland coast and return south along the Baffin Island side of Davis Strait to take advantage of prevailing winds and currents. The *Beothic*, with E. Falk as captain, by contrast was able to serve more stations, establish one RCMP post at Bache Peninsula on the central Ellesmere Island coast (1926) and another at Lake Harbour on Hudson Strait (1927), cross Hudson Bay to Chesterfield Inlet (1930), and make forays deep into the Parry Channel, once as far west as Melville Island. Officers from the department, notably J.D. Craig (1922 and 1923), G.P. Mackenzie (1925, 1926, 1930), and Major D.L. McKeand (1927, 1928, 1929, 1931 and after), directed the patrols, which also carried six to ten policemen, scientists from government and universities on surveying and research work, a ship's doctor to examine and treat patients at the ports of call, sometimes a legal party, and occasional guests such as Dr. F.G. Banting and A.Y. Jackson in 1927. By the end of the twenties the Eastern Arctic was opened to greater scientific study and policing and health services, and it was rapidly becoming a regular, though still remote, part of the Canadian state.

With the onset of the Depression, the chartering of an entire ship was discontinued. In 1932 space was rented in the annual HBC supply ship for the Eastern Arctic, the ship *Ungava* being used in 1932 and the famous *Nascopie* thereafter. Government cargo included 300 to 450 tons of freight each year, mostly building materials, machinery, and boats, gasoline and oil, food supplies, and relief supplies such as reindeer hides to make clothing for needy Inuit. Passengers carried on the government account included as before the patrol staff, the police detachments, government anthropologists, biologists, geologists, land surveyors, astronomers, an officer of the Post Office Department to handle the growing amounts of regular and philatelic mail, engineers to study radio reception and broadcasting problems, and approved non-government personnel, who were usually scientists from the universities proceeding to their research assignments and an occasional artist, such as F.H. Varley in 1938.

Since the patrol now operated in conjunction with the Hudson's Bay Company's business activities, the route had to be negotiated in advance. The usual procedure was to sail from Montreal to Churchill, stopping at Port Burwell at the mouth of Ungava Bay and sometimes at Nain or other Labrador centres en route. As Churchill was now a railway terminus, considerable interchanges of passengers and freight were often made there. From Churchill the ship sailed north along the Keewatin coast to Chesterfield Inlet, to Southampton Island, into Davis Strait and north to the various Baffin Island stations, after which it continued north to Ellesmere Island and Thule, or sometimes journeyed west along Lancaster Sound. In 1937, in fact, the *Nascopie* followed Lancaster Sound, then turned south into Prince Regent Inlet to Bellot Strait, where it met the company's *Aklavik* coming from the west, the purpose being to establish the short-lived Fort Ross at this remote spot.

Besides supporting a permanent Canadian presence in the Eastern Arctic, the Eastern Arctic Patrols had the added purpose in the 1920s of dispelling lingering doubts concerning Canada's sovereignty over the entire archipelago. That this question was concluded satisfactorily was one of the major successes achieved in the administration of the North during the interwar period. The main challenge was not so much claims that parts of the archipelago belonged to other powers but rather the attitude that certain areas were, in Knud Rasmussen's often-repeated words, "No Man's Land" and completely open to activities of citizens of other lands. True challenges to Canada's sovereignty may have existed less in fact than in the minds of suspicious Department of External Affairs officials, who were inclined to worry that every sign of interest in the land, the wildlife, or the inhabitants of the Arctic Archipelago by foreign (that is, non-British) scientists might be used to forward sinister national designs against the territory. To be fair, however, when private expeditions began obtaining proper exploring licences in advance, the Northwest Territories administration strongly supported their research activities to increase the knowledge of the region.

Its support of such researches owed much to the excellent results of one of the first, Knud Rasmussen's Fifth Thule Expedition, 1921–24, whose genesis had aroused so much concern in 1920–21. The diplomatic exchanges between Denmark and Britain concluded, Rasmussen applied for and was granted Canada's permission to undertake his wide-ranging archaeological and ethnological study of Northern Canada. Rasmussen and his associates, Kaj Birket-Smith, Thirkel Mathiassen, and Peter Freuchen, investigated Inuit bands and Inuit remains in the country along the west coast of Hudson Bay and Foxe Basin from Churchill to northern Baffin Island and including Southampton Island. Rasmussen himself studied the bands from Repulse Bay across the Boothia Peninsula and King William Island west along the coasts to Nome, a task that continued to 1924 and constitutes the main subject of his book, *Across Arctic America* (1927). The expedition produced invaluable, extremely thorough studies of every aspect of the Inuit bands in Arctic Canada just when many of them were coming under the fuller influence of the white man. Unfortunately, the administration could not, or would not, follow Rasmussen's advice and take the initiative in guiding Inuit adaptation to the pressures of the outside world that was rapidly closing in on them.

The storm in a teacup over Rasmussen's earlier activities had been the catalyst for the annual voyages of the Eastern Arctic Patrol and the opening of permanent police posts to patrol areas where Canada's title seemed most open to question. The 1922 Patrol, a member of which was Major R.A. Logan, sent to make an aeronautical review of the archipelago and select sites for future air stations, established RCMP posts at Pond Inlet and at Craig Harbour on the southeastern corner of Ellesmere Island; that of 1924 set up another at Dundas Harbour on Devon Island to oversee Lancaster Sound and Prince Regent Inlet. Another post was planned for central Ellesmere Island to supervise overland travel to the little-known islands farther west first explored by the Sverdrup Expedition some twenty years earlier and not yet visited by a Canadian. Since the *Arctic* was unable to reach the locality, it was only in 1926 that the *Beothic* delivered the supplies to the Bache Peninsula, the site chosen for the strategic post.

By then Canada had confronted its most overt challenge and had been driven to open affirmation of its sovereignty over the archipelago. The challenger was the United States in the person of the educator D.B. MacMillan, the protégé and exploring successor of Robert Peary, who after spending the years 1913–17 exploring Ellesmere Island and other islands of the Sverdrup Group had continued visiting the High Arctic, for instance in 1924 crossing Ellesmere Island to Bay Fiord. In 1925 MacMillan became involved in a plan of Lieutenant-Commander Richard Byrd and the U.S. Navy Department to examine the Arctic

Ocean north of Alaska from the air for still-undiscovered land, using the Canadian archipelago for caching supplies to support the flying operations farther west. The official nature of the proposed expedition so alarmed the Canadian authorities that they set up an interdepartmental Northern Advisory Board on April 23, 1925, and sent officers to Washington to appeal to the U.S. State and Navy Departments to request permission to enter Canada's territory. That territory was described in the House of Commons on June 10, 1925, by the Minister of the Interior as the lands enclosed by the sector lines extending northward from mainland Canada to the North Pole. Legislation introduced on May 27 and given assent on June 27 required exploring expeditions to secure permits before entering the territory.

The Byrd-MacMillan Expedition set out on June 20, however, without securing the requisite permit, and by the time it was accosted on August 19 at Etah, Greenland, by the Eastern Arctic Patrol it was already at the point of returning to the United States because of problems with the three Navy amphibian aircraft and difficulties in placing the caches. Byrd, questioned about his authorization, said MacMillan had advised him "that he was already in possession of a permit from the Canadian Government to carry on flying operations over Ellesmere and other islands in the Canadian Archipelago"[4] – an untruth that could not be checked at the time. The sequel was a stiff note (December 9, 1925) for the British ambassador in Washington to convey to the U.S. Secretary of State that directly challenged Byrd's assertion and listed the expedition's violations of three Canadian statutes: the Air Board Act, the Customs Act, and the recently amended Northwest Territories Act. No official apology was forthcoming, but U.S. expeditions operating in the Canadian North thereafter were careful about complying with the licensing and other regulations.

In any case, Canada had begun taking measures that brought the whole archipelago under effective administrative control. The entire region was designated the Arctic Islands Game Preserve, closed to any but resident hunters and traders, by an order in council of July 19, 1926. From the key RCMP post opened at the Bache Peninsula Staff-Sergeant A.H. Joy made two long patrols in 1926 and 1927 over and around the islands of the Sverdrup Group, the second of which was a fifty-nine-day, 1,320-mile circuit west from the Bache Peninsula to Cornwall and Graham islands. Later, in 1929, he made an extraordinary eighty-day, 1,700-mile journey west along Parry Channel to Winter Harbour, then north across Melville, Lougheed, King Christian, and Axel Heiberg islands to the Bache Peninsula. As there were no Inuit residing north of Parry Channel except the two families imported to each RCMP station to help the policemen live and work in the Arctic, these and other patrols by T.C. Makinson and E. Anstead were made purely to support parallel diplomatic efforts aimed at securing unquestioned recognition of Canada's sovereignty over the whole of the Arctic Archipelago.

The steps taken in 1925 to affirm Canadian sovereignty over the Sverdrup Group brought out a new challenge, this time from Norway on the basis of the Sverdrup Expedition. After having requested five times a statement of Canada's position and having received no response whatever, the Norwegian government finally (March 26, 1928) notified Canada of its intention to affirm its rights in international law. The one action that followed, however, was a letter (April 22, 1929) from the aged Otto Sverdrup himself stating that the Norwegian government's "rights" would be "definitely relinquished should I at any time so desire," and proposing that E. Bordewick, the CPR agent at Oslo, arrange "a suitable compensation" from Canada to pay for his expedition's important and arduous four-year effort.[5] Prolonged negotiations ensued with Bordewick and with the Norwegian government, the upshot of which were an *ex gratia* payment of $67,000 to Sverdrup from the Canadian government and the affirmation by the Norwegian government that they "do not as far as they are concerned claim sovereignty over the Sverdrup Islands, [but] formally recognise the sovereignty of His Britannic Majesty over these islands." The Norwegians affirmed their acceptance of Canada's assurance that should the status of the closed game preserve be altered, Canada would treat applications by Norwegian citizens to operate in the region "in most friendly manner."[6] Norway's recognition of Canada's sovereignty preceded Sverdrup's death on November 26, 1930, by little more than a fortnight.

Thus Canada completed the process initiated by the British order in council of 1880 transferring Britain's claims to the Arctic islands to her and had gained unchallenged title over, and effective control of, the Arctic Archipelago. Following a last 1,400-mile patrol by Corporal W.N. Stallworthy in 1930–31, in which he circled Axel Heiberg Island in search of the missing explorers H.E.K. Krueger and A.R. Bjare, the Bache Peninsula station was closed as no longer needed, leaving Craig Harbour as the sole RCMP detachment on Ellesmere Island. Although Canada had maintained persistent, patient, low-key diplomatic offensives against three essentially uninterested foreign powers, it had really achieved its goal by establishing unquestionable practical control over the region that wiped out the potential claims of other nations based on earlier discoveries of their nationals.

CHAPTER 8

The North in the Second World War

I

During the Second World War the North participated in a far greater way in the national war effort than it had in the First. By then industrial frontiers had advanced far into the Middle North, and the many lumber camps, pulp and paper plants, mines, and large hydro-electric power stations could furnish an appreciable fraction of Canada's material wartime requirements. The agricultural frontier, too, had been pushed some distance into the Subarctic forests and its several thousand farms were better equipped than in 1914 to contribute foodstuffs, man-power for wartime industries, and men and women for the armed services. Thus the North had an important role to play in serving the needs of a modern nation caught up in a desperate all-out war.

The demand for strategic minerals and forest products strained the capabilities of previously under-utilized industrial plants, but the higher production levels attained were available thereafter for equally large post-war efforts. The great mining camp of Sudbury in particular felt the impact of unlimited markets for nickel, copper, platinum, and rarer metals. During the six years of war as much ore was mined in the Sudbury Basin as in the previous fifty years of the field's history. In the Saguenay, the production of the Aluminium Company of Canada at Arvida was increased from 200 million pounds a year to 985 million pounds in 1943, exceeding the 1939 world output. That greater pro-duction, in turn, was a direct result of the development in 1943 of the 1.2-million-horsepower Shipshaw generating station and the building of additional reservoirs in the headwaters of the rivers feeding Lac St Jean to regulate the water level of that great natural reservoir. Labour flocked to the Saguenay's wartime industries from the surrounding

203

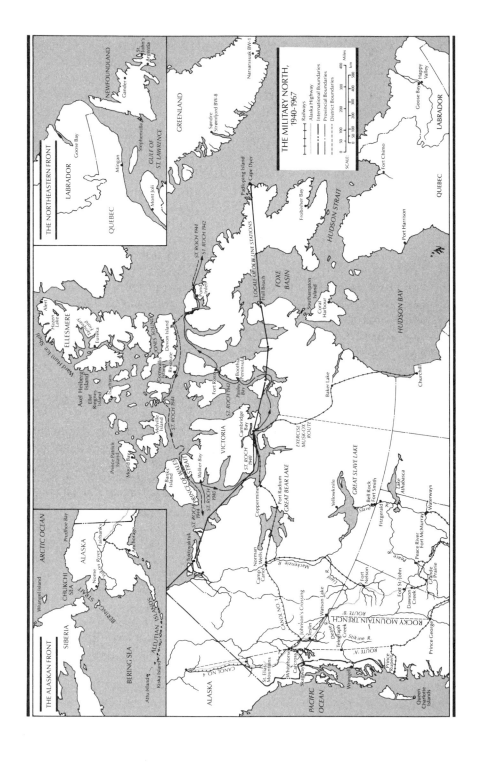

THE MILITARY NORTH, 1940-1967

Railways
Alaska Highway
International Boundaries
Provincial Boundaries
District Boundaries

SCALE

0 50 100 200 300 400 500 km
0 50 100 200 300 400 Miles

THE NORTHEASTERN FRONT

St. John's
Avondia
NEWFOUNDLAND
Gander
Stephenville
GULF OF ST. LAWRENCE
Goose Bay
LABRADOR
Mingan
Mont Joli
QUEBEC

GREENLAND
Narsarssuaq BW-1
Sandre
Strømfjord BW-8
Cape Dyer
Padloping Island

THE ALASKAN FRONT

ARCTIC OCEAN
Prudhoe Bay
ALASKA
Yukon River
Fairbanks
Anchorage
Nome
CHUKCHI SEA
Wrangel Island
SIBERIA
BERING STRAIT
BERING SEA
ALEUTIAN ISLANDS
Kiska Island
Attu Island

Tuktoyaktuk
ST. ROCH 1944
PRINCE OF WALES STRAIT
Banks Island
Maud Bay
Prince Patrick Island
Melville Island
Axel Heiberg Island
Ellef Ringnes Island
Isachsen
Resolute
Cornwallis Island
Devon Island
LANCASTER SOUND
ELLESMERE
Alert
Hazen Lake
Mould Bay
Eureka
Pond Inlet
ST. ROCH 1942
Ward Hunt Ice Shelf

ST. ROCH 1944
VICTORIA
Walker Bay
ST. ROCH 1942
Fort Ross
Pasley Bay
Boothia Peninsula
Cambridge Bay
ST. ROCH 1940
Coppermine
Port Radium
GREAT BEAR LAKE
LOCALE OF DEW LINE STATIONS
Hall Beach
FOXE BASIN
Southampton Island
Coral Harbour
Frobisher Bay
HUDSON STRAIT
Port Harrison
Fort Chimo
QUEBEC
LABRADOR
Goose Bay
Happy Valley

EXERCISE MUSK-OX ROUTE
Baker Lake
HUDSON BAY
Churchill

Yellowknife
GREAT SLAVE LAKE
Bell Rock
Fort Smith
Slave
Fitzgerald
Lake Athabasca
Peace River
Fort McMurray
Waterways
Camp Canol
Norman Wells
Mackenzie R.
CANOL NO. 1
Fort Nelson
Fort St. John
Dawson Creek
Grande Prairie
Peace R.
Liard R.
Watson Lake
Johnson's Crossing
CANOL NO. 4
St. Elias Mountains
Skagway
Whitehorse
Carcross
Teslin
Dease Lake
Telegraph Creek
Stikine R.
Wrangell
ROCKY MOUNTAIN TRENCH
ROUTE 'B'
ROUTE 'A'
Prince Rupert
Prince George
Queen Charlotte Islands
PACIFIC OCEAN
ALASKA

rural areas and elsewhere in Quebec, so that the population of the district increased from 143,187 in 1941 to 174,300 in 1943 and eventually settled down to a post-war level of 165,000. There was also significant activity in Canada's metal-mining centres, where all-out efforts were made to wrest as much copper and base metals as possible from the existing mines and smelting plants. Record productions of 816,000 tons of nickel, 1.8 million tons of copper, and 1.6 million tons of zinc were secured, but at the cost of neglecting underground development work and seriously impinging on future supplies.

The federal government made special efforts to secure metals and other critical commodities by means of purchase contracts and cash loans and by building access roads and supplying equipment to developers and operators. A noteworthy drive to obtain badly needed mercury led to the opening of two mines in the Omineca district of British Columbia. The Pinchi Lake plant of Consolidated Mining, acclaimed as the largest mercury producer in the British Commonwealth, operated from June 1940 to July 1944, the smaller Takla mercury mine of Bralorne Mines between November 1943 and September 1944. Their total of four million pounds of mercury made Canada for a time the second-largest producer in the world. But as soon as foreign supplies were again available the operation became uncompetitive and production in Omineca ceased. The hope of obtaining a large domestic source of petroleum also led the federal government to assist in the attempt to develop an economical separation process so that the vast bituminous sands beds of the Athabasca district could be exploited. Consolidated Mining received a non-profit contract to take over the pre-war plant of Abasand Oils and develop feasible processes. The effort failed; the new plant burned down, and the government handed the operation, still a long way from success, back to Abasand. On the Pacific Coast a Crown corporation named Aero Timber Products was set up to procure Sitka spruce for aircraft manufacture. As in the Great War, eight logging camps were opened in the Queen Charlotte Islands, and another six floating camps harvested pockets of spruce along the coasts of Vancouver Island. The emergency having subsided, the operation was closed in 1944 and immediately after the war ended was sold to the Powell River organization.

The government was particularly eager to return the dormant silver-radium mine of Eldorado Gold Mines to operation because of the crucial importance of the Allied powers' atomic energy researches. The mine was secretly reopened by Eldorado in 1941 at the urgent request of C.D. Howe, and for two years the federal government financed the work, had the mine drained and cemented to permit removal of ore from beneath Great Bear Lake, and employed prospectors to search for additional uranium deposits. At the same time the company carried on its sales and research programs in the midst of mysterious dealings with agents of the former Belgian monopoly and unedifying scandals that finally led the government to expropriate the company and its properties (including Northern Transportation Company) under the War Measures Act, paying the shareholders $1.38 a share, the prevailing low stock market price. When the shareholders complained, a secret government inquiry, headed by J. Grant Glassco, was held in 1945 to review the activities of the company. Though evidence of misconduct by certain officers was uncovered, the shareholders received no further compensation. From Port Radium (and the slag dump at Port Hope) came much of the fissionable material that went into making the first atomic bombs and ushered in the nuclear age.

A different sort of treatment was accorded the gold-mining industry. We have seen that gold was the prime force extending Canada's industrial frontiers northward and that the dozens of gold mines and camps across the Subarctic brought production to record heights. The coming of war further stimulated gold mining when the Canadian dollar was devalued by 10 per cent, and gold was needed to pay for swollen imports from the United States. The mines were accordingly at first given high priorities for supplies and manpower. But as financial arrangements improved between the United States and Canada, gold mining was reclassified as a non-essential industry, and its priorities were withdrawn in October 1942. Thereafter production declined steadily as workers were subject to the draft for military service or were directed to more vital employments, and machinery and supplies became difficult to procure. The great Hollinger operation at Timmins cut its milling rate from 4,500 tons to 2,634 tons daily, and at Kirkland Lake, where 4,600 men had laboured in 1939, employment fell to just 2,000 persons. The recently opened mine at Goldfields closed forever in 1942, and at the promising Yellowknife camp one mine closed in 1942, three more in 1943, and the fifth and last in October 1944.

Lumber, woodpulp, and newsprint also were vital to Canada's war effort, and production records were achieved despite shortages of workers and materials and the problems caused by price and wage controls and other governmental regulations. The output of lumber increased from 3,768 million f.b.m. in 1938 to 4,935 million in 1942 and newsprint production from 2,625,000 tons in 1939 to 3,257,000 tons in 1942; in the same period, woodpulp exports were more than doubled. But these were the peaks, for there were increasing shortages of manpower and to some extent of hydro-electric power. Furthermore, price controls had been imposed before the industries had fully recovered from their Depression levels, so that as the war proceeded lumbermen were caught in an inexorable price squeeze. Newsprint producers, similarly, were allowed only modest price increases. Accordingly, the forest industries eagerly awaited the return of peace and dismantling of the controls.

To harvest the requisite two million acres of woodlands each year, 150,000 seasonal workers, some 100,000 man-years in all, were needed. The armed services and more lucrative war industries drew heavily on the men who customarily made up the bulk of the workers. Operators had little to offer them, for the employment was temporary, camp amenities were even worse than usual, and pay rates were low. A great propaganda effort was therefore mounted each autumn to lure workers back to the woods. Labour was also secured from among the alternative service detainees (conscientious objectors), the Japanese detainees, and Axis prisoners of war, but this reservoir was only marginally helpful. Pulpwood reserves were short by some 1,750,000 cords by the spring of 1943, and the situation worsened thereafter. Output of pulp was maintained largely from the pre-war inventories, and as these were used up production failed to sustain the higher levels. The output of lumber fell by 10 per cent, and the industry was often forced to market inadequately seasoned material. Small-scale production did expand markedly, however, in response to heightened demand for railway ties, telephone poles, fence posts, pit props, wooden boxes, and lumber for local construction. Fire-killed timber also was harvested to furnish logs for the pulp mills. Many small northern lumber mills prospered greatly from the heavy demand for their products created by nearby military camps and related civilian construction.

Although shortages were plaguing the logging and lumber industries, the newsprint industry found itself with excess capacity from the unwise overbuilding during the twenties. Held back by pulpwood and hydro shortages, it operated at only 80 per cent of capacity during the war. Output at hydro-electric installations increased from 8.29 million horsepower in 1938 to 10.28 million in 1945, making it possible to ease hydro restrictions in 1943 and lift them altogether in the autumn of 1944. The war brought increased concern for future supplies of wood. Surveys revealed that the forest resources then capable of exploitation were markedly inferior to those already being used. Government and company foresters called for efforts to reduce the heavy losses from fire, insects, and plant diseases, more efficient use of the timber harvested, and the institution of vigorous reforestation and forest management programs. Royal commissions of forestry were at work soon after the war in British Columbia and Ontario and in New Brunswick, attesting to this concern.

Northern agriculture also was regulated in line with the needs of a nation at war, and farmers, too, faced shortages of machinery, fertilizers, gasoline, and especially labour. The government discouraged wheat culture in such areas as the Peace River and Lac St Jean districts by maintaining a low price and small delivery quotas for wheat while it encouraged the growing of oil seeds (rapeseed, today named canola, was introduced in 1943) and forage crops, which would increase quantities of the meat, dairy products, and eggs that were deemed more important to the war effort. Northern farmers switched so wholeheartedly to raising hogs that swine marketings from frontier areas reached record levels in 1943 and 1944. Large block orders from Britain, the requirements of the military establishment in Canada, plus improvements in the diets of working Canadians created much larger markets for meat and eggs, butter, cheese, fluid milk, and fresh vegetables. Northern farmers responded, particularly where near-at-hand war industries or military bases provided unprecedentedly good local markets for their fresh produce. In Northern British Columbia a symbiotic relationship developed between farmers and the large home-defence units stationed there, the farmers being assisted to expand their vegetable-growing, hog-raising, dairying, and other operations to meet the needs of the district's camps by the servicemen released in large numbers to help them out at key times of the year.

Pioneer farmers who had struggled to become established on the land during the Depression were given a chance at last of finding less onerous and more rewarding work. Thousands from the frontiers of Northern Ontario and the Prairie Provinces joined the armed service, their pay and allowances helping their families to stay on the land and carry on subsistence farming pending the return of husbands and fathers. Many others, like the recently arrived Sudeten settlers, found work at war factories or in war-related industries and moved away as families, abandoning farming altogether. As a result, there were sharp reductions in the farming populations of many northern frontier districts but not in the Peace River district or the Abitibi-Témiscamingue region, where local conditions favoured continuing agricultural expansion. Northern Saskatchewan, for instance, lost so many of the farmers attracted there during the Depression that "by the middle 1950s . . . the gains of the Dirty Thirties had all been lost. The total population of the north was comparable with that of 1928, although sprinkled over a far wider area."[1]

The war also afforded opportunities of alternative employment for large numbers of native persons. As they had in the Great War, many served in Canada's armed forces – more than 2,600, including some women – and 170 died while on active service. Hundreds more Indians and Métis left the Middle North to work in war industries outside or found employment locally in industries with war-depleted staffs such as railways and lumber mills, on farms and in fisheries. Where military activities impinged on their homelands they found work as guides and hunters, at unskilled labouring and maintenance tasks at the bases, and occasionally as truck drivers. In addition, the camps furnished markets for local produce and services. Many native families earned higher incomes and enjoyed better nutrition, housing, and clothing than ever before. Their experience of the material comforts and ways of the majority society so separated them from the old mode of life that they could not readily have returned when conditions changed – even if they had so desired.

For the many natives and others who continued the hunting, fishing, and trapping life, the war also brought significant changes, few of them for the better. Muskrat and beaver catches increased, muskrat by 50 per cent, beaver by 100 per cent, thanks to growing production from earlier managed programs and the start of new ones. Catches of other fur-bearers fluctuated, but total production remained much as before. Prices, however, failed to rise as they had during the Great War. Overseas markets were lost, and the United States did not provide the same profitable outlet as before; at home, comprehensive price and market controls, heavy wartime taxation, and a prevailing mood of austerity adversely affected the Canadian market for furs. As military activity burgeoned in the North and northerners turned to other employments, a noticeable decline in numbers of furs trapped was registered. Although the many transitory military and civilian newcomers created a small, casual local market for furs and other products, they also engaged in much careless hunting that added to the havoc caused by the permanent camps and roads built in many hunting and trapping areas and especially by the widespread forest fires that accompanied the wartime activities. The war left a much poorer environment for wildlife in large sections of the North, greatly reducing the prospects for a healthy post-war industry.

II

Particularly important for Canada's future development was the unanticipated heavy involvement of northern parts of the Subarctic and the Arctic in the Second World War, a direct consequence of the impact of a shrinking world upon military strategy in the air age. The war provided a dramatic beginning for the modern age in the Canadian North comparable to the Klondike Gold Rush in its time. The repercussions, moreover, were felt very widely all the way from Labrador to the Alaskan boundary. In the Northwest the war opened up the sparsely inhabited, only partly explored district between the Peace River area and Whitehorse and also embraced the District of Mackenzie. In the Northeast the Subarctic and Arctic were affected by the air transport system developed to supply the European war theatre. A complex of airfields, highways, and oil pipelines was constructed in the Northwest, a string of airports and weather stations in the Northeast. Workmen and military personnel swarmed into the North – as many as 40,000 in the Northwest at the height of construction in the summer of 1943, far outnumbering the scattered native and resident white populations. The influx into the Northeast was smaller, though here, too, thousand-man contingents were landed in localities where the presence of a score of human beings would once have been a memorable event. By the time the war ended, the North had acquired an elaborate array of transportation and communications facilities, and much new information had been gained regarding the nature of the region and the problems of living and working there. The North could never be the same thereafter.

These developments were a minor, even trivial, outcome of the worldwide military-strategic planning of the United States, and the heavy expenditures of manpower and matériel in Northern Canada were undertaken purely to help defeat the Axis powers. Hence locations and construction were determined by American rather than Canadian priorities, and their value for the future development of the North was incidental. Still, the operations were on such a gratifyingly generous scale that the Americans' efforts were received gladly in Canada, especially by those interests and populations that expected to benefit from them. Canadians enthusiastically welcomed the involvement of the United States in the war as a friend and ally whose military might ensured ultimate victory to the cause of the Allies. While the extent of the American presence in Northern Canada created difficulties and aroused some fear and resentment, the public was disinclined to look the gift horse in the mouth while the war continued. Nevertheless, the experience heightened Canadian sensitivities when the post-war international crisis brought renewed American involvement in the North.

The northern wartime construction programs of the United States exemplified the close collaboration between Canada and the United States that followed the overrunning of Western Europe by the Nazis in the summer of 1940 and the signing of the Ogdensburg Agreement by the leaders of the two countries. Military collaboration was exercised principally through the Permanent Joint Board on Defence (PJBD) set up under that agreement and composed of a five-member section appointed by each sponsoring government. It was this board that received proposals, mostly from the U.S. section, to push forward with enterprises designed to put the geography and resources of the Canadian North at the disposal of the common war effort.

Projects were pressed on an often reluctant Canada by the much larger, more exuberant American partner and were executed with the verve and technical skill that characterized the U.S. military-industrial machine. The American planners appeared to regard their country's capacities as virtually without limit; their military chiefs made fullest provision for every conceivable contingency and disregarded costs almost completely. The Canadian war effort, by contrast, was firmly under the control of the political chiefs, who, ever conscious of the nation's limited means, weighed options, established priorities, and selected courses of action according to the likeliest possibilities. Most of the grandiose projects proposed by the United States were considered to have too little military value to warrant diverting Canada's scarce resources to carry them out. The Canadian government was on the whole content to allow the United States to make whatever expenditures in Canada it desired and concerned itself chiefly with arranging for eventual Canadian control of the projects. Ultimately, the limited military use made of the projects justified the Canadian government's unwilling attitude.

The one joint activity the Canadian government wholeheartedly supported was the fashioning of a link with Alaska. Long before the Ogdensburg Agreement, indeed since the twenties, the United States had been interested in an overland route to Alaska. British Columbians also had long desired such a highway for its effects on the undeveloped north of their province. Special commissions from both countries had studied the matter in 1930–31 but had reached no conclusive decision. Interest revived late in the thirties as the international situation darkened and American West Coast businessmen grew uneasy over the power of the International Longshoremen's Association to interfere with shipping to Alaska. A campaign led by Warren G. Magnuson of Seattle and Premier Pattullo of British Columbia swept the Pacific Coast. The two countries appointed five-man commissions during the autumn of 1938 "to enquire into the engineering, economic, financial, and other aspects of the proposal to construct the said highway to Alaska,"[2] and sittings were held throughout British Columbia and Yukon during 1939 and 1940.

The American commissioners, predictably, favoured Route A, a western path that would serve Alaska Panhandle communities via a 1,000-mile road in Canada through Hazelton, Atlin, and Whitehorse. The Canadian commissioners, however, seemed because of engineering, climatic, and economic considerations to prefer Route B, north from Prince George by way of the Rocky Mountain Trench. From east of the Rockies came pleas for a highway that would follow a still more easterly route from established railway and road systems, which the Canadian commissioners rejected because of "the Order-in-Council creating the Commission specifically confining its consideration to routes through British Columbia."[3] The preliminary report, made public on May 10, 1940, expressed dissatisfaction over the lack of information on all the routes and urged further surveys, particularly of the A route.

In the meantime, the threatening situation in the Pacific increased the desire of both nations to improve the air route to Alaska that was being used under a 1937 airmail contract by the Canadian firm United Air Transport. The Civil Aviation Branch had this North-West Staging Route (NWSR) surveyed during the summer of 1939 with a view to improving it for year-round flight by wheeled aircraft. Notwithstanding the outbreak of war, the government provided funds in 1939–40 to improve the airports at Grande Prairie, Dawson Creek, and Peace River town, while the airline itself constructed landing fields at the remoter Fort Nelson and Watson Lake stops. The newly formed PJBD reviewed the highway and airway projects at a session in Victoria on November 13, 1940, and recommended further improvement of the air route to enable it to handle a greater volume of air traffic between Edmonton and Fairbanks. At that time it ruled against construction of a highway in view of advice that the project was not justified from a military standpoint and the continuing lack of agreement on the best route. Indeed, that situation remained little changed for the next year. A conference held in Washington in March 1941 again disagreed over the route, while Charles Stewart, the chairman of the Canadian section of the Alaska Highway Commission, added to the confusion by reminding those interested that routes east of the Rockies remained to be considered. As late as October 1941 the U.S. Secretary of War, H.L. Stimson, still gave an Alaskan highway a "low-priority rating" though he conceded it was "desirable as a long-range defense measure."[4]

In the meantime, following the decision on the air route, Canada began early in 1941 to equip the airfields with paved runways, radio-location facilities, and intermediate landing strips. Work was relatively easy at the main airports on railway lines and at Fort St. John, which was accessible by good road from the railhead at Dawson Creek. The real difficulty was with the two isolated interior bases, Fort Nelson and Watson Lake. During February 1941 tractor trains and trucks rushed supplies from Dawson Creek to Fort Nelson over the frozen muskegs until an early thaw turned the route into a quagmire. The freight that had only reached the Sikanni Chief River was delivered on scows after the spring break-up. Watson Lake had to be supplied by river during the springtime high water from Wrangell via the Stikine, Dease, and Liard waterways to Lower Post on the Liard. From there it was hauled by truck the remaining twenty-six miles to the airfield, an excellent site on a gravel beach projecting into the lake. By autumn, 4,400-foot runways were ready at both airports, and by the end of the year airport radio stations offered a guidance system for planes over the entire route. During the summer of 1941 a few U.S. military aircraft were able to make their way to Alaska over the newly built Canadian NWSR.

Earlier, the fall of France in the summer of 1940 had directed the immediate attention of both North American countries to problems of Atlantic defence, to coastal patrol work, and above all to air routes for ferrying airplanes and air crews to Britain. The Department of Transport had built or improved airports at Dorval, Mont Joli, Sept-Iles, Moncton, and Sydney, while the RCAF had been assigned to assume control of the Newfoundland airport at Gander. Under terms of the destroyer-bases agreement with Great Britain of September 2, 1940, the United States received ninety-nine-year leases to establish bases at Argentia and Stephenville in Newfoundland and the use of Gander airport. Canada early in 1941 also secured a wartime lease to a base at Torbay near St. John's. From November 1940 onward, American-built planes in increasing numbers began to be flown across the Atlantic using this route. Delivered to Dorval from the factories, they usually went by way of Gander to Prestwick, Scotland.

In the sixteen-month interval between Ogdensburg and Pearl Harbor military planners considered various aspects of the northeastern routes to Europe. It was now recognized by meteorologists (German as well as Allied) that Greenland and Arctic Canada were most valuable locations for weather stations to help with forecasting Atlantic and European weather conditions. The urgent need for shorter-range fighter aircraft in Britain also required the adoption of more northerly "stepping stone" routes via Labrador, Greenland, and Iceland. A further factor was the certainty of congestion at Gander, which was also subject to frequent fogs. Following passage of the Lend Lease Act in March 1941, larger numbers of planes began to be flown to Britain. The United States took Greenland under protective custody in April 1941 by agreement with the Danish ambassador in Washington and proceeded to build airports at Narsarssuak (Bluie West-1 or B.W.-1) near the southern tip of the island and farther north at Søndre Strømfjord (B.W.-8).

Both Canada and the United States sent out survey parties to seek both additional airfield sites and sites for weather stations (known as Project Crystal) in Labrador and on Baffin Island. A major find was made in June 1941 by Eric Fry of the Mines and Geology Branch of the

Department of Mines and Resources near the junction of the Hamilton and Goose rivers. The site, as he described it,

> . . . proved to be a huge sandy terrace or bench extending for several square miles. Bulldozers could level a square mile smooth as the top of a billiard table within a few weeks. The sand was as deep through as the height of the bench down to the level of the river bed. That took care of drainage. The only disadvantage I could see was the fact that the location was over 100 miles inland from the sea. I didn't know at that time how far inland Lake Melville, Goose Bay and Terrington Basin might be navigable. It turned out afterwards that vessels drawing 21 feet could be brought right up to the head of Terrington Basin.[5]

In fact, ships could be unloaded just a mile from the future airport. The climate also was ideal; the airport registered almost twice as many flying days monthly as either Gander or Torbay.

Fry's party was soon joined by the American party under Captain Elliott Roosevelt, and highly favourable reports of the site were submitted to both governments. The PJBD authorized Canada to undertake construction of the Goose Bay airport, and the government began the assignment with alacrity. After speedy surveys, the construction contracts were let in early September. During the autumn, supplies and equipment were delivered and workmen began round-the-clock shifts to prepare 7,000-foot runways. By December 9, 1941, surfaced with packed snow, the landings were ready to receive aircraft with further supplies and men from Dorval or Moncton.

Full-swing construction continued in 1942. Ten million f.b.m. of lumber were manufactured, a gravel plant was opened, and the dock was enlarged to handle four ocean-going ships simultaneously. After cement supplies arrived, the runways were paved with six-inch layers of concrete. The RCAF took control of the station in March 1942, and an American air force detachment moved in during the following month. At first both groups used the Canadian facilities, but beginning in July, a separate camp with three hangars and housing for 1,000 permanent and 1,200 transient personnel was built for the Americans on the opposite side of the field. By 1943 the American base was over twice as large as the Canadian. Authority over the area – by now a small modern city in the Labrador wilderness – remained in Canadian hands. In fact, in 1944 the Newfoundland governing commission granted Canada a ninety-nine-year lease of the base, thoughtfully back-dated to September 1, 1941. For all the many privileges the United States secured from Prime Minister Churchill, Canada probably gained the major prize in the post-war aviation sweepstakes that lay in the gift of the island dominion.

III

The course of the war was sharply altered on December 7, 1941, when the United States was suddenly precipitated into the armed struggle by the Japanese attack on Pearl Harbor. Eight of nine battleships of the American Pacific fleet were destroyed or immobilized, throwing the Pacific front into immediate danger and making overland communications with Alaska an urgent necessity. Canada took further steps to strengthen its coastal defences in British Columbia and stationed a large number of home-defence troops along the Prince Rupert branch of the CNR. The threat became reality in June 1942 when carrier-based planes harried Dutch Harbor, Alaska, and Japanese troops occupied Attu and Kiska, westernmost islands of the Aleutian chain.

The U.S. War Department in January 1942 had rushed squadrons of bombers and pursuit planes over the NWSR, only to lose nearly 30 per cent of them because of inclement weather, inadequate radio communications, inaccurate maps, poor airport facilities, insufficiently winterized planes, and inexperience of air crews with northern flying conditions. To prevent a repetition of that fiasco the effort to improve the staging route was renewed. Once more tractor trains, trucks, and riverboats rushed supplies for a 1942 round of improvements that would equip the interior airfields with 6,000-foot runways, radio communication and direction-finding equipment, control towers at main airports, and a string of intermediate landing fields to take care of shorter-range planes or emergencies. Work continued in 1943 and beyond to enlarge and improve the route further in line with plans to mount an attack on Japan from Alaska and supply the USSR with planes for its massive counter-offensives. As a result of Canadian involvements elsewhere, the United States assumed increasing control over the construction, placing one of its engineering regiments on the work. The final cost of constructing the NWSR was given as $55 million, about $37 million of which was spent by the United States.

The emergency situation also brought about construction of the long-awaited Alaska Highway. The inability of the U.S. Navy to guarantee uninterrupted communications with Alaska encouraged the military to push ahead with the highway so as to be assured of reliable connection with Alaska. In fact, even a possible Prince George-to-Alaska railway was investigated. Colonel J.H. Graham, a logistics expert from the Great War and dollar-a-year assistant to the U.S. Undersecretary of War, was commissioned by B.B. Somervell, the commanding general of the U.S. Army Service Forces, to assess means of supplying the Alaskan front. Graham rejected the railway proposal on the grounds that the War Department did not envisage a large enough force in Alaska (200,000 to 300,000 men) to warrant its construction. Instead, he recommended building a sixteen-foot gravel road to connect and service the string of air bases between Edmonton and Fairbanks. His recommendation was accepted by the U.S. Cabinet and endorsed by the PJBD. The ensuing agreement with Canada provided for the United States to construct, maintain, and operate the highway until six months after the end of the war, after which the Canadian part of the road would be handed to Canada to become "in all respects an integral part of the Canadian highway system."[6]

The location of the Alaska Highway was decided by the same considerations that had inspired the earlier decision on the air route plus the need to supply the airports and mark the route for pilots unfamiliar with the area. In the following year, J.F. O'Connor, Commanding General, Northwest Service Command, defended the choice of this so-called Route C in the following terms: "The primary purpose of this road was the airfields. The secondary purpose was to have an additional route to Alaska in case of difficulties in the Pacific. At the time this road was initiated, our fleet, of course, was knocked out and we had grave fears. Our sole aim in our construction here has been to give a road that would serve the military purpose and not have what we call up here a peacetime road."[7] The selection was a bitter blow, however, for the West Coast interests who had counted on the project and had planned long and carefully to have it located according to their desires. A headline from Seattle bluntly asserted, "New Route Not Alaska Road At All,"[8] while A.J. Dimond, the Alaskan delegate to Congress, branded the decision "a mistake so great that it verges on tragedy."[9] Congressman Magnuson of Washington and Senator William Langer of North Dakota demanded inquiries into the selection of Route C, and the matter became one of the many investigations conducted by the Truman Committee (the Senate Sub-Committee Investigating the National Defense Program).

By early 1942, Dawson Creek, the railhead in northeastern British Columbia, was bulging with American troops and their equipment. One unit alone, the 35th Engineering Regiment, was accompanied by no fewer than 165 railway carloads of mechanical equipment. Seven such regiments of engineers, some consisting of black troops under the segregated system followed by the U.S. Army, succeeded in building the entire 1,611-mile pioneer road between Dawson Creek and Fairbanks in the single summer of 1942 – an achievement that warrants comparison with construction of the Burma Road built about the same time by tens of thousands of basket-carrying Chinese. Since the C route had never been fully explored, the 850-mile section between Fort St. John and Whitehorse first had to be located and marked on the ground. The location followed a succession of high ridges and avoided the many muskegs and interbraided streams south of Fort Nelson, skilfully skirted outliers of the Rocky Mountains (its maximum elevation is 4,251 feet), then selected a newly discovered direct alignment via the Rancheria and Swift river valleys to Teslin, from which point the road was carried into Whitehorse. The construction was effected by stationing separate regiments at Dawson Creek, Fort Nelson, Watson Lake, Teslin, Whitehorse, and Fairbanks to work in both directions from the four intermediate centres and flying bridge-building crews to major river crossings to complete their work ahead of the road-making units. Several miles could be built during a single long, bright, summer's day, and finally on November 24, the last remaining gap was closed at a ceremony on a scenic promontory overlooking Kluane Lake, with the lofty snow-covered peaks of the St. Elias Mountains for a backdrop.

This pioneer road was to have been used by fifty-four civilian contracting firms – thirteen of them Canadian – to build a paved highway to full U.S. Public Roads Administration standards: thirty-six-foot wide pavement, gentle curves, and grades accommodating the seventy m.p.h. speed limit. But the military situation having changed, the road specifications were downgraded on April 2, 1943, to a twenty-two-foot gravel strip, and it was decided simply to improve the pioneer road to that standard. Much repair and reconstruction work was needed to overcome the severe ravages of the winter of 1942–43, and in addition the grades and alignments were greatly improved and the most hazardous bridges and approaches were replaced. Branch roads were built to the airfields and intermediate landing strips. The important 154-mile cut-off road that linked Whitehorse with Haines Mission near Skagway gave the Yukon Territory its first direct highway link with the Pacific Coast. A teletype-telephone system along the highway with connections to the various airports, control towers, and weather stations was also in operation between Edmonton and Fairbanks by November 19, 1943. Including this last, the total cost of the Alaska Highway to the U.S. Treasury was $147.5 million.

Nor was this all. Concern for the security of the Alaskan front after Pearl Harbor also spawned the Canol Project, surely one of the most incredible of all Second World War enterprises. Planning for the defence of the Northwest region included the possibility of making the region self-sufficient in petroleum, that all-important requirement of modern warfare. Again Colonel Graham was summoned to inquire into the matter. Having heard about the oilfield at Norman Wells, he discussed with Imperial Oil officials the possibility of developing it into a major supply source. They did their best to discourage the plan. He also convoked a board of high-ranking but unqualified military officers who expressed a requisite degree of interest in having a regional petroleum supply made available. Then he drafted a one-page memorandum recommending a drilling program in the Mackenzie valley to develop production of 3,000 barrels a day, construction of a 590-mile, four-inch pipeline to move the crude oil to Whitehorse, and the erection there of a surplus oil refinery from Corpus Christi, Texas, that would be adapted to supply the requirements of the air route and the highway. General Somervell issued a directive ordering the project forward, and in this seemingly lightheaded fashion the United States was launched upon a highly questionable $135-million enterprise that one critic called "a gigantic boondoggling project for opening the Canadian wilderness."[10]

The Truman Committee stigmatized the project as extravagant, improvident, and failing to safeguard the interests of the United States. Be that as it may, the Canadian members of the PJBD were more than reluctant to have the Americans undertake the task. So sceptical were they that the American sponsors took the proposal direct to the Canadian Cabinet instead. That body merely authorized the United States to proceed on its own to build and operate the project during the war, subject to observation of Canada's mining and business laws. Afterwards it would have to be disposed of at a price based on its commercial value, the Canadian government to have the first refusal; thereafter it might be disposed of to any other parties approved by Canada for whatever the United States could get.

Thus was launched one of the strangest, most versatile enterprises of the entire war. Imperial Oil entered into a contract with the U.S. government to drill new wells besides the nine that were producing 1,500 barrels of light crude daily. Later in 1942, when the planners decided Alaska might be used as an assault base on Japan, they increased the objective to 15,000 to 20,000 barrels a day. New contracts followed with Imperial Oil and with an American drilling company to undertake a vigorous prospecting program over much of the Mackenzie and Liard river basins. The results were disappointing; the only additional supplies found were within the original 4,325-acre Norman Wells field. In any case, these were more than adequate, since the strategy for which the extra production was wanted was very shortly abandoned.

To build the pipeline the United States selected Bechtel-Price-Callahan, a consortium of nine American companies, which as "constructor" received a fixed $1.5-million fee (subsequently substantially increased) for managing the project. The major task entailed delivering thousands of workers and more than 100,000 tons of pipe and other equipment from Waterways to Norman Wells, a distance of over a thousand miles. Before that phase was completed the project had mushroomed to include fleets of river vessels and barges brought up from the Mississippi River system, a miscellaneous collection of airplanes (some said to have been used in Hollywood films), tractor trains, and trucks. It also entailed building shipping, storage, transfer facilities, and housing along the length of the waterway, 1,129 miles of temporary winter tractor roads, and eleven dirt or gravelled landing strips. These "East Side Transportation Routes" added over $20 million to the cost.

An elaborate installation, Camp Canol, was built at the oilfield, where Imperial Oil, subsidized by the U.S. government, was bringing sixty more wells into production. To meet increased nearby requirements the company's local refinery was enlarged from 250 to 1,200 barrels daily capacity. The pipeline to Whitehorse, which had to be carried over innumerable muskegs and along steep, barren mountainsides with a maximum 5,860-foot elevation, required ten pumping stations. The engineering troops and workmen in addition built a road, a telephone line, and midway along the route a landing strip. At Whitehorse the knocked-down refinery was rebuilt to a new design. Besides the main Canol pipeline from Norman Wells, others were built in 1942 and 1943 – Canol No. 2, Skagway to Whitehorse (110 miles, four-inch pipe), No. 3, Carcross to Watson Lake (265 miles, two-inch pipe), and No. 4, Whitehorse to Fairbanks (596 miles, three-inch pipe). These facilitated moving petroleum products to points on the Alaska Highway and NWSR west of Watson Lake and also permitted them to be imported to Whitehorse by way of Haines Mission, to which it could be readily delivered from the south by ocean tankers over the now safe sea route.

Indeed, the danger to ocean transport had largely passed by mid-1943, if it had ever really existed, and the northwestern theatre could be supplied far more easily by the regular maritime routes. Because shipping was in short supply, however, Prince Rupert began to be used as never before to serve Alaskan and Yukon points. As early as February 1942 the PJBD agreed on the use of Prince Rupert as an embarkation point, and facilities there were quickly improved. From the large installation the Americans built at Port Edward a shipping movement running at a high point in July 1943 of 95,000 tons of cargo and 12,600 personnel was begun. By August 1945, some 940,000 tons of cargo, besides large tonnages of bulk liquid fuel cargoes, had been delivered from Prince Rupert. The White Pass and Yukon Railway also was taken over and virtually rebuilt to handle materials forwarded to Whitehorse for highway and airway points.

Concurrent with these large-scale operations in the Northwest, plans were developed to build still more airfields in the Northeast to assist short-range tactical aircraft to cross the Atlantic to the large U.S. Army Air Force establishment based in Britain. In May 1942 the PJBD was handed a detailed proposal of which the U.S. chairman, Fiorello La Guardia, wrote, "The plan itself challenges imagination. It is gigantic and dramatic. It took our Canadian colleagues by surprise and frankly they have not yet recovered."[11] Project Crimson was discussed at the June 1942 meeting of the board, where it was accompanied by a submission that traffic would reach a peak of one hundred fighters and forty transport planes daily, and was approved as its Recommendation No. 26. Crimson was impressive indeed, projecting three separate air routes across Canada extending to bases on Baffin Island, Greenland, and Iceland. Airports were to be built for the easternmost route at Fort Chimo and on Baffin Island, for the central route at Moose Factory, Richmond Gulf, and Baffin Island, and for the western route at The Pas, Churchill, Southampton Island, and, once again, Baffin Island. The Americans also received permission to build thirty weather stations in connection with the plan.

The Minister of Transport, C.D. Howe, felt that constructing such remote bases would be enormously difficult, and he doubted that Canada would be able to assume these new responsibilities. But having first driven out the Canadians by the magnitude of their program, the Americans began to scale it down. The central route was abandoned altogether, and it was decided to build permanent airports only at The Pas and Churchill. Runways of compacted snow would serve at the Crystal weather stations of Fort Chimo, Frobisher Bay, and Padloping Island. Canada undertook to build only the airport at The Pas, the others being left to U.S. construction. A little later, in October 1942, the United States obtained permission to build an airport on the North Shore at Mingan, only eighty miles from the RCAF station at Sept-Iles, as an emergency field for aircraft proceeding from Presque Isle, Maine, to Goose Bay. The PJBD gave the United States authority over all these stations, The Pas included.

Work was begun at once on the airbases. The Pas and Churchill were relatively easily built, but work on those at the Crystal bases and Southampton Island was set back when a German submarine sank a supply ship off Labrador on August 27, 1942. The remaining supplies went forward by other ships and by air, and by the end of 1942 unpaved but usable runways were ready at each location. During the summer of 1943 a thirty-five-ship American convoy made its way north with stores, equipment, and materials for the Arctic bases, carrying 1,500 civilian workmen and 100 servicemen for the Frobisher Bay base alone. But the pace of construction slackened after 1943, again as a result of the changing military situation. As the submarine menace diminished, it became feasible to deliver short-range aircraft by ship. Other planes were able to fly the safer if roundabout South Atlantic route, particularly useful after the war spread into the Mediterranean sector. Finally, the range of some fighter aircraft was greatly extended by equipping them with disposable extra fuel tanks under the wings.

The American section of the PJBD proposed in May 1943 to abandon the western arm of the Crimson Project, stop work at The Pas, Churchill, and Southampton Island (Coral Harbour), and turn the bases over to Canada. Construction proceeded on the eastern arm only, where the Mingan, Fort Chimo, and Frobisher Bay airports were given paved runways but were maintained only as emergency landing fields. The planned thirty weather stations were similarly curtailed. In July 1943 it was decided to limit observing and forecasting services to five airports, plus another eleven observing stations. These services, in addition to the radio facilities, helped overcome gaps in radio reception and afforded much-needed information on weather and ice conditions in the Hudson Bay and Labrador regions.

IV

Much of the United States' wartime construction quickly fell into desuetude from mid-1943 onward as the military situation improved. In the Northeast, the need for the Crimson airfields was disappearing even as they were being built. Though large numbers of American-built planes continued to fly the ferry route direct from Gander, or by way of Goose Bay and Greenland, little traffic ever used the Crimson routes. Only five RAF planes flew them during the summer of 1943, and apart from these, "air supply, aerial photography, and other miscellaneous operations accounted for most of the aircraft arrivals."[12] Frobisher Bay recorded a mere 323 arrivals during the whole of 1943, fewer than one a day; Fort Chimo registered only 85 during 1943 and 87 in 1944, two thirds of these in connection with ice patrol work. At Coral Harbour, fifty- and eighty-day intervals passed without arrival of a single plane recorded.

In the Northwest, the Japanese were driven from the Aleutians in July-August 1943, and sea communications with the Alaskan front were no longer subject to any danger. In September 1943, too, the Joint Chiefs of Staff abandoned any plans for using Alaska as a major base for an assault on Japan in view of the success of the naval and island-hopping campaigns in the mid-Pacific sector. These developments greatly reduced the need for the Canol, airway, and highway enterprises. The Canol Project, which had barely got under way by 1943, was drastically curtailed. By the time oil from Norman Wells began arriving in Whitehorse in April 1944, supplies were far easier to procure by tanker from outside. Indeed, the Joint Chiefs on October 26, 1943, quietly dropped a proposed Canol No. 5 pipeline (Fairbanks to Tanana) and deleted a new process from the Whitehorse refinery plans. The *New York Times* after the war (October 9, 1946) suggested that it had been decided in 1943 not to cancel the Canol project outright principally to deceive the Japanese into holding large forces in the Kurile Islands against possible invasion of their homeland from Alaska. At the end of 1945, when fewer that four tankerloads of petroleum had been delivered from Norman Wells, the pumping stations and refinery units began to be closed down. From a military standpoint, the $135 million spent on Canol was almost an utter waste, comparable to the Coral Harbour, Fort Chimo, and Mingan airports. Yet it was a useful project locally. The refinery and subsidiary pipelines supplied and distributed oil and gasoline over a 900-mile stretch of highway and air route between Watson Lake and Fairbanks. Imperial Oil's refinery at Norman Wells also processed 457,506 barrels of oil for United States use in the Mackenzie region – most of it, however, for the Canol enterprise itself.

The Alaska Highway also was affected by the reduction of operations, but it did perform a useful function throughout the war and still remains an important transportation artery for a large section of the Northwest. Travel was very hazardous at first because of the ice-clad hills, dangerous hairpin turns, and winter temperatures that quickly froze men and engines if they had to stop for any length of time. After the pioneer road was completed, however, freight began moving in large truck convoys while servicemen and civilians travelled in Greyhound buses chartered to the U.S. Army. The all-weather road, completed during 1943, and maintenance and repair stations placed at fifty-mile intervals, improved travelling conditions to a point where a bus service could operate on a regular schedule between Dawson Creek and Whitehorse. Nevertheless, the volume of traffic did not reach the levels anticipated by the planners in either 1943 or 1944, thanks to the revival of shipping via Prince Rupert and the changing military plans in 1945 because of Japan's sudden surrender.

Only the North-West Staging Route could be said to have achieved most of its military purposes. Its facilities were used throughout the war by Canadian and American transport and communications units supplying the Alaskan front. In June 1942, following the invasion of the Aleutians, swarms of airplanes from eleven private aviation companies under contract to the U.S. government were rushed over the

NWSR, some before the Canadian authorities had been properly briefed. During the ensuing months another 750 planes were delivered over the route to the 11th Air Force to bolster Alaskan defence and aid the recovery of the islands. Canadian Pacific Air Lines (the successor of United Air Transport), the Department of Transport, and the RCAF also maintained flying operations along the route. The RCAF establishment, in fact, grew from a Communications Flight, organized in October 1942, to a Transport Squadron (No. 165) in April 1943, became the North-West Air Command in May 1944, and took over control of the route after October 1944. U.S. traffic was preponderant throughout, however. The most important function from 1942 onward was the Alsib Movement, which forwarded lend-lease aircraft for the Russian front. In November 1942 the first planes began reaching Fairbanks, where Russian pilots took delivery, and the movement reached its peak of 403 planes for one month in August 1944, by which time virtually all lend-lease aircraft for the USSR were being flown by this route. By August 1945, when deliveries ceased, 7,926 American-built planes had been ferried from Great Falls, Montana, to Fairbanks for use on the Russian front – with incalculable effect on the war's outcome.

While Canadians appreciated and welcomed the U.S. involvement with Northern Canada, many aspects of the conduct of its military forces caused annoyance and sometimes resentment. One of these was empire building; the commanders insisted on becoming as self-sufficient as possible, regardless of existing Canadian facilities, even to the point of duplicating entire air stations, as at Goose Bay. Duplication of services was especially common in weather forecasting and communication. At some bases there were both Canadian and American forecasting centres, and for a time American commercial airlines even operated their own meteorological sections. Most of the difficulty was created by the Chief of the U.S. Army Air Force, who defied the agreement that the NWSR was to have one combined service, ruling that his airforce would provide its own meteorological service at all airports from which its planes operated (throughout the Crimson and Mackenzie River air routes, and at Goose Bay as well as over the NWSR). In fact, since Canada could not have provided enough meteorologists for all the programs, the Americans' facilities were needed in many places. The Americans supplied the meteorological, coding and decoding, and other equipment, and in some places they also controlled the communications facilities, which enabled them alone to secure and transmit weather information. Canada, however, possessed the better system along the Mackenzie – the RCCS network – for transmitting observations to Edmonton or to Fort Nelson. Weather stations on Vancouver Island and the mainland were linked by an RCAF teletype system

with Prince Rupert and Prince George. Indeed, one of the most important advances during the war years, as far as the North was concerned,
was the vast improvement in communications and in meteorological
facilities and services that had been so paltry in previous years.

The American presence in the North aroused some anxiety in the
Canadian government because of the very large numbers of servicemen and civilians stationed there, particularly in 1942–43. Some
administrators worried, with justice, over the impact so many Americans might have on the native peoples of the remote districts in which
they were stationed. The scale of American spending put heavy strains
on supplies and manpower throughout the North and greatly disturbed
the operation of the wartime wage and price control system among the
inhabitants. At the same time the high wages paid American civilian
workers and the lavish spending by American servicemen kindled local
discontent and resentment. The efforts of the Americans to try their
servicemen accused of offences against Canadians and Canadian laws
in their own military courts caused further annoyance. Worst of all,
American officers frequently acted on their own initiative, ignoring
proper Canadian civil and military authorities, and individuals sometimes conducted themselves as though the United States were a conquering occupation force rather than an ally and partner. Loose talk
about even larger plans extending into the post-war period added still
more apprehensions.

The uneasiness reached the Dominion Cabinet on March 31, 1943,
when the War Cabinet received a report from Malcolm MacDonald, the
British High Commissioner in Ottawa, on his recent trip through the
Northwest. MacDonald sounded a note of urgency and alarm: the U.S.
effort was on an immense scale that had to be seen to be believed; it
was proceeding with little or no reference to, or apparent control by,
Canada; and it was being "planned and carried out with a view to the
post-war situation."[13] In response to this representation and to many
other complaints over a year and more of offhand treatment by American agencies and personnel, the government appointed Major-Gen-
eral W.W. Foster to act as Special Commissioner for Defence Projects
in the North-West, in a liaison capacity between the military services
of the two countries.

The government's concern was not restricted to military matters.
Fears were also expressed that the large scale of the American activities
might reflect a design, hope, or excuse to establish a post-war foothold
in the region. As MacDonald warned, ". . . certainly many influential
American individuals who have had a hand in these developments in
the North-West have no serious thought that the interest which they
represent shall withdraw. . . . One can imagine some of these people

stirring up quite an unpleasant agitation in Congress circles to force the hands of the Administration."[14]

Prime Minister King had already sensed some such insidious design behind a proposal that originated with the Joint Economic Committees of the two countries in August 1942. The North Pacific Planning Project called for a comprehensive, systematic study of the resources and problems of the vast region embracing Northern British Columbia and Alberta, the District of Mackenzie, Yukon Territory, and Alaska, ". . . one of the large undeveloped sections of the world in which we find a challenge to resource development and settlement. Here a strong community of interest has already provided a framework and habit of cooperation, and results may be expected that will serve as a demonstration of the fields, methods and possibilities of international collaboration toward advancement and security."[15] King had taken exception to the project when it was discussed at a meeting of the War Committee of the Cabinet on December 30, 1942. He confided to his diary that "efforts . . . would be made by the Americans to control developments in our country after the war, and to bring Canada out of the orbit of the British Commonwealth of Nations into their own orbit."[16]

Nevertheless, the project went forward, and the national sections were organized in January 1943, the American section directed by B.H. Kizer, utilizing federal agencies and private groups to study Alaskan resources and problems and the Canadian section headed by Charles Camsell, drawing on personnel from the departments of the federal, British Columbia, and Alberta governments. King's growing uneasiness led to the dismantling of the Joint Economic Committees in 1944 and a decision for Canada to proceed on its own along the lines of the agreed agenda. The Canadian section continued with its work and eventually in 1947 published a report.

While the war proceeded, the Canadian government became increasingly determined to acquire or otherwise dispose of every American establishment on Canadian soil, and in the case of Canol to make no commitments beyond a vague one of maintaining a strategic oil reserve in the North that would be available to the United States in the event of future difficulties. In the meantime, its concern to reduce the American "occupation" of large sections of Northern Canada was reflected in the careful arrangements it made to secure control over the operations of the several projects and assure eventual total withdrawal of American forces and interests. As the number of Canadian meteorologists increased, they took over the weather forecasting work at Prince George and the Mackenzie River airfields, the stations between Edmonton and Whitehorse, between The Pas and Churchill (including the American-owned teletype system), and finally, the Arctic stations. A few stations were closed and observations at others were reduced in frequency, but all in all, Canada emerged from the war with a very useful group of northern weather stations and ancillary communications facilities.

Canada also took over maintenance of the Alaska Highway by the winter of 1944–45, and traffic control over the Canadian section was handed over to the RCMP on July 1, 1945. Finally, the Canadian Army took formal charge of its maintenance and operation on April 1, 1946, in line with the original agreement, as part of the Canadian highway system and "subject to the understanding that there shall at no time be imposed any discriminatory conditions in relation to the use of the road as between Canada and United States civilian traffic."[17] While Canada received the highway gratis, as agreed, it paid $9,342,208 for the telephone and teletype system, which it took over on July 1, 1946. In the following year the United States rented back some of the circuits to maintain contact with Alaska.

In contrast, Canada made no effort whatsoever to take over the unwanted Canol Project. On August 31, 1945, it announced it would not exercise its option to purchase the remaining Canol properties, which were left to be disposed of in ways and to buyers acceptable to Canada. Most of the shipping facilities introduced in the Athabasca-Mackenzie waterway had been removed by Marine Operators, the subcontractor, in 1944; the remaining ships, barges, buildings, and housing were sold to local operators or to the now nationalized Northern Transportation Company. Camp Canol was handed over to Imperial Oil on April 1, 1945. That company later also purchased the Whitehorse refinery, dismantled it once again, and shipped it to Alberta for installation in connection with the recent discovery at Leduc. Imperial claimed that the one-million-dollar price was no bargain because by the time the refinery was re-erected at Leduc it would cost as much as a new plant; the real advantage was availability, for such equipment was still in very short supply. Lifting the Canol No. 1 pipeline entailed the greatest trouble of all. The section between Norman Wells and Johnson's Crossing was sold for scrap in June 1947 to a U.S. company for $700,000, the pipe being taken up and removed during the winter of 1947–48 and shipped back to the United States either from Skagway or from Camp Canol by water to Fort McMurray. The road and airstrip quickly fell into disuse and decay. The subsidiary Canol pipelines were left in place and continued in use after the war, the most important surviving remnant, with the East Side landing fields, of the costly ill-starred project.

The American-built airports were a different proposition, since aviation was expected to play an enhanced role in the post-war world and the federal government considered the airfields useful for the future development of the Canadian North. Under an agreement of June 27, 1944, the government agreed to repay the United States $76,811,551 for the airfields and flight strips plus the Edmonton-Alaska telephone system, and to cancel the $29,599,963 spent by Canada on airfields on the United States' behalf. These payments covered the full cost of the airports of the Athabasca-Mackenzie route and the flight strips along the Alaska Highway, 84 per cent of the United States' expenditures on the North-West Staging Route, and 80 per cent ($31,631,310) of the permanent facilities of the Crimson Project, including the airports at Mingan and Goose Bay, on which the United States had spent $39,494,000. Altogether, Canada reimbursed the United States to the tune of 87.5 per cent of its expenditures on the airports and landing strips, useful and useless alike, extending across the Canadian North – including $543,000 for its spending on the Goose Bay airport, which was not even in Canada.

Thus eventually all the facilities built by the United States on Canadian soil were disposed of, in line with Recommendation No. 28 (January 15, 1943) of the PJBD. Unfortunately, the careful precautions to protect Canadian autonomy against any potential U.S. threat were largely illusory. Even before the war's end, Canadian military planners were expecting to maintain the defensive alliance in the North, as much to forestall steps by the United States on its own to safeguard its security as to avert any as yet perceived Soviet threat. The troubled international situation after 1945 quickly reversed the American withdrawal from Northern Canada, and soon United States servicemen, and some civilian employees, too, were back at some of the wartime bases in the Arctic and at many others as well, raising renewed concerns about maintaining Canada's authority and even its sovereignty.

The expenditure of up to $500 million on building transportation and communications infrastructures in many parts of the Canadian North during the war undoubtedly gave that region incomparably better preparation for travel, administration, economic development, and settlement in the future. By making large parts of the North far more accessible, the United States' wartime activities had brought the region's resources appreciably closer to the stage of profitable exploitation and had even gone a long way towards changing the character of "the North." The undeveloped northern parts of certain provinces – particularly British Columbia and Manitoba – and of Labrador were brought much nearer to the "developed" and organized condition of their provincial heartlands, and in the minds of Canadians "the North" became more closely restricted to the Arctic zone, and, in geographical terms, to the Yukon and Northwest Territories.

Thanks to the war, post-war inhabitants of the Northwest could list such improvements as the reconstructed White Pass and Yukon Railway; the airports, landing strips, and oil pipelines of the North-West Staging Route; the Alaska Highway (including the long steel bridge that replaced the inconvenient ferry across the Peace River south of Fort St. John); and the telephone system that provided the whole region (including the Peace River district settlements) with its first telephonic connections with the outside world. Along the Mackenzie waterway there were the new docks and wharves, transfer and shipyard facilities at Prairie between Waterways and Fort McMurray, at Bell Rock below Fort Smith, at Wrigley Harbour at the head of the Mackenzie River, and at Norman Wells, an improved portage road system at Fort Smith, and new shipping techniques (such as large steel tanker barges) borrowed from Mississippi River operations. Expensive airports could now be found at such unlikely Eastern Arctic locales as Coral Harbour, Frobisher Bay, and Fort Chimo, at which (and elsewhere) weather observing stations provided information on climate and ice movements; radio and telephonic communications had been greatly improved in the Hudson Bay basin and Labrador regions. Everywhere across the North individuals and organizations were able to take over and convert to peacetime uses all sorts of military equipment: military buildings became community halls, companies added trucks, tractors, and boats to their transport equipment, and airplanes were acquired for transport, survey, or forestry patrol work.

The peoples of the North, white and native, also underwent many changes as a result of the American and Canadian wartime collaboration. The military establishments made the fullest use of the local populations, who responded by flocking enthusiastically to take up the employment opportunities and markets for their produce or services laid so fortuitously at their doorsteps. The airports at Goose Bay, for instance, attracted whole families, the men to work on construction or maintenance of the bases, the women to help in the clerical sections, kitchens, canteens, and hospital. The high wages and other perquisites afforded the recipients a standard of living luxurious beyond anything in their experience. The bases provided other benefits as well – entertainments, religious services, medical treatment (including mercy flights), and welcome personal contacts through servicemen's visits to settlers' homes in the new village of Happy Valley.

Military requirements had important effects on many communities. Prince Rupert, for instance, had acquired greatly improved shipping facilities and access to natural trading markets in the Alaska Panhandle, from which it had previously been excluded. Now it could look forward to developing closer contacts with that region, especially as Alaska approached statehood and emancipation from the metropolitan dominance of Seattle. Dawson Creek experienced a sixfold increase in population from a pre-war 700 to 4,293 in January 1943 overflowing the 320-acre townsite into four new subdivisions and creating difficulties for water supply, sanitation, and fire protection that were only slowly overcome. Smaller centres along the Alaska Highway such as Fort St. John, Fort Nelson (a new site at Mile 300 of the Alaska Highway, six miles from the fort), and Watson Lake were affected to a smaller extent. Stopping places and maintenance camps had sprung up at intervals along the highway, the twenty-eight camps of 1945 including 187 families with 124 school-aged children. A modern social pattern – perpetuated by the continuing traffic along the highway – had been superimposed on the traditional native-trader-policeman-missionary pattern that had previously characterized this remote sector of the primitive North.

The sparsely populated but gradually changing Mackenzie valley felt similar effects, thanks to the Canol Project and the presence there of American Engineering Corps and other service personnel. The Canol "East Side Transportation Routes" expanded a dozen communities between Waterways and Norman Wells, notably the portage centres of Fitzgerald and Fort Smith, providing a basis for them to acquire larger post-war populations. The Canol activities at Norman Wells broadened the industrial base of that centre as well, turning it into an important settlement. Farther east, on Great Bear Lake, Canada's involvement in the atomic research activities of the Allies had also revived the mining operation at Port Radium.

The community that was most affected, however, was Whitehorse, the railway terminus town of 600 inhabitants that found itself at the very heart of construction and operations for wartime projects in the Northwest – the air route, highway, railway, pipeline, and telephone system, and the oil refinery besides. Suddenly the unorganized settlement was overwhelmed by some 10,000 U.S. servicemen and employees of a dozen large contracting organizations, who poured into the neighbourhood with all their equipment and came and went incessantly. By August 1944 the settled population of Whitehorse mushroomed to over 8,000, occupying several surveyed sites and shacktowns along the river flats, the bench above, and the heights beyond.

Though the newcomers brought unheard-of prosperity to local businesses, they strained to breaking the minuscule facilities of the settlement and of the Yukon government that administered the town. The pre-war traffic regulations were completely unsatisfactory, and in any case, like everything in the Yukon, were inadequately enforced; the four-man volunteer fire department was hopelessly insufficient; the venereal disease rate was rising beyond control; and unchlorinated local water supplies threatened at any moment to cause a serious epidemic. The newcomers quickly took charge of the situation. To meet the fire problem the U.S. area commandant appointed a captain to act as fire marshal over the American installations and an experienced fireman from a civilian company that owned a modern firefighting outfit became the fire chief. A comprehensive fire code covering the town as well as the camps and enforced on public buildings (including the RCMP's) by American soldiers assigned to that duty speedily appeared in the *Whitehorse Star* over the signature of an American second-lieutenant, all without reference to the territorial authority.

It was the same with the more serious health problem created by the increasing amounts of sewage dumped into the Lewes (now Yukon) River with the possible spread of dysentery and typhoid among users of the untreated water, which included town residents and businesses as well as the military establishments. Once again the Americans took the situation in hand. Following protracted discussions on a joint water supply and sewage disposal program, the Americans eventually built their own water purification and sewage treatment plants and ran their primary water and sewer systems across the town to service their own installations. Many townspeople were able to make connections with the Americans' lines, but the town would eventually have to build a new trunkline system and treatment plants for its long-term needs.

In this way the presence of the Americans pushed the residents of Whitehorse into a situation they would otherwise not have had to face for many years and into expenses they were not yet in a position to meet. In providing for their own needs and riding roughshod over the authorities of the town and Territory, the U.S. armed services transformed Whitehorse willy-nilly into a modern community and urban society. Whitehorse would have to become a self-taxing, self-regulating, incorporated municipality – in fact, a city – as quickly as possible. The situation at Whitehorse exemplifies in microcosm wartime relations in the Canadian North. After the departure of the Americans, the 3,000 to 4,000 Whitehorse residents remained in the squatter areas and in some former military camps, while Canadian units involved with airway and highway maintenance occupied others. The wartime changes raised Whitehorse to a position of pre-eminence in the Yukon that soon brought it the functions and population of a territorial capital as well.

Government agencies active in the Arctic and Subarctic also had to adapt to the war situation. Surveying and museum collecting activities were suspended, and staff members were transferred to other work. The RCMP, on the other hand, was compelled to increase its staff in the North from 85 to 120 men, new posts being opened at Alaska Highway and Canol Project points, at the Eldorado mine, at the Arctic air stations, and at Port Harrison, Quebec. Its added duties included enforcing wartime regulations regarding enemy aliens, registering firearms, administering price and foreign exchange controls, collecting wartime taxes, and registering manpower. The activities of thousands of workers and their relations with adjacent native groups also had to be watched. There were marked increases in cases of vagrancy, drunkenness, supplying liquor to Indians, creating disturbances, violent assaults, and offences against morality until the construction phases passed their peaks, and vagrancy remained at a higher level thereafter. An important, onerous new responsibility was added when Family Allowances were instituted in 1944; in the Inuit country and many Indian districts, policemen were required to register all eligible children and see that the allowances were received and spent according to the rules.

Even the High Arctic was affected to some degree by the Second World War. The government's ice patrol ships *N.B. McLean* and *Saurel* assisted shipping along the Labrador coast and in Hudson Bay, delivering supplies to defence projects in the region, while *Nascopie* continued its annual voyages on HBC business, transporting the Eastern Arctic Patrol and military supplies as appropriate. At the same time the RCMP continued its program of Arctic patrolling – in fact, one of the most remarkable dogteam and boat patrols was made in 1943–44 by Constable C.L. Delisle, an arduous 3,551-mile journey from Pond Inlet to investigate and act on an Inuit homicide case in the vicinity of the then abandoned Fort Ross. The most celebrated exploits of the *St. Roch* also were accomplished during the war years. It crossed from Vancouver to Halifax via the Arctic Coast route in 1940–42 (wintering at Walker Bay, Victoria Island, and at Pasley Bay, Boothia Peninsula) and returned from Halifax to Vancouver in just eighty-eight days in 1944 via Lancaster Sound and Prince of Wales Strait. Thus *St. Roch* became the first vessel to traverse the North-West Passage from west to east, the first to navigate it in a single season, and the first to negotiate the passage in both directions. The technological impact of the war in the Eastern Arctic also was strikingly shown when *Nascopie* proved unable to break through to isolated Fort Ross for two years in succession. The staff was instructed by radio to abandon the post, a U.S. Army Air Force plane flew to the site in November 1943, dropped a parachutist to locate a suitable landing area, then landed and brought out the residents. Obviously the Eastern Arctic had become far more accessible for post-war travel and development.

Many Inuit in whose midst the Crimson airbases and Crystal weather stations had been built were profoundly affected by the wartime experience. In 1939 the 7,700 Inuit were living so completely from the wildlife resources that J.L. Robinson could correlate their population distribution with the lengths of seacoasts from which they secured their needs. But wartime developments, "the clatter of tractors and the clang of military bugles,"[18] drew hundreds to day-labouring jobs that were far more rewarding and much less arduous than life on the land. Participating in the strange work and alien wage relationship produced strains among groups and within individuals that weakened traditional relationships based on hunting prowess or possession of magical powers. The self-reliance of the erstwhile hunters was undermined, and they grew dependent on the white man's bounty. Thus their first exposure to modern civilization was quite traumatic for many Inuit, particularly in the Eastern Arctic. Having seen at first hand the comfortable, want-free, luxury-filled lives of the servicemen and the civilian employees, the huge amounts of valuable equipment and the extravagant, wasteful ways in which it was used, they came to feel that if conditions became difficult the white man would provide for their wants and share his wealth with his fellows in need.

The scale of the wartime activities in Northern Canada, well publicized by press and radio, created a powerful tide of public interest and attracted scholars and research scientists to investigate the North and its problems. The Social Science Research Council of Canada, for instance, arranged for university scholars and government specialists to study the region in 1943 and 1944. The resulting reports were published in scholarly journals and then, under the editorship of Professor C.A. Dawson, in a book, *The New North-West* (1947). The Canadian section of the North Pacific Planning Project also commissioned a large number of field and office studies of that region's geology and mineral resources, forests and arable soils, fish and wildlife, waterpower, climate, recreational resources, transportation facilities, and local populations, backed up with extensive, wide-ranging topographical, geological, geodetic, and hydrographic surveying and mapping operations by various agencies. The final report, a sober factual survey, *Canada's New Northwest* (1947), was intended as a reference handbook for administrators and potential developers of the Northwest region's natural wealth rather than a guide to future policy. At the same time the great interest in the Eastern Arctic led to the incorporation in Montreal in 1944 of a research foundation formed for the purpose of promoting Arctic development through scientific research – the Arctic

Institute of North America (AINA). Inspired by the wartime "collaboration" in the North and determined to continue it in time of peace, the institute was established and financed by private Canadian and American citizens in "recognition of the fact that only properly coordinated scientific study can furnish a sound basis for the thoughtful planning upon which the development of North America's last frontier should be built."[19]

Canada's public, now considerably better informed about the opportunities, challenges, and problems inherent in northern development, began insisting that governments show more concern for the region and establish a larger presence there. Keeping up the surviving wartime facilities alone called for higher government spending and more involvement with the North than previously. After the lavish scale of U.S. spending and the attendant social transformations, postwar Canadian governments found relegating the North to the obscurity and neglect of pre-war days both undesirable and politically dangerous. Thus the American "invasion" forced a much greater role in the North on post-war Canadian governments. That meant new national priorities: taking a stronger position on how the Arctic would be utilized in the defence of North America and the "Free World," providing greater supervision and aid for its future economic development, and designing and applying new social programs that would lead its people (especially the native sector) to satisfactory adjustment to the demands of modern life. From this suddenly awakened concern stemmed much of the administrative activity and assistance Canadian governments have directed since 1945 toward the northern territories.

CHAPTER 9

Development at Any Cost: The Megaproject
Reaches the Provincial Norths, 1945–1967

I

As the tide of war began to turn, so did the plans of mining and forestry corporations for peacetime expansion. The wartime regimen of steady prices and assured markets had given businessmen a good position for the future, as witness the reorganization in 1945 of the giant Abitibi Power and Paper Corporation, which had been administered since 1932 by an Ontario government-appointed receiver. Mining companies had accumulated large reserve funds to finance deferred maintenance and development work and to undertake large-scale prospecting programs in new districts. Vistas of unimpeded growth stretched before the industries. The domestic market was full of corporations and individuals putting wartime savings to work on long-delayed construction programs, and there were nearly one million war veterans setting up homes and businesses. The changing lifestyle that caused Canadians to flock to the new suburbs gave local authorities and private developers the gargantuan task of building streets and houses and extending the full range of utilities and public services throughout the mushrooming communities. The heightened demand for lumber, industrial minerals, cement, hydro-electric power, fuel oil, and gasoline kept production of these commodities as high as during the war.

Still larger markets for many of these commodities beckoned outside Canada, particularly in the rebuilding after the wartime devastation in Western Europe and in supplying the needs of a rapidly expanding U.S. economy. Continuing international tensions generated further heavy

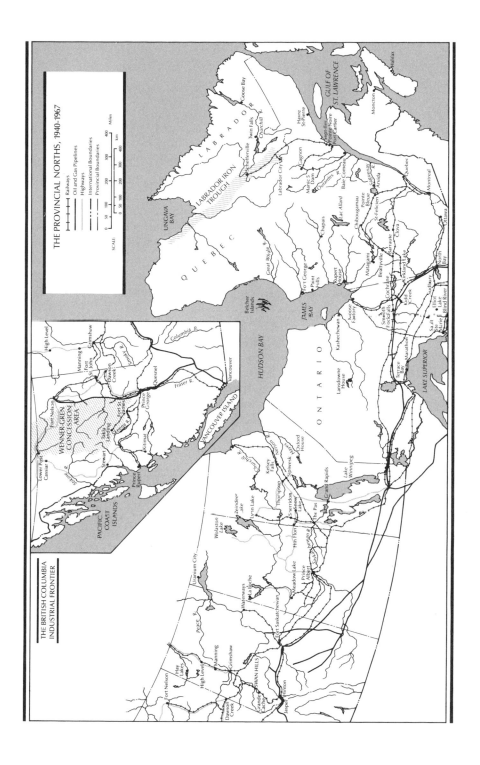

THE BRITISH COLUMBIA
INDUSTRIAL FRONTIER

THE PROVINCIAL NORTHS, 1940-1967

Railways
Oil and Gas Pipelines
Highways
International Boundaries
Provincial Boundaries

SCALE:

0   50 100   200   300   400   Miles

0 50 100   200   300   400   km

demands for uranium and other key metals and directed United States procurement efforts to Canada as a "safe" supply source. The dimensions of the United States' long-term needs were highlighted in 1952 with the publication of the so-called Paley Report, which prophesied that the country would need to import large quantities of nickel, lead, copper, zinc, aluminum, and other materials by 1975. As a result, Canada's forest and mineral resources enjoyed good markets, and much American capital was attracted to their development, extending searches for further supplies in the still-undeveloped norths of the provinces and the territories beyond.

The resource development drive was assisted also by important war-induced technological breakthroughs. For instance, aircraft capable of delivering tons of cargo over thousands of miles had been developed and mass produced; now they were available for commercial use in Northern Canada, where airfields, radio and radar communication facilities, and weather stations had been set up during the war. The highways and tractor trails could be used by improved varieties of motor vehicles, some of them also extremely useful for earth-moving and construction tasks. The development of air photography had transformed surveying and prospecting operations into a most effective instrument, while radar and other electronic advances increased geologists' ability to discover and analyse interesting terrains and underlying geological formations from the air. Magnetometers and other geophysical instruments became available for ground surveying, while researches in atomic energy had developed more effective methods for detecting radioactive minerals. Thus after 1945 opportunities for the development of Canada's outlying natural resources had arisen that seemed comparable with those the prairie grasslands had held out to pioneering land seekers half a century earlier.

The new onslaught on the resources of Northern Canada had the benefit of an altered view of the appropriate role of government in natural resource development. Governments had not only determined to become more active in directing the economy and society than in pre-war days but had also had their means and purposes for so doing greatly changed by the war. Social concerns – the attainment of a higher national standard of living bolstered by comprehensive social welfare programs for needy, disadvantaged sectors of the population – now dominated their plans. Governments depended more than ever on specialists and experts to determine goals and work out ways to implement them. Future social and economic programs were to be based on the findings of research science and apply the latest social techniques.

In these post-war plans natural resource development was a central ingredient. Because most developable resources belonged to the provinces, those governments expected to play the leading part in developing them, in the process emerging from their wartime subordination to the federal government. The federal government, however, possessed greater taxing powers and jurisdiction over the increasingly important fields of interprovincial and international trade and communications, to say nothing of certain important new industries, such as uranium production. It employed a large staff of expert civil servants, which enabled it to take a leading part in future resource development and social programs for which it might negotiate agreements with individual provinces on subjects of mutual interest. During the forthcoming expansion developers were assisted as never before by government surveys and resource assessments, roads, airports, and improved waterways providing better access to and transport for products, publicly financed hydro-electric power stations, housing for employees, and even the expanded social security system that protected them against hardship and want.

Many of these advantages were apparent in the drive that opened central Labrador – a part of Canada after 1949 when Newfoundland entered Confederation – to modern industry and society. It came about as the direct result of the depletion of high-quality iron ore in the Lake Superior iron ranges of the United States during the Second World War and the consequent need of American and Canadian steel makers to find safe, convenient new sources of supply. The vast, rich iron deposits in the Labrador Trough had been known for over fifty years, but exploiting them had been uneconomic while more accessible supplies were available. Foresighted interests prior to and during the war had secured concessions from the Newfoundland and Quebec governments that were taken over by Hollinger Consolidated Gold Mines (controlled by Jules Timmins of Montreal) and the M.A. Hanna Corporation of Cleveland. Their subsidiary company, Labrador Mining and Exploration, conducted extensive drilling during 1943 and 1944 and by 1947 had uncovered sufficient high-grade ore extractable by open-pit methods around Knob Lake to warrant the heavy investment of bringing the beds into production – chiefly a $250-million outlay to build a 357-mile railway to a shipping port on the Gulf of St. Lawrence. Hollinger-Hanna found the necessary capital and market by forming a consortium with six leading American iron and steel companies, which acquired over 80 per cent ownership of the Iron Ore Company of Canada, the subsidiary that was to carry out the project. The route for the Quebec, North Shore and Labrador Railway was surveyed, the extensive deposits were prepared, and eventually a permanent townsite, Schefferville, was built on the shores of Knob Lake. The railway, mine, townsite, power plant, and extensive port facilities at Sept-Iles were completed between 1949 and 1954.

The first direct-shipping ore was delivered to the owner companies in 1954, and full production (12 million tons) was achieved by 1956. By then Iron Ore and another company, Wabush Mines, were working on a second location some 130 miles south of Schefferville, where they planned to concentrate the mined ore to upgrade it and reduce the shipping weight. (Later they also formed it into pellets better suited to the steelmaking process.) The concentration plants at the new centres of Labrador City and Wabush, unlike Schefferville, required year-round labour forces. The Wabush mine was connected with Iron Ore's railway by a forty-two-mile branch over which its concentrated ore moved to its own port on Sept Iles Bay, Pointe Noire, where the pelletizing plant was located. The mine went into production in 1962 and the plant in 1963. A United States Steel subsidiary, Quebec Cartier Mining Company, developed a fourth enterprise about one hundred miles southwest of Wabush in the Manicouagan River watershed of Quebec. The mine, concentrator, and townsite of Gagnon were linked by a privately owned 197-mile railway to Port Cartier, a specially built port on Shelter Bay, the $200-million project going into operation in 1960. American companies also were responsible for an iron-titanium mining operation at Lac Allard, inland from Havre St Pierre and linked to that port by a thirty-seven-mile railway.

These projects inspired others. Many iron prospects were investigated during the 1950s – notably north of Gagnon, around Ungava Bay, along Great Whale River, and on the Belcher Islands. But none of them were followed up because of some shortcoming: unsatisfactory properties of the iron, shipping difficulties, or lack of financing or assured markets. Parallel studies of the plentiful waterpower resources of the Labrador peninsula undertaken for the iron companies, however, had important consequences. Iron Ore built a small station for its requirements and the Hamilton Falls Power Corporation started a 120,000 horsepower plant at Twin Falls in 1960 for local users. These were precursors of the huge projects of Hydro-Québec on the Manicouagan and Outardes rivers and of British Newfoundland Corporation (Brinco) at Churchill Falls on the Churchill River of Labrador that followed in the 1960s.

These enterprises brought a remote, previously completely undeveloped region into the ambit of modern industry and society. The town of Schefferville (population 3,178) was the first organized municipality in Nouveau-Québec, and Sept-Iles, formerly a sleepy fishing and pulp-log collecting village, swelled into an important transportation and industrial city of 14,196. As might be expected, almost the whole of the iron ore was exported to the United States, transforming Canada from a large importer into a considerable producer and exporter of iron. The anticipated scale of the shipping movement (20 to 40 million tons a year) and its direction (up the waterway to Lake Erie), plus the powerful political influence of the American owner companies, were major influences leading the United States to participate in building the long-delayed St. Lawrence Seaway, which added still more fuel to the post-war construction boom.

Across Canada a similar process was under way in British Columbia. During the war the Aluminium Company of Canada (Alcan) had expanded almost to the limit of its available water resources in the Saguenay district. Anticipating still larger peacetime markets for aluminum, the company began looking for suitable new power sites. Such an opportunity existed in Northern British Columbia, with its excellent harbours, vast, untapped hydro-electric power resources, and provincial government eager to foster industrial development in remote regions. Responding in 1948 to a government invitation, Alcan selected Kitimat at the head of Douglas Channel as the site for a port, smelter, and townsite. A large hydro-electric power supply was secured by reversing the eastward flow of the main headwaters of the Nechako River and turning them west to Kemano, where a tunnel through a mountain dropped the water almost to sea level, the resulting generated power being transmitted fifty miles to the Kitimat smelter. Construction of the 400,000-horsepower generating station (eventually increased to 750,000 horsepower) began in 1951, and the plant went into operation on schedule. But when a soft market situation delayed expansion to the planned-for capacity and no other industries were attracted, Kitimat did not grow as much as anticipated. Still, the project led to a substantial construction boom that fed British Columbia's continuing prosperity during the fifties, brought the communities of Kitimat and Kemano into being, created employment and generated wealth in the district, and put the waterpower resources of a sizeable part of central British Columbia into commercial use refining aluminum.

Another noteworthy regional development based on mining, this time in Northern Manitoba, was occasioned by depletion of reserves elsewhere and the favourable post-war markets for nickel and base metals. This was true of the Sherritt-Gordon Mining Company's operation in the Flin Flon district. The company therefore proceeded in 1951 to develop a large nickel-copper deposit at Lynn Lake, some 250 miles farther north. The CNR built a connecting line to the new mine in return for a twenty-year traffic and rates guarantee. Sherritt-Gordon developed two small hydro sites to supply its concentrator, then shipped the copper concentrates to the Hudson Bay Mining and Smelting refinery at Flin Flon and the nickel concentrates to a nickel refinery it constructed at Fort Saskatchewan, Alberta, to take advantage of cheap natural gas available there. Buildings were hauled by tractor trains in winter from the former camp at Sherridon to the new townsite of Lynn Lake. Hudson Bay Mining also discovered and developed several base metal deposits in the Snow Lake district to supply additional ore for its large Flin Flon operation. A townsite from a failed neighbouring gold mine was moved to the new location, and arrangements were made in 1959 for the CNR to build a fifty-two-mile branch line to connect the new mines and townsite with Flin Flon.

These were preludes to a much larger operation undertaken by INCO, which in view of the gradual depletion of its mines at Sudbury had put prospectors and geophysical survey parties in Northern Manitoba from 1946 onward. The Thompson nickel-copper deposit was staked in 1954, and the company decided in December 1956 to establish a large, fully integrated nickel-mining operation there. Rail transport was provided by a thirty-mile branch from Sipiwesk on the Hudson Bay branch of the CNR; Manitoba Hydro developed a 210,000-horsepower site at Kelsey Falls on the Nelson River, fifty-three miles northeast of the mine, with considerable assistance from INCO itself. The company constructed a large modern town with a full range of utilities and amenities for a planned population of 19,000 but then adopted a hands-off stance toward the settlement. The city of Thompson, at first administered by a provincially appointed official and in due course by an elected council, was officially opened in March 1961.

Mineral production in Northern Manitoba was trebled during the 1950s, with more to come as the newest mines reached their full output. About 20,000 inhabitants were added to the pre-war 25,000, and the region had gained modern towns, several hydro-electric power plants, new railway branch lines, roads, air services, and eventually major highways from The Pas to Thompson (202 miles) and from Thompson to Lynn Lake (195 miles).

A very different sort of expansion was associated with uranium mining, which, because of its strategic importance, was closely regulated by the Atomic Energy Control Board, established in April 1947. While the government continued to support its Crown corporation Eldorado Mining and Refining Company, it also resorted to the private sector to discover, develop, and operate other uranium mines as business enterprises. The principal market, the United States, wanted as much uranium oxide (U_3O_8) as "Free World" sources – Canada, the Congo, South Africa, and the United States itself – could provide. A system was worked out by March 1948: the Canadian government negotiated large block contracts with the Atomic Energy Commission of the United States that set prices and quantities for five-year periods; then it appointed Eldorado its agent to fill the contracts, which Eldorado did from its own mines or by subcontracts with other producers. Arrangements with approved producers took the form of five-year contracts based on their productive capacities, with prices set under a generous formula related to their costs, including adequate dividends and speedy amortization of their investments. In addition, governments looked after roads, hydro-electric power, and a full range of social and administrative services for the mines; the federal income tax laws offered generous depletion allowances and exempted new mines from taxation during their first three years of production. Seldom, if ever, had an entire industry enjoyed such favourable conditions.

In the decade after being opened to private enterprise, the industry mushroomed. Under the impetus of the Korean War, the United States doubled its price for uranium in 1950, then almost quadrupled it in 1953 to encourage its domestic high-cost producers. Prospecting for new supplies immediately jumped to boomtime levels in Canada and elsewhere. Eldorado's original Great Bear Lake source was mined to exhaustion. A second northern locale on the north shore of Lake Athabasca was developed between 1945 and 1953 by Eldorado, Lorado Uranium, and Gunnar Gold Mines (a new operation directed by Gilbert LaBine), all three of which built treatment plants to concentrate their own ore and that from the six or eight other mines in the region. The camp reached full production in 1958. A single townsite, Uranium City, was established in 1952 near Eldorado's mine, buildings being moved from the abandoned pre-war community of Goldfields and electric power drawn from its nearby hydro station.

Northern Ontario was the locale of the largest prospecting rush. Hundreds of prospectors combed the Precambrian Shield searching for developable uranium occurrences. F.R. Joubin concluded that an enormous tonnage of low-grade uranium lay within an eighty-mile stretch of a distinctive geological formation near Blind River. Backed by J.H. Hirshhorn, an American mining financier, Joubin organized a "staking blitz" by a corps of prospectors in July 1953. Other groups followed suit, staking claims, floating companies, and raising funds to develop their finds to the stage of receiving contracts from Eldorado. The first plant, Pronto, was in production by October 1955, and eleven mines and ten mills were operating in the district by the end of 1956, working on contracts worth $500 million, soon raised to $1.1 billion. By 1958 the plants could handle a combined 34,000 tons of ore a day, and Consolidated Denison's 6,000-ton plant was the largest of its kind in the world. To serve the population attracted to the district, the

Ontario government established the model town of Elliot Lake for an estimated 12,000 settlers. It was equipped, in the manner of long-established towns, with paved streets and brick homes. At a smaller operation in the Bancroft district, 250 miles to the southeast, another four companies worked on small contracts.

Part of the $275 million invested in the industry at Elliot Lake was provided by established mining organizations like the Rio Tinto group of Great Britain and by investors in company shares, for the rapid rise in prices of uranium stocks brought excited investors running to participate in Canada's and Ontario's windfall. Most, however, was provided by bonds issued on the security of the contracts awarded successful companies. Canada's uranium oxide output reached a peak of 31,784,000 pounds worth $331 million, representing nearly one seventh of the value of the nation's entire mineral production in 1959. About 80 per cent of it was derived from the Ontario mines and most of the remainder from the Lake Athabasca mines, with small amounts from the District of Mackenzie.

The largest, most important post-war resource industry of all, petroleum and natural gas, entered its modern phase in Western Canada with the Leduc oil discovery in 1947. It was another major force for expansion as prospectors ranged over the sedimentary basin between Edmonton and the Arctic coastline – and beyond. Directed and financed mainly by American, British, European, and Canadian oil companies, thousands of surveyors, technicians, and oil geologists, drillers, pipeline workers, and other labourers fanned out across the region seeking developable pools. Because bringing such finds into production depended on markets, expansion had to march hand in hand with the building of pipelines that brought such markets within economic range. The consequent expense and delay of waiting for production to start favoured the large, wealthy foreign companies, which in addition enjoyed tax advantages over Canadian companies in this phase of operations.

Expansion of the industry proceeded northward in step with pipeline building, first the oil pipelines from Edmonton to Ontario and to Vancouver, then the natural gas lines from Edmonton to Ontario and from Fort St. John to Vancouver. To feed these long-distance pipelines, extensive gathering systems snaked out to ever more remote oil and gas fields, each extension making the next all the more accessible and nearer development. Thus the industry prospected, discovered, and developed oilfields in the Swan Hills region, and by 1967 operations extended to the Rainbow and Zama Lake fields adjoining Alberta's northern boundary. In the meantime, natural gas discoveries in British Columbia extended the exploitable gasfields from Fort St. John to Fort

Nelson, and across the 60th parallel to Pointed Mountain in the Northwest Territories. Far ahead of the developers raced the prospectors, seeking to discover and claim promising pools for their principals. By 1960 the Mackenzie valley, where the small oilfield at Norman Wells was still producing 350,000 barrels a year, was being prospected all the way to the delta of the river, and the Arctic islands were beginning to attract interest. The industries brought activity and disruptions to formerly undisturbed trapping grounds, spawned several new communities in the norths of the two provinces, and contributed greatly to the prosperity of the Peace River district, an important locale of producing wells, trunk pipelines, scrubbing and sulphur recovery plants, and service firms.

Gold mining alone failed to display the expansiveness of the other mining industries. With the return of peace, resumption of the pre-war state of affairs was anticipated, and the prospectors began returning to centres such as Yellowknife. Old mines were reopened and work was started to bring new mines into operation, using immigrant labourers from Europe in place of the miners who had moved to other work during the war. Unfortunately, the price of gold, unlike that of other minerals, failed to budge from the $35 an ounce fixed by the U.S. Treasury, and producers speedily became squeezed between that price and their rising costs. New development quickly ground to a halt, and once profitable mines threatened to close, imperilling the communities that depended on them.

The ensuing outcry from the companies and the people who depended on them persuaded the now interventionist federal government to rescue the industry from complete collapse. Under the Emergency Gold Mining Assistance Act, enacted for a three-year term on December 11, 1947, gold mines could apply for subsidies equal to one half the cost above $18 an ounce of producing their gold. These subsidies helped keep some marginal mines alive and encouraged better ones to expand production, so that the industry revived almost at once and the legislation was renewed again and again over the next two decades. Older mines were closed, but greater production was achieved from newer mines in northwestern Ontario, the gold belt of Quebec, and the Northwest Territories. By 1967 the eighty-seven auriferous quartz mines of 1948 had dwindled to forty-four, 90 per cent of which were receiving subsidies under the act. The arrangement was successful in that the cost – perhaps $11.2 million annually – was small in comparison with the benefits to mineowners, workers, and communities. Instead of collapsing overnight, the industry's life was prolonged for decades, giving time for those dependent on it to move to better prospects and for the mining towns to find new industries, as happened for Timmins in 1966 when a large lead-zinc mine was opened at Kidd Creek nearby. But gold mining would not return to its thirties role of throwing open the northern frontiers of Canada.

The expansionary role of mining is readily apparent because operations are centralized and concentrated and because they usually involve wealthy, semi-monopolistic international companies. Expansion of the forest industries has been less noticeable for the resource is spread across the continent and operations in the post-war period were carried on mainly by existing companies. In production terms, however, forestry expanded even more than mining; ten years after the war lumber production was 75 to 80 per cent above peak wartime levels, newsprint double, and woodpulp exports had increased by a million tons annually. Over the period to 1967, production in the various categories increased by between 40 and 250 per cent, with significantly larger proportions being drawn from previously unexploited forests in the Subarctic and Cordillera sections of the provincial norths.

For the forest industries benefited from an unparalleled stream of innovations that vastly enlarged their potential markets and improved their productivity. The lumberman was the beneficiary of prefabricated and preshaped components in construction and new processed materials such as wood veneers, plywoods, pressed and composition woods. For the pulp industry, it was the development of new artificial fibres and fabrics, plastics, and building materials that displaced wood and metals in many uses. Specialty papers also found new uses replacing jute bags, tin cans, wooden boxes, and even cloth in packaging anything from milk to cement and in innumerable household uses.

The character of the industries changed almost beyond recognition. The colourful, skilful axe-wielding lumberjacks of the shanties and the springtime log drives were replaced by operators of gasoline-powered chainsaws, who cut down the trees and trimmed their branches, and by diesel tractor operators, who gathered the logs and hauled them to the sides of the roads where they were cut to length and piled for loading on large truck trailers for delivery to the mills. Productivity in the woods operations increased several fold, greatly reducing manpower needs. Smaller numbers of professional, year-round, unionized workers carried out the exacting tasks. Many woodsmen now lived in villages and commuted to their work daily by car or company bus or stayed overnight at the camps during the work week and returned home on weekends. The new pattern displaced thousands of seasonal workers who had combined work in the woods with making a scanty livelihood from farms and migratory labourers who had to be retrained and relocated in other occupations.

New techniques also entered the sawmill, as kiln-drying equipment improved the grades of lumber produced and new woods were put to use. The trend was toward large, diversified mills that could manufacture logs for veneers, plywood layers, or lumber, or exchange undersized logs with pulp mills for good sawlog material. The pulp and paper industry developed new pulps using hitherto-rejected poplar and hemlock logs and established on-site units to manufacture the chemicals needed in quantity for their operations. Larger, more efficient paper-making machines were able to manufacture thinner paper and run much faster than before; the process was put on a continuous seven-day basis. All these innovations increased the productivity and profitability of the industries, enabling forestry to expand all the more readily in response to favourable conditions. The timber harvest rose each year to about 50 per cent between 1945 and 1966, although it fluctuated between the 34 million cunits (100-cubic-foot units) of 1951 and 1956, and the 28.5 million of 1958, to the 38 million in 1966. Lumber production, the largest single use, increased fairly steadily, while in pulpwood, the main raw material of the pulp and paper industry, the quantities fluctuated in response to general economic trends and others specific to the newsprint industry, such as renewed competition from Scandinavia and new competitors in New Zealand and Chile, the growth of a newspaper-making industry in the southern United States, and especially the impact of television on advertising revenues and newspaper circulations.

The reactions of the paper companies to post-war opportunities and challenges are illustrated by Price Brothers, which added a kraft pulp mill and paperboard-making machine to their large newsprint plant at Kénogami, built two hydro stations on the Shipshaw River for more electric power, and began drawing more timber from their large reserve holdings north of the Saguenay. New operations in Northern Ontario included the Abitibi Power and Paper works at Smooth Rock Falls on the Mattagami River and the plants of the two American subsidiaries north of Lake Superior at Marathon and Terrace Bay organized before the war but only in full operation after 1945. Along the Pacific Coast another American company established a plant on Watson Island off Prince Rupert, the former wartime U.S. base, drawing timber from the Skeena and Nass valleys under licence. Alberta acquired its first pulp mill at Hinton, near Jasper, which utilized a lodgepole pine and white spruce reservation awarded by the Alberta government in 1951. Many other prospective locations were investigated, especially in unexploited sections of forest that were becoming accessible or where provincial governments were ready to offer generous concessions to secure their development. Sawmilling operations also advanced into newly opening districts, notably in British Columbia, whose production, thanks to expansion of lumbering on Vancouver Island, the adjacent mainland coast, and in the Quesnel, Prince George, and Bulkley districts of the interior, increased by 135 per cent to make up almost two thirds of Canada's total.

Overexpansion continued to hurt the pulp and paper industry. The excess capacity of the twenties had barely begun to be absorbed in the late forties when a new round of construction in the fifties renewed the threat. Because specialty pulps were less threatened than newsprint paper, most of the new mills were designed to produce kraft pulp, kraft paper, and products other than newsprint. The result of the overexpansion and overproduction was that companies began diversifying their operations and absorbing rival or related firms, initiating a process of corporate mergers that increased in scale as the economic situation became more threatening. Efficiency, the all-important consideration, dictated eliminating redundant manpower, closing uncompetitive plants and operations, and abandoning lower-yielding timber areas for newer, less-depleted sources of supply. Thus development of the forest resources after 1945 created problems as well as opportunities.

The advances of the mining and forestry frontiers were matched by parallel expansion of hydro-electric power installations to supply the energy needed on those frontiers and to help meet the seemingly insatiable demand from distant urban centres. Power station constructions were still important events in their own right, entailing multi-million-dollar investments, roads capable of carrying thousands of tons of cement, steel, and heavy machinery, dormitories, serviced trailer parks, or houses, schools, and public halls for the large workforces. Construction villages lasted only about two years, after which they were usually abandoned except by the two or three families needed to maintain and operate the power station. The many large installations along the northern industrial frontiers contributed in a major way to a phenomenal growth of Canada's developed hydro-electric power capacity from the 10-million-horsepower level in 1943–47 to 31.3 million horsepower (23.4 million Kw, under the new system of measurement) in 1967. An average of 1.4 million horsepower was added annually throughout the fifties, with record 2.5-million-horsepower additions in 1958 and 1959.

The new frontier of hydro-electric power-generation resembled the others in that the installations tended to be built in more remote, usually more northerly, sites after accessible resources were developed and problems of long-distance transmission of electricity were overcome. Ontario Hydro, for example, to meet the heavy needs of the industrialized South, completed the St. Lawrence Seaway stations in the late forties, turned in the early fifties to the Ottawa River, and moved in the later fifties and early sixties to the Mississagi River and, beyond the height of land, to the Abitibi and Mattagami rivers (three large plants). When these proved insufficient, Ontario Hydro began building expensive coal- and natural gas-fired electric power stations, then nuclear-powered plants. In like fashion Hydro-Québec, newly formed in 1944, completed development of the Beauharnois site near Montreal, followed by plants on the upper Ottawa and two large developments on the Betsiamites River by 1960. Then it started work on the distant Manicouagan-Outardes project and began planning for future supplies from the Hamilton (Churchill) River of Labrador and the rivers of the James Bay basin. In the West, hydro projects were built along the frontier to serve local industries such as the mining operations in Northern Manitoba or the Alcan project, although they also included the development of the power potential of the Peace River for the distant Lower Mainland urban market.

Providing needed transportation was another side of northern resource development, and interestingly, it brought a revival of railway construction, the first since the twenties. The newly established resource-based industries had to ship large tonnages of raw, semi-processed, and manufactured mineral and forest products within the region and to the ouside world, a service best provided by the railway. Hence resource developers gave thought to building their own lines or made arrangements for them to be supplied by other parties, while the railway companies, eager to tap large valuable sources of long-distance traffic, began building branch lines to take advantage of the new opportunities in the Middle North. As we have seen, in undeveloped Labrador–Nouveau-Québec the iron-mining companies attended to their own needs. In the more advanced areas of Northern Manitoba, developers arranged with existing railways to meet their requirements. The CNR, in addition, built branch lines on its own account where potential traffic from several or many sources warranted, for example the developing district north of the National Transcontinental division in Quebec. Expanding industry and settlement accompanied and inspired construction in stages of a northerly looping line from Barraute to Beattyville, Chibougamau, and finally (1959) to a junction with the Lac St Jean branch at St Félicien. That line helped open more than half a dozen base-metal mines and stimulated considerable expansion of lumbering, pulp and paper operations, and some farming, together with the building of new communities along this latest frontier of Quebec.

Governments, too, joined in assisting railway construction, for

some retained the old faith in the railway as an appropriate development tool. This was true particularly of British Columbia, which
already owned a railway whose deficits burdened the province's treasury. During the fifties, after once more failing to interest the national
railways or the federal government in taking over the Pacific Great
Eastern Railway, the provincial government determined to complete
the original objectives of the railway and then extend it to other
regions to foster their growth. The railway was built to Prince George
in 1952 and to a better southern terminus in North Vancouver in 1956.
Construction north from Prince George was started in 1954, and in the
next few years a 324-mile extension was completed through the Rockies by way of Pine Pass, after which it divided, one branch proceeding
to Fort St. John, the other to Dawson Creek and a junction with the
Northern Alberta Railways. The railway both assisted and benefited
from the resource boom in the Peace River area based on expanding
petroleum and natural gas and forestry industries and in the early sixties from construction of the huge hydro-electric power project on the
Peace River, besides the prospering agricultural industries of the
region. These generated large amounts of British Columbia traffic for
the suddenly prospering railway, which offered reduced rates on farm
produce to attract freight from Alberta besides.

Throughout the period the federal Department of Transport carried
on a generous policy of airfield and airport construction and of provision of ancillary services. The extended air services made possible
prospecting for minerals and other resources by specially equipped
planes and haulage of bulky equipment, supplies, personnel, express,
and mail by cargo-carrying aircraft and scheduled air services. Indeed,
it is doubtful whether a single industrial project could have been successfully developed or conducted in the North during the post-war
period without the use of aircraft.

Roads were similarly indispensable to industrial progress, whether
they were tractor-train trails or paved highways. Tractor trains were
still widely used for a month or two each winter, notwithstanding their
great expense. Several tractor routes later became summertime roads
and eventually gravelled or paved highways or railway lines. The winter trail of the twenties from Lac St Jean to Chibougamau became first
a year-round road, then the Beattyville-St Félicien railway branch.
Another running from the town of Peace River to Great Slave Lake was
improved in the late forties into the all-season Mackenzie Highway as
a federal-Alberta project and later was the route for the Great Slave
Lake Railway. Similarly, the British Columbia government extended
the provincial highway system to the Peace River district to provide
the rest of the province with a link to that region and to the Alaska

Highway and to give Peace River settlers their long-awaited direct outlet to the Pacific Coast. The John Hart Highway, built from Prince George through the Pine Pass to a junction with the Peace River district's road system after 1945, pioneered the route to be followed by the PGE. As necessary, the provincial governments extended their regular roads systems in the wake of industrial development and settlement to new farming areas or to new resource centres such as Kitimat, Uranium City, and Thompson.

The one frontier able to carry a full tide of settlement and modern society along with it, northern agriculture, failed to expand appreciably after the Second World War. "Since southern Canada is almost filled, at our present standards of living, the only direction in which our population *may* expand is northward. This past decade has seen the transportation expansions; the next decade should see the northward migration of people," wrote J.L. Robinson in 1954.[1] Nevertheless, agricultural colonization did not revive after 1945, chiefly because the lands available for settlement were not attractive and far fewer persons were willing and able to undertake the tasks of agricultural pioneering. Besides, governments no longer followed a blind, hands-off policy toward colonization but discouraged unpromising colonists and occupation of unsuitable localities.

On the other hand, the provinces that still promoted agricultural pioneering now furnished settlers with ready prepared farms that could be expected to provide adequate livelihoods within a short time. British Columbia, for instance, inspected and evaluated potential farmlands and laid out 320-acre units containing 200 cultivable acres. Both British Columbia and Alberta made modern equipment for clearing brush and breaking land available to settlers and financed the cost of these operations, estimated at twenty-five to fifty dollars an acre depending on the forest cover. Alberta even arranged with contractors to clear large acreages in new districts before opening them for settlement, both contractor and government to recover their outlays from the farmers' produce over time. Such efforts encouraged continuing expansion of farming in the northlands of these two provinces, which not only possessed some of the best remaining potential farmlands but were also in the midst of industrial development and non-agricultural settlement that created local markets for produce. The Hart, Alaska, and Mackenzie highways and the PGE opened sizeable arable areas to new settlement and gave district farmers a means to ship their produce by road to northern communities or by railway to world markets.

Prospects for expansion of farming were far more restricted in the northern counties and districts of Ontario and Quebec, where would-be colonists faced poorer soils and climates but were offered more attractive alternative employments than their counterparts in the westernmost provinces. The governments, too, seemed to have given up trying to encourage colonization because of the disappointing results from past efforts. As in the West, the new industries and the building of transportation arteries encouraged some new settlement, such as that on the outskirts of the Saguenay–Lac St Jean region, around the developing mining and forestry enterprises in Abitibi and Northern Ontario, and along the new highways and railways opening districts farther north. The agricultural population of the two Lac St Jean counties declined from 1951 onward, while those of Abitibi and Témiscamingue maintained their farming populations until 1956, when agriculture apparently became less appealing to the latest generation of Quebeckers. In Northern Ontario, however, the farm populations of the Districts of Cochrane and Timiskaming had declined steadily after 1941 – from 21,583 persons to 14,236 in 1961. Altogether, the rural farming populations of the six frontier census districts from Lac St Jean to Cochrane declined from 104,444 to 87,889 persons in the decade 1951–61 (almost 16 per cent), and that at a time when the total populations of the six districts stood at 577,669. Agricultural pioneering obviously was spent as a force for expansion in the norths of Quebec and Ontario. Instead, forestry and mining, especially, had become the main dynamics extending the Canadian *ecumene* northward.

II

The resources boom continued virtually without pause for more than a decade, fuelled by massive investments, particularly from the United States. But after 1956 a prolonged recession (or series of recessions) set in that occupied most of the ensuing decade, apart from a spell of prosperity during 1963–67. Immigration, which had achieved a postwar record of 282,164 persons in 1957, slumped badly as the European economy improved and the West German "economic miracle" took hold. Concern that markets might not be able to absorb the products of the newest mining and forestry plants led to a slowdown in further capital spending on resource development. Record federal government deficits in 1958–59 and 1959–60, an open division on monetary policy between Prime Minister Diefenbaker and his more strictly monetarist colleagues, and the federal government's sometimes contradictory statements on foreign policy and other questions weakened investor confidence. The economic malaise was intensified by Britain's approaches to the European Common Market and difficulties with U.S. trade and foreign policies that included annoying protectionist measures from both sides. Fears of undue control of the Canadian economy by American interests were fanned by the studies and final report of the Royal Commission on Canada's Economic Prospects (the Gordon Commission), though, ironically, Canada's trading orientation toward the United States continued to increase in part because of restrictions imposed by Europe against Canada's exports.

These setbacks, coming so close on the heels of the unprecedented expansion of the 1945–56 period, made federal and provincial authorities redouble their efforts to renew the drive to develop resources. Increasingly they moved into the risky, untried field of sponsoring, organizing, and participating directly in developmental enterprises that appeared to serve the public interest. Successive federal governments took commanding initiatives through general programs such as Roads-to-Resources or incentive grants to improve the economies of depressed regions. The provincial governments, as we have seen, increased their direct involvement in railway building and hydro-electric power development programs through provincial Crown corporations; they also responded eagerly to the challenges from competing governments and the blandishments of developers, as "entrepreneurial skill and financial resources moved around the nation seeking the best deals, stimulated by volatile politician-statesmen such as Newfoundland's Joseph Smallwood, the new Thatcher cabinet in Saskatchewan, or the more colourful members of the Robarts cabinet in Ontario."[2]

The changed economic climate was most apparent in the uranium-mining industry. The high prices and other incentives that had encouraged expansion of Canadian production had also spurred efforts in the United States, South Africa, and elsewhere so that there was an oversupply of uranium oxide just as the U.S. government was drastically reducing its military purchases and reserving the market that remained for American producers. Its Atomic Energy Commission decided to terminate the arrangements with Canadian suppliers when the existing contracts were fulfilled in 1958. Behind the scenes, the federal government strove from 1955 onwards to win concessions, but the only victory it gained was the extension of the contracts with the AEC to 1966 to give Canadian firms more time to adjust. When this decision became known in December 1959, the industry abruptly went into shock. Buoyant optimism turned to dejection as deliveries to the all-important, high-price ($10.50 a pound) market declined by stages from 16,000 tons to 1,100 tons in 1966, and the price fell by more than half. Efforts to find satisfactory replacement markets were disappointing. A 12,000-ton contract over a ten-year period was secured with the British nuclear authority at a price of $5.03 a pound, followed by a further contract in 1962. Other sales were made to Ontario Hydro and to authorities and companies in other lands, and in 1965 the federal government started to stockpile uranium oxide, for which it paid $4.90 a pound.

The decline of the industry could not be averted. Production fell steadily from the peak 12,700 tons of 1959 to 3,900 tons in 1966 and 4,100 in 1967. In an agonizing period of shrinkage, the poorer and weaker mines (with their contracts) were taken over by stronger companies that could fill the contracts more profitably. By 1968 Eldorado Nuclear, Denison, and Rio Algom alone survived at Elliot Lake, and only Eldorado at Uranium City. Employment tumbled from 13,600 in August 1959 to about 2,000 by 1963, when the 8,000 workers in Algoma had dwindled to a mere 1,000. The dependent towns underwent severe attrition as settlers and businesses departed, and the surviving residents had to struggle to sustain the institutions of former days. Despite large proven resources and even larger prospective supplies, Canada's uranium-mining industry faced decades of attrition until expanding peacetime markets might again make it a significant force pushing Canada's mining frontier forward.

Although governmental decisions were all-important in the deflation of the uranium-mining industry, its collapse reflected the same conditions faced by other resource industries: much stronger worldwide competition and greater protectionism in major markets. The situation in the mining industries was confused. The total dollar production, strongly influenced by rising oil and gas outputs, increased steadily from 1958 to 1967, but the value of metallic minerals dropped slightly in 1961. Zinc production declined sharply in 1959 when the United States imposed a quota on sales; the 1958 production level was not regained until 1962. Iron ore, too, was affected by adverse economic conditions in the United States; despite steady increases in capacity, output underwent declines in 1958, 1960, and 1961 before resuming an upward climb that reached 40.6 million tons in 1966. Gold production, tied to the fixed price, lapsed into a decline from the 4.6 million ounces of 1960 to below 3 million ounces in 1967. The forest industries suffered small drops in output and shipments in 1958–59, but these were overcome by 1960. Capital investment also declined as railway branch line construction was slowed and additions to hydro-electric power capacity plummeted, though the time required to complete installations already under way delayed the impact until 1961 and 1962.

Faced with these setbacks, the Diefenbaker government newly returned to power in 1958 strove to revive natural resource development as a means of returning the nation to the paths of prosperity.

In keeping with its "Northern Vision" and economic nationalist stance, the federal government in that year launched the large Roads-to-Resources program, which featured widespread surveys of natural resources and federal financial aid on an equal-shares basis to help the provinces build federally approved highways into areas with developed or developable natural resources. The decade-long program (1959–70) aided construction of some four thousand miles of new roads, most of them in northern parts of the provinces. Among them were a road connecting Cassiar with a seaport at Stewart, British Columbia, to give an asbestos company a more direct export route for its production; the all-weather Peace River–Hay River road (called the Great Slave Lake Highway and extended around that lake to Yellowknife) and a highway east from that road across Northern Alberta toward Wood Buffalo Park; a road from La Loche, Saskatchewan, northeast, paralleling Reindeer and Wollaston lakes towards Uranium City; and the highways linking Thompson, Lynn Lake, and Norway House with the Manitoba roads system. Ontario and Quebec used their grants to build highways into several remote mining camps, such as those from Amos to Matagami and from Chibougamau to Lac Albanel in Quebec. The federal government independently assisted the CNR to construct the Great Slave Lake Railway from the Peace River district to the large lead-zinc mining development at Pine Point, NWT. The new highways and railway, it was hoped, would significantly improve the position of existing resource industries and assist the establishment of new mines, plants, and industrial communities based on hitherto-neglected natural resources of the Middle North.

The Roads-to-Resources program involved more than mere construction. Deciding where the highways should be located called for the services of both provincial and federal agencies, the lead being taken by the federal government's Department of Mines and Technical Surveys (1950–66). Its increased budget enabled it to bring to bear all the technological and scientific advances. The Geological Survey of Canada, for instance, put its new-found capability into a joint investigation with Ontario of a 50,000-square-mile district in the northwest of the province "in connection with the Federal Government's Road-to-Resources Program":

The resultant geological, geophysical and geochemical maps enabled the respective departments to select the areas most likely to produce mineral wealth and to select the routes for the roads to these areas. The success of this venture prompted the Federal Government, through the Geological Survey, to begin in 1961 an

$18,000,000 federal-provincial program of aeromagnetic surveys of the Canadian Shield and bordering areas to be completed within 12 years.[3]

Federal interest in other natural resource fields was indicated by the passage in 1961 of the Agricultural Rehabilitation and Development Act (ARDA), which through federal-provincial agreements encouraged better use and conservation of soils. Noteworthy, too, was the establishment in 1960 of the federal Department of Forestry to co-ordinate researches, encourage governments to adopt standard practices for investigating and administering their forests, and subsidizing desirable programs of forest protection and reforestation. Early results of a nationwide inventory of the forests (coinciding, perhaps, with new and less stringent classification standards in keeping with the greater ability of the users to process inferior grades of timber) vastly increased the estimate of "productive forest land." Large-scale operations were expanded during the 1960s into hitherto neglected areas, notably the interior of Northern British Columbia and northeastern Quebec.

It was in hydro-electric power development that provincial governments became increasingly involved. Electric power not only was now indispensable to everyday living but cheap, plentiful energy also offered important cost advantages to existing industries and attractions for new ones. The success of Ontario Hydro in promoting its province's economic and social development was a ready and excellent model for other provinces. Close governmental regulation was imperative to enable this industry to function as the desired regional monopoly and public utility, and the economic characteristics of hydro development made it logical to finance new construction by loans raised on the credit of the provinces. Continued federal taxation of privately owned electric utilities added an incentive for the provinces to construct new installations and assume ownership of the old. In Quebec there was the added motive of reducing French Canada's dependence on outside, "alien" interests and striking out towards becoming truly "*maîtres chez nous*." The improvements in transmitting electricity over long distances also made public involvement desirable so as to guarantee adequate supplies to rapidly growing and politically powerful urban areas and help with making arrangements for exchanging large but uneven power surpluses with adjacent provinces or states (planning for a "National Power Grid" was under way by 1960).

Regulatory commissions to oversee industries that served the public were common, but provincially owned systems on the model of Ontario's were slow to materialize. Then two noteworthy advances occurred in 1961 and 1962 when British Columbia and Quebec took over the principal private power corporations within their borders. Eleven companies cost Quebec over $600 million. The resulting Crown corporations emerged as the most important providers and distributors of power in their provinces, and huge construction programs, financed by the credit of the provincial governments, speedily followed. Hydro-Québec began large-scale development of sites on the Manicouagan and Outardes rivers north of Baie Comeau that envisaged an output of 7.3 million horsepower from eight plants. The largest of these, Manic 5, which included an enormous 4,000-foot-long, multi-arched dam, rising over 700 feet above the bedrock, was a showplace for Québécois engineering competence and a source of strong nationalistic pride. Then the ambitious, power-hungry utility turned its attention to still more distant sources of supply to help sustain Quebec's industrial growth and economic prosperity and to earn new revenues from surplus power.

Hydro nationalization in British Columbia was the personal decision of Premier W.A.C. Bennett, taken to secure speedy development of the power potential of the Peace River as part of his program for developing the northeast and northern interior of the province. To accomplish his objective, Bennett expropriated the large B.C. Electric Company to give the Peace River plant a guaranteed market in the urbanized southwest of the province while he disposed of power rights in the Columbia River basin to the United States for a cash consideration. Construction was started on the large dam and the 2.3-million-horsepower installation at Portage Mountain in 1963, with the first power to be delivered in 1968.

To the east, the strengthened Manitoba Hydro system began construction of a 600,000-horsepower plant at the Grand Rapids at the mouth of the Saskatchewan River, and the Saskatchewan Power Commission undertook another at Squaw Rapids, higher up the Saskatchewan. Manitoba Hydro, looking ahead to a large market for power in the adjoining United States, also began planning to harness the hydro potential of the Nelson River augmented by water diversions from the adjoining Churchill River basin.

In contrast with this trend, Premier J.R. Smallwood followed the traditional method to secure development of the huge power potential of the Hamilton River of Labrador by private enterprise. He offered Brinco, a consortium of seven companies formed in 1953, very large concessions in forest, mineral, and hydraulic resources under easy terms and performance conditions. Following surveys, Brinco organized a subsidiary, the Churchill Falls Corporation, to undertake development of the Churchill River (so renamed by Smallwood to honour the British wartime prime minister, his personal hero) and find both the capital for construction and the markets for the power that would be generated. Technical conditions made it impractical to export this power by any route except through Quebec, so that construction had to wait until terms satisfactory to the company (in which Hydro-Québec, through Shawinigan, held a substantial interest) and to the two governments could be arranged. In the end, virtually the whole of the generated power had to be contracted to Hydro-Québec at low prices fixed for a forty-year term before construction of the great $937-million project could begin. Work commenced on the Churchill Falls station in 1967 and power generation started at the end of 1971; the full output from the eleven generators was attained by 1976. Like so many of Smallwood's projects, the realized dream brought only meagre rewards to Newfoundland in exchange for the long-time surrender of Churchill Falls, the veritable jewel of his province's natural wealth.

Premier Bennett's nationalization of B.C. Electric, while not unique in his career, was the exception rather than the rule. In the main he relied on the private sector, encouraged by generous grants and a government that boasted of its receptivity to the entrepreneur's every need, to develop the rich natural resources of his province. In fact, this takeover grew from an earlier gigantic concession that quite eclipsed any of Premier Smallwood's. In November 1956, following two years of negotiations, the Bennett government earmarked a 40,000-square-mile tract extending along the Rocky Mountain Trench from near Prince George to the Yukon boundary for a multi-resource development program by the Wenner-Gren Foundation, a Swedish organization that had some experience in this sort of activity. In return, the foundation deposited a $500,000 performance bond with the province and committed itself to start on a 400-mile railway between the PGE and the Yukon boundary by mid-1960. Extensive surveys were carried out by specialist firms under contract to the organization, while the principals made plans to develop the tract's resources.

From the outset the abilities and good faith of the developer were questioned, while the deal was criticized as too hasty and dangerously improvident. The doubts were intensified when the would-be promoter seemingly lost interest in the forest and mineral resources but determined to proceed with developing the enormous hydro-electric potential of the Peace River at Rocky Mountain Canyon, for which purpose the subsidiary Peace River Power Development Company was formed. It was the inability of this company to proceed with construction because it could not find markets and raise finances that led the British Columbia Power Commission to take control of the hydro-electric power system of the province. The subsequent failure of the Wenner-Gren organization to carry out its railway undertaking (proposed as a high-speed monorail system) marked the complete collapse of the ambitious project.

Far more typical of the Bennett government's management was its program of large, long-term forestry concessions under which most of the timber resources of the British Columbia interior were awarded to private interests. On top of an existing system of Forest Management Licences and Public Working Circles inaugurated in 1948, a new system of Pulpwood Harvesting Areas was instituted in 1961 under which large tracts – many of them already licensed to lumbermen – were granted to pulp mill developers who could cut the small-diameter trees and had exclusive rights to use material left over from the sawmills of their areas. The result was beneficial to all three parties: the sawmills because they now could dispose of formerly worthless waste material, the pulp mills because they received large supplies of cheap, convenient woodchips suitable for pulping, and the province because the forest was being used far more efficiently than heretofore. But the system also accelerated the consolidation of the lumber industry into a few large permanent mills and once more (in conjunction with similar changes elsewhere) encouraged overbuilding of pulp and paper mills, creating excess capacity and contributing to a new round of mergers and corporate reorganizations.

Agreements were negotiated with several qualified licensees, who almost invariably included a major foreign partner to supply capital, expertise, and markets for the products. Most of the Rocky Mountain Trench and the forested areas farther west (including the former Wenner-Gren concession, part of which was being inundated by the large lake forming behind the Peace River dam) were awarded to consortia of Canadian and foreign companies during the revived boom of the mid-sixties. By 1968 three new kraft pulp mills were operating at Prince George and a fourth at Prince Rupert (its second); others were under construction at Quesnel, Kitimat, and Mackenzie, a new town 125 miles north of Prince George incorporated in 1965. The new mills benefited from the Peace River hydro-electric power and from special freight rates on the PGE Railway, which began a new round of construction after 1963 from Prince George to Mackenzie (1966), Fort St. James (1968), Takla Landing (1969), and in 1971 north from Fort St. John to Fort Nelson. These 426 miles of new branch lines extended sawmilling and pulp chip-making operations into newly opening districts of Northern British Columbia and fostered mine and oil and natural gas well development. With all its faults, the Bennett government's northern natural resources development program was the most extensive in the province's history and a major explanation for British Columbia's prolonged great economic prosperity.

The Bennett program assumed that development of the northern resources with the aid of the most modern, efficient technology automatically benefited the residents of the new centres, regardless of background, and also the province as a whole. A similar approach motivated the governments of Alberta, Manitoba, Ontario, and of course Newfoundland and Labrador. The CCF government of Saskatchewan, and to a lesser degree the post-1960 governments of Quebec, on the other hand, took a more direct part in the planning and development of natural resources, and were more concerned with non-economic goals, such as creating employment for large indigenous populations that had outgrown the fish, game, and fur resources of their regions. For Quebec, strengthening the "French fact" was of great importance. Besides involving themselves heavily with the enormous expansion of Hydro-Québec, the governments of Quebec in the 1960s created Crown corporations through which the province participated directly in development of natural resources (Sogefor and Rexfor for forestry, Soquem for mineral prospecting) or specific manufacturing industries (Sidbec for steel production), financed ultimately out of the large Quebec Pension Plan and other funds controlled by the provincial government. In line with their penchant for economic planning and promoted development they also established the Direction-Générale du Nouveau-Québec to oversee the economic and social development of that northernmost part of their province.

Saskatchewan's CCF government, elected in 1944, was committed to state planning and the use of public corporations to promote development of the long-neglected northern third of the province for the best social as well as economic interests of the region and its people. Its program of economic and sociological studies, for instance, was designed to "show ways and means of coping with current integrated problems of resource conservation and development in the region, and in so doing contribute towards the rehabilitation of the Metis by leading to the ultimate optimum development of the region's resources."[4] The Northern Administration District (later Northern Affairs Branch) set up in 1948 managed the region with field officers and area administrators and co-ordinated the activities of other agencies of government there. Its tasks included extending medical, social welfare, and co-operative programs into the region; developing local government institutions; constructing roads, public buildings, and housing; organizing the hunting, trapping, and fishing industries; and promoting the wildlife and other industries. Crown corporations were set up to provide air services and to help market furs, fish, and timber. The Saskatchewan Timber Board, for instance, directed custom cutting for mining and other companies, for export as pulpwood or cordwood, for manufacture into lumber for local consumption, or for supply to a provincially owned box factory. Over the years the social programs were expanded and made more effective, the resources inventory was pushed forward, the region became more accessible, and uranium and base-metal mining industries were started.

The election in 1964 of a Liberal government dedicated to reintroducing "free enterprise" put a new face on resource development. Premier Thatcher, like other premiers of the day, resolved to attract large-scale, economically competitive modern industries to develop the region's natural wealth, its forest resources in particular. Plans were made to establish two sawmill–pulp mill complexes to provide significant wage employment for resident whites and natives. Parsons & Whittemore, an international company specializing in organizing and building pulp and paper mills in underdeveloped countries, was commissioned to build and manage a 600-ton-per-day kraft pulp mill at Prince Albert, the province guaranteeing most of the construction bonds and agreeing to provide roads, electric power, and the wood for processing. This last task was handed over for the first few years to the Timber Board, which continued to manage the local forestry operations. Construction was begun in 1966 and the mill was in operation in 1968, the pulp being marketed in the United States through the management company. Despite criticism of alleged company profiteering and governmental improvidence, the project was judged "a qualified but important success for Premier Ross Thatcher."[5] When the CCF (now NDP) returned to office in 1970, however, they cancelled the second mill planned for Meadow Lake.

The favourable assessment of the Prince Albert project owed something, perhaps, to events in Manitoba that revealed how many pitfalls could lie in the path of an unsophisticated government eager to encourage resource development. Manitoba, like Saskatchewan, aspired to establish an industrial complex based on the forests of the district centred on The Pas, but the result of its endeavours was "a grotesque horror story and a scandal of international proportions."[6] Failing to interest Canadian companies in the plan, the Liberal government of the 1950s commissioned an American consulting firm to prepare reports on the project, then advertised for a developer with little success.

In 1966, on the eve of a provincial election, the successor Conservative government chose an unknown Swiss company called Monoco A.G. to construct and operate the project under arrangements that appear improvident beyond belief. For instance, funds for the local company, Churchill Forest Industries, were supplied by the Manitoba Development Fund, a provincial agency, which used money raised on the credit of the province and paid the accounts presented with little or no checking. The company supplied little capital or expertise but relied on contracting companies (some closely connected with itself) to carry out the operations. The government funds were siphoned through a management company before being disbursed to the suppliers, inflating costs by an estimated 50 per cent above the physical worth of the properties. Lawsuits only revealed how difficult it was to bring unco-operative foreign principals to book and how little they were affected by threats of court action. Construction of the sawmill, machine plant, kraft pulp and kraft paper mills proceeded from 1966 until an NDP government elected in 1969 put the company in receivership in January 1971. The project reached completion and began serving the intended purpose later that year, but the heavy debt burden (including interest) from its difficult gestation made it unlikely the enterprise would ever become profitable.

Alberta did not feel the same urge to assist resource developers because oil and gas companies were well able to finance their own projects and pay handsomely for the privilege. The drive to exploit the enormous Athabasca oil sands, however, was an exception in that it was such an inordinately expensive proposition that governments desired to see it achieved mainly for nationalistic reasons. Would-be developers, accordingly, were offered special royalty and tax arrangements, agreed prices, markets for their product, even loans and direct investments to bring plants to the production stage. The government was even more directly involved with resource development in the Alberta Resources Railway, undertaken in 1965. The main purpose for this long-sought line between the CNR west of Edmonton and the Peace River district was to help develop a large coal-mining operation on the Smoky River at Grande Cache that McIntyre Mines was developing with financial aid from, and under contract to, Japanese interests. The province paid for the railway out of its large oil royalties fund and had the CNR build and operate the line on its behalf. The outcome was unfortunate in that the costs of building and operating the line far exceeded expectations, while the developed resource failed to meet them. The closing of the coal mine in the seventies brought hardship to the settlers and the owning company and complete frustration to Alberta's experiment with development railways. In this unsatisfactory outcome Alberta resembled most of the provinces that strove to force the pace of natural resource development in their northlands to bring back the resource-based prosperity of the period 1945–57.

III

The remarkable advances of the industrial frontiers into the provincial norths between the Second World War and 1967 represented many economic and technological triumphs but also introduced social, environmental, and national problems. The new industries, extending from Churchill Falls to Cassiar across Canada, were organized as natural resource-using plants with adjoining communities to house their workers. Most, except those situated in farming districts, were surrounded by the forests, bush, muskegs, and lake-studded country that were the permanent habitats of native bands still subsisting from hunting, fishing, and trapping. The approximately 250,000 settlers along the resources frontier made almost no use of these surroundings except for recreation. Despite the distance separating them from their heartlands in the South, the residents and industrial operations were tied to the "outside" by a lifeline of highways, railways, air routes, and communications networks over which they moved the products of the mines and mills to market and received their supplies and services.

The new communities mirrored the large-scale, capital-intensive, technologically advanced resource-extracting industries that were their *raisons d'être*. The first comers were the contractors and hundreds of workmen and tradesmen, who constructed the mines, mills, or hydro stations, the transportation and electric power facilities, and the townsites. When their work was finished, the construction crews moved to other projects, leaving the townsite to the employees of the industrial firm, its permanent residents. Because of the vast scale of both the investment and the companies' means, the townsites generally incorporated advanced town-planning theory, almost regardless of costs, which after all were minor in terms of the overall investments. Besides, only well planned, built, and equipped communities could provide the living conditions needed to attract and hold the highly educated, upwardly mobile key personnel and the skilled, trained, reliable workmen the enterprises required. The Central Mortgage and Housing Corporation (CMHC) and sometimes provincial agencies powerfully assisted the companies' efforts at community-building.

These communities were mostly single-industry company towns in which the firm employed virtually all the adult residents, and which possessed distinctive, much studied societies and social structures. The companies' recruitment and employment practices set the demographic, ethnic, and religious composition of the settlements; place in the corporate hierarchy in the main determined the social as well as the economic status. The single men and limited-term employees were

usually accommodated in apartment-type buildings with common din-
ing rooms. Single-family or multiple-family dwellings were available
for the managerial and specialized technical personnel. Since labour
turnover was high because of the isolated locations of the plants, company managements were at pains to encourage desirable wage employees to take root by offering them very attractive arrangements for
home purchase and buy-back. Provincial laws and corporate self-inter-
est may have reduced most of the unpleasant features of company
towns by this time, but the company's presence was still overwhelming, especially as it often had to provide all important services whenever outside agencies were unable to do so. Most communities
advanced toward local self-government in accordance with provincial
laws, but even then the fullest co-operation of the employer and almost
sole taxpayer was essential for the system to function successfully.

Given the power of the management and the residents' close identification with the company, trade unions might have been expected
to find difficulty becoming established in such communities. Before
1939 employers had generally been able to use economic pressure to
stop efforts to organize their workers and were usually backed by
provincial authorities. By the post-war period, however, most jurisdictions, following the federal government's wartime lead, had
enacted labour legislation that provided for union certification, collective bargaining, and formalized union-employer relations. Most
large companies no longer resisted unions. As owners of several or
many plants, they were already dealing with unions on a nation-wide
or continent-wide basis and had learned how to work with them.
Union locals were formed with relative ease in the northern plants to
defend workers' interests and provide a channel for settling their
grievances. Occasionally, however, jurisdictional disputes between
rival unions, industry-wide or company-wide strikes, or dissatisfaction with the policies of distant union headquarters disturbed the normal smooth functioning of employer-union relations at the local level.

Time would reveal serious social problems in these communities.
Because the original workforces were usually relatively young, the
communities after a few years faced heavy tax burdens for education
and recreation. Later would follow the exodus of energetic young
people as local jobs failed to offer attractive enough opportunities or
adventure to satisfy them – or to live up to big-city tastes and standards
propagated by schools, press, motion pictures, and, most influential
of all, television. Still later, the communities would face a no-growth
stage of advancing age combined with the problems of elderly, dis-
heartened, resigned inhabitants. The passage of time brought obso-
lescence of plant, equipment, and operations (an ever-present danger

in an age of such rapidly changing technologies) and of community buildings and amenities, depletion of the best and cheapest raw materials, and increasing environmental pollution from years of unsupervised and unchecked operations.

Obviously, the well-being of the communities was completely dominated by the fortunes of the owning companies and quickly reflected their periods of prosperity, expansion, and growth or of austerity, slowdown, and depression. Outside ownership and control, often beyond Canadian borders, was universal. Decisions promulgated by head offices in New York, San Francisco, Boston, Montreal, or Toronto were based purely on corporate considerations and took little or no note of the local situations in Northern Canada, even though those decisions profoundly affected the fate of plant operations and the lives of the employees. Changes of corporate ownership or governmental interventions could also at any time disrupt the even flow of life in the industrial settlements. Community improvements were hampered by the uncertainties inherent in the absentee-landlord relationship and by the residents' inability to take full charge of local affairs. In times of drastic retrenchment or shutdowns, the feeling of powerlessness could affect the mental health of entire communities. Thus the economic marginality of the resource-using industries arising from their northerly locations was duplicated by the fragility of the societies they engendered.

The branch-plant form that natural resource development followed in the provincial norths created national problems as well as local difficulties. Many of the industries were foreign-owned or -controlled, and chiefly by U.S. corporations and investors since the resources boom of 1945 to 1967 was largely inspired and directed by American industrial, commercial, and financial interests. Canadians' pleasure at the resulting prosperity was offset by increasing uneasiness over the transfer to the United States of profits and employment opportunities, together with control over an important and growing sector of the Canadian economy. Even the usually supportive St. Laurent government was moved in 1955 to appoint the Royal Commission on Canada's Economic Prospects, chaired by Walter L. Gordon, a Toronto economic nationalist. That commission's report, issued in 1959, noted that foreign investments in Canada (77 per cent of which were from the United States) had accounted for 13 per cent of all new capital investment in the 1950–54 period but then had soared to an incredible 40 per cent in 1955 alone.

This investment took the form chiefly of equity ownership rather than fixed debt and was concentrated mainly in the manufacturing and natural resource development sectors, parts of the economy that were rapidly appreciating in value, so that the capital actually transferred to Canada was far less than the worth of those investments. In fact, over half the increase in foreign investments during the 1950s was derived from the retained and reinvested earnings of foreign-owned concerns already in Canada. Thus foreign investments were snowballing, making it all the harder to arrest or reverse the process. Moreover, while Canadians invested a large part of their savings, they were in the main spent on roads, hydro utilities, railway lines, city works, and similar infrastructures and little on developing the new resource industries, which, as a result, were left almost as an open field for foreign investors.

Certain characteristics of the resource extracting and primary processing industries (oil and gas, aluminum, iron ore, nickel and other metals, lumber, and pulp and paper) made them particularly liable to foreign ownership and control. As the Gordon Commission's report explained,

> Connections with a parent or affiliated company in the United States or abroad often mean advantages which could not be duplicated by a purely Canadian enterprise or could be duplicated only at considerably greater cost. Availability of capital is important but so too . . . are technology, research, product development, technical and managerial personnel, training facilities, access to markets, access to sources of supplies and accumulated experience over the whole range of business activity. . . . Most of the output of many of Canada's basic industries cannot be consumed at home and must be exported. In such circumstances the assured market which foreign parent companies can often provide to their Canadian subsidiaries may be imperative to offset the heavy risks which otherwise would be inherent in the large-scale capital investment required to develop these industries.[7]

The report's main concern was that the large amount of foreign control over important sectors of the economy could be exercised in ways that might be harmful to Canada's interests. The commission suggested that special efforts should be made to have foreign-controlled firms employ Canadians in senior positions and secure the supplies, materials, equipment, and services their Canadian subsidiaries needed as much as possible in Canada. They should clearly differentiate their Canadian operations from those of the parent company, with separate records that would be subject to disclosure. Governments should use their control over natural resources to insist that grantees be incorporated in Canada and fully subject to Canadian law. Foreign-owned subsidiaries should appoint Canadian directors, and Canadians should be able to acquire equity stock in them. Larger Canadian participation in resource developments should be encouraged by permitting trust and insurance companies to invest in them; Canadian-owned oil and gas companies should have the same generous depletion allowances as the American companies received. This would not only encourage participation of Canadians but also enable Canada to exert greater control over the activities of foreign-owned companies.

For all the publicity the report gave to the question of foreign ownership and control, and the continuing proofs of the accuracy of its analysis, few realistic efforts were made to implement its suggestions during the 1960s. By 1959, recession gripped the economy, and the large transfers of foreign capital to Canada that had caused such alarm began a three-year decline. In fact, the transfers were hardly needed any longer; by the early 1960s and the arrival of the next investment boom, expanded American ownership and control were largely financed from retained earnings of subsidiaries in Canada and borrowings raised in Canada itself – Canadian loans to underwrite takeovers of Canadian industries by foreign enterprises! Federal governments of all stripes displayed reluctance to take drastic action for fear of possible American reprisals and assured domestic outcries. Instead, they turned to plans like setting up the Canada Development Corporation to direct Canadian investment funds into Canadian enterprises. Provincial governments, for their part, viewing the vast expanses of their underdeveloped "empty" northlands and the growing populations for whom gainful employment had to be found, continued to spare no effort to have the natural resources of their territories developed as swiftly as possible. The Canadian response to the question of foreign ownership and control in the 1960s was in the end not the economic nationalism of the Gordon Report but the actions of the development-minded premiers, Smallwood, Bennett, Thatcher, and Roblin.

Although uncontrolled natural resource development by profit-motivated private enterprise was not impeded by governmental action, there were still important indications in the 1960s that forces were emerging that would gradually slow the pace and change the direction of that development in the coming decades, perhaps for the long term. For one thing, the unchecked flow of certain natural resources to the United States in response to economic forces began to be challenged in the light of the national interest, and governments began taking steps to ensure that their citizens would derive maximum benefit from all such trade. Energy was a field that invited intervention by governments. After 1945, for instance, Alberta's oil and natural gas conservation authority would not permit natural gas exports to Montana until it was satisfied that the transaction would not endanger supplies available to Alberta users. During the decade 1947–57 the federal government, which was constitutionally empowered to regulate inter-provincial and international trade, had quite readily authorized oil and natural gas pipelines built mainly to export these fuels to the United States. One such proposal – to lend government funds to the American owners of the Trans-Canada Pipe Lines system for building a line to deliver natural gas to markets in the American Midwest, with eventual extension at governments' expense across Northern Ontario to serve markets in Central Canada – created a public outcry and parliamentary crisis that contributed to the downfall of the long-entrenched Liberal government.

The coming to power of the Diefenbaker government was followed by the appointment of the Royal Commission on Energy, chaired by Henry Borden, a Toronto lawyer and corporate executive, to inquire into and advise the government on policies for regulating the production, distribution, marketing, and exporting of energy and energy sources. The Borden Commission recommended the creation of a permanent board independent of government to license interprovincial movement of oil and natural gas and exports from and imports into Canada. The board would constantly monitor and evaluate the Canadian energy situation and deal with other federal, provincial, or foreign government bodies on such matters. The primary concern of the National Energy Board that emerged was to promote a National Oil Policy aimed at expanding Canadian production, gaining a greater share of the U.S. market, and eventually enlarging the domestic market by extending pipelines, notably to Montreal, so as to encourage a higher level of production that would ensure healthy growth of the Canadian oil industry. Its authority soon was significantly broadened to include regulation of electric power exports and oil and gas pipelines and hydro transmission lines falling under federal jurisdiction. A subsequent action that indicated the federal government's continuing interest in the energy supply question was the board's intervention to prevent sale of the large Denison uranium-producing company to prospective American buyers. The question of a somewhat comparable export – fresh water from northern lakes and rivers to water-deficient areas in Western Canada but especially in the southwestern United States – commanded wide attention in 1965 and thereafter. Periodic suggestions of such an export to the United States evoke such condemnation as to make it difficult for the proposal to advance beyond the talking stage.

Development by private entrepreneurs usually entailed exploiting a single natural resource deemed capable of profitable development

under the current economic and technological conditions, with con-
comitant neglect of or even harm to other uses of resources that were
less susceptible of profitable development. That approach invited
criticism from a number of perspectives. Moralists deplored the dominant place of the profit motive in the process; socialists decried the
profits going to private developers and investors rather than to the
public, i.e., the state. Economists and conservationists inveighed
against the waste and duplication inherent in single-resource rather
than multiple-resource development, and environmentalists condemned subordinating non-economic to economic resources and
overlooking intangible for purely materialistic values. Later in the seventies the discussion acquired a new dimension – the interests and
rights of original inhabitants of areas undergoing industrial development, particularly Indians, Inuit, and Métis.

Planners looked askance at the unorganized, apparently chaotic
nature of development and summarily rejected the classical doctrine
of a beneficent "invisible hand" working behind free enterprise.
Planned multi-resource development, in contrast, entailed a regional
approach – selecting a geographical area, surveying and evaluating its
potential resources in toto, and establishing an order for proceeding
to develop the entire spectrum as completely and efficiently as possible. (Even scenic, cultural, aesthetic, and environmental resources
were considered to have an economic dimension through their tour-
istic and recreational value.) The regional approach was frequently
adopted for the developing world by United Nations agencies and by
the USSR. A few efforts also were made to adopt the approach in whole
or in part in the Middle North of Canada during the period 1945–67.
The germ of the idea appeared with the North Pacific Planning Project,
which simply prepared a comprehensive inventory of the known and
potential natural resources of the Northwest but made no suggestions
as to any program of integrated development. In contrast, planning
was fundamental to the CCF philosophy, and when that party came to
power in Saskatchewan the multi-resource economic and social planning approach was adopted for developing the north of the province.
Since Northern Saskatchewan did not experience the same pressure for
rapid industrial development exerted on its neighbours Northern
Alberta and British Columbia, the administration had time to implement its program in gradual stages. The abortive Wenner-Gren project
in Northern British Columbia in the late 1950s, too, was conceived as
a multi-resource development program for an undeveloped region. A
much more ambitious scheme that transcended provincial boundaries
was Richard Rohmer's Mid-Canada Development Corridor concept. In
the planning stage in 1967, Rohmer envisaged mobilizing govern-

ments, corporations, and individuals in a great co-ordinated program to develop the resources of the continent-wide Subarctic, Middle North, or Taiga band as a national challenge. The project generated a pair of books by Rohmer, a number of articles, and a conference at Thunder Bay in 1969 but failed to accomplish much beyond training a few persons and collecting data for future development programs.

Running through the idea of regional development was a conservationist drive for more effective use of natural resources. The work of the Commission on Conservation had highlighted the concept of conservation in the sense of making the most efficient use of natural resources. That cause had been overridden by the imperatives of two World Wars, the Depression of the thirties, and, unfortunately, by the eager drives for profits during the boom times of the twenties and after 1945. Nevertheless, the economic rationality of the conservationist approach was not to be gainsaid. Economists, following A.D. Scott's landmark *Natural Resources: The Economics of Conservation* (1955), strove to determine the most appropriate methods and management systems for developing the several resources, and progressive companies employed specialists to improve the efficiency of their operations. Managers of public resources were constantly striving to apply more efficient, rational programs; British Columbia's royal commissions and successive programs for the important field of forestry afford excellent illustrations of the traditional conservationist approach in action.

Resource ministers and their officials began meeting regularly to discuss and concert plans of action and lobby their cabinets for appropriate regulations. Pressures grew for the federal authorities to take the lead in stimulating and co-ordinating researches in the natural and biological sciences and to see that the findings were applied in everyday administration. Early in 1958 Prime Minister Diefenbaker announced a plan to convoke a very ambitious Resources for Tomorrow Conference to bring together specialists and administrators concerned with every aspect of resource management and make Canadians fully aware of the situation. Before the year's end advisory groups had been formed to arrange the studies and discussions for a conference "in which resources management problems of agriculture, water, regional development, forestry, wildlife, recreation, and fisheries are considered, including their research, jurisdictional, administrative, and information-extension characteristics."[8] By the time the conference met in October 1961, a total of eighty learned papers had been prepared as a basis for the three days' discussions, and the conservationist and environmentalist viewpoints were aired as never before.

Environmentalism was emerging by then as a cause distinct from economically motivated conservationism, which was concerned primarily with management of resources that were capable of profitable use. The gradually emerging new attitude gave greater attention to protecting the non-economic aspects of the environment. It drew its strength from widely held feelings of disgust over profligate despoiling of the environment by, and on behalf of, private interests and from fears that essential resources were being dangerously used up to a point where the quality of everyday life was threatened. Particularly serious and glaring examples in Subarctic Canada were the widespread polluting of the air and waters by chemical and noxious wastes discharged from pulp mills and mining plants, the destruction of forests by lumbering and of landscapes by strip-mining and quarrying operations, the deliberate drying up of the Peace River all the way to the delta by the Bennett Dam, and the equally destructive permanent drowning of parts of the Rocky Mountain Trench behind that dam – a scenario typical also of the Manic 5 Dam and most other hydro-electric power projects across Canada.

Social changes of the time made a highly propitious climate for emergence of the environmentalist conscience as a powerful public and political force: more leisure time and longer vacations, increased automobile ownership and travel, the growth of a "consumerist" viewpoint, the impact of television and other media in shaping individual tastes, the responsiveness of governments to pressure groups and mobilized public opinion. Television was particularly effective in depicting and dramatizing harrowing situations and arousing the viewers' emotions against environmental degradation. Demands grew that social, aesthetic, recreational, moral, and ethical considerations be included along with the economic in deciding how resources development should be organized and managed. Economists even began to consider how these values might be incorporated into the hitherto purely economic form of cost-benefit analysis: ". . . economists . . . are only now beginning to attack the problem of non-marketable benefits (such as recreation and aesthetic values, and the indirect effect of one activity on another), which are often of critical importance in natural resource management," wrote Peter H. Pearse in 1966.[9]

Thus the post-war resource development booms encountered increasing resistance as time went on in the form of heightened economic nationalism directed against foreign investment and control, social and other priorities injected by governments, opposition based on environmental grounds, and (by 1967) the beginnings of pressures from advocates and supporters of native land claims. These new currents strongly affected the governments' attitudes and policies and led them to attach conditions based on social desirability to the subsidies and grants they offered to groups proposing to undertake projects of industrial development in depressed areas of Canada. Monetary inducements were held out to industrialists to upgrade or remodel existing plants, introduce pollution-abatement machinery, or employ native persons. After 1967, economic considerations no longer bulk so large as in the past in natural resources development, and development by private entrepreneurs begins to proceed in greater conformity with state-imposed conditions and priorities.

Since the northern territories had barely attained the threshold of industrial development before 1967, these retarding forces reached them almost in company with the modern resource developing industries. The region that offered the severest natural obstructions to development was thus the one in which the counterpressures were most persistent, and the northern territories became something of a battleground between pro- and anti-development forces. The territories' constitutional situation contributed to these results. The authority controlling their natural resources had less to gain from developing them than had the provinces from theirs. Furthermore, it was the authority most likely to be swayed by the anxieties and values expressed in media-shaped, big-city public opinion. Industrial natural resource development therefore found far less support after 1967 when it sought to expand Canada's frontiers northward past the 60th parallel than it had received in the provincial norths during the hectic megaproject-dominated decades after 1945.

CHAPTER 10

The Native Peoples since the Second World War, 1945–1967

I

The widespread destruction of wildlife habitats by industrial activities that extended into districts hitherto left to the hunter and trapper and the resulting declines in the supplies of game and fur has been a fundamental element in the difficult situation Northern Canada's native peoples have faced since the Second World War. Their position was aggravated by the rapid increase in their numbers, which as Malthus had warned reduced each family's possible share of the available game and fur. It was reported from Northern Saskatchewan in 1959, for instance, that "the population in many areas is now outstripping its inadequate renewable resource base bringing increasing poverty."[1] In addition, social changes were drawing native families off the land and gathering them in settlements, causing the nearby districts to be overexploited while the distant ones were virtually abandoned.

Yet in some districts native families still were able to continue securing the major part of their livelihoods through hunting and trapping. Hugh Brody, who studied the 1,006 Cree, Beaver, and Slavey Indians of northeastern British Columbia in 1978 when that region was still a partly developed frontierland, reported that the eleven bands had followed prior to 1960 and still were following a highly mobile hunting routine, almost constantly on the move in lengthy seasonal circuits radiating outward from their home reserves. In the proper seasons they hunted game for food and grease, trapped fur-bearers in winter and spring, caught fish, and picked berries. Their hunts were punctuated by visits to trading posts to exchange furs for staple foodstuffs and hunting and trapping supplies or visit fairs and rodeos. On the basis of three of the bands Brody estimated that the meat from their hunts provided nearly 59 per cent of their livelihood, followed by the returns from fur and handicrafts (over 31 per cent), minor incomes (over 8 per cent) from wages earned by guiding and casual labour, with social payments far in the rear (below 2 per cent).[2]

In certain Arctic districts, however, a very different situation prevailed. In the interior of Keewatin, for instance, a few hundred nomadic Inuit waged an incessant struggle to wrest a hazardous, precarious livelihood from the migrating caribou herds and sometimes perished when they failed to find the herds and the fishery was insufficient. One of their many tragedies in the early 1950s was advertised to the world by Farley Mowat, who had been introduced to Keewatin in 1952 as a member of a federal wildlife party investigating the caribou. His sensational book *The People of the Deer* powerfully moved readers and pushed governmental and private agencies into action. Government parties visited the district to evaluate the situation and provide relief, the RCMP began to patrol from Churchill dispensing Family Allowances and other aids, and the missions hastened to extend their work in the district. The unfortunate nomads were encouraged to abandon the Keewatin Barrens and resettle in centres along the Hudson Bay coast where employment opportunities and social assistance would provide a more secure livelihood. Other Inuit were moved from overcrowded hunting and trapping areas to ones that were under-utilized, the most striking examples being the transfers of families from older settlements in Arctic Quebec or Baffin Island to Resolute Bay and Grise Fiord in the Queen Elizabeth Islands or to the Belcher Islands, and in the Western Arctic from Tuktoyaktuk to Banks Island.

The need to enlarge the precarious food supply of the northern native and place much-needed income in his hands led administrators to promote fuller development of the coastal and inland fisheries. The object was to offer individuals the opportunity of integrating fishing with hunting and trapping so as to provide more adequate and reliable sustenance. Fishermen of the Pacific Coast bands, benefiting from the elimination of Japanese competition, increased their participation in the ocean fishery by working as fishermen and as operators or crews of boats and in canneries, freezing, and other processing plants. In the Subarctic the new roads made possible the extension of the inland fishery to numerous large, previously inaccessible northern lakes. To assist native fishermen the authorities organized Indian-operated fisheries for goldeye, sturgeon, Atlantic salmon, and other varieties, installed freezing plants, storage sheds, and ice houses, and lent individual fishermen the money to purchase nets, boats, and other equipment. By the mid-1960s Indians were taking an estimated 20 million pounds of fish for home consumption from the inland fisheries plus a like amount for commercial purposes. The non-native fishing enterprises were encouraged to employ natives as fishermen and in their filleting and fish-processing plants and to train natives for future management roles. Among the provinces Saskatchewan, for one, organized northern residents into local fishing co-operatives and established a central fish marketing agency to sell their surplus production. Hundreds of northern natives thus were transformed into commercial fishermen, for whom hunting and trapping became secondary sources of income. Indians and Métis were also encouraged to harvest and market the wild rice of their marshlands, pick blueberries, dig seneca and ginseng root, and collect frogs in the appropriate seasons. For Inuit, the Department of Northern Affairs organized beluga fishing expeditions and Arctic char fisheries, attempted unsuccessfully to establish an eiderdown collecting industry, and even started limited agricultural projects in Northern Quebec and other localities.

The Indian Affairs Branch, in co-operation with the provincial authorities responsible for lands and forests, also encouraged Indians to participate as fully as possible in developing the forest resources of their reserves and districts. The branch owned many portable sawmills (at least forty-five in 1957) and operated them on the Indians' behalf on the reserves to manufacture lumber for use in local housing and other construction or for sale to other users. Besides gaining the lumber and the workers' wages, the bands earned sizeable stumpage fees and royalties that increased their trust funds. By the 1960s most forests on reserve lands were no longer auctioned but were developed by the bands themselves. A few Indians were trained and gained certificates as timber scalers. Some bands also were assisted to secure cutting rights to other Crown lands to supply logs and pulpwood to commercial markets. In the northern parts of most provinces hundreds of Indians and Métis obtained seasonal employment (some as logging contractors) in forest industry operations in log driving and transport, sawmilling, and manual labour at lumber-milling centres and pulp and paper establishments, others as forest rangers, in reforestation work, and as firefighters. Thus while forestry for the most part complemented the hunting and trapping life, it also became an increasingly valuable part of the native's livelihood, reducing dependence on the declining wildlife.

Some northern natives committed to the traditional life earned supplementary income by working as outfitters, guides, and camp workers, particularly in tourist operations. This was a useful aid in certain districts such as Southern Yukon or Northern Saskatchewan and Manitoba, but the benefits were not as great, nor did they increase as rapidly, as administrators hoped. Small hunting parties requiring the service of guides continued to come to the Yukon but were becoming less fashionable elsewhere. The great majority of tourist hunters and fishermen did not employ guides at all but simply motored to the locale of their activity with their foodstuffs, camping equipment, and other supplies and took their quarries home with them. Serious sportsman hunters and fishermen more often were flown to the seasonal tourist lodges or hunting camps that required employees at the servant level, most of them the operator's family and friends.

Native Canadians also were finding it harder to share in the new-style tourism, and then only at relatively low levels. Guiding was becoming increasingly formalized and regulated; authorities required considerable equipment, capital investments, and high standards from the guides they licensed, which ruled out most native aspirants. The same was even truer of the licences to operate tourist camps and hunting lodges. There were allegations that the regulations were rigged to achieve those results, which may indeed have been the case in a small, tightly knit community like the Yukon, but the interests of natives were undoubtedly better protected in other jurisdictions, notably the Northwest Territories.

The administration in that area, taking advantage of the improved access by road and air and the great publicity the region was receiving, began promoting tourism in the late 1950s. The goal was to develop a new source of badly needed employment and income, particularly for the native sector, and also to reinforce the acculturative process by bringing isolated native groups into stronger contact with modernity. To develop sport fishing and hunting for tourists it encouraged the opening of camps and lodges, some operated by native entrepreneurs with its financial backing, for sport fishermen on and around Great Slave and Great Bear lakes, at Arctic and Hudson Bay coastal points, and elsewhere. To attract big-spending sportsman hunters, Wood Buffalo Park was opened in 1959 to licensed hunters and outfitters under conditions that assisted native involvement, and when that hunt had to be suspended because of an outbreak of anthrax among the bison, a similar arrangement was extended to the Mackenzie Mountains for mountain sheep and bears. To encourage sportsman visits to the Arctic, regulated hunts of beluga and seals, too, were started, and by 1967 hunts of caribou and polar bears were being studied.

Natives in many localities earned important additional income by manufacturing handicrafts and art objects. Following a decline in production during the war years because of more lucrative employments, many artisans resumed making baskets, sports equipment, clothing

(beaded and decorated moccasins, gloves, leather garments, and Cow-
ichan sweaters), model totem poles, and Inuit dolls and miniatures, for
which insatiable markets existed that could be sustained indefinitely
by judicious publicity. A particularly successful promotional campaign
was mounted in the early 1960s to market Ookpik, an engaging toy
owl made of seal fur with round moosehide eyes, designed by Jeannie
Snowball, a Fort Chimo woman.

Artistry expressed in argillite, jade, and silver carvings and lapidary
work received encouragement. Soapstone carving achieved sudden
importance as a considerable source of income and upbuilder of Inuit
morale through the efforts of James A. Houston on behalf of the Canadian Handicrafts Guild, starting at Port Harrison in 1948. The guild's
outstanding success in marketing Inuit carvings in Southern Canada led
the Department of Northern Affairs to subsidize Houston's work and
help him extend it to other centres. For some years Houston and his
wife (who also trained Inuit women in homemaking arts and crafts)
travelled about the Arctic, identifying and encouraging talented native
artists to produce original, attractive, saleable soapstone carvings and
securing them on the government's behalf for sale in retail outlets.
Houston also arranged to send essential materials such as soapstone to
places where they were lacking and taught individuals to express
themselves in other media, such as printmaking and painting on sealskin, that won new markets for the native artists' works. Production
centres were set up by craft development officers of the department
at Baker Lake, Rankin Inlet, Holman Island, and elsewhere, and by
other patrons, such as Father André Steinmann at Povungnituk. Indian
Affairs officials made similar efforts to furnish Indian artisans and artists with prepared skins, beads, coloured cord, and other materials,
arranged for the training of Indians in decorative pottery making,
weaving, felt working, and carving, and helped market their products.
Later they copied the highly successful methods used in popularizing
Inuit art to publicize the work of the more eminent Indian artists and
artisans.

The campaign to promote Inuit art attained great popularity in and
after 1958, thanks to vigorous help from the CBC, National Film Board,
and other official and private media, and from well-attended, critically
acclaimed exhibitions of the Department of Northern Affairs in Canada
and abroad. These facilitated sales of the displayed pieces and greatly
enhanced the reputations (and incomes) of the artists, some of whom
attracted followings of their own and gained art dealers as sponsors.
To enlarge the market, new art forms were introduced: carved caribou
horn, walrus ivory or antique whale ribs, sealskin prints and stone rub-
bings, colour prints and etchings, embroideries, tapestries, even pot-

tery and ceramics. The artists were encouraged at first to concentrate on the bold, honest, flowing depictions of Arctic creatures, persons, and activities that had so captivated many critics and viewers. But gradually as other forms besides sculpture grew popular, the work was broadened to include mythological and abstract subjects as well.

To sustain the quality of the art and match the supply to the demand, the government set up a Canadian Eskimo Art Committee in 1961. By 1963 an estimated two thousand Inuit were producing art items for sale in their homes or art centres, and Inuit art was becoming an important income source in several Arctic settlements. Their artistic accomplishments brought fame and considerable fortune to several highly gifted individuals and did a great deal to uphold Inuit self-esteem. Moreover, recognition of their talent encouraged scholars and a variety of artists to study and record the traditions, crafts, culture, and way of life of the Inuit. The achievements they discerned made Inuit culture a subject for serious study and enormously enhanced the public's already highly favourable opinion of the Inuit people and their lifestyle.

The efforts to expand all these alternative sources of employment and income could not, however, offset the serious declines in the hunting and trapping returns that had once provided the complete livelihoods of northern peoples. Although the numbers of fur-bearing animals were in fact reduced, the declines were partly masked by periodic fluctuations, and at the same time most types of wild fur fetched almost constant low prices over the entire period. What with sharp cyclical fluctuations of the catches and dramatic swings in prices, natives who depended on furs for a major part of their livelihood were always in difficulties. For instance, the earnings of the Inuit who trapped the long-haired Arctic or white fox almost exclusively fluctuated between annual extremes of $800,000 and $130,000. Even in the best years the native trapper's earnings seldom kept pace with constantly rising costs for supplies and the family's needs.

The poor returns from trapping inspired efforts to improve the prices natives received for their furs, most of which they traded outright at local trading posts. The newly elected CCF government of Saskatchewan, eager to improve the economic position of its large northern native population, established the Fur Marketing Service in 1945 to market all beaver and muskrat pelts produced in the province. The system was like that of grain marketing boards – producers received small advance payments when they delivered the furs and second payments when the fur was sold. Native trappers, forced to accept lower initial payments, ran up debts while waiting for final payments that invariably did not cover their debts. Since the two main fur crops were assigned to the marketing service, little was left to sell to the trader. The trapper therefore could obtain little or no credit for a future outfit and was forced into a hand-to-mouth life, supported by welfare and other social grants. Eventually the government had to run the marketing service as a more voluntary agency. Indian Affairs officials a little later began encouraging the more sophisticated native trappers to market their furs through local co-operatives, or, as white trappers did, at auction centres, notably the Ontario Trappers Association's three annual fur auctions at North Bay, where expenses were smaller and returns were prompt.

The introduction of the co-operative movement was a noteworthy attempt to arrest the deteriorating position of the native hunters and trappers. In the Northwest Territories, the administration, copying Saskatchewan's programs, embarked on a series of comprehensive area economic surveys to improve the harvesting of renewable resources and organized local co-operatives to enable the inhabitants to help manage the economic development of their regions. Following consultations, two co-operatives were organized in 1959 in the Ungava Bay district to exploit previously under-used resources that an area survey had indicated were commercially feasible, an Arctic char fishery at Port Burwell and a logging and lumbering industry at George River using timber stands higher up that river. Two other co-operatives organized in 1959 and 1960 at Cape Dorset and Povungnituk concentrated on developing and marketing the artistic talents of their carvers and printmakers, while another was formed at Aklavik to operate a fur-garment manufacturing industry. More followed in swift succession until the number, spread across the Northwest Territories and Arctic Quebec and including a few Indian co-operatives organized by the Indian Affairs Branch, approached thirty.

Most co-op groups concentrated on fishing, seal hunting and fur marketing, manufacturing handicrafts and artistic pieces, logging and lumbering, house building, managing housing projects (as at Frobisher Bay), or operating tourist facilities (as at Cape Dorset). They also operated retail stores and imported essential supplies such as fuel oil in bulk. The administration provided organizers and technical experts, development funding, and working capital, but Inuit soon assumed larger roles in managing the local groups, some of which became financially self-supporting. Total sales, of which 40 per cent were derived from merchandise sales, 32 per cent from handicrafts and carvings, 8 per cent from fur, and smaller amounts from fish, fur garments, and lumber, in that order, soared from $750,000 in 1964 to $2,096,000 in 1967.

The co-operatives directed a fuller development of the renewable natural resources of their districts and the human resources of their members. The members obtained good returns for their products, and the wages and salaries were welcome additions to local income. By involving whole settlements the co-operatives moulded community cohesiveness and diminished the power of family or clan-based approaches to life. Their successes increased Inuit confidence in their ability to handle their problems through collective action and gave their morale a strong boost. Many persons, moreover, were trained in managing businesses, forming a cadre of educated, self-assured young persons to lead their people across the unknown terrains of modern life. The co-operatives helped many Inuit adapt to contemporary economic, philosophic, and political realities.

The movement also broke down the isolation of Inuit communities and enlarged the Inuit world. Delegates from eighteen co-operatives from all parts of the Arctic met at Frobisher Bay in March 1963, "the first time in history that such a large number of Eskimo from so many different places had the opportunity to meet with each other."[3] A second conference at Povungnituk in April 1966 was attended by representatives from twenty-two co-operatives and another eight in the process of formation. That meeting took up the plan for a central marketing and bulk purchasing agency set up by the Co-operative Union of Canada. By 1970 Canadian Arctic Producers, Limited, had emerged as a major supplier and regulator of sculptures and other Inuit artistic products.

But these efforts at diversification still did not reach most native hunters and trappers who could no longer maintain themselves from the old pursuits. To continue their life on the land they needed extra income from wage employment – or social assistance. Accordingly, they sought casual work for wages, particularly in the summers. When outside work was plentiful and trapping prospects were discouraging, they tended to work as long as possible and reduce their trapping effort. But when work was scarce or trapping seemed lucrative, they were likely to leave their wage employments abruptly to return to the trapping life. The call to abandon the old life altogether was strongest in the younger generation: ". . . the year's activities seemed to confirm the tendency for the younger people to find their way into other occupations."[4] Individuals who found congenial full-time employment might become regular town dwellers, bringing their families with them and forsaking the hard, uncertain life on the land except for occasional visits to enhance the appeal of their new urban lifestyle, or keep the old in reserve should the new life prove too difficult. By 1960 it was reported from British Columbia that "more and more Indians were and are on the move . . . in search of a more stable form of economy than existed in their home reserve area . . . Indians from small isolated bands have moved into centres where employment was to be found and the benefits of Unemployment Insurance were available in the off seasons."[5]

II

The efforts of the Indian Affairs Branch to help its clients overcome their economic difficulties were largely indirect, at least prior to 1960, when the branch at last set up an Economic Development Division. A $1-million revolving fund was made available for loans for purchasing farm equipment and livestock, fishing equipment, power saws and sawmills, clearing and breaking land, handicraft and tourist operations, and other development purposes. The branch also paid a varying portion (40 to 80 per cent) of the costs of building thousands of Indian houses and renovating as many others and of improvements to reserves, other shares of which were met by band funds and private persons. These and similar projects, of course, created employment.

The branch also began employing a staff of placement officers in the sixties for such duties as placing Indians in suitable existing jobs, developing new employment opportunities, training men for particular jobs, and helping them adapt to life in non-Indian communities. They contacted and worked with employers, trade unions, vocational and social agencies, the plethora of new government bodies (the National Employment Service, the Unemployment Insurance Commission, the Area Development Agency of the federal Department of Industry), and especially managers of winter works programs.

Besides the more obvious work on their homes, gardens, and improvements to their reserves, Indians (and Métis, too) found seasonal employments in river transport and coastal shipping or stevedoring work, clearing and piling timber on the new long-distance highways, railway branches, and pipelines, which work sometimes continued through several seasons. Permanent employment was also available to northern natives who could carry out assigned duties and adjust to the new living conditions, as in the great resource development enterprises such as the Labrador iron towns, the many hydro projects, or the northern airfields and radar defence lines. These provided more large-scale and continuing employment that sometimes attracted natives from hundreds of miles around. Naskapi Indians who had settled at Fort Chimo to work on the military installation later moved to Schefferville to work on the iron-mining operation; it was reported (1957) that "Rupert House and Waswanipi Indians have found jobs at Chapais, and Indians from Mistassini are working at Chibougamau and Clova.''[6] Some northern natives were regularly employed at northern mines (even underground) – at Kirkland Lake and a few northwestern Ontario camps, in the Territories at Keno Hill and Yellowknife. Government agencies provided another source of full-time employment for a few other Indians, mostly in unskilled maintenance and general labouring tasks but also as teachers, nurses, clerks, and administrators. In 1960, for instance, the Indian Affairs Branch employed one hundred status Indians as teachers (nearly 9 per cent of the total).

Employment opportunities were far fewer for the Arctic-dwelling Inuit than for Indians and Métis in more settled parts of Canada, though there was less competition in their homeland for such work as they were capable of performing. Employment was mainly associated with government and military activities, the agencies of which did what they could to hire Inuit. In several localities they found work on the defence facilities, which gave full-time work for a few and part-time work to many others. Inuit were also recruited for a part-time defence force, the Arctic Rangers. Many had regular seasonal employment on transport and freighting operations or assisting the numerous prospecting, surveying, and scientific parties at work in the Arctic. Temporary and longer-term local employment could be found on civil government construction at Inuvik, Frobisher Bay, and smaller settlements. In the Arctic, the government services were more likely than the Indian Affairs Branch to seek Inuit not only for unskilled tasks but also as interpreters and translators, medical, nursing, and teaching assistants. Traders, co-operatives, tourist enterprises, and the like employed some Inuit. Employment in industry often arose from governmental pressure on companies working in the North and sometimes included undertakings by employers to train Inuit for more advanced positions, such as operating well-drilling equipment.

Yet all these employments could not overcome the enormous income gap. Another part of that gap was filled by the proliferating social programs and by payments from band funds built up by forestry, petroleum, and natural gas royalties, fees, and other revenues; the remainder was closed by what was hoped would be temporary welfare assistance (relief) dispensed locally on behalf of the various agencies. The most significant income-support program was Family Allowances, paid monthly from 1945 to mothers of every child in Canada below the age of sixteen. Aimed at ensuring that children were adequately fed, clad, and sheltered, the allowances at first were paid in kind in most northern districts, and traders imported fresh fruit and vegetables, eggs, milk, and other approved goods to serve this new cash market. Because receipt of Family Allowances was conditional on school attendance, they were a strong force for increased enrolment and settlement of native families in communities. Other programs followed: in 1948 special allowances for natives past age seventy (at first $8 a month, increased to $25 in 1950, eventually absorbed into the national Old Age Security Pension), Old Age Assistance benefits for persons aged sixty-five, Blind Persons Allowances, Disabled Persons Allowances, and in some provinces Needy Mothers Allowances, the last four administered by the provinces, or insofar as they were instituted in the territories, by the territorial administrations. Each was intended to give the northern natives income that would assist them to care for the persons who were most at risk. Indeed, as early as 1948–51, when nearly all the Inuit still lived on the land, these payments were their largest source of cash income, exceeding even the returns from fur. They also had value for the entire native community: "The eligibility of the Indians to all provincial and federal social allowances, pensions and benefits has helped to stabilize economic conditions."[7]

Notwithstanding these aids, a large number of indigent natives still had to be assisted with relief for all or part of the year. Prior to 1959 such relief took the form of rations supplied by the branch or the territorial administration. The total amount was large but indefinite, varying from year to year according to weather, agricultural and employment conditions, and especially the vagaries of the fur-trapping economy. Later, Indian Affairs reformed the relief system by giving recipients cash to purchase the family's food needs, with clothing, housing, and heat still being handled by the administration. The change was intended "to place more responsibility on Indian families to manage their own affairs, to remove the stigma of relief as much as possible and to maintain the morale and self-respect of persons who must receive assistance."[8] The rates were also brought into line with payments that municipalities made to persons in comparable circumstances, and in Ontario, at least, many reserves began administering their own programs under the provincial system, the federal government paying 50 per cent of the cost, the province 30 per cent, and the band 20 per cent.

These changes probably reflected a shift in the sort of persons requiring the bulk of the assistance – Indians who no longer depended on the land but lived on reserves or in towns and were employed intermittently or not at all. The Hawthorn-Tremblay Report, *A Survey of the Contemporary Indians of Canada*, the product of an extensive three-year investigation commissioned in 1963 by Guy Favreau, Minister of Citizenship and Immigration, described the situation mainly of wage-earning Indians in 1965:

. . . Indian households are heavily dependent on welfare (i.e. relief payments, in money or in kind) and other supplementary income. More than one-third (33.5 per cent) of all households in the sample depended on welfare grants from the Branch. . . . A number of Indian bands with larger band funds and revenues look after their own welfare needs. All types of transfer payments in the social security category to Indians including unemployment insurance, and family allowances, old age security and old age assistance, and welfare payments from band revenues as well as from public bodies, in the aggregate amounted to 31.4 per cent or almost one-third of total earnings from employment.[9]

The most acceptable way for natives to achieve a desirable standard of living and be freed from dangerous dependence on relief, experts agreed, was through vocational training in usable trades and occupations to prepare them for full participation in the rapidly growing professional and service sectors of the national economy:

Many of the young people are realizing that a higher standard of education and the advantage of vocational training are prerequisites to competing on the labour market today. In the face of a tightening overall economy it is evident that if our Indians are going to find employment and security they must be in a position to compete with non-Indians in the employment fields.[10]

After-school training programs were greatly expanded during the 1960s for Indians and Inuit at middle-sized local schools and at large new vocational schools opened at northern regional centres. Selected students were sent in ever greater numbers to institutes in southern cities. Many enrolled simply to achieve basic literacy but most of the teen-agers and adults also received training in skilled trades, from carpentry and bricklaying to welding and electronics, and in other work. There were domestic arts and child-care programs for women and girls. Courses in leadership training, practical social work, community organization, and managing co-operatives also were offered.

All the while large numbers of native persons continued to turn away from the land. Those who remained in their homelands could look forward only to the stagnating, demoralizing existence exemplified by Oxford House, a fur-trade centre on the upper Hayes River northeast of Lake Winnipeg. Between 1940 and 1960 that settlement "saw the end of family trapping as a way of life, a resulting change from nomadic to sedentary, village-orientated existence, the emergence of wage labour to replace trapping, and the introduction of modern communications."[11] Summer employments such as freighting disappeared, but from 1943 onward men from the village went outside to work on the harvests or on the roads and railways. Village life became stabilized with the opening of a primary school:

> a few permanent jobs became available in the village. . . . In the early 1960s poverty was relieved by the spread of welfare payments, which became an acceptable means of earning a living. Government subsidies provided grants for brush-cutting projects in winter, and house-building and commercial fishing in summer. Despite these efforts to create new employment, by 1978 between 60 and 80 per cent of the Oxford House population were receiving assistance in one form or another.[12]

The Hawthorn-Tremblay Report confirmed the trend: "Dozens of bands across Northern Canada who up until recently supported themselves at a meagre subsistence level in hunting, trapping and fishing economies, have now forsaken their traditional activities and become almost entirely dependent upon government welfare and relief."[13] Unfortunately, the training programs of which so much was expected had limited success, for most northern districts developed too slowly to employ the trained persons in their home localities. Moreover, the training was usually unequal to the task of preparing native persons to compete successfully for positions that did present themselves in outside communities.

Large numbers of young Indians continued to drift from their home reserves to nearby or distant cities, however unfriendly, in quest of work and more interesting experience. Many, having few marketable skills or opportunities for securing regular employment, became discouraged, fell in with the substratum of urban society that existed on casual, low-income labouring and welfare, and shared their unfortunate lives. Some, however, who "made good" established permanent roots in the cities. Indian Affairs reported in 1961 that approximately 26 per cent of the Indians "live off reserves, the majority in non-Indian communities,"[14] and the Hawthorn-Tremblay Report stated that while more than a quarter of the Indian population it sampled were living off the reserves but still retaining their band memberships, "a possibly larger number and proportion have left permanently and fitted into White society on various levels."[15] The ones who returned after a time to their home reserves or districts joined the unemployed or partly employed northerners performing what casual work they could and depended mainly on social assistance and relief to sustain themselves and their families. The lack of gainful employment and the enforced idleness combined with the other frustrations of their socio-cultural situation to lead many down the trail of drunkenness and family abuse and some to criminal behaviour.

The Hawthorn-Tremblay Report proposed that the federal government meet this challenge head-on and embark on a vigorous, thoroughgoing, and expensive program of integrating the northern Indians into the industrial society moving so relentlessly into their territories. It condemned past economic development programs of the Indian Affairs Branch as wholly inadequate, consisting merely of ". . . innumerable small bits-and-pieces of local resource development projects – a fishery here, a logging project there, and a land clearing or fur conservation program somewhere else. Most of these appear to be in the category of make-work or employment-relief programs, designed primarily for the bands suffering the worst degree of unemployment and dependency."[16] It felt that the enormous problem demanded a far different strategy that would secure more and better-paid work in the construction, sales, or service trades that were the fastest-growing sectors of the national economy. The renewable resources industries, by contrast, should be administered as "a sort of holding action to enable decreasing numbers to derive their livelihoods from this source."[17]

"The main avenue of improvement in the economic status of Indians," the report concluded, "must lie in speeding up their absorption into outside wage employment."[18] The scores of industrial and commercial communities springing up near Indian reserves and hunting territories held out full-time employment opportunities for large numbers of underemployed Indians. But since almost nothing was being done, "the economic role of Indians in such communities appears to be, at best, that of casual, temporary and unwelcome visitors, customers and spectators of White society."[19] The report proposed that Indian Affairs should actively encourage and assist Indians to resettle in centres with good employment prospects by promoting job training and placement and making removal and housing grants available to them.

Northern Affairs, however, had reached an opposite conclusion for its far smaller and less threatened Inuit clientele. Diamond Jenness, the renowned Inuit scholar, had expressed the same conclusion as Hawthorn-Tremblay in 1963 when he suggested that the Inuit could be encouraged (as residents of other high unemployment regions were encouraged) to move to the South where many more employment opportunities existed. The proposal was dismissed without discussion either because of bureaucratic inertia or, more likely, from a feeling that the Inuit should be encouraged to remain in the Arctic and work out their destiny regardless of economic considerations. In the meantime, the Inuit continued to abandon the land for settlements handy to defence stations, administrative centres, or other locales of possible employment. Despite the best efforts of the administration to find or provide employment for them, the amount of available work fell far short of satisfying the needs of adult Inuit displaced from hunting and trapping, let alone the growing numbers leaving school. In 1967 most employed Inuit still were unskilled or semi-skilled workers, and many of the employments were short-lived. The sum total of work available in the Arctic was simply too small to accommodate the rapidly increasing numbers of job-seeking Inuit. A socio-economic catastrophe, comparable with that faced by the Indians though far smaller in scale, seemed in store for the Inuit of Arctic Canada.

III

The exodus from the land resulted only in part from economic necessity. As strong or even stronger were the social programs the federal and territorial governments held out to the native people and the way in which they delivered those services. The nomadic lifestyle of the northern natives multiplied immeasurably the difficulties and expense of providing those services; indeed, educational, health, welfare, and other services could be supplied effectively only at established centres. There administrators hoped "to modify an existing social order until it approximated the minimal social and economic conditions within which existing governmental programs were designed to operate."[20] After the war, the Indian Affairs Branch started its policy of centralization in Nova Scotia, with the idea that "the establishment of the Indian on . . . reserves, where education and medical care can be more easily provided and where supervision is more effective, will result in a steadily increasing improvement in living conditions."[21] Over the next few years new Indian reserves were created in various provinces to collect scattered Indian families from isolated locations (as along the transcontinental railway in Northern Ontario) and for many of the nomadic bands in former wilderness districts that were undergoing industrial development, such as the Quebec North Shore and Northern Alberta. In more developed localities – Abitibi – and in the vicinities of Yellowknife, Sept-Iles, Mayo, Fort Smith, and other northern centres, small acreages were secured "to provide a residential site for members of the band who have been living in that area"[22] that could be supplied with electrical, water distribution, and sewage disposal systems.

The influx of native families from the land was accompanied by "intensification and broadening of programs in the fields of education, economic development and social welfare."[23] The federal agencies installed their schools, nursing stations, and other facilities at existing settlements like Norway House, Old Crow, and Fort Norman and at new communities formed especially for the purpose such as Rae-Edzo,

Easterville, Manitoba, Kashechewan, Ontario, and Paint Hills, Quebec. These centres accommodated the trained persons from the South (whose presence necessitated the installation of these utilities) who carried out the various functions, and they also attracted many native families from the surrounding districts to avail themselves of the amenities (often including housing for natives as well as civil servants) and the opportunities available in them. Sometimes the advantages proved insufficient. After six bands had been drawn from a large section of northwestern Ontario to a central location at Lansdowne House, the Indians discovered that the local game could not sustain their numbers. They accordingly returned to their home districts, followed by the schools and other government services and the churches, leaving behind a very deflated planned administrative centre.

The Inuit, too, were on the move; "between 1956 and 1959 alone no fewer than 1,104 Eskimos (10 per cent of the population) left their homes and migrated to other places in search of work, or of better living conditions."[24] As more government agencies were installed, the movement accelerated. A dozen years later Graham Rowley, a noted authority on Inuit and the Arctic, described the process in these terms:

Urbanization is proceeding rapidly; families are deserting their old hunting camps and moving into a small number of large settlements, where there are schools, stores, and nursing stations. This trend has been accelerated recently because the government's housing programme has meant, in effect, that an Eskimo who wants a house for his family has no alternative to moving into these settlements. Soon, practically the whole Eskimo population will be concentrated in about thirty settlements. A second stage of urbanization, with movement towards fewer, larger centres may then set in.[25]

Though the educational and housing programs have been singled out, the most successful social programs were in the health field. The health of the native people, formerly so bad as to constitute a national shame, showed improvement almost at once after the Department of National Health and Welfare took over the health services of the Indian Affairs Branch in November 1945 and those of the Northwest Territories administration to Inuit in 1947. The new department was able to recruit far more physicians and nurses to its Indian Health Service and Northern Health Service than their predecessors had been able to do. Hospitals turned over by the Armed Forces – Miller Bay near Prince Rupert, The Pas, the Jesuit College Hospital at Edmonton – were converted into tuberculosis sanatoria, and the existing northern hospitals, many owned and operated by the missions, were enlarged and re-equipped. Nursing stations and treatment centres were built on many reserves, along strategic transportation arteries, in fur-trading centres, and in barren Arctic settlements. Whenever epidemics of disease broke out in isolated localities, as at Cape Dorset, where some sixty Inuit died of typhoid fever in 1945, medical parties were flown in to treat the sick and institute preventive measures. A large specialized medical party now travelled annually with the Eastern Arctic Patrol, sailing from 1949, following the sinking of the HBC ship *Nascopie*, in government icebreakers, notably the *C.D. Howe*.

An especially determined effort was made to isolate and treat active cases of tuberculosis in order to eradicate from the North the dread disease that had been making such tragic inroads in the past decades. By the end of the forties many Indians and Inuit were under treatment, and when the limited facilities in the North were overtaxed they were sent south to hospitals and sanatoria, the Inuit usually to Quebec City and Hamilton, the Indians and Métis to Edmonton. More than 3,500 Indian patients were hospitalized for tuberculosis in 1954 55, the largest group at the Charles Camsell Indian Hospital in Edmonton. At the peak of the Inuit program in 1956 "approximately one Eskimo out of every seven"[26] was hospitalized; 1,356 persons were treated in 1955 and 1,578 in 1956, and the Territories administration expressed the hope that the disease was being wiped out. To help the large numbers of Indian and Inuit patients, teachers and counsellors of their own language groups worked with them in the hospitals. A large rehabilitation centre was set up at Frobisher Bay to aid Inuit returning home from prolonged sojourns in Southern Canada re-adapt to northern conditions.

Another feature of the program was a full range of health tests for the entire native population. Indian Health Service dentists, equipped with mobile clinics, visited the reserves of their districts. Preventive work was begun under the new order: children were inoculated or vaccinated against various diseases, and doctors acting as local health officers examined and reported on actual or potentially dangerous situations and conditions. Native girls trained as nurses aides and as health workers worked on reserves to promote better sanitary conditions by enlisting the interest and co-operation of the residents.

In the early 1960s health care for most Indians living in the provinces came under the provincial hospital insurance schemes, and the bands were encouraged to negotiate their own health service arrangements until the comprehensive medical care (medicare) system was instituted. Under these programs the hospital care and medical treatment of Indians became merged with that of the general populations of the provinces, and the role of the Indian Health Service was mainly one of directing public health activities for Indians and paying their subscriptions to the programs. In the northern territories, however, the Indian and Northern Health Services (merged in 1962 as the Medical Services Directorate) were the *de facto* department of health, responsible for the health care of all elements of the population, and they continued as before to provide this service for their native inhabitants.

The Medical Services' drive to extend the benefits of health care to the scattered Inuit settlements and camps was a noteworthy feature of the effort in the 1960s. Modern hospitals primarily for Inuit patients were opened at Inuvik (1961) and Frobisher Bay (1964). By 1967 specialists were being appointed to the staffs of the Arctic hospitals, other specialists from southern institutions regularly visited and checked the hospitals and nursing stations, and southern hospitals and universities arranged to assist health care in certain sections of the Arctic. In addition, nursing stations were installed at all main Inuit settlements, each staffed by two registered nurses and auxiliary helpers, to serve as centres for public health and preventive medical work and treat minor surgical and obstetrical cases. Doctors could be consulted by radio-telephone, and in emergencies serious cases could be evacuated to the main hospitals. To reach still more remote groups, health stations operated by lay dispensers were set up, and isolated camps were supplied with Eskimo Family Medical Packs. Doctors and supervisory nurses also travelled extensively throughout their districts "to provide supervision and guidance and to hold regular clinics in all communities."[27] The main problems in expanding the program were not funding but inability to recruit and retain enough qualified staff and the scarcity of trained Inuit assistants. Nevertheless the full-time medical staff stationed in the Districts of Keewatin and Franklin jumped from thirty-nine in 1960–61 to one hundred in 1965–66.

The outstanding success of the health program was measured by the gratifying increase in numbers of native people, utterly reversing the previous stationary or downward trend, that was recorded by every census from 1951 onward, particularly in the case of the Inuit:

> Eskimo mortality is probably the most sensitive barometer of what is happening in the North and it is significant that the crude death rate for Eskimos from all causes has been reduced from 29 per 1000 of population in 1956 to 12 per 1000 in 1966. . . . The Eskimo birth rate is now also tending to fall slightly but still stands at around 55 per 1000 of population, one of the highest birth rates recorded in the world. The Eskimo vital index in 1966 was 4.33, i.e. for every Eskimo death there were 4.33 live births.[28]

That crude birth rate was over three times the national average of 17.6 per 1,000 in 1968. The Inuit vital index had improved still further in two years' time, so that the department's annual report for 1968–69 observed that "the Eskimo population is still increasing annually at over 4.5%, the highest rate of natural increase now being recorded anywhere."[29] The total Inuit population of Canada (about a third of which now lived outside the Territories, mostly in the Arctic sections of adjacent provinces) grew from 9,733 in 1951 to 11,385 in 1961, then soared to 17,550 in 1971, an increase of above 48 per cent in the decade of the sixties and over 81 per cent for the twenty-year period.

The Indian population increased nearly as rapidly. Despite the removal of many names from band registers and several hundred enfranchisements each year, the numbers of status Indians rose, thanks to a birth rate that was three times that of the non-Indian community and represented a natural increase of 3 per cent per annum. During the two decades between 1944 and 1964 their numbers rose from 125,946 to 211,389, an increase of 67 per cent, and a milestone was passed in 1963 when it was pointed out that there were then probably as many Indians as there had been before the coming of the white man to Canada. In the two territories, the figures did not show as rapid an increase as did the national figure, for they declined between 1944 and 1949 before turning upward. If the period 1949–1964 is taken as a basis, the Northwest Territories' Indian population rose from 3,586 to 5,383, an increase of 50 per cent, and the Yukon's from 1,443 to 2,215, an increase of 53.5 per cent. In the same period, the Indian population as a whole increased by 55 per cent.

No health system, of course, could surmount every hazard of northern living. Small settlements and groups continued to be harried by contagious diseases and diseases arising from insanitary conditions, and individuals fell prey to the many perils of northern living. A dangerous revival of tuberculosis at Eskimo Point and elsewhere even mocked the massive campaign of a few years earlier to eradicate that plague from the North. Still, the system now in place was in a position to react quickly to accidents and health crises and to start curative and preventive work to check the spread of the epidemic diseases.

Nor could the system prevent the spread of unhealthy conditions brought on by the changing social and economic situations, particularly in the Arctic. As the Royal Commission on Health Services observed, "the provision of good health also necessitates measures securing proper housing, sanitation, and water supply as well as adequate livelihood."[30] Traders may have imported milk and fresh fruit and vegetables for children, but they also brought in unhealthful, even harmful goods such as candy, soft drinks, and starchy, sugar-laden processed foods, so that many natives' store-based diets were far inferior to the old staple hunted or gathered foods. Besides, many native mothers lacked means or knowledge to make effective use of the processed foodstuffs. Nutritional deficiencies began to undermine the undoubted advances made by health services, resulting in a population that displayed signs of malnutrition and higher incidences of gastro-enteritis, tooth decay, heart disease, and cancer. In parallel fashion, respiratory illnesses increased because fur and skin apparel was replaced by store-bought clothing and the housing was deplorable. The practical problems caused by the new conditions led the district nurses, home economists, and vocational teachers to try to teach native women healthful habits and practical homemaking arts in addi-tion to basic reading. Health pamphlets in Inuktitut were prepared and distributed to the Inuit, as was the "Q" (Quajivaallirutissat) Book of Wisdom to provide information "on just about everything – educa-tion, health, welfare, equipment maintenance, household hints, gov-ernment services, and laws."[31]

It was clear that adequate shelter for the nomadic persons trying to settle into community life in the Subarctic and Arctic was vital to their health and comfort. It was not hard to build cabins or houses for forest-dwelling Indians or Métis, and large numbers of houses (over 10,000 in the decade after 1948) were built on reserves, mostly by the Indians themselves, assisted in part from band funds. Some part of the cost was contributed by the Indian Affairs Branch, which also supplied housing for the indigent. Many other houses were repaired, remodelled, or rebuilt under similar arrangements. The branch, assisted from band funds, also supplied or arranged building of roads and utilities, occa-sionally planning the creation of whole new communities on sites selected by its engineers. But in spite of these efforts, however, many of the houses were still classed as poor because of the wear and tear on existing housing and, ironically, improving housing standards. The growth of population meanwhile created much overcrowding. As a result, the branch reported a shortage of no less than 12,000 houses in 1966 and announced a five-year program to cost $112 million to pro-vide needed housing and related utilities.

In the Arctic, material for modern housing had to be imported at great expense from outside, but because of the severe climate it was needed even more than it was on reserves or in the forests to the south. Housing was provided for government or company employees almost as a condition of employment, so it was not surprising that the Terri-torial administration decided to make better housing available as well to native residents as a contribution to good health. In 1959 the North-ern Administration Branch began shipping small prefabricated houses for Inuit settlers, to be erected as far as possible by local labour. As in the South, wage-earners were expected to purchase their homes by monthly payments with the aid of a thousand-dollar subsidy, but some houses were provided free to needy families.

The high costs of fuel and power, the small size of the houses, and the inability of many Inuit to carry the payments led the administration in 1965 to inaugurate a rental housing program based on ability to pay, the houses to be "serviced with electricity (where available), fuel oil, sew[er]age and water, and basic maintenance."[32] Local tenant associations were to maintain the houses and administer the maintenance funds (rents and government subsidies) under contract. The program continued to expand until by 1974 (when housing for Indians also was included) it embraced more than 2,200 dwellings in the Territories, over 1,500 having three or more bedrooms. By then it was a $20-million investment with an annual $3-million operating budget, of which rents accounted for only $500,000.

Despite all these aids, the situation that many natives drawn from the land encountered in the settlements was charged with socio-psychological difficulties. The challenges to be faced are well stated in this picture of life of Inuit newcomers at Frobisher Bay:

> This situation is not entirely the consequence of wage employment, although this lies at the heart of the problem. It also stems from the requirements of the whole new cultural order – sending children to school, observing modern health and sanitation measures, abiding by numerous Government laws and regulations, ranging from the RCMP rule requiring the leashing of dogs to filling out Federal income tax returns, and so on. It also stems from the restrictions the new social order has imposed on the Eskimo's traditional mode of life. Most notable in this regard is the limitation placed on his freedom. The wage employed Eskimo, for example, is no longer free to hunt when he pleases, to let his dogs roam unleashed, to pitch his tent whenever he pleases, nor to build winter houses from scrap lumber and other discarded materials. Even his home is no longer a private domain, for it is subject to periodic inspection by health officials. In many other ways he has become a helpless captive of Western civilization.[33]

The presence of white workers and administrators generated further problems of adjustment. Many natives observed and copied their dress, diet, games, dances and amusements, manner of spending money, use of alcohol, and treatment of women. In absorbing these attitudes and standards young natives were drawn farther away from the ancestral lifestyle and from the authority and wisdom of their elders, sometimes with disturbing results. A particularly destructive force that further undermined the fragile native social order was alcohol. After authorities made it available to native drinkers in the 1960s, the increase in consumption was accompanied by rising alcohol-related family violence, criminal actions, and accidental deaths. Despondent drunken natives began copying their white counterparts, and instances of abused wives and battered children, once a rarity, grew more frequent. Native women even more than their white sisters found it difficult to turn to the courts for redress because of familial tradition, the harm to their children and themselves that would result if their husbands were fined or imprisoned, and the utter lack of anywhere else to go. Hence few wives would sign complaints authorizing prosecutions.

Rowley described the sad, worrisome human situation developing in the Arctic:

> Many settlements in the north have very grave inter-related social problems in drunkenness, juvenile delinquency, prostitution, unemployment and underemployment, and abject poverty. These problems and the resulting crime and illegitimacy rates are worst at such places as Frobisher Bay and Inuvik, where it is easy to buy alcohol and where the white population is of significant size. On the other hand, the more isolated settlements have little to attract the young, who have learnt at school about the wider world. Juvenile delinquency or juvenile despondency is sure to follow unless there are satisfying outlets to absorb their energies and imagination.[34]

The principal means of raising the native population to a position of economic and social equality with other Canadians was to prepare the children and young adults for their future lives through schooling: "Throughout the entire Indian education program a continuing effort is being made to fit young Indians to take their place eventually in the larger Canadian community."[35] The depth of that commitment was shown by the unceasing expansion of the program. Half or more of the annual budgets of the Indian Affairs Branch went to education; expenditures soared from $2.29 million in 1944–45 to $52.25 million by 1967, by which date some 95 per cent of the school-aged Indian children were enrolled. The numbers rose steadily from 14,000 to 65,000, illustrating the growth of the Indian population, more complete enrolment (attributable in part to Family Allowances), and the earlier commencement of schooling. The branch operated 1,291 classrooms in 355 schools and employed 1,549 teachers, and in addition half the 64,439 Indian students went to schools outside the branch's system.

A feature of the new system was its secular character. The missionary societies were regarded as well meaning and devoted, but their schools were now considered pedagogically antiquated and entirely unsuited for coping with the rapidly changing northern socio-economic environment. Besides, the denominations (the Church of England in particular) lacked the means to serve all the greatly enlarged native constituency. The missions continued to operate some sixty-five residential schools across the north for a fairly constant 8,000 pupils, but even there the instructors were employees of the Indian Affairs Branch. As time passed many of the residential schools became housing units for pupils who were attending Indian day schools or provincial schools. New residential schools were built and owned by the branch but were operated under contract by the missions. Old buildings were replaced by new, larger ones at centres like Carcross, Moose Factory, and Norway House. The new centres also were the sites of schools – La Tuque, Fort George, Sept-Iles, Pointe Bleue, and Amos in Quebec, The Pas in Manitoba, Hay Lake in Alberta, and Lower Post in British Columbia.

The numbers of day schools, which the administrators preferred because they kept children with their families and helped the effects of schooling permeate the family, also increased by as many as twenty and thirty a year until the mid-sixties, when some one-room schools were closed in favour of sending children to consolidated or integrated schools. The numbers of children taught in the day schools exceeded those in residential schools from 1947 onward, rising from 8,178 in 1947–48 to 19,829 in 1960–61 and 32,040 in 1965–66.

The branch's teachers were accorded civil service status and benefits, and they were paid in line with current teaching and government salaries, with extra allowances for remote locations. Nonetheless, turnover rates were as high as 30 per cent (1965). Growing numbers of the teachers, however, were properly certificated, and their work was regularly reviewed by branch and provincial inspectors. Special seminars and conferences helped them improve the quality of their work with native pupils. The branch sought to employ as many status-Indian teachers as possible, and as Indians graduated from normal school they were added to the staff. The branch also employed "welfare teachers" for isolated day schools and hospitals, who investigated welfare problems and dispensed medicines as well as instruction, and some three dozen seasonal summer teachers "to meet, in so far as possible, the educational needs of children of Indians who follow a nomadic way of life."[36]

Since the goal of the education was "to assist acculturation . . . and to prepare Indian youth for economic competence and social stability,"[37] the schools followed the curricula of the provinces in which they were situated, adjusted in some areas to serve functional needs such as combatting the spread of tuberculosis or training in beaver conservation. Because most beginners spoke ancestral dialects but fewer than half were fluent in English or French, much attention was given to improving their command of basic English and starting kindergarten classes to train preschool children. Little effort was made to adapt teaching to the language or culture of the Indian groups.

At the same time the provincial and territorial governments took a growing part in the work. These jurisdictions operated larger, fully developed systems that made the Indian Affairs schools redundant. They were already instructing on a fee basis large numbers of status Indians who lived in the cities or in the settlements within the special regional school districts (for example, Alberta's Northland Division) that the provinces set up to provide local schooling for children of all ethnic groups. The small but increasing number of children proceeding beyond Grade 6 (the upper limit of instruction offered at most Indian day schools) had to transfer to the public systems. Besides, the principle of preparing Indian children to be members of the majority society and to compete for economic positions required that they receive educations equal to those given other Canadians, preferably in the same institutions. Integrated education had other benefits, too, as the Northwest Territories administration pointed out: "It is most important that segregation by race in education be avoided. The mingling of all children – whether Indians, Eskimo, part-blood or white – in common schools in their formative years will have important social and psychological advantages in the north."[38]

Empowered by the revised Indian Act of 1951, the Indian Affairs Branch accordingly made arrangements with provincial educational authorities and individual school boards for Indian children to be instructed in integrated classrooms and schools. In fact, in 1955 it merged its entire Northwest Territories operation (a dozen or so Indian day schools and three or four residential schools) with that of the Territories for efficiency and greater uniformity of service, forming one single system for all the children. Less comprehensive arrangements had to be made with other jurisdictions. In the Yukon, Indian pupils moved from mission or Indian schools or residential schools into the public and separate schools provided for the predominantly white settlements under direction of the territorial school superintendent and his teaching staff. In the provinces, the branch assisted school boards by contributing to the cost of additional construction or equipment, sharing in the operating costs of the integrated schools, and paying fees for pupils who were its responsibility; it arranged for transporting an eventual 16,700 pupils daily from their reserves to and from school. By 1966 the branch was spending some $15.5 million on behalf of 15,550 pupils in outside schools, including most of the children at the secondary and post-secondary schools. It also extended scholarships and sometimes living allowances to selected senior students to pursue their vocational or higher educational studies. Some of these and other students attending integrated schools were accommodated in hostels such as Shingwauk at Sault Ste Marie, Akaitcho Hall at Yellowknife, and the public and Catholic hostels at Whitehorse.

Paralleling the efforts of the Indian Affairs Branch were those of the Northwest Territories administration, which was responsible for educating all the Inuit, Indian, Métis, and white children living in industrial towns, trading centres, and scores of native camps scattered about its vast jurisdiction. Educating the hundreds of native children in the native camps was a special problem that could not be met solely by enthusiastic special teachers prepared to travel with the bands while holding summer schools. Besides, the results were unsatisfactory when the children remained in their home environments. The territorial administration, therefore, decided to gather these children together in day schools operated in conjunction with large residential hostels – desirable educational and acculturative settings away from the deleterious conditions of the camps. Such large hostels and day schools were built at Fort McPherson, Inuvik (originally intended for Aklavik), Fort Simpson, Fort Smith, and Frobisher Bay, to which hundreds of pupils were brought by plane from the camps each year. The total school enrolment in the Northwest Territories in 1958–59, 3,692 pupils, included 52 per cent of the native children of school age, a figure that rose to 70 per cent in 1969.

The system, however, was increasingly attacked as unnecessarily traumatic to the children in the hostels and the families from whom they were separated. It was also said to expose uprooted children to undesirable influences at the schools and adjoining towns. The children tended to make poor academic progress, initially because they were inadequately prepared at home for the type of schooling offered and subsequently because of their personal problems. In an attempt to deal with these conditions and to provide schooling for the children of the growing Inuit and Indian settlements, the administration constructed one- to four-room schools at some thirty-five smaller communities along with eight- to twelve-pupil hostels for children from adjoining districts. By 1967 the goal of universal education seemed in sight with 90 per cent of the school-aged children in regular attendance – 2,975 Inuit, 1,495 Indian, and 3,350 "Others" enrolled in fifty-seven schools that ranged in size from Inuvik (1,024 pupils) and Fort Smith (840) down to Padloping Island (16), Fort Liard (15), Discovery (13), and Jean Marie River (11).

The forty-five predominantly native local schools, in turn, gave families added incentive to move to the settlements to be near the schools, thereby enlarging the communities and reducing the numbers of families living entirely on the land. Thus the school system had harmful as well as beneficial effects for the native population of the Territories:

> The system achieved, as well, the creation of a generation of "hostel children", picked up in annual massive airlifts in the fall, and returned home ten months later, year after year, until the child no longer fitted into his home community. They created communities around the schools where there had not been communities before, and where game was insufficient for a permanent settlement, so that men who had been hunters lived on welfare, while their children attended the schools. Men went home trained to operate machinery, but there was no need for their skills because the machines did not exist in their communities. And no tiny settlement was so remote that it could remain untouched.[39]

Besides the primary schools, secondary schooling on the southern model was available in larger towns, mainly for Euro-Canadian students but also for qualified native pupils. The only predominantly Inuit settlements with high school classrooms in 1967, however, were Tuktoyaktuk and Frobisher Bay. A start also was made with preschool and kindergarten programs to help native children adapt to the unfamiliar educational environment. Vocational training schools were set up at Frobisher Bay, Inuvik, and Yellowknife that received pupils from all parts of the Territories.

The territorial administration, like Canadians generally, believed devoutly in the efficacy of formal education for preparing its native charges for participation in the national life and, like its Indian Affairs counterpart, assumed that its system was in the best interests of the native children. Its schools and curriculum followed those of Southern Canada. The teachers were southern trained and qualified, attracted north by a sense of adventure and the federal scales of pay and benefits. After brief acclimatization workshops they were dropped into the schools to cope with the very special needs of their native pupils. Little heed was paid to the socio-psychological development of the Inuit pupils, barely emerged from a primitive existence, and no more than lip-service was paid to the ideal of a distinctive northern curriculum adapted to their experience and traditions. After the system came increasingly under attack on this score, however, some small but significant steps were taken to design a less blatantly southern curriculum. Inuit classroom assistants were employed "to assist the younger children to adapt to the school system."[40] In contradistinction to the policy of Indian Affairs, work was started on developing standard Inuktitut orthographies, and material in syllabic script began to be published in a small way, notably newsletters and instructional brochures, and the Northern Affairs department's magazine *Inuktitut*, started in

1962. A rapidly developing cultural renaissance flowed from these small linguistic beginnings, fostered by Inuit Tapirisat and related associations.

Education epitomized the dual nature of government-sponsored social services. The new social programs of the post-war decades reflected the increasing involvement of the federal government in areas that were essentially under provincial jurisdiction. Ordinary citizens benefited, receiving an enhanced level of social services from competing provincial and federal authorities. But the status Indians could not enjoy this largess since they were solely the responsibility of the federal government, which extended its services to this relatively small, highly dispersed population as best it could. The Indian Affairs Branch realized that aligning or integrating its social programs for Indians with those the provinces provided for their citizens was the simplest and fairest way of ensuring Indians of adequate services.

Such integration already was largely achieved in the health care field, where Indians were included, like other Canadians, under the mandate of the federal Department of National Health and Welfare. Efforts were proceeding to replace the inferior segregated educational system with one in which Indian children would be taught in multiracial schools. In like fashion, Indian Affairs made cost-sharing agreements with the provinces and other agencies for bands to participate in welfare assistance, employment, winter works, and other programs on the same basis as non-Indian groups. Several provinces proved ready to meet the branch halfway by extending their social programs to Indians as individuals or to reserves as they would to municipalities.

In short, "the concept of the Indian as a 'ward' of the crown, and a special and exclusive responsibility of the federal government is weakening," as the Hawthorn-Tremblay Report approvingly observed, and "existing trends strongly support the policy of extending provincial services to Indians providing that suitable arrangements can be made with the provinces and Indians are in favour of such changes."[41] Such arrangements, the report felt, should be promoted to ensure that Indians received the full complement of benefits available to other Canadians and were not condemned to fall farther behind the general population. Instead, they should be fully accepted into Canada's social welfare-oriented society.

IV

Equal citizenship, the ruling philosophy of native administration during the period 1945–1967, was entirely in harmony with the liberal egalitarian mood of the post-war era. Government and public were determined to undo the harmful effects of past policies based on the concepts of tutelage and wardship and improve the lot of natives to a point where they could "attain the full rights and . . . assume the responsibilities of Canadian citizenship."[42] A joint committee of both houses of Parliament was set up in 1946 to examine the situation of the native peoples and study the Indian Act with a view to removing its undesirable features. The committee held 128 sittings over three years, heard 122 witnesses, and studied 411 written briefs. Much of the testimony from a large number of Indians and Indian bands revolved about practical subjects such as health conditions, education, housing, welfare, and economic prospects, but the recommendations dealt mainly with political and administrative matters. The committee was still not prepared to abandon the wardship, assimilationist approach, however. Its final report (June 22, 1948), while setting out a goal of facilitating "the gradual transition of Indians from wardship to citizenship and to help them to advance themselves" at the same time recommended retaining the restrictive provisions of the existing act in order to protect "such Indians as are not sufficiently advanced to manage their own affairs."

The report called for a tighter definition of the term "Indian" and a complete revision of the existing band membership lists, giving Indian bands greater control over their own affairs (including possible incorporation as municipalities) and Indian women an equal voice in band councils. It recommended reducing Indian legal disabilities under the criminal code (but, significantly, retaining the prohibition of alcohol on reserves) and suggested that a claims commission be set up to deal with complaints against alleged violations of the terms of Indian treaties. Individuals should be fully eligible for pensions and other social programs on the same basis as other Canadians and should be given the vote in federal elections "as part of the education and preparation of the Indian to assume his place in the Canadian body politic." The committee, reflecting the many complaints against the missionary-directed system of education, similarly recommended educating native children wherever possible in conjunction with other children "in order to prepare Indian children to take their place as citizens."

The legislation revising the Indian Act along the lines of the committee's conclusions had to await a reorganization of the federal bureaucracy in November 1949, which transferred Indian Affairs from the unwieldy Department of Mines and Resources to the newly created Department of Citizenship and Immigration, in keeping with the current assimilationist philosophy. As Prime Minister St. Laurent explained the move:

> Once the decision had been reached to recommend the establishment of a Department of Citizenship and Immigration, it was

considered that the minister responsible for this department should, in addition, be given the responsibility for the Indian affairs branch. I believe it is the policy of all members of the house to attempt to have the Indian affairs branch administered in such a way as to bring the original inhabitants of Canadian territory to citizenship as quickly as that can reasonably be accomplished. . . . Having citizenship, immigration and Indian affairs in the one department would indicate that the purpose of the activities of that department was to make Canadian citizens of those who were born here of the original inhabitants of the territory, or those who migrated to this country.[43]

He pointed with approval to the transfer in 1945 of responsibility for Indian health and welfare to the federal department of National Health and Welfare, which, he said, "creates a good psychological effect . . . that the health of the Indians is a matter which is of the same concern to the public as the health of those who enjoy full citizenship in Canada."[44]

As he predicted, all parties in the House welcomed the move. M.J. Coldwell of the CCF, for instance, was "pleased . . . that our Indian population is to be encouraged more and more to assume its place in the life of our country."[45] The Progressive Conservative spokesmen, while not challenging the objective, expressed concern at the irony of placing Indians "in the same department as displaced persons from abroad, because they have on occasion suggested that they were displaced persons at home," and complained that leaving the words "Indian Affairs" off the title of the new department, which its importance merited, would cause the public to regard the branch "as just tacked on."[46]

The bill revising the Indian Act was introduced in 1950, then withdrawn because its deficiencies and lack of meaningful Indian input came under attack. A second revision was successful, and the new Indian Act was passed in 1951. Some disabilities such as the crime of attending a potlatch and the prohibition against hiring spokesmen to pursue lawsuits on Indians' behalf were abolished. Yet the little-used compulsory enforcement provision was repealed only in 1961, and the proposed Indian Claims Commission was not appointed until 1968. The new act also failed to improve the political status of the Indian, still restricting the federal franchise to Indian war veterans and Indians residing off reserves. Indians who continued to live on reserves and did not waive their special taxation privileges could not enjoy the vote. The extension of the franchise did gradually follow over the ensuing decade, first in several provinces beginning with British Columbia, and finally, after a second Joint Committee on Indian Affairs (1958–61), in federal elections in 1961.

The most significant feature of the act was its new provision for an Indian register that would carry the names of all persons entitled to Indian status; thereafter holders of Indian status would be legally defined simply as persons listed on the register or descended from such persons in the male line, unless that status had been lost through enfranchisement, usually as a result of Indian women marrying non-status men. The new register ignored ethnicity, cultural background, and lifestyle, the qualities that constituted the Indians' special status and their need for special treatment. Inevitably, many instances of unfairness arose that required special consideration by administrators, negating the simplification that was an ostensible aim of the measure.

The gradual extension of the franchise to status Indians greatly increased their political influence and their ability to participate in the determination of their future treatment by officials and legislators. Frequent consultations between Indian spokesmen and administrators became the norm, and Indian affairs became a regular subject of standing parliamentary committees and of the second lengthy special committee, to say nothing of federal-provincial conferences. Individual Indians were included in the growing complex of social programs and aids under the same conditions as other Canadians, including the Veterans' Re-establishment grants (more than 1,600 by 1960).

A noteworthy side of the new attitude was the effort to encourage Indian bands to take greater responsibility for matters of local concern, as by forming school committees to work with local school authorities. As the balances in the Ottawa-managed Indian Trust Funds swelled with the annual income from oil and gas revenues and other sources, the branch returned larger portions of the windfall to the bands concerned, allowed their councils more say in how those funds were to be spent, and gave them a greater hand in the distribution. Some councils also were permitted to manage local welfare, community planning, and economic development programs. But as only relatively few bands, and those the most progressive of all, proved willing to accept these added responsibilities, the majority of reserves remained almost completely under supervision by Indian agents and administrators. Many more years of advances in educational and social attainments and of agitation would elapse before Indian self-government would become a realizable goal.

One dubious result of the liberalizing trend and of the Indians' advance to fuller citizenship was the relaxation of the prohibition against consuming alcohol. Various provincial governments gradually eased their restrictions during the 1950s, and bands were given power to authorize private consumption of liquor on their reserves. Some natives used money from wage earnings and transfer payments to seek solace in liquor from individual feelings of hopelessness and resignation, as temporary escape from the drabness and vicissitudes of their everyday lives, or as "a means of blunting the intra-personal conflicts and tensions that arise from overcrowding and friction with kin and others."[47] The escalation of alcohol consumption, with its deplorable effects on family relationships, work habits, and law-abiding behaviour, went far to undermine the programs intended to promote Indian betterment.

The position of the Inuit differed sharply from that of the Indians. They parted administrative company from the Indians in 1950, for they remained the responsibility of the departments that managed northern affairs – Resources and Development from 1950 to 1953 and Northern Affairs and National Resources from 1953 to 1965 – whose Northern Administration Branch (under various names) was charged with attending to their welfare. The fact that the same department controlled administration of the Northwest Territories (in which the majority of Inuit resided) made it far easier to integrate governmental services to Inuit with those offered the rest of the community than it was in the provinces, where federal services for Indians remained separate from (and unfortunately inferior to) provincial services for non-Indians and integrating the two systems entailed prolonged, suspicion-laden legal and financial negotiations between the two levels of government.

Through the Northern Administration Branch the Inuit received a greater expenditure of money, time, and effort, more direct supervision, and more innovative programs, and were subjected to far more investigation by social scientists, geographers, and economic development specialists (all in per capita terms) than the status Indians, who outnumbered Inuit by about ten to one. The mandate of the Indian Affairs Branch, in contrast, was nation-wide; its programs were planned on a national basis and were implemented uniformly in the North as elsewhere, whereas the well-financed, vigorous, innovative Northern Administration Branch could design programs exclusively for Inuit. The Department of National Health and Welfare, the other agency heavily concerned with the acculturative process, established a Northern Health Service to discharge its responsibility for the peoples of the territories more effectively. Thus the Inuit, who had suffered a woeful lack of health and other services, thanks largely to the work of these two northern agencies became one of the most heavily assisted, administered, and studied groups on earth.

While the two federal administrations for native peoples had the same objective of bringing their charges into a position of real equality with other Canadians and used economic and social programs to that end, their approaches differed. Indian Affairs (down to 1967 at least) remained wedded to the principle of assimilating the Indian into the mainstream of Canadian society. The broad purpose of the branch was described in 1954–55 as "the achievement of full-fledged citizenship for the Indian. Its program is essentially one of developing human resources and is designed to help them to contribute to and share in the national growth in full proportion to their heritage."[48] The Hawthorn-Tremblay Report described the objective in similar terms, and even its much-praised "Citizens Plus" concept referred more to extending extra and unusually large material aids to Indians to bring them up to the same economic and social levels as other Canadians than to setting them apart as a distinct segment of Canadian society.

The Northern Administration, on the other hand, had moved some way by 1967 in promoting both material and cultural survival of the Inuit. Its approach was understandable, inasmuch as most Inuit were fairly primitive and were just then entering the process of social and cultural change. Moreover, the acculturative forces capable of effecting their transformation were relatively few in the near-empty Arctic: there was less incentive to assimilate the Inuit because other Canadians could not live off the country or participate in other aspects of its development as well as the Inuit themselves; indeed, Inuit were encouraged to continue making the Arctic their home. Recognition of the artistic talents of certain Inuit also enhanced a feeling among Canadians that the Inuit were a distinct cultural entity that should be preserved and not allowed to disappear. In any event, Inuit skill in developing the co-operatives into a force for people and culture as well as for economic benefit, the stimulation of worthy self-image and pride, and the rise of a cadre of trained leaders seemed likely to assure their cultural survival into the foreseeable future.

Hence by 1960 the Northern Administration began to be aware that if its programs for the Inuit were to be effective they would have to harmonize with Inuit traditions, mores, modes of thought, and psychological outlook; moreover, its programs ought to deal with Inuit as they were and not as proto-white men. The educational program was therefore changed to involve Inuit in the schools, and the Inuktitut orthography and publications helped heighten their ethnic sensitivity. J.H. Sissons, the first Justice of the Northwest Territories (1955–66), was in himself a powerful force by his constant striving, during his circuits of his vast jurisdiction, to reconcile Canadian laws with native traditions on matters of marriage, inheritance, and adoption or violations of the Liquor Ordinance and the territorial game laws. His trials, judgements, and point of view were widely discussed, adding to the strong interest and public support for native causes that had flourished throughout Canada since 1945.

For the plight of the native Canadian and the seemingly ineffectual efforts to better his condition certainly had not gone unnoticed, especially after 1960 when "public sympathy for the Indian cause was unquestionably enhanced by the civil rights and anti-poverty movements in the United States and by the emerging nationalism of decolonizing third-world nations."[49] Innumerable pieces in newspapers and periodicals and on radio, film, and television kindled widespread interest and brought much voluntary aid for Canada's native peoples. The IODE in every province, for instance, arranged to send clothing, furniture, and games to reserves and supplied books and other materials to schools they adopted in remote areas. The IODE, the churches, and other agencies co-operated to set up native friendship and recreation centres in many cities and towns, while their members visited and helped hospitalized natives.

The churches continued their efforts to assist Indians in social and material as well as spiritual ways on the reserves and extended their services to those living in new and urban settings. They reshaped their outreach to increase use of native languages in their work and gave their native workers more prominent positions. In these reforms the churches perceived the need to combat the inroads of new evangelical sects propagating their faiths by airplane and to curb the spread of hedonistic attitudes and behaviour by young Indians on vacation from distant secondary schools. The churches, IODE, and other groups also exerted what pressure they could on politicians and administrators at all levels on behalf of the native peoples. In this they were supported by non-partisan public interest groups such as the Indian-Eskimo Association of Canada, formed in 1960 and reorganized in 1972, in recognition of its non-native antecedents and its acceptance of a new subordinate role, as the Canadian Association in Support of Native Peoples.

A significant change of approach was emerging in the 1960s as natives were beginning to find their own leaders and take a hand in determining their proper place in Canadian society. The apathetic acceptance by older Indians of decision-making by outside forces was coming under attack from three sides. Liberal-minded Canadians were developing a concern for the rights of all minority groups to "cultural and linguistic expression" and becoming convinced of their need for self-determination in these fields. In 1964 the Indian Affairs Branch, suddenly interventionist and anxious to "inspire self-determination and confidence in the communities, at the same time lessening their dependence on branch superintendents," inaugurated a program that placed "young and enthusiastic community development workers, who were committed to changing the traditional ways of Indian Affairs management,"[50] on Indian reserves. Their role of "grass roots activism," continued by the Company of Young Canadians (1967), helped undermine the existing authority structure and encouraged native bands to organize to serve their own interests. Finally, and most important, was the emergence of young, articulate, impatient, somewhat belligerent leaders, intolerant of the old paternalism and determined to lead their people to take full control of their destiny. In the atmosphere of racial and ethnic self-assertiveness exemplified by Black Power and Red Power movements in the United States and the *séparatiste* movement in Quebec, the attitude that the economic and social plight of the Indians could be solved by putting them on the same footing as other Canadians no longer seemed "progressive" or acceptable.

Thanks to these altered perceptions, native organizations, supported and largely financed by governments imbued with the trendy philosophy of social animation, gained new prominence and influence. When Andrew Paull, a British Columbia Indian, organized the Native Brotherhood of British Columbia in 1942, he had found it impossible to form a national organization, although several provincial organizations did come into being. Those of the four western provinces joined in 1961 to establish the National Indian Council, which set up a national office (1963) that the federal government recognized as the Indians' spokesman and assisted with funding. Unfortunately, the council soon disintegrated because of the differing interests of status and non-status Indians and Métis. The last two groups withdrew to form new provincial organizations for their own interests and the Métis eventually to set up the Native Council of Canada (1970); the status Indians went ahead to form the National Indian Brotherhood in 1965 with which the regional Indian organizations affiliated themselves.

The federal government's retreat from its long-held purpose of incorporating the Indian into the Canadian mainstream can be seen in those provisions of the Government Organization Act (14–15 Eliz. II, Chap. 25) of May 1966, which transferred management of Indian affairs from the Department of Citizenship and Immigration to the new Department of Indian Affairs and Northern Development that replaced the Department of Northern Affairs and National Resources. Thus with little discussion or debate the two services for native peoples, with their differing styles and approaches, were combined in the same department. The change seemed reasonable and natural in that it ended the anomaly that made Canada's oldest inhabitants and "first citizens'' the responsibility of a department primarily concerned with recently arrived immigrants. Indeed, many felt the department had given its Indian Affairs Branch little support and had done little (and that mainly after 1963) to make it a vehicle to deal effectively with its clients' many problems. Northern Affairs, on the other hand, in its thirteen years had demonstrated great concern for, spent heavily on, and devoted much manpower to its small constituency of Inuit and had introduced many programs to promote their well-being and ease their adjustment to modern conditions. In the union, therefore, it was hoped that the experience, initiative, and attitudes of the Northern Administration Branch might prevail throughout the new department and help overcome the tradition-bound views and ultraconservative practices of the Indian Affairs Branch.

That the old habits of the 2,893-man Indian Affairs Branch (1966 figure) were still in the ascendant, however, was speedily shown by the Trudeau government's White Paper on Indian Policy of 1969, which was the culmination of the assimilationist approach that had dominated the branch in its Citizenship and Immigration days. By throwing itself into the campaign against the White Paper and the highly publicized confrontations with government that characterized the 1970s, the National Indian Brotherhood speedily won great prestige and wide influence among sympathetic Canadians. Successive governments since 1967, belatedly grown sensitive to demands by the native peoples for autonomy and cultural survival, have striven through many frustrations and at great expense to achieve the contradictory goals of improving their material condition while sustaining as intact as possible a culture and value system derived from a largely archaic hunting and trapping lifestyle.

CHAPTER 11

The Federal Government and the Development
of the Northern Territories, 1945–1957

The highways, airfields, buildings, and communications systems installed north of 60 during the war made a propitious opening for the post-war resource-based development boom already sweeping the rest of Canada. The public's interest in the North and awareness of its potentialities probably were stronger than at any time since the Klondike excitement. Journalists fostered interest by writing about the North, artists found it a source of inspiration, and scientists (Canadian and foreign) increasingly took up investigation of the region's natural and social phenomena. Young people saw development of the territories as a challenge, a mission, and an opportunity in which they were ready to participate. Moreover, the war had added a new dimension to Canadians' perception of the North by revealing its considerable strategic importance in the air age, which continuing tensions of the Cold War made all the more evident.

The federal government, long cognizant of its responsibilities for the region but negligent in its duties there, was now in a position to plunge actively and directly into northern development. It commanded ample enough revenues not to let considerations of expense deter it from mounting a large-scale program there, and it could draw on a large pool of useful specialists from the armed services or the wartime civil service in applying its programs in the North. Post-war planning to sustain employment and prosperity in Canada dictated a serious effort to promote development of the untapped natural resources of the territories. The nation-wide social services and the newly awakened concept of minimum standards of health and educational services available to all regardless of income were particularly applicable to the northern territories, whose large native population was very much in need of these aids. Supplying these services was both incentive and reason for

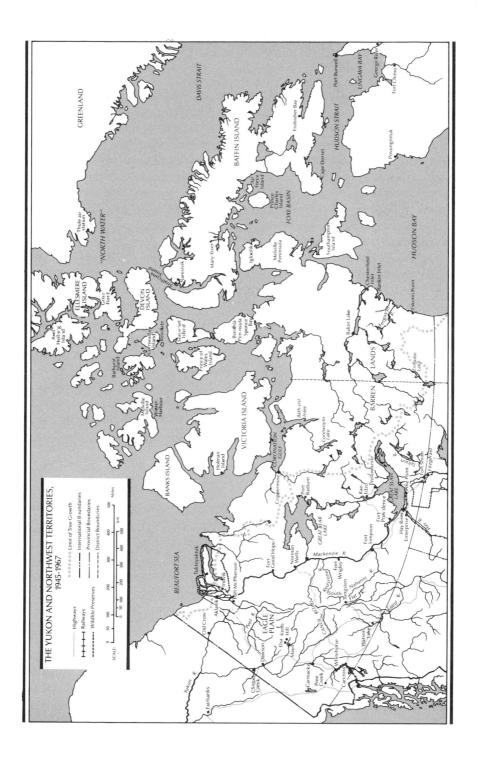

THE YUKON AND NORTHWEST TERRITORIES,
1945–1967

SCALE:

Highways
Railways
Wildlife Preserves

Limit of Tree Growth
International Boundaries
Provincial Boundaries
District Boundaries

GREENLAND

DAVIS STRAIT

"NORTH WATER"

Thule air station

ELLESMERE ISLAND

Alex Heiberg Island

Axel Heiberg Island

Grise Fiord

DEVON ISLAND

Resolute

BAFFIN ISLAND

Foxe Island

Prince Charles Island

Frobisher Bay

Cape Dorset

HUDSON STRAIT

Port Burwell

UNGAVA BAY

George River

Fort Chimo

Powungnituk

HUDSON BAY

Eskimo Point

Ferguson R.

BARREN LANDS

Rankin Inlet

Chesterfield Inlet

Baker Lake

Southampton Island

Melville Peninsula

Igloolik

FOXE BASIN

Mary River

Pangnirtung

Santsuvik

Bathurst Island

Melville Island

Winter Harbour

BANKS ISLAND

Holman Island

VICTORIA ISLAND

Prince of Wales Island

Somerset Island

Boothia Peninsula

Spence Bay

Cornwallis Island

Bathurst Inlet

Contwoyto Lake

CORONATION GULF

Coppermine

Port Radium

GREAT BEAR LAKE

Rae Edzo

Yellowknife

Fort Providence

Fort Simpson

Fort Wrigley

Fort Good Hope

Norman Wells

Mackenzie R.

BEAUFORT SEA

Tuktoyaktuk

Aklavik

Inuvik

Fort McPherson

Peel R.

Old Crow

EAGLE PLAIN

CANOL ROAD

Yukon R.

Fairbanks

Dawson

Clinton Creek

Elsa Keno Hill

Mayo

Carmacks

Pine Creek

Whitehorse

Carcross

Watson Lake

Fort Liard

Liard R.

Nahanni

South Nahanni R.

Flat R.

Redstone R.

Keele R.

GREAT SLAVE LAKE

Pine Point

Hay River

Enterprise

Fort Smith

Fort Fitzgerald

Fort Resolution

Emmerton Lake

Taltson R.

Slave R.

km

Miles

greater federal involvement with the territories that were its constitutional responsibility.

Two shadows clouded but did not efface the rosy vision of rapid
northern development: the minor one was the need to preserve the
northern environment so often abused in the past; the more serious
one was the deplorable condition of the native inhabitants and their
poor prospects under whatever changes might take place. The first was
not considered insoluble, for extending the operations of the government's forestry, wildlife, and other protective agencies to the northern
territories might correct the situation. Confidence that the worst of the
native peoples' problems could be overcome also grew stronger as
resource-developing industries resumed their advance and especially
as public, industrial, and military spending on construction projects
reached a crest in the early and mid-fifties. When the boom brought
many natives into the workforce, the notion was strengthened that
their difficulties could be solved by using the new social programs to
alleviate their poor health and poverty, educating them to participate
in the coming industrial development of the territories, and applying
scientific knowledge to improve the productivity of the traditional
industries among those who still had to rely on the land. As the federal
government insinuated itself into every aspect of the region's development it found a new type of public servant to direct and operate its
northern programs: the products of the Canadian universities' new
graduate programs in the natural and social sciences, who considered
promoting northern development a patriotic, personally satisfying
cause.

I

The quintessential sign of the federal government's serious and growing interest in the North after 1945 was the rapid growth within the
bureaucratic hierarchy of the agency charged with its administration.
In just eight years it was transformed from a very lowly position within
a large department of state to the leading role in a department created
expressly for it in 1953; in only five years more, northern development
was to be made the keynote theme of the federal general election campaign of 1958.

At the war's end, the Bureau of Northwest Territories and Yukon
Affairs was a minuscule agency employing some forty persons, a small
part of the Lands, Parks and Forests Branch of the Department of Mines
and Resources, the ungainly department thrown together mostly for
economy on December 1, 1936. An advantage of its situation, perhaps,
was that its personnel enjoyed close contacts with the staffs of the

National Parks Bureau and the Dominion Forest Service, which belonged to the same branch, and of other departmental branches, especially the National Museum of Canada, the surveying elements of the Mines and Geology, and Surveys and Engineering branches, and officers of the Indian Affairs Branch with similar involvements and experience with the territories. Most of those direct connections were lost in the administrative shuffle of 1950 when Mines and Resources was abolished and its mining and surveying units were combined in the new Department of Mines and Technical Surveys, while Indian Affairs was placed within the Department of Citizenship and Immigration. The remaining elements were gathered into another new department, Resources and Development, presided over by R.H. Winters, among which the northern agency, now renamed Northern Administration Division, formed part of the Development Services Branch.

Resources and Development was one of the shortest lived of all government departments, destined to endure no longer than three years. A further reorganization in 1953 replaced it with the Department of Northern Affairs and National Resources that seemed at first only a semantic change inasmuch as the new department contained the same agencies as its predecessor. But the change of title was significant: the function of the department had been redirected to make northern development its main thrust and purpose, and this its vigorous minister, Jean Lesage, and his deputy minister, the able R.G. Robertson, proceeded to do. The northern division, elevated to the status of the Northern Administration Branch, received new functions and new administrative structures, and its staff was enlarged again and again. Branch spending had increased six times over by 1957–58 and with 35.6 per cent of the budget it was now the largest branch in the department. The insignificant agency of a dozen years earlier had mushroomed into a large multi-functional, six-divisional administrative organization by 1957, headed by a director and two assistant directors, with a staff of some 1,000 persons, 343 of whom were dispersed full time across the length and breadth of the northern territories.

At the same time the branch underwent a significant change of style. Prior to 1945 the bureau had been tightly curbed by financial constraints and the close scrutiny of R.A. Gibson, the director of the Lands, Parks and Forests Branch, a colourless single-minded bureaucrat who had headed the branch and the northern administration since the early thirties and presided over them until he retired in October 1950. Gibson enjoyed the support of his long-time deputy minister, Charles Camsell, and minister, T.A. Crerar, both of whom were concerned mainly with keeping down expenditure, and he fully earned it by his frugality and conscientious attention to detail. Under Gibson the administration lost the drive W.W. Cory and O.S. Finnie, its leaders in the 1920s, had displayed. The surviving officers, aging and tied to Depression-time salaries, were confronted by the burdens associated with the Second World War when enlistments had depleted the bureau of its doctors, administrators, and legal advisers, and heavy workloads had undermined the health of the staffs who conducted its swollen wartime business at Fort Smith and Yellowknife, Whitehorse and Dawson. The minuscule Yukon administration had been handicapped throughout by the continuing poor health of Controller G.A. Jeckell, who was often absent on extended leave outside the territory, especially during the crucial winter of 1942–43. Within months of the ending of hostilities most of the leading officers – Major D.L. McKeand, Superintendent of the Eastern Arctic, A.L. Cumming, Superintendent of the District of Mackenzie, Controller Jeckell, and Deputy Minister Camsell – had retired. Camsell was succeeded as Deputy Minister and Commissioner of the Northwest Territories by H.L. Keenleyside, who brought more firm, confident, and innovative leadership to Northern administration.

In the decade after Gibson's departure the Northern Administration Branch became a far more self-directing arm of government in keeping with the trend throughout the federal public service, which grew enormously in size, complexity, and degree of specialization while Parliament and public became less able to criticize or direct its operations in detail, perhaps from lack of interest. Legislation was more and more confined to setting out general policies or programs, leaving the Cabinet to spell out the enactments in detail by orders in council and regulations drafted mainly with the advice of the civil servants charged with administering the legislation. In the case of northern administration – an area that enjoyed the support of expansionist, ambitious ministers after 1950 but did not normally attract much detailed public attention, affect many voters, or command much political power – the branch had a great deal of initiative. In native affairs, especially, the administrators enjoyed an almost free hand to operate existing programs and initiate new ones conceived by well-intentioned, usually benevolent officials. The resulting programs often lost something by the way they were implemented in the North, and they did not always achieve the results intended by the formulators in Ottawa.

While the Northern Administration Branch was concerned exclusively with the northern territories and stationed a comparatively high percentage of its staff there, it was far from being the sole, or even the preponderant, arm of the federal government represented in the North. "Government Activities in the North, 1957," one of a series of annual reports initiated in 1953, described the efforts of no fewer than thirteen government departments and ten special agencies, whose combined spending in the territories more than trebled the $10.6-million outlay of the Department of Northern Affairs and National Resources. National Defence also far outdistanced Northern Affairs in numbers of full-time employees stationed in the territories. In all, the federal government in 1957 employed 3,233 full-time, 2,015 seasonal, and 177 part-time workers in the territories, the number including 302 full-time employees in the District of Franklin (127 of them in the Arctic Archipelago) and sixty-nine in Keewatin. Government service, employing over 3,000 persons full-time in a region whose permanent population (themselves included) was only 31,500 in 1956, was rapidly becoming the main source of paid employment in the territories.

A major part of the large government presence in the territories reflected the heightened concern for the welfare of the native inhabitants, whose deteriorating state became a continuing preoccupation of the administration. Before 1939 the missions, with small support from government, had provided social services to the natives as part of their religious work and duty. As the administration took more direct control over those services it introduced its own staffs to deliver the various programs to the Inuit and Indians of the North. The results were a great increase in the numbers of civil servants living in the North and considerable shuffling of the roles of the traditional agencies. As we have seen, the missions had to adjust their northern operations drastically, while the role of the police, at first enlarged, eventually was diminished as more and more administrators arrived to deliver and regulate the various services to natives. Traders' relations with their native clients were weakened and their operations were increasingly regulated, but on the other hand the purchasing power and new tastes acquired by the natives meant good opportunities for profitable trading through general store operations.

During the fifties, the administration invested funds and efforts in the programs to bring the native northerner to a position of being able to participate in the coming industrialization of the North. He had, if he desired, the alternative of joining the economic mainstream in Southern Canada, in keeping with the then administration's belief that "the complete assimilation of the Inuit was inevitable within two generations, and [it] was anxious to reach this end as soon as possible"[1] to minimize the accompanying strains. By 1955 it already saw its programs as succeeding in this objective:

> As the native people engage more actively in the economic development of the northern territories, they will develop increasingly a sense of personal responsibility, and the solution of these problems of economic and social adaptation will emerge.

The task of implementing a broad plan of Eskimo development will be long and probably expensive. A carefully developed program – and substantial progress has been made on such a program – can, however, transform Canada's Eskimos from a financial liability to a national asset. The results in human terms will be of the highest importance.[2]

To administer the programs directed at bettering the condition of the native residents civil servants trained in many different specialties were introduced to the Northwest Territories: forestry and wildlife officers, policemen, doctors and nurses, teachers and "welfare teachers," crafts development officers, program administrators. A new sort of official, the Northern Service Officer (NSO), began to be appointed in 1955 "to co-ordinate field activities and to supervise developments in various areas."[3] He was also a welfare officer trained to help natives readjust following their return from hospitalization in the South. By 1958 eight NSOs were stationed at points ranging from Great Whale River and Churchill in the east to Cambridge Bay and Tuktoyaktuk in the west to help Inuit find wage employment in military and other construction and in other activities appropriate to their home districts. These were succeeded, in turn, by Area Superintendents stationed at nearly every important settlement to oversee industrial development, conduct area economic surveys, and supervise the growing numbers of civil servants and services located in their districts. In 1956 the first social worker arrived in the Arctic, a reflection of the need for something more than economic guidance to lead the Inuit through a period that was swiftly erasing the main guideposts of their traditional way of life.

Besides the large numbers of full-time government employees stationed in the territories, hundreds of others worked there on a seasonal basis each year for National Defence, Public Works, Transport, Mines and Technical Surveys, and other departments carrying out their own programs. The scientific agencies in particular greatly stepped up their activities after the Second World War because of the greater accessibility of the northern territories, the advances in science and technology that reshaped their missions and made their operations more effective there, and their own stronger administrative and financial positions. Many agencies had already investigated the resources of the Yukon Territory and District of Mackenzie in connection with the North Pacific Planning Project. The Department of Agriculture, following its soil surveys, opened experimental sub-stations after the war at Fort Simpson and Yellowknife, and a larger one for the Yukon at Pine Creek west of Whitehorse. The Fisheries Research Board on the basis of its surveys of the large lakes of the region established a quota and opened Great Slave Lake for commercial fishing. The Dominion Water and Power Bureau extended its stream measurements program to northern rivers and investigated the power potentials of several sites adjacent to industrial centres.

The wartime studies of the Dominion Forest Service also revealed the need for proper measures to protect the neglected, much-ravaged forests of the region. Accordingly, field organizations were set up during 1946 and 1947, headed by superintendents stationed at White-horse and Fort Smith. Full-time forestry officers and modern fire-fighting equipment were placed at seven centres in the District of Mackenzie with assistance from part-time wardens and firefighters. The forestry staffs enforced the game regulations as well. Specialists were secured for the Dominion Wildlife Service to conduct researches on various species, and on harvesting practices; mammalogists inves-tigated the fauna of Wood Buffalo Park, the Mackenzie delta, and the caribou of the tundra between the Mackenzie and Hudson Bay.

The surveying branches were especially eager to extend their activ-ities into the third of Canada within the northern territories that was still largely uninvestigated. In the summer of 1947, the first "normal" season after the war, the Geological Survey sent six parties to the ter-ritories while units of the Surveys and Mapping Bureau (as it then was) were carrying out township outline surveys and legal surveys of air-ports and settlements and making astronomical fixes for the aeronau-tical charts being compiled from air photographs supplied by the RCAF's active program. The Hydrographic Survey, using a specially designed vessel, began charting the Mackenzie waterway route. The Dominion Observatory, assisted by the RCAF and a U.S. Navy icebreaker, estab-lished nineteen magnetic stations in the Arctic, located the current position of the North Magnetic Pole (on Prince of Wales Island, two hundred miles northwest of the site reported in 1831), and arranged to open observatories at Baker Lake and Resolute Bay. Each year the operations extended farther afield and were conducted on larger, more sophisticated lines.

The activities of the Geological Survey, particularly significant for mining, with its key place in the plans for industrializing the North, highlight the rapidly changing character of the work. Fixed-wing air-craft and helicopters speeded reconnaissance surveying tenfold, to the point where most of the 185,000 square miles of Arctic tundra west of Hudson Bay could be mapped on a scale of eight miles to the inch in only three seasons, the entire southern half of the Mackenzie basin west of the Canadian Shield (in Operation Mackenzie) in 1957, and most of the Queen Elizabeth Islands (in the momentous Operation

Franklin) in 1955. That last-named enterprise was headed by Y.O. Fortier, who had first visited the islands north of the mainland in 1947 as an observer with the Dominion Observatory's pioneering magnetic survey. During 1955 the twenty-eight-man party (including eleven geologists trained in various sub-sciences) surveyed a 200,000- square-mile tract, consisting of shallow straits and seas and the islands from Bathurst to northern Axel Heiberg and from western Melville to southwestern Ellesmere. So many favourable structures and showings were discovered that the keen attention of the international oil and gas industry was immediately drawn to the Arctic islands and seas. To facilitate its work in the Arctic the Geological Survey soon established a marine geology unit to deal more effectively with the geology of the sea-covered areas and also began more intensive study of the surficial geology, the fragile soils exposed by the latest land rises and glacial recessions.

The geologists, of course, did not work in isolation. The base maps on which they depended were prepared from photographs provided by the RCAF's air photography squadrons (sometimes the photographs were used directly). They also represented the continuing work of the astronomical and geodetic services in fixing the latitudes, longitudes, and elevations of the key features. Submarine geological work similarly depended on the hydrographic charts being made of Arctic and Hudson Bay waters. Besides its more spectacular large-scale operations, the Geological Survey each year spread a dozen or more parties across the territories to study their geological phenomena by detail work on gold, uranium, and other mineral deposits and tectonic studies of cordilleran structures in Northern Yukon-Mackenzie and the mountainous eastern parts of Baffin and Ellesmere islands, and of fossil-bearing sedimentary formations in the western islands. Sweeping aeromagnetic and geophysical surveys were conducted from the air. By 1958, reporting of the geology of the enormous region north of the 60th parallel was assisting prospectors to fan out everywhere seeking to bring its mineral resources under active development. Thus the several surveying agencies laid a basis for the development of transportation facilities and future exploitation of the mineral and other resources of the northern regions.

II

The government's concern to make the territories more accessible and attractive to modern industry inspired a program of major public construction and investment that explained the large numbers of employees of the Departments of Transport and Public Works and those of National Defence, now maintaining the Alaska Highway, stationed there. The program was intended to reduce the costs of transportation and of fuel and power to something approaching those in pioneering districts in the provinces and to supply urban townsites and modern utilities to attract the workforces to man the future industries. Reliable, convenient, reasonably priced transportation facilities and services were of paramount importance. Water transport in the District of Mackenzie in 1945 was quite efficient, handled by the well-equipped government-owned Northern Transportation Company and the updated Hudson's Bay Company service, although the latter abandoned the role of public carrier (except for certain remote routes) after 1948. But it was still relatively expensive and quite inconvenient because its seasonal character forced industries to maintain very large inventories or hire expensive air transport to bring in supplies in winter. Southern Yukon was reasonably well served by its railway and recently built highways, but industries north of Whitehorse still had to depend on river or air services.

Efforts were accordingly made to push all-weather highways into the settled and settling parts of the territories, building on foundations laid before or during the war. Of particular importance for the District of Mackenzie was the improvement of the former winter tractor road between Grimshaw and Hay River into a permanent highway. Hay River became the head of navigation for Great Slave Lake and points beyond and the point of departure for boat trips, airplane flights (in which the young flyer and entrepreneur Max Ward participated), or over-ice deliveries to Yellowknife. The road was upgraded and was gradually extended around the west end of Great Slave Lake to Yellowknife, the mile-wide Mackenzie River being crossed by a ferry installed below Fort Providence. A similar highway was completed north from Whitehorse to serve the mines in the Keno Hill area and then to Dawson, ending the need for water transport altogether and laying up the historic Yukon steamboat fleet. Although most of the Canol Road fell into disuse following removal of the pipeline, its southern part continued to be maintained for travel to and from the Ross River country.

These main road arteries made the southern parts of the territories far more accessible to sportsmen, trappers, prospectors, and commercial fishermen and improved northern living conditions. A study of the impact of the Mackenzie Highway on life in Yellowknife (1962) reported sharp reductions in the cost of perishable foodstuffs and great improvements in quality (such as fresh milk to replace the reconstituted variety), the inauguration of garages, restaurants, motels, and tourist facilities, and, above all, a striking bettering of settlers' morale because the feeling of isolation from the outside world was lessened.

Abundant, reliable, cheaper supplies of energy, being a requirement of industrial expansion, the federal government determined to make electric power available to northern industries and settlements as a development aid. First it constructed a larger 8,350-horsepower hydro station at Snare River north of Yellowknife, primarily to help Giant Yellowknife Gold Mining Company bring its large mine into operation. Then, in 1948, it established the Northwest Territories Power Commission (renamed Northern Canada Power Commission in 1956) on the model of Ontario Hydro to supply northerners' energy needs as economically and efficiently as possible and yet recover the investments in twenty years. The commission built a second $4-million hydro plant on Mayo River to serve the mines in that area (1952) and installed a diesel electric plant at Fort Smith (1950) for government offices and other customers. During the fifties diesel electric plants were installed at other main centres, the Mayo and Snare River hydro stations were enlarged, and in 1958 the commission completed its largest hydro plant to that date (15,000 horsepower, costing $7.2 million and amortized over forty years) at Whitehorse Rapids. As in the provinces, private groups developed smaller plants in collaboration with the commission at Whitehorse and Hay River. Since it was not yet feasible to equalize the rates, they varied according to local circumstances and were generally higher than in the provinces. Still, the commission supplied northerners' requirements as cheaply as possible, relieved developers of having to finance such costly installations, and made it possible for residents to live more safely and comfortably than in the past.

The "human" concerns, the needs of the territories' inhabitants as distinct from the economic aspects, were the particular responsibility of the Northern Administration Branch. This branch oversaw the development of local government and the functioning of local institutions in conjunction with the councils provided for both territories, which were to legislate and provide services to inhabitants other than status Indians. The Yukon Council was fully elective, financed its operations largely out of local taxation, possessed its own consolidated revenue fund, and employed a territorial civil service to provide for education, welfare, public works, wildlife management, and so on. The Northwest Territories Council enjoyed similar legislative authority but at war's end had almost no financial means of its own and no civil service except for the small staff operating the territorial liquor system. Local services were supplied by the Northern Administration Branch. In addition, this council depended so heavily on the branch for information, administrative know-how, and financial support that officers of the branch to a great extent determined the policies for the territory, while the council's functions were "limited to legislative matters, and to giving advice on such questions of major policy as might be referred to it by the Commissioner."[4]

The character of the Northwest Territories Council underwent major changes after 1945 as the federal government determined "to streamline and strengthen the administration and simultaneously to make the reformed Council a more democratic institution as well as a more exclusively legislative body."[5] Beginning in 1946 a series of small steps were taken to reduce its identification with the federal civil service and make it more representative of the residents. J.G. McNiven, a manager of a Yellowknife gold mine, became the first resident and first non-government member to be appointed to the council, which also received two new councillors from departments other than Mines and Resources. Beginning in 1951 the voters in the Yellowknife, Fort Smith, and Aklavik districts elected three members to council and a fourth in 1954. From 1960 the appointed members were selected from outside government, chiefly from business and academic circles, and by 1964 only the commissioner and assistant commissioner were still being drawn from the civil service.

The style of the council also changed. Prior to 1945, sessions had been informal, almost casual one-day meetings scattered through the year at intervals of a few weeks. In 1951 it was decided that the council should hold two long sessions yearly, one in Ottawa, the other at some centre in the Territories to bring the council closer to the people and better acquaint its members with conditions in the North, the process being inaugurated in December 1952 with a session at Fort Smith. Earlier, the electors of the District of Mackenzie had received the federal franchise when the Yukon constituency was enlarged in 1947 to include their district. Since the experiment proved unsatisfactory, provision was made in 1952 for a constituency of Mackenzie River on its own in succeeding parliaments until 1958, when it was enlarged to embrace the Northwest Territories and was renamed accordingly. The franchise was extended to native persons from 1950 for territorial and federal general elections.

The Yukon, too, benefited from the new approach as well as from the local prosperity that gave the elected council greater confidence to press for constitutional changes. Accumulated wartime savings and liquor profits were large enough to enable the territorial government to function without any federal grants in aid for a year or two (1945–47). A brief experiment with levying a territorial income tax gave the Yukon a lever with which to negotiate a five-year tax rental agreement with the federal government in 1948 comparable with the Dominion-Provincial Taxation Agreements of the day, an arrangement extended to the Northwest Territories Council in 1952. In keeping with the post-war growth of the territory, indicated by the increase in its population from 4,914 in 1941 to 9,096 in 1951, two more elected members were added to the council in 1952. A year later, also, the territorial capital at last was transferred from the decaying community of Dawson to Whitehorse, the centre of the post-1942 growth, which had become a city with its own municipal government in 1947.

Both councils agreed with the Northern Administration Branch that the industrial and administrative development of the territories depended on settlers from outside, who would have to be attracted by being offered living conditions as secure, healthful, and comfortable as prevailed elsewhere. Many existing settlements had isolated and unsatisfactory sites and lacked public utilities and improvements. Before the war settlers (or their employers) had attended to their own needs, and most settlements had grown up in haphazard, unplanned, even dangerous directions. Since the administration had to build schools, hospitals, and other modern public buildings and equip them with the essential utilities, it seemed logical to add serious efforts at site consolidation and community planning. The principal need in the Yukon was to modernize archaic facilities and locate or relocate settlements to meet modern conditions.

A more pressing situation existed in Yellowknife, where the original settlement had sprung up on a lakeside site that was difficult to provide with public utilities and in any case was too small to accommodate the population being attracted to it. A new townsite on relatively sandy ground one mile inland was surveyed in 1945, and building lots were offered for lease to housebuilders and businessmen, ownership being retained by the Crown. In 1946 the Department of Public Works prepared the townsite's roads and streets and a franchise for a telephone system was awarded. By the end of 1947 a modern, well-equipped forty-bed Red Cross hospital and a splendid school (to be complemented by a separate school in 1951) were in place, while the heated and chlorinated water and sewer systems were completed in 1949. The Local Trustee Board established in 1940 gradually took over the operation of local utilities and such functions as fire prevention, for which a municipal staff was acquired. Initially the board had been appointed, but by 1947 five of its nine members were elected by the ratepayers, and in 1951 it was replaced altogether by an elected mayor and five-member council.

Similar attention was paid to providing roads, services, schools, and public buildings for other leading settlements. The Northwest Territories administration remained responsible for maintaining and operating these, except in the organized municipalities of Yellowknife and Hay River. By 1957 Local Improvement Districts were being established for communities like Fort Smith and Fort Simpson in which the administration levied taxes on townsite properties for local purposes, established site control regulations, and arranged with CMHC to prepare urban development plans and carry them out.

Ambitious and very expensive plans to create a completely new town in the Mackenzie delta region to replace Aklavik were made in 1953. Certainly Aklavik was unacceptable as a regional metropolis. It was subject to flooding and impossible to drain, was gradually subsiding into the surrounding mud flats, and lacked a year-round airfield. The new town, planned as the administrative and research centre for the region, would be located on a higher, well-drained site suitable for installing and operating the full complement of modern amenities. With all the latest advances in Arctic construction and community organization in practice, New Aklavik would become a showplace, "consciously designed to demonstrate the possibility of building a northern town with as many of the features of our urban civilization as possible."[6] A site east of the East Channel of the Mackenzie River "East-Three," about thirty-five miles from Aklavik, was selected, and preliminary construction was begun in 1955. Builders had to master the techniques of building on permafrosted ground, and seven years elapsed before Inuvik (the official name given the site in 1958) was completed. The outstanding features of the town were its oil-fired central heating and electricity plant, specially insulated buildings, and circulating utilidor (an elevated, boxed-in system housing the steam heating, water, and sewage disposal lines) to serve the homes and buildings.

The residential school and government offices went into operation, and the town quickly filled with white and Inuit settlers. Persons and institutions transferring from Aklavik were compensated for making the move. But the main purpose was not attained, for Old Aklavik despite its inconveniences did not wither away. It remained the fur-trapping and trading centre of the delta area, and most Indian, Métis, and Inuit continued using it as their base. Thus building Inuvik only introduced another community to the district, negating the government's effort to consolidate facilities and tending to divorce the white settlers from the large part of the native population which gravitated to Aklavik or to Tuktoyaktuk. Besides, the plan had not made allowance for the attractiveness of the modern town to native persons from the surrounding district. A shacktown soon grew up beyond the utilidor-serviced core, creating a sharp divergence in lifestyles and undesirable inequalities (marked by the presence or absence of utilidor services and government-subsidized living expenses) and kindling tensions among residents.

It was much the same with planned settlements from Whitehorse to Frobisher Bay – indeed, all around the Third World. Modern government-dominated centres planted in the midst of primitive societies offered casual employment, medical and educational services, novelty and entertainment, and comfortable, more abundant living that tempted impoverished persons to leave the land and flock to them. There they squatted on traditional campgrounds, in the rundown older sections of the towns, or more often in unorganized areas adjoining the surveyed subdivisions while the newcomers occupied the modern townsites or newer subdivisions of old settlements. The squatters along Canada's northern frontier were mainly, but not invariably, persons of native origin. At Whitehorse, where squatters formed about a third of the total population, they included many non-native seasonal workers, impoverished and "problem" families, and persons who preferred the lifestyles of the unorganized communities or simply chose to avoid the taxes, expenses, and responsibilities that went with residing in the official townsites.

The reasoning for making the comparatively large public investments on amenities and infrastructures had been to hasten the development of the North. New industries that could compete in outside markets would now have to be developed. From the outset it was recognized that agriculture and forestry were most unlikely to be among these; they would be developed only to serve local needs, helping to improve employment and living conditions and to relieve the heavy dependence on outside supplies. On the other hand, mining and, to a lesser extent, commercial fishing were capable of producing for large distant markets and should be fostered accordingly. Some mines already were at that stage, and there was every likelihood that there would be many more, since the territories must contain developable mineral resources in the same proportions as the rest of Canada.

But production and employment from the mining industries did not always come up to expectations, even though extensive prospecting activity aroused high hopes and the future of properties under development remained good. There were closures or obvious declines of some existing mines: cancellation of the Canol Project had at once reduced oil production at Norman Wells to the small requirements of the regional market (about 300,000 to 600,000 barrels annually) and although the wartime mining operation at Port Radium continued, after reaching peak uranium production in 1954 its output rapidly declined, and the mine was closed in 1960. Negus, the smallest and richest of the Yellowknife gold mines, the last to close during the war and the first to reopen thereafter, was soon worked out and ceased operations in 1953. Yukon Consolidated strove throughout the period to regain its pre-war levels of gold production, but the steadily declining grade of the remaining Klondike sands and reduced annual returns presaged closure in the not too distant future.

These were offset by the coming into production of two large new mines that promised long-term survival, the Giant Yellowknife, mining a large low-grade gold deposit beginning in 1948, treating an eventual 1,000 tons a day, and the United Keno Hill Mines, a new company mining rich, newly discovered silver-lead ores after 1947 at Elsa in the Mayo district. In addition, three smaller but unfortunately short-lived mines were brought into production. A small, rich gold producer, Discovery Yellowknife, went into operation in 1950 but showed signs of depletion before the end of the decade, and the Rayrock mine, a small high-grade uranium producer on Marian Lake north of Yellowknife, opened in 1957 but ran out of ore in three years, even before its production contract was completed. More noteworthy was the small nickel-copper mine at Rankin Inlet on Hudson Bay, 270 miles north of Churchill, that also went into production in 1957. To solve the employment problem the management adopted the unusual, highly significant policy of hiring a mainly Inuit workforce to operate the mine and concentrating plant. The concentrates were shipped to Churchill, thence by rail to the Sherritt Gordon nickel refinery near Edmonton. Unfortunately, the Rankin Inlet operation lasted only until 1962, when the deposit was worked out. The maximum value of production from all these mines did not exceed $26 million a year for the Northwest Territories and $16 million for the Yukon, and peak employment for the Territories was 1,255 (1957). Yet even in that year, mining accounted for 82 per cent of the entire net production, by value, of the two territories.

Besides these, a number of other mines in various preliminary stages heralded a more promising future for the industry: a tungsten mine in the southwestern corner of the Northwest Territories that at first was accessible only from the Yukon side, another small gold mine on the tundra 150 miles northeast of Yellowknife, and especially the huge long-known lead-zinc deposit at Pine Point south of Great Slave Lake. Consolidated Mining and Smelting started a large-scale diamond drilling program to outline the deposits in 1951. In the following year it built a townsite complete with water mains and sewers in anticipation of arrival of a railway, when a large output tripling mineral production in the Territories would start. Still other mines were foreshadowed by the extensive searches for gold, silver, uranium, tungsten, asbestos, and other minerals that persisted throughout the period and were extended into ever more remote areas.

Less certainty surrounded the widespread prospecting carried on along the Alaska Highway, in the Yellowknife district and north to Great Bear Lake, and around the northwestern and southeastern coasts of Great Slave Lake. The search extended even into the Arctic islands, so much so that the Arctic and Hudson Bay Mining Division recorded the largest number of mineral claim stakings of any division in 1957 and 1958. The authorities had adopted a new policy of awarding very large mineral concessions to attract the prospecting companies, and three of these in the Coppermine-Bathurst Inlet region, totalling 1,720 square miles, went to groups that undertook to spend a million dollars apiece exploring and developing their holdings. A similar 500-square-mile concession was awarded in the Ferguson River area of Keewatin on which the concessionaire spent over $1 million for development in 1952 alone. The Rankin Inlet mine inspired many stakings along the Hudson Bay coast between the Manitoba border and Chesterfield Inlet. Prospectors staked iron ore beds on the Belcher Islands, on the Nastapoka Islands along the eastern shore of Hudson Bay, and on the Foxe Peninsula, the southwestern spur of Baffin Island. One company in 1957 staked a lead-zinc occurrence on Strathcona Sound in northwestern Baffin Island – an area that had attracted the Bernier expedition of 1910–11 – which eventually (1976) became the Nanisivik mine.

Even greater optimism was generated by oil and gas prospecting and developmental activities. Activity around the Norman Wells field and in the Hay River–Fort Providence area was followed after 1950 by the entry of major oil companies, first in southern Mackenzie and Yukon, then in the latitude of Fort Simpson, and by the mid-fifties in the far norths between Fort Good Hope and the Mackenzie delta in Mackenzie and on the Peel Plateau and Eagle Plains of Northern Yukon. Under regulations instituted in 1953, exploration rights to large (two- to three-million-acre) tracts were put out for competitive bidding, the successful applicant receiving exclusive rights to undertake developmental operations on the tract. Eventually, if the obligations were met and the operator desired to continue to the well-drilling stage, he could apply to lease part of the original permit area, surrendering at least 50 per cent of it to the administering authority. The obvious purpose was to encourage participation by the wealthy companies capable of carrying their enterprises to production. Outstanding exploration permits totalling 32 million acres in 1957 brought expenditures (which had first passed the $1-million level in 1953) of $3.6 million.

By the middle 1950s the developers were already affecting the local economies by providing work for guides and casual labour and business for hotels and stores. A more questionable result of their efforts was to open and scar remote areas with survey lines, trails, roads, and campsites. Few productive discoveries were made (no oil wells and only a few gas wells, which were kept capped for lack of markets), but the feeling persisted that a large oil strike could come at any moment that might unleash a boom like the one that followed the Leduc, Alberta, oil strike of February 1947.

A surer but localized new industry was commercial fishing, inaugurated on Great Slave Lake after the war. The Fisheries Research Board survey of 1944 had set a five-million-pound fish quota for the lake (soon raised to nine million), and the largest operator on Lake Athabasca immediately moved equipment from that lake and began fishing the large, relatively untouched new supply source. Refrigerating equipment was transferred to a base at the entrance to Rae Arm, where a good summer catch of lake trout and pickerel was filleted, quick-frozen, and shipped in refrigerator barges to the railhead at Waterways. A winter fishery for lake trout and whitefish was started in 1947–48 at the western end of the lake, handy for shipping whole fresh fish by refrigerated trucks from Hay River over the Mackenzie Highway to the railhead at Grimshaw or direct to Edmonton. The fishery achieved a peak nine-million-pound catch (10 per cent of Canada's freshwater total) in 1949–50; more normal catches were in the range of six to seven million pounds. These did not seem to reduce the fish stocks overall but quickly depleted the lake trout, the largest and best species for sales, compelling the fishery to rely on less valuable species. When efforts to extend commercial fishing to nearby large lakes met with little success, the industry remained virtually restricted to Great Slave Lake. It employed some 500 men, most of them seasonal fisheries workers or farmers from the Prairie Provinces. Nevertheless, the industry gave Hay River a considerable boost by creating local employment and business in fish processing, boat outfitting and repairing, trucking, and other activities.

III

While the government agencies were thus active in the territories north of 60, a very different force was also pouring huge sums into the region, particularly its northernmost sector, and affecting development in many important ways. This was the joint Canadian-United States program to protect the North American continent against possible airborne attack by a potential Cold War adversary. As part of the worldwide strategy of containment, transport and travel facilities

were vastly improved throughout the North, thousands of construction and transport workers were brought in for the great building projects, and hundreds of servicemen and civilians were stationed in the
region for years at a time. The defence program exerted a wide influence on the Inuit, helping many of them become familiar with the
opportunities and challenges of modern life. With public attention
focused on the Arctic region, many scientific and technological
researches were undertaken, inspired and largely supported by funds
and practical assistance from the defence departments. The Arctic and
its people were brought under modern influences and introduced to
industrial development as never before.

As the Second World War drew to its close, Canadian and U.S. military planners viewing the growing international tensions and the new
strategic situation created by long-range aircraft and nuclear weapons
foresaw that the Arctic had an important place in the future defence
of North America. Canadian diplomats thought of the Arctic as more
properly a locale for international scientific programs; Canadian military chiefs tended to believe that the empty, inhospitable environment was the region's best insurance against being used for military
purposes by an invader. Both groups, however, agreed that Canadian
agencies would have to maintain an active presence in the Arctic, and
the wartime collaboration with the United States in Northern Canada
would have to be continued, at the very least to head off undesirable
unilateral actions by a United States alarmed for its own security.

Shortly after the war ended a military training experiment, Exercise
Musk-ox, was carried out to test the functioning of a mechanized force
in Arctic and Subarctic terrain. A forty-man force, periodically supplied by RCAF planes, travelled from Churchill to Baker Lake, Cambridge Bay, Coppermine, Norman Wells, and Fort Nelson, thence over
the Alaska Highway to Grande Prairie between February 14 and May
5, 1946 – a 3,000-mile journey, 2,600 miles of it in entirely roadless
country. The exercise was a test of the operation of all kinds of vehicles, aircraft, and communications equipment, along with clothing,
gear, and rations in all manner of situations and under extreme climatic
conditions. Throughout these gruelling months the men remained in
good health: "No frostbite, snowblindness or sickness occurred, nor
was any sickness introduced among the natives."[7]

They brought back useful knowledge of the lands traversed and left
equipment in place that found good future use, some becoming incorporated into a weather observation and scientific research base at
Baker Lake. Their valuable experience in improvising airstrips and
parachuting supplies could be applied throughout the Arctic in future
military, scientific, and prospecting operations. Musk-ox was deemed

a success in demonstrating both the ability of men and machines to function under Arctic conditions and the limitations of conducting large-scale military operations there. In any case, it was thought that the main threat was long-range military aircraft, whose potentialities were revealed in May 1945 by the Arctic flights of *Aries*, a modified RAF Lancaster bombing plane. In a series of 5,000-mile sorties from Britain, *Aries* investigated problems of navigating in high latitudes and the reliability of magnetic compasses in the vicinity of the North Magnetic Pole, in the process demonstrating that transpolar flights by long-range planes were entirely feasible.

The United States also began to take steps against the danger perceived as emanating from the north. During 1946 the U.S. Navy tested aircraft carrier and seaplane operations in polar waters, while the U.S. Weather Bureau made plans to establish weather stations in the Arctic, one of them on Melville Island. Rumours circulated that the United States wanted "a system of northern frontier air bases to be maintained and equipped as part of the general defensive machinery of this continent,"[8] and negotiations were initiated with Canada that reaffirmed the wartime relationship (including the key role of the PJBD) but on more voluntary, equal lines, in keeping with Canadian sensitivities.

The first public indication of the new Canadian-American role in the North purposely stressed its scientific value. On March 4, 1947, C.D. Howe reported that the government intended to establish nine Arctic weather stations during the next three years, the United States having "undertaken to assist Canada in the establishment and operation of these northern stations, which will, of course, be under the control of the Canadian government, which will supply the officers in charge."[9] The opening of five joint air weather stations (JAWS) at widely separated points in the northerly Queen Elizabeth Islands followed, at Resolute on Cornwallis Island (September 1947), Mould Bay on Prince Patrick Island, and Isachsen on Ellef Ringnes Island (April 1948), and at Eureka Sound (April 1947) and Alert (April 1950) on Ellesmere Island. These stations were linked with others on Baffin Island and Greenland and with the regular weather systems of both countries. The five stations were equipped and at first supplied by the United States.

By 1948 the United States was considering a further sort of protection against possible attacks from the north by planes carrying nuclear bombs, such as the USSR was now capable of sending: a chain of radar stations extending across the continent able to detect attackers quickly enough to allow defending forces to take action against them and launch retaliatory strikes against their homeland. The United States first built the Pinetree radar defence system across the continent in the vicinity of the 49th parallel, Canada agreeing to pay a third of the cost of extending it over the Canadian Subarctic east from Manitoba and of operating the stations in Canada. On its own initiative Canada built and operated an automated electronic detecting system approximately along the 55th parallel, the $200-million "McGill Fence" or Mid-Canada Line, to serve as a back-up for a far grander system the Americans were building much farther north.

That system, the Distant Early Warning (DEW) Line, was to be located along the northern coastline of the mainland and across Baffin Island at approximate latitude 69° North. The United States was to pay the entire cost of building and operating the system, the Canadian government being kept fully informed and to be free to inspect construction undertaken in the 2,000-mile-long Canadian sector. Canadian firms and personnel were to be employed as much as possible in equipping, supplying, building, and manning the sites. Canada was to have the right to use the stations' non-secret facilities, and the United States agreed that its personnel and operations would comply with all appropriate federal and territorial regulations and undertook to protect the wildlife and native population of the region. Under Western Electric, the general contractor for the line, and its Canadian sub-contractors, Foundation Company of Montreal and Northern Construction Company of Vancouver, the arduous, costly work was pushed forward. "Construction of the Line had cost over $500 million and nearly 30 lives, but on 31 July, 1957 it became officially operational."[10] The entire system thereupon was turned over to Federal Electric Corporation of New Jersey to operate.

There were forty-one DEW Line stations in Canada, of three different sorts. Four main stations (Cape Dyer, Hall Beach, Cambridge Bay, and Cape Perry) served as regional headquarters and were equipped with giant scanning radars enclosed in fifty-five-foot plastic bubbles to locate and identify aircraft, collate reports from stations, and transmit warnings of unidentified planes to command headquarters. The second type were similarly equipped auxiliary stations built at hundred-mile intervals between the main bases that constantly scanned the skies and transmitted their reports to the main stations. Finally, there were I-sites, small intermediate stations with fixed radars whose signals echoed off objects crossing their beams and were picked up by the larger stations. The main bases required staffs of about forty civilians and military officers (five RCAF and two USAF), the auxiliary stations twenty-man complements, and the I-sites three to five men. As far as possible the stations were constructed of standard prefabricated wooden modular units, 16 by 28 by 10 feet, joined together to bring as much of the living and working quarters as possible within a "self-contained, life-supporting environment."[11] About fifty such units were required for a main station, but even a small I-site was comprised of "three small buildings, one small house, two bulk fuel tanks, a communication tower, landing strip and the short road connecting the airstrip and with the building site."[12]

Detecting intruders was only half the U.S. program for defending North America and the "Free World." The other half was a powerful retaliatory force kept in constant readiness to deter aggression by the threat of "massive retaliation," thereby creating a "balance of terror." The second aspect grew all the more dominant during the fifties as more deadly nuclear weapons were developed and it was not entirely certain that they could be prevented from reaching their targets. Deterrent forces of the Strategic Air Command (SAC) were stationed at some forty locations around the world, among them Goose Bay and Frobisher Bay, air bases the Americans had used in the Second World War. The United States resumed control over the Frobisher airfield in 1951 and installed a powerful radar station there in 1952. The runways were paved and lengthened, and large fuel storage tanks and appropriate buildings for maintenance and personnel were built. The Goose Bay establishment, which was an RCAF base besides, was even larger. While manned bombers were considered the main threat during the fifties, squadrons of fighters and long-range bombing planes ready to go into action were based at these stations. In addition, considerable civil and military transport traffic was handled, particularly in connection with DEW Line construction and resupply, but also with the transatlantic and transpolar commercial air services established since the war.

Building and operating the northern JAWS, DEW Line, and SAC stations put unprecedented strains on existing transportation facilities that expanded them enormously thereafter and opened up the High Arctic for future activities. The weather stations were supplied at first by air from Thule and Resolute, but beginning in 1953 with the *d'Iberville* and the *Labrador* in 1954, Canadian icebreakers and chartered freighters delivered supplies each year to Resolute and occasionally to Winter Harbour, or ploughed northward into Jones Sound towards Eureka or along Nares Strait towards Alert. Mould Bay, Isachsen, Alert, and often Eureka had to be supplied by air. The RCAF Air Transport Command was called to ferry supplies from Thule or Resolute to the JAWS bases, and after larger, longer-range Hercules aircraft became available, from Namao near Edmonton. The annual supply operations to the Queen Elizabeth Islands were not inconsiderable in view of the heavy amounts required for the JAWS stations (estimated as nineteen tons a man annually) and the other activities: RCMP and other government stations, a sizeable Canadian Army base at Alert, and numerous scientific projects.

Yet these demands were dwarfed by the gigantic transport requirements of the DEW Line. More than 200,000 tons of building material, equipment, and supplies had to be moved north by sea in 1955 alone. Most DEW Line freight was shipped during the summers of 1955 and 1956 in convoys from Montreal or Halifax. Some ships, supported by government icebreakers, pushed through the heavy ice of Hudson Strait and Foxe Basin to supply the bases in that sector; the remainder proceeded north to deliver supplies to the Baffin Island sites or still farther in the Queen Elizabeth Islands. The westernmost bases were supplied from Seattle and by the Northern Transportation Company's Mackenzie waterway service, which deposited the DEW Line freight at Tuktoyaktuk, whence it was distributed along the mainland coast.

Other DEW Line freight was delivered by planes, especially during the winter of 1954–55 to hasten the start of work. Tractors urgently needed for the initial construction stages were loaded into Globemaster freighter aircraft and parachuted to the sites to prepare runways for the cargo-carrying planes that would deliver the vast quantities of steel, lumber, cement, machinery and equipment, and foodstuffs and the workmen. A few inland sites, especially on Baffin Island, had to be built and supplied entirely by air, usually from Churchill via Coral Harbour. In all, "something in the order of 106,000 tons of air freight moved in the space of about one year over an estimated average distance of 1,500 miles . . . over some of the wildest country in the world, much of it at the worst time of year in a savagely relentless climate." [13]

These air operations represented an unprecedented windfall for the Canadian air industry. One company secured a valuable contract to help with the preliminary air surveys and ground support operations, and eleven airlines, flying many types of aircraft, received very lucrative work during the hectic construction phase. The large planes delivered the heavy freight to airfields at Goose Bay, Fort Chimo, and Frobisher Bay, which smaller planes then distributed to the individual sites. The high profits transformed some of the companies – Pacific Western, Maritime Central, and Transair – into sizeable regional air carriers. Air travel to and from the Arctic was made infinitely easier by all the installations after 1945 and by the considerable traffic the many stations generated. Scheduled air services were regularly flown from Montreal, Winnipeg, and Edmonton to Frobisher Bay, Cambridge Bay, and Resolute. The DEW Line itself was a busy air route for military and commercial aircraft delivering supplies, transferring staffs, and bringing in inspecting officers, doctors, clergymen, and visitors. By 1958, it was asserted, "as one measure of the profound change wrought by the DEW Line, you may now fly completely across the North American Arctic without losing sight of the lights of a human habitation, and rarely being more than 25 miles from an airstrip." [14]

A large part of the $500 million the United States spent on constructing the DEW Line went for on-site building and installation activities. Between 10,000 and 20,000 highly paid employees from engineers to cooks and general labourers were injected into the Arctic sites of the stations for varying periods of time. Many Canadian manufacturers and distributors of electrical and motor machinery and equipment, building supplies, and other necessities became involved with the DEW Line and established continuing connections for future northern activities. Servicing the completed line required smaller but still quite considerable annual supplies and transport services; a sealift in 1962, for instance, delivered 5,000 different items weighing 45,000 tons, about 65 per cent being petroleum products, the remainder food and comforts for the employees.

The DEW Line stations and other military bases of course had noticeable impacts upon Arctic society. The line employed some 1,000 permanent employees (about 10 per cent of them Inuit) and smaller numbers of RCAF or USAF personnel, who were generally posted on one-year tours of duty. Most of the civilian employees were hired by Federal Electric under eighteen-month or twelve-month contracts at high enough rates of pay to enable them to save for a more abundant future, which was their main incentive for taking the jobs. DEW Line workers led quiet, comfortable, though monotonous lives under conditions that were purposely made as similar as possible to those Outside. They lived and worked in well-heated buildings with individual bedrooms and hot and cold running water, enjoyed excellent food, and received paid vacations. For recreation there were camp libraries, hobby rooms, and movies three time a week, while doctors, dentists, and clergymen paid regular visits to the stations.

All this contrasted sharply with the lifestyles of the natives and the old-time whites (fur traders, policemen, missionaries) near the stations. The bases drew natives from the land to sometimes completely new settlements close to the stations, where they could find work for wages, interesting recreation and entertainments, and assistance for the needy (sometimes retrieved from the refuse dumps and camp discards). Some natives gained steady work and became permanent settlers in houses provided by the government: "They tasted wages, the security of food from a grocery . . . the comfort of oil-heated housing – and stayed."[15] Each station (in the Tuktoyaktuk sector at least) employed two or more Inuit who derived entire livelihoods – monthly salaries of $200 or $300 plus houses and heating for their families – from their work. At Tuktoyaktuk itself as many as a quarter of the local men worked on DEW Line construction while many others found casual employment on the annual supply and maintenance activities, using the income from this work to supplement their returns from hunting and trapping.

Most bases were two or three miles from the nearest settlements, far enough away to control visits of natives to the camps while permitting employees to visit the settlements as they wished. Thus most Arctic communities were made up of two or more distinct settlements or neighbourhoods (three in the case of Cambridge Bay, four at Frobisher Bay) with social mixing depending on the attitudes of individual whites and natives, the relationship tending to be more formalized at the larger communities. In Frobisher Bay, much the largest of these and owing something perhaps to the military nature of the SAC base, Inuit were barred from the military clubs and servicemen were discouraged from associating with Inuit women. Besides the unquestioned material benefits they offered, the stations had profound social and psychological effects on the Inuit from the surrounding areas.

The dozen years of increasing governmental involvements with the northern territories after 1945 had transformed that region by 1957 from a neglected, little-known backwater into a region that was gradually being elevated to the foreground of the national consciousness. Its main centres of industrial activity in the Southern Yukon and Mackenzie waterway were becoming "normal" parts of Hinterland Canada; the Arctic, stretching from the Belcher Islands to Alert, the northernmost permanent settlement in the world, was becoming the latest frontier of activity. Much of the drive was inspired by the defence priorities of the United States, and the Canadian government was being prodded to assume a larger role and more prominent presence in the Arctic by nationalists concerned about "foreign domination." The extravagant spending by the United States for military purposes, and the Canadians' smaller outlays (both government and private sector) in themselves were enough to give the territorial economies a considerable boost and lay a firmer base for future development.

Nonetheless, the efforts of the private sector were insufficient to carry the region's future development forward unaided and permit the governments to reduce spending on aids to development. The private agencies had been largely separated from their function of sustaining the native inhabitants against the encroaching modern society. The programs the federal government instituted in their place were achieving some notable successes in the fields of health and education. But they were failing to meet the challenges of a multiplying native population, a declining wildlife resources base, and a quickly changing socio-economic environment. In some respects they were even aggravating the situation. While the administration had recognized the scale of the problems by increasing its commitments of staff and money, it still did not appear to comprehend fully its complexity or its subtlety. "Throwing money at the problems in hopes they would go away" would continue to characterize government policy in the coming decade, but the even greater efforts would bring little or no better results.

CHAPTER 12

The Northern Vision and Afterwards, 1958–1967

The concept of developing the North as a national duty reached political centre-stage in February 1958, when Prime Minister Diefenbaker launched a federal general election campaign by proclaiming his Northern Vision as a main goal of his administration. The Vision, which embraced the provincial as well as the territorial norths, had the inestimable political merit of being a unifying rather than a disruptive theme that could appeal to every regional, sectarian, or class interest, like the transcending national development programs espoused in times past by Macdonald and Laurier. Diefenbaker's unprecedented success at the polls in part indicated how the public's consciousness of the North had been heightened by governmental and private activities and publicity ever since the United States had "discovered" Northern Canada in connection with the Second World War.

I

The Diefenbaker vision was not simple political expediency. National growth based on economic development had been a constant theme of Conservatives from the day of Sir John A. Macdonald onward. After both World Wars, Conservative M.P.s – Meighen and R.J. Manion after 1918 and J.R. MacNicol (M.P. for Toronto Davenport) after 1945 – had argued vehemently that stimulating the development of Canada's northern natural resources was an appropriate way to exploit the technological breakthroughs and sustain the spirit of dedication inspired by the wars, at the same time being a highly practical method for helping the country achieve peacetime prosperity. The prime minister, a long-time resident and M.P. for the northward-looking small city of

Prince Albert, was far better attuned to the importance of northern development than any earlier prime minister had been. An outsider by temperament, he understood northerners' and westerners' resentment of the preponderant influence of the Central Canadian heartland over federal governments and was determined that hitherto neglected regions would receive their proper shares in formulating future policies and of government benefits. A convinced egalitarian and humanitarian, he could also view northern development in other than material terms, as the achieving of national purposes by improving the condition of the North's inhabitants and placing them on a more equal footing with the other Canadians. Though realizing that these objectives might call for disproportionate amounts of government spending and involvement, the prime minister, a prairie populist, was unlikely to allow financial considerations to deflect him from carrying out what he regarded as a national duty.

Under the impetus of the Depression and the Second World War, the development-minded Liberal governments of the period from 1945 to 1957 had moved toward widespread intervention in the economy and society. They had adopted the redistributive role suggested in the Rowell-Sirois Report and advanced in the direction of social welfare by introducing important social programs and greatly increasing the federal part in achieving social goals. They had applied these policies throughout Canada, but they had also paid special attention to the needs of their northern populations to the point of establishing a distinct department of state charged with administering the concerns of the territories. They had introduced special social, educational, and economic programs to help ease the natives' adjustment to the modern world and committed large sums for transportation and communications facilities, power plants, and building new communities. Yet rather than defend these considerable accomplishments, in 1958 the Liberal party preferred to downplay them and to ridicule the Diefenbaker program as reckless sensationalism – in L.B. Pearson's long-remembered quip, building roads "from igloo to igloo."

The program of aggressively assisted northern development was announced with great fanfare in Winnipeg at the outset of the 1958 campaign, then echoed and amplified in subsequent speeches. Its key ingredient was building "Roads to Resources" to uncover natural resources and make them accessible. The provinces would be assisted on a cost-sharing basis, and the federal government itself would undertake a separate $100-million program for the northern territories. Other benefits to the territories included a railway to Great Slave Lake, improved navigation on the St. Lawrence and Hudson Bay routes that might include nuclear-powered icebreakers, a $75-million plan to

build a modern Arctic city at Frobisher Bay, a greatly expanded scientific research effort in the Arctic, and fuller self-government for the
territories with provincial status as the eventual goal.

Though the prime minister credited M.W. Menzies, a policy adviser
and writer on economic subjects, with inspiring much of the national
development program, many of its elements had already been investigated by Northern Affairs officials, and some were being implemented. The department, which viewed itself as the custodian of the
interests of the northern territories and peoples, was a frequent source
of new programs. The Inuit housing plan, for instance, has been
described as having been "conceived, developed, and administered
entirely within the realm of non-elected officialdom."[1] So, too, was
the very controversial plan of dividing the Northwest Territories into
two new territorial entities, which the Territorial Council formally
proposed in 1962. The novelty about the Northern Vision, perhaps,
was the government's eagerness to proceed with northern development as a national priority, speed up programs already in operation,
and embark on new fields of activity, plus highly visible commitments
to implement certain costly, ambitious programs.

The free-wheeling initiatives of the administration relied largely on
and patronized a growing body of scientific and scholarly researches
into all manner of northern phenomena. The value of such studies for
the development of the North, and their proliferating number, had led
in 1954 to the creation of the Northern Co-ordination and Research
Centre (NCRC) within the Department of Northern Affairs and National
Resources. As its title indicates, the centre encouraged and regulated
northern researches by public and private groups, maintained records
on all of them and publicized their findings, and commissioned special
projects of interest to the administration. It took over issuing the permits required since 1926 for every scientist and explorer working in
the Territories and maintained files on their proposals and findings. It
also published commissioned studies on social anthropology and
resource development topics prepared by university scientists and bib-
liographies, reports of government operations, and the like, compiled
by its staff.

An important function of the NCRC was to administer and dispense a
system of annual research grants to scholars intending to carry on studies in the North. These at first were issued on an individual basis, but
beginning in 1962 block grants were made to university and institute
committees that allocated the funds and supervised the assisted programs. The funds were subsequently increased, and administering the
awards became important activities and incentives for universities to
build up their multi-disciplined northern studies programs.

Many scholars drew support for their scientific programs from private granting agencies, chief among them the AINA, which by 1970 had given financial aid to some seven hundred research projects in the North American Arctic. By the 1950s a few universities (particularly McGill and Laval) had begun organizing northern studies programs and fostering northern studies as adjuncts of their natural or social science departments. The movement really got under way in 1960–61, no doubt in response to the heightened attention the Arctic was receiving, and in swift succession many universities launched northern research committees or institutes. At least two of these, Saskatchewan and McGill, also established field stations in the North as research and training centres. The McGill base at Knob Lake (Schefferville), opened in 1953 and financed mainly by contracts with the Department of Transport for supplying meteorological services, trained four or five graduate students a year. The Institute for Northern Studies at Saskatoon opened its Arctic Research and Training Centre in 1967 at Rankin Inlet with the goal of making it a multi-disciplined teaching as well as research institution.

The university-based northern science programs transformed Canada's universities into "a principal instrument for developing interest in our northern lands."[2] Their involvement injected an intellectual approach into northern problems, while their research programs helped sustain graduate programs in the natural sciences, engineering, medicine, and the social sciences. A new generation of scientists and professionals, made familiar with the land and its people, could attempt to solve their problems when they attained important positions in government, industry, and academic life.

The Department of Northern Affairs and National Resources, headed from October 1957 to August 1960 by Alvin Hamilton, who was credited with being the prime minister's *alter ego*, began to receive far more money to expand its activities, and for a few years its mood became one of innovation and experimentation rather than civil service caution. The staff of the Northern Administration Branch (previously Northern Administration and Lands Branch) was greatly enlarged, its Arctic Division was split into Industrial (chief D. Snowden) and Welfare (chief W. Rudnicki) divisions and the director, B.G. Sivertz, was given two assistant directors, R.A.J. Phillips and F.A.G. Carter.

The further growth of the branch changed direction in 1960, however, with a decision to transfer many of its functions to region and area centres in the Territories, headed by an Administrator of the Mackenzie (stationed in Fort Smith) and an Administrator of the Arctic (headquartered for the time being in Ottawa). For Mackenzie there were three regional centres at Fort Smith, Yellowknife, and Inuvik, plus four area centres. The Arctic administration similarly maintained regional headquarters at Churchill (with four local centres) and Frobisher Bay (with three). The Administrator of the Arctic also supervised five centres in Nouveau-Québec that delivered services to the Inuit population, the subject after 1962 of an increasingly acrimonious jurisdictional dispute with the province. The Ottawa "line" or function-based divisions became mainly policy-formulating and co-ordinating agencies while the regional and area centres began employing their own specialists in various fields. The Ottawa-based establishment declined slightly after 1961 while its full-time employees stationed in the North increased from 338 in 1957 to 791 persons in 1963, including 213 in the Arctic administration.

The process continued after 1963 under the succeeding government. The number of local administration centres and their staffs were almost doubled as thirteen new centres were opened between 1961 and 1967, by which date the full-time personnel stationed in the North stood at 1,981, six times the number in 1957, just a decade earlier.

The branch was still only a part, though quite a large one, of the total federal presence in the territories. In 1963, for instance, the Department of Northern Affairs accounted for nearly 41 per cent ($31.7 million) of a total federal expenditure in the northern territories of $72.9 million and a little more than 20 per cent of the 3,889 full-time staff, National Defence being far in the lead, Transport a fairly close third, and the RCMP and National Health other significant employers. The trend, moreover, was towards increasing the relative presence of these other departments (except for National Defence). Indeed, Northern Affairs' share of government expenditures in the territories declined to as little as 32 per cent of the total in 1965.

The duplication of effort between the Ottawa-based and field units of the Northern Administration Branch and among the several other arms of government acting on the same small population attracted the attention of the Royal Commission on Government Organization (named the Glassco Commission for its chairman, J. Grant Glassco), which was appointed in 1960 and reported in January 1963. Accepting the paramount role of the Department of Northern Affairs and National Resources for the region, the commission sought to bring the plans and operations of the other agencies into line with those of that department. In a chapter entitled "Co-Ordination of Federal Activities in the North" the report proposed transferring authority over the territories' status Indians (from Citizenship and Immigration) and over the Northern Transportation Company (from Trade and Commerce) to Northern Affairs.

To improve effectiveness (or reduce adverse effects), the report encouraged regional and area administrators to examine and report on the activities of other government agencies in their districts. In fact, it recommended that "consideration be given to relaxing the restrictive effect of federal regulations in the territories, within appropriate limits, and local officials be given specific direction and the requisite authority to make the best use of local human and material resources."[3] Accordingly, the department began to give regional administrators greater leeway to make transportation and other arrangements and simplified the procedures for transferring property from other government agencies such as Defence Production.

The commission, in words that greatly encouraged the growing autonomist movement in the territories, also recommended greater local participation in the administration of the territories: ". . . remote control and a cautious paternalism are no substitutes for local enthusiasm and a local sense of responsibility, particularly if the outsiders are of a different culture and speak a different language from the group that is being helped."[4]

Taking action on the Glassco Commission recommendations fell to the new Liberal government that assumed office following the federal general election of April 8, 1963. The usual northern issues figured in the election in a small way – the meagre results of government expenditures in inducing development of the territories, charges of extravagant and mismanaged spending (the Dawson City Gold Rush Festival was singled out as a glaring example). More crucial, though less directly related to the North, was the major issue of Canadian air defence, which split and paralysed the Diefenbaker government and led to its collapse. In 1957 that government had quickly accepted the tightly integrated North American Air Defence Command (NORAD) with centralized command at Colorado Springs and regional headquarters for Northern and Eastern Canada at North Bay. NORAD functioned in conjunction with the newly developed semi-automatic ground environment (SAGE) computerized system of communications centres (one in North Bay) that reduced the time needed to check and react to possible threats from hours to minutes. To improve Canada's ability to react, the government after much soul-searching adopted the Bomarc missile, a relatively economical American ground-to-air weapon still in the development stage. It was its inability to accept the necessity of arming these Bomarc missiles with nuclear warheads for which the weapon had been designed that toppled the Diefenbaker government.

Inasmuch as the Conservatives had made northern development a very effective partisan political issue, the Liberals seemed likely, after scrutinizing the programs of their predecessor carefully and critically, to adopt a distinctive program of their own. Their return to power did give an opportunity for questioning by nationally known commentators Blair Fraser, Charles Lynch, and Scott Young and by, among others, Bob Hill and Ralph Armstrong, the roving northern correspondents (Canada's first!) of the *Edmonton Journal*. Fraser, for instance, in a piece entitled "Our double image of the North" (October 17, 1964), wrote:

> In the past dozen years the Canadian government has poured hundreds of millions of dollars into its Arctic and sub-Arctic regions to pay for various versions of politicians' "visions of the north" . . . .
>
> It is too soon to say these programs have failed – but they have certainly not succeeded. Today's reality is a far cry from the most publicized of the visions of revolutionary developments in the north, that of John Diefenbaker.
>
> Indeed, Arthur Laing, the present minister of Northern Affairs, openly refers to the north as "a problem area" and openly welcomes counsel on how the problem can be solved. . . .[5]

The new government did not completely reject the northern policy of its predecessor nor dismantle the Northern Administration Branch. Instead, it continued the programs while it strove to redirect the effort more efficiently and more in keeping with its own priorities. Continuity was encouraged by the appointment of Arthur Laing as minister. Laing, a Vancouver lawyer and former leader of the British Columbia Liberal party, had a West Coast businessman's boosterish approach to resource development not unlike that embodied in the Northern Vision pursued by his predecessors in office, Alvin Hamilton and Walter Dinsdale. At the same time the Liberal government's more acute sensitivity to social issues contributed a stronger concern for the needs of the native sector and a proportionate expansion of its activity in that direction.

In keeping with the Liberals' advertised spirit of investigation and inquiry, Laing made frequent well-publicized visits to the North accompanied by groups of officials, businessmen, journalists, and scientists, sponsored and attended many professional and scholarly conferences, increased government funding to scientific agencies and researches at the Canadian universities, and approached foreign governments to exchange Arctic experience and know-how. He saw his role as encouragement of "private investment and development, especially in tapping the mineral resources" so that the North could "start to stand on its own two feet" and relieve the government and Canadian taxpayers of some of the heavy burden that being the main support of the territories imposed.[6] He readily adopted the Conservatives' northern roads program because "lowered transportation costs would benefit all residents and borderline operations which could then take advantage of known resources."[7] He also supported other aids that would "make it economic for investment and risk capital to enter the country" and "narrow the cost of living for those who fight the North."[8] These included, besides the usual infrastructures, commissioning studies by consultants of specific questions like the feasibility of establishing base-metal smelting plants at Pine Point or Ross River or plans for the development of the Yukon Territory to the year 2000.

Laing saw the North as "dependent upon massive and continuing importations of risk capital from Outside,"[9] so he took issue with the nationalist-protectionist attitude of the previous regime, represented in the current one by Walter Gordon. Against his colleague's views he argued that

> risk capital from outside Canada should be permitted to contribute to . . . the Northwest Territories' mineral development. . . .
>
> In a nation like Canada, with its fantastic expanse and enormously dispersed resources, it appears to me to be foolish to require risk capital to carry a passport. And of all parts of the country, the biggest welcome mat of all should be placed at the door of the Northwest Territories.[10]

To induce risk capital to invest in the North he advocated more government incentives, tax reliefs, assistance grants, and direct investments. Under Laing the Northern Vision remained alive and well.

The Glassco Commission's recommendation regarding the anomolous position of the Indian Affairs Branch was ultimately responsible for a momentous change in northern administration. By an order in council the Indian Affairs Branch was moved from Citizenship and Immigration and was attached to the Department of Northern Affairs and National Resources, the reorganized Department of Indian Affairs and Northern Development beginning operations effective January 1, 1966. The move was ratified retroactively by legislation only in May 1966, buried within an omnibus Government Organization Act (14–15 Eliz. II, Chap. 25) that created five new departments. While the bill moved through the House of Commons the new department received very little discussion compared with some of the others, and what discussion there was focused on the disappearance of the "National Resources" aspect of the former department. There was little or no discussion in Parliament of the implications or effects of uniting the Indian Affairs and Northern Administration agencies.

The merger raised forebodings among the Northern Administration staff, who felt they could only lose their previously exalted, innovative, satisfying position and rapid promotions in a department whose name had confirmed their special status. Now they expected they would be overshadowed in a department that was concerned principally with the needs of the Indians and would be bound to subordinate northern affairs to those priorities. The fears were largely confirmed. The main thrust, administration of Indian services, was intensified as Indians' problems coincidentally were approaching political crisis with the growth of native nationalism and the emergence of native organizations. At the same time, expansion of the Northern Affairs Branch of the new department was being curtailed because the territorial administrations were assuming more and more of the functions of provinces.

More fundamentally, Northern Affairs' primary goal of encouraging modern resource development through attracting capital investment and white settlers ran counter to the socially oriented, basically anti-development policies and approaches of the dominant Indian Affairs side of the department. Indeed, the Northern Vision's emphasis on production and wealth-getting was being supplanted by the Liberal government's consumer-oriented obsession with programs of social welfare, and northern development, no longer recognized as a special priority, was being made subject to the normal processes of Liberal-style administrations.

II

The emphasis on improving transportation and communications facilities as a necessary prelude to developing the North led both Conservative and Liberal governments to push ahead vigorously with these and other infrastructures, the change of government making little difference. Laing so readily made the Conservatives' program his own that during the 1965 election campaign he spoke of continuing the road-building program at a level of $10 million a year for another ten years, with greater emphasis than in the past on directly assisting mining and tourist development. Under the Conservatives, important regional roads had been built, including one from Whitehorse to Ross River that was extended onwards to the Nahanni Range to service the tungsten mine at Tungsten, N.W.T. The Mackenzie Highway was completed to Yellowknife (with a branch to Pine Point) and extended from Yellowknife towards MacKay Lake to assist developing gold-mining developments there. Two extremely ambitious plans to push highways all the way to the Arctic Ocean were launched. One, a highway and telephone line from Enterprise, on the Hay River, was to proceed down the Mackenzie River to the Arctic, but construction of the road was blocked near Fort Simpson. The telephone system with its sixteen-foot right of way, however, was completed to Inuvik, 1,040 miles distant, in 1966, its unimpeded progress contrasting sharply with the controversies that soon developed over the Mackenzie Valley Pipeline Corridor. In the Yukon, as an aid to oil prospecting, the Whitehorse-Dawson Highway was extended north to the Eagle Plain area. Officially named the Dempster Highway in 1963, it eventually was extended to Inuvik, which then became the northernmost town on the Canadian roads system.

Even more spectacular was the penetration of the Northwest Territories by the Great Slave Lake Railway. It was built primarily to permit cheap transport of large tonnages of lead-zinc concentrates to the smelter of Consolidated Mining (renamed Cominco in 1967) at Trail, B.C., and thus bring the mine at Pine Point into production. The railway in addition would make the Mackenzie waterway far more useful for shipping heavy freight to and from the northern parts of the Territories, materially assisting development of those areas. Accordingly the Conservative government provided most of the funds ($86.25 million) for building the railway, the mining company contributing a subsidy in the shape of a long-term tonnage and freight rate contract. For some time location of the line became a political football between advocates of an eastern route north from Fort McMurray and of a western one north from Peace River that was only resolved in 1961.

The 432-mile railway was built by the CNR from Roma, Alberta, north along the route of the Mackenzie Highway and crossed into the Northwest Territories on August 19, 1964, to the accompaniment of a public ceremony. It reached Pine Point and Hay River soon afterwards, and the first trainload of hand-sorted ore left the mine in November 1964. In Alberta, the railway assisted northward expansion of agriculture and helped create the new towns of Manning and High Level. Hay River received a boost as a shipping point at the expense of Fort Smith. The waterway was virtually split at the Slave River portage into a southern section, served from Waterways and terminating at Fitzgerald, Alberta, and a northern one based on Hay River. Highway connections in the shape of a branch road from the Mackenzie Highway to Pine Point and Fort Smith were no real substitutes for that settlement's lost pre-eminence as the gateway to the District of Mackenzie, which became all the worse when Yellowknife was selected as the territorial capital.

Though the government's effort mainly concentrated on land transport, the other modes were not neglected. The water route was continually improved by dredging and better port facilities. The Northern Transportation Company spent its profits on more powerful equipment, steel barges, and improved wharf facilities, notably at Hay River and Tuktoyaktuk. Aviation and communications facilities, greatly expanded by the sac and dew Line activities, benefited from the Department of Transport's $2.6-million annual expenditures on aviation facilities in small settlements, jaws bases, and important prospecting centres such as Contwoyto Lake or Mary River, Baffin Island. The department's Meteorological Branch expanded its network until by 1967 fifty-five stations north of 60° were regularly reporting weather and climate data. It furnished forecasts and ice advisory services for travellers and workers in the North and significantly improved the accuracy of weather reporting elsewhere in Canada. Canadian National Telecommunications (cnt) established telephone service over the land line and by high-frequency transmitting/receiving equipment at many isolated points. The cbc extended its radio service throughout the territories, increased local programming and broadcasts in native languages, and by 1967 was making preparations to bestow television on the North's inhabitants.

The task of extending electric power for industrial and household use had already been taken in hand by the Northern Canada Power Commission. Another large hydro project, a $9-million, 25,000-horsepower installation at Twin Falls on Taltson River, thirty-five miles northeast of Fort Smith, was built between 1963 and 1965 and connected over a 175-mile transmission line with Pine Point. Mining activity in the Yukon was similarly assisted by local diesel plants and eventually by a 225-mile transmission line from the Whitehorse hydro plant to Faro. That added market necessitated increasing the generating station's capacity by 11,000 horsepower and installing a 9,000-horsepower diesel plant at Whitehorse. At Dawson the procedure was reversed; a diesel generating plant replaced the antiquated hydro station on the Klondike River and also supplied the new mine at Clinton Creek over a transmission line. At the same time other diesel plants were installed to meet local markets at communities ranging in size from Inuvik and Frobisher Bay to Fort Resolution and Coppermine. Private power companies purchased most of their power from the ncpc and supplied local customers over their distribution networks. All told, electricity consumption increased by about 248 per cent between 1961 and 1968. Private companies criticized the ncpc for interfering with their self-proclaimed role of retail distributors (particularly in the Yukon), and the Territories council complained it was not making enough effort to equalize the rates, urging it to set an upper limit for small settlements. But all the same, the success of the NCPC as an agent for northern development could not be gainsaid.

The program of providing communities that would attract the mining staffs and public servants the territories required was continued, notwithstanding frequent changes of direction and delays occasioned by fluctuating military requirements or natural disasters such as springtime floods. At Inuvik work continued on the public buildings and serviced housing that made up the $35-million price tag for the project. The Diefenbaker government planned an even more dramatic program for Frobisher Bay; for an anticipated 5,000 inhabitants there were to be multi-storey interconnected service and apartment buildings (to conserve heat), a nuclear power plant to supply electricity and steam heat for the town, and even plastic domes enclosing the main part of the community. But while the government was in the middle of a building program completing the townsite's water and sewer systems, hospital, school, and residences, the Americans suddenly withdrew the SAC base. Sunk without trace were the grandiose futuristic plans for the experimental Polar City made proof against the Arctic weather.

Most of the public construction on these communities was carried out by the Department of Public Works, and the CMHC assisted private building by planning and financing construction by corporations and individuals. Since northern building costs exceeded national norms, the territorial governments had to supplement the loans to builders with loans of their own. In this fashion new communities were built at Pine Point, Faro, Clinton Creek, and other locations and government complexes and new residential subdivisions were added to older communities at Fort Smith, Hay River, and Fort Simpson. At Whitehorse, however, the city was able to expand into already serviced government subdivisions as those were relinquished. The federal government appeared to leave no stone unturned to provide for the new settlers in the North, including the large sector comprised of its own employees.

It also offered many direct incentives to the mining industry to undertake the large investments needed to bring the territories' resources under development. It extended the income tax holiday for new mines beyond the initial three years. It lowered acreage fees for oil and gas exploration, extended the time limits for fulfilling permit conditions, and introduced favourable tax measures such as faster write-offs of expenditures. And in line with the current mood of economic nationalism, in 1960 it announced that only Canadians could file for land in the territories and in 1966 that Canadian-owned mining and oil companies were eligible to received 50 per cent of their approved exploration expenses from the Northern Development Loan Fund (a loan that would be forgiven unless, or until, profitable production ensued). These changes were designed to encourage Canadian operators to join in the hunt for minerals and fossil fuels and induce foreign-owned companies to establish Canadian subsidiaries, both desirable objectives highlighted in the Gordon Commission report.

Tourism had been a major activity in the Yukon ever since the completion of the White Pass and Yukon Railway, but it was far less important in the Northwest Territories, where the administration, out of concern for native welfare, had not been especially anxious to encourage unregulated travel. Now, in the late 1950s it, too, proposed to make tourism a major industry. Campsites, tourist camps, and information centres were opened along the highways and in Yellowknife, government officers formed a tourist organization to train local operators and co-ordinate their efforts, and appropriate amendments were made to the game and liquor ordinances. The administration encouraged the opening of hotels, motels, and several camps and lodges for sport fishermen and organized licensed hunts to attract big-spending sportsman hunters.

In the Yukon the territorial government administered tourism and controlled the wildlife resource. It was especially eager to promote a sportsman hunting enterprise that could cater to between 150 and 250 hunters who would spend about a thousand dollars apiece and employ some twenty licensed outfitters and thirty chief guides each year. The industry was carefully regulated through periodic inspections of hunters and guides. The federal government, as in the Territories, provided aids to encourage upgrading of existing tourist facilities and build new ones and helped organize the operators for their mutual support and benefit. The National Parks Branch strove to establish a national park in the scenic Kluane Lake district to attract visitors to the peaks and icefields of the St. Elias range, only to have the plan blocked for many years by successive Yukon councils dominated by mining interests.

Less controversy was aroused by a program of the National Historic Sites Branch (another arm of the National Parks) to preserve and restore historic buildings at Dawson and surviving river sternwheelers as tourist attractions. In 1959 the National Parks Branch acquired the Palace Grand Theatre and four laid-up sternwheelers and started an expensive reconstruction program. Over $500,000 were speedily expended, and a heavily subsidized Dawson City Gold Rush Festival was held in 1962 to show off the refurbished theatre, the highlight of which was a commissioned musical, *Foxy*, based on Ben Jonson's *Volpone* and featuring well-known writers, composers, and performers. Despite a blast of publicity, tourists and tourist spending increased only moderately, and the sequel was even less happy. More modest later festivals, lacking a sought-for legalized gambling casino, drew even fewer visitors, and Dawson relapsed to its former condition, as real estate prices fell to earlier levels and "every week cars, trucks, planes and suitcases . . . [carried] away the goods and chattels of bygone days."[11] Moreover, the restoration expenses and the mounting deficits from the festivals, including an ill-starred attempt to take *Foxy* to Broadway, excited bickering among citizens and between governments. The program became a laughingstock in press and Parliament that reflected adversely on the Northern Vision program.

The prime object of the Northern Vision was to foster rapid development of the territories' resources by making it easier to establish more modern industries, especially mines. Government efforts did help carry new mines to the production stage, notably the large lead-zinc mine at Pine Point, the future tungsten mine at Flat River in the Nahanni district, and a gold mine at Matthew Lake, 165 miles east of Yellowknife, none of which went into production until after the fall of the Diefenbaker government. The search for minerals ranged widely across the territories, especially when metal prices improved in the early sixties and the government instituted the system of Prospectors Assistance Grants (1962). Gold showings were staked in the Contwoyto Lake and Coronation Gulf districts east of Great Bear Lake, west of Carmacks in the Yukon, and at Ennadai Lake in the interior of Keewatin, base-metal occurrences in the Redstone River and Ross River areas astride the Yukon–Northwest Territories boundary, and iron beds at Snake River in Northern Yukon and at Mary River, inland from Eclipse Sound, Baffin Island. These last attracted a good deal of public attention and considerable governmental planning and spending on local facilities, notwithstanding the negligible chance that they would be developed speedily, or ever.

Oil and gas companies conducted large-scale seismic and test drilling operations on the Eagle Plain and Peel Plateau of Northern Yukon and along the lower Mackenzie. Deep wildcat wells were drilled northwest of Fort Good Hope, at Tununuk Point and the north shore of the Mackenzie delta, and three on the Arctic islands in 1961–62. These multi-million-dollar activities helped bring prosperity to Inuvik, Fort McPherson, and Dawson as transport bases and employee recreational centres, and furnished lucrative traffic for the transport services. No commercial production was achieved, but the effort kept hopes alive that the territories would soon be transformed from endless drains on the national treasury into generators of wealth through sales of oil and gas lands and royalties.

Nevertheless, mining production actually declined by 25 per cent between the mid-fifties and the early 1960s. In 1958 the industry still reflected the effects of the Korean War and Cold War; but during the next few years economic recession reduced prices and markets for metals, while certain mines ran out of extractable ore. United Keno Hill alone managed to withstand the tide by increasing its annual silver production to 6.6 million ounces, which was over one fifth of Canada's entire silver output between 1958 and 1964. Exhaustion of mineable ore closed the two uranium mines and the Rankin Inlet mine. Gold output declined as Yukon Consolidated began winding down its operations to a final close in 1966; Discovery Yellowknife's ore was so reduced that it was expedient to truck 1,500 tons of ore 400 miles from a closed pre-war mine to keep the mill operating efficiently in 1963. In that year rising costs and diminishing profitability so affected gold mining that three of the Territories' four lode gold mines were receiving subsidies under the Emergency Gold Mines Assistance Act. Even the tungsten mine, ready to go into production in 1962, remained closed because Asian supplies flooded the market and the price of tungsten took a precipitous fall. Thus mining failed to live up to the Diefenbaker government's ambitious hopes for a speedy economic breakthrough, delaying the advance of the territories to prosperity and economic self-sufficiency.

The change of government, however, coincided with a marked improvement in the economic climate that brought renewed prosperity and expansion. Important new mines, mainly highly mechanized open-pit operations under development before 1963, joined the ranks of the producing companies and mightily transformed the territorial economies over the next few years. With better prices for tungsten, Canada Tungsten put its troubled mine into production in 1964, although a fire that destroyed the mill soon forced it to close. Tundra Gold Mines (formerly Taurcanis) started milling ore at its mine on Matthew Lake. Activity even returned to Port Radium when Echo Bay Mines began mining the original Eldorado mineral showings for their silver and copper.

Above all, 1964 brought the start of production at the lead-zinc deposits at Pine Point south of Great Slave Lake, which transformed the economy of the District of Mackenzie as no other post-war mining operation had done. By 1965 Cominco, through its subsidiary Pine Point Mines, was ready to proceed to production; the mill started operating in November 1965, and full production was attained by 1966. All promising ground surrounding Cominco's holdings was staked, more than 24,000 claims involving over eighty companies in 1964–65 alone. Some of these developed their properties, and Pine Point Mines absorbed one of them (Pyramid Mining), significantly increasing its own resource base. The value of Territories mineral production quadrupled in a single year from $18.6 million in 1965 to $75.4 million in 1966, and vaulting to $115.0 million in 1967.

In Yukon, a similar upsurge in mineral production occurred toward the end of the decade, when three important new mines replaced the now vanished Yukon Consolidated and dwindling operations at United Keno Hill. New Imperial Mines began shipping copper ore in April 1967 from an open-pit operation only seven miles from White-horse to a Japanese firm that advanced some of the development cap-ital. Later in 1967, at Clinton Creek, forty miles northwest of Dawson, a short-staple asbestos deposit was brought into production by Cassiar Asbestos to supplement the long-staple product from its mine in North-ern British Columbia. More time was needed to bring the large mine in the Ross River district into production. As at Pine Point, news of zinc-lead discoveries by Alan Kulan in the Vangorda and Anvil creeks area and subsequent development work there sparked a staking rush that led to 5,500 claims being recorded in 1965 and 10,000 in 1966, when thirty companies spent over $5 million on geological investi-gations and diamond drilling in the area. The main company, Cyprus Anvil Mining Corporation, a merger of several interests, developed a large open-pit mine and concentrator at Faro that went into produc-tion in 1969. The scale of production lifted Yukon mineral output from $14.7 million in 1967 to $21.4 million in 1968 and $37.7 million in 1969 and when all three mines were in production, to $77.5 million in 1970 and eventually to $229 million in 1975.

Mining was the main reason for the marked expansion of the terri-tories' economy after 1958. It contributed to noticeable increases in the populations of both territories. Thousands of transient workers came to the region for longer or shorter periods to carry on pros-pecting and development work, build trails, mines and mining plants, hydro stations and mining communities, and man the expanded trans-port and other services. Hundreds of permanent settlers arrived to operate the mines or provide the facilities and services the mining com-munities required. The population of the Northwest Territories rose by 25 per cent in the first half of the decade (22,998 to 28,738) and by 21 per cent in the second half, to 34,807 in 1971, although part of this resulted from growth in public employment (particularly after 1966) and considerable natural increase in the native population. The impact of mining was more marked, perhaps, in the Yukon, where the pop-ulation actually declined slightly during the first five years, mainly because of reduced military, military-related, and metal-mining activ-ities. In the later sixties, when Yukon mining boomed the territory's population soared by nearly 30 per cent from 14,382 in 1966 to 18,388 in 1971. The Clinton Creek mine led to the building of a new town for some seven hundred people on an attractive site overlooking Forty-mile River, five miles from the mine, and Faro gave rise to a community about twice as large. As for Whitehorse, the New Imperial Mine (employing 135), the expanded transportation operations, and developmental work on another half dozen properties created work for all who might want it and caused a serious shortage of housing and rent increases. Thus the approach of Canada's centenary was marked in the Yukon and Northwest Territories by a booming economy and period of growth that stirred the enthusiasm of the inhabitants and inspired confidence in the future of the lands north of 60°.

III

Economic activity in the shape of large-scale oil and gas prospecting and development was extended into the High Arctic during the period of Northern Vision. The advance flowed directly from the findings by the Geological Survey's Operation Franklin and by subsequent studies that confirmed the potential of the Arctic Archipelago as the locale of large, rich oil and gas fields worth developing. In 1959 the Diefenbaker government was caught unprepared by requests from oil companies for permits to explore in the western half of the archipelago. No appropriate regulations being in place, the administration gave applicants priority listings until 1960, when proper exploration permits covering 40 million acres were issued to large international companies and to small and medium-sized Canadian companies. The cost of prospecting and drilling in this remote region, plus the obviously difficult marketing problems, encouraged companies to pool their investments and efforts to spread the risk. During the first few years the permit areas were prospected, mapped, and studied, and many promising structures were uncovered. The Peter Bawden Drilling Company of Calgary drilled a pioneer test well to a 12,000-foot depth at Winter Harbour, Melville Island, and one each on Cornwallis Island, near Resolute, and Bathurst Island in 1961–62. All three were disappointing, though they demonstrated the possibility of working in polar regions. The limited results, the operating difficulties, and the high costs led the companies to abandon much of the original acreage in 1964 as the lowest rental period (5¢ an acre) expired.

Greater incentives clearly were needed to encourage the companies to persevere with the long, costly, unremunerative quest. The Liberal administration met the situation with a policy of more direct government participation that also reflected its economic nationalist stance. J.C. Sproule, a Calgary consulting geologist involved in the Arctic from the start of activity, proposed forming a largely Canadian-owned company made up of interested firms that would contribute land holdings and capital to a common pool. The new company, aided with a government subsidy, would carry on work on behalf of the participants. The plan at first failed to win enough backing, but in 1966 a second attempt succeeded. Panarctic Oils, Limited, was formed along the original lines, but the government's $9-million contribution was not a subsidy but a 45 per cent interest in the company. The remaining 55 per cent was shared by twenty private companies, foreign and Canadian, some of which contributed land they held under permit or lease (43 million acres) and the remainder, among them such major Canadian firms as Canadian Pacific, INCO, and Noranda, funds to help carry on operations. Dome Petroleum agreed to manage the company until Panarctic secured its equipment and built up its own staff. The original partnership being 76 per cent Canadian-owned was eligible for all the subsidies and other concessions available to Canadian firms. The resources continued to be developed with no returns to the developers, but governmental participation and spending over the next decade of its involvement in the Panarctic syndicate would mushroom to gigantic proportions.

The islands were also the locale of much scientific activity by governmental agencies and civilian groups, the latter subsidized mainly by military and economic interests. During the most intense Cold War period, in fact, most field researches were directed towards assisting military operations and were conducted by military personnel. Military sources also supplied large sums to support Arctic researches by universities and the binational AINA, which made good use of the military's Arctic facilities. The U.S. Office of Naval Research, in particular, helped support much field research by individuals and sustained the preparation of the monumental but never published "Encyclopedia Arctica," to which the elderly Stefansson devoted much of his energies.

The Defence Research Board (DRB), among its many other projects in Ottawa and at Churchill, sent parties to the High Arctic. On northern Ellesmere Island, the long-term Operation Hazen was launched in 1957 to study the little-known inland Lake Hazen area, first explored by the A.W. Greely expedition during the First International Polar Year seventy-five years earlier. The operation was supported by the RCAF, which gained valuable Arctic experience making landings on glaciers and ferrying supplies from coast depots to the camps by helicopter, while military personnel helped with the practical tasks as part of their Arctic acclimatization. Each year relays of government and university scientists were flown to the area to study the physical, biological, and archaeological features of the region. In the early sixties the researchers were shifted from Lake Hazen to Tanquary Fiord and along the north coast of Ellesmere Island. An important part of that work was investigation of the Ward Hunt Ice Shelf, which extends seaward into the Arctic from northern Ellesmere Island and is the main source of the enormous ice islands that constantly revolve about the Arctic Basin, imbedded in the polar ice pack.

In its oceanographic and climatological studies the DRB drew heavily on the scholarly resources of McGill University (on whose campus the AINA was housed), which assembled a very able research and training faculty in the related fields of Arctic oceanography, glaciers and sea ice, and climatology. In 1959, McGill initiated the Jacobson-McGill Expedition, an important investigation of the temperature regime of the Axel Heiberg–Ellesmere–Nares Strait region. This gave rise, in turn, to the ongoing North Water Project, the object of which was to study the changing extent, location, and characteristics of the large polynya southeast of Ellesmere Island that reflects the climatic changes in the surrounding district and in turn affects the climate over much of the North Atlantic.

Many government agencies besides the surveying branches took advantage of the improved accessibility of the Arctic islands and the presence there of the JAWS and other permanent stations to extend their work to the archipelago as part of their Canada-wide coverage of their fields of study. The Canadian Wildlife Service's ornithologists and zoologists, for instance, investigated particular species and population dynamics and ecological balances in specific districts. The Fisheries Research Board made parallel studies of the plankton, bottom fauna, and fishes of Frobisher Bay and other areas and studied fish and marine mammal populations in many localities. The National Museum of Canada collected specimens and prepared reports on fish, mammal, botanical, and entomological species, or the natural histories of specific districts, while its Anthropological Branch conducted important archaeological researches in the islands, Northern Yukon, and at many prehistoric Inuit settlements.

The involvement of the Geological Survey and the other branches of the Department of Mines and Technical Surveys in the western part of the Arctic Archipelago in which oil and gas prospecting companies were manifesting such interest – the mostly submerged parts of the continental platform on which the islands stand – led the department in 1958 to establish the Polar Continental Shelf Project (PCSP), a program that the prime minister singled out as part of his Northern Vision. During the first few seasons the project concentrated on the 1,500-mile-long western margin of the shelf with its islands, operating from a base at Isachsen, then at Mould Bay, both JAWS stations. After 1967 the focus shifted to the centre of the archipelago and the base was transferred to Resolute. Many governmental agencies participated by sending eighty or so employees to the area each year, where they investigated a broad range of physical aspects of the seabeds, waters, and islands or studied the entomological, botanical, fish, and mammal life of the region. The efforts of the government agencies were supplemented by those of university scientists working under contract to the agencies or supported by research grants from funding agencies, so that by the mid-1970s as many as 150 different projects annually were being carried on under, or in conjunction with, the PCSP.

Independent researchers found such bases very helpful from a logistical point of view. They reduced the heavy expenses of operating in faraway districts by making transport and communications, accommodations, scientific and transport equipment and gear, and lower-cost fuel oil and local air services available to researchers in the field. On the other hand, there were some complaints that the existence of the bases led researchers to concentrate on nearby districts, to the possible neglect of other important but more distant areas. Still, the stations were so helpful to researchers that others were soon established elsewhere, notably at Inuvik. There the government opened an important regional research station for permanent research projects of several government agencies and visiting scientists, who could use the offices, library, workshops, storerooms, and facilities for photographing and preparing scientific specimens. The permanent staff made advance arrangements and assisted the research parties in the laboratories and while in the field. The Inuvik Research Laboratory at once became invaluable to scholars investigating all manner of subjects in the Mackenzie delta and adjacent lands and throughout the Western Arctic. Other stations at Devon Island, Igloolik, Rankin Inlet, and elsewhere were similarly helpful to researchers in those areas as, to a lesser degree, were the military, weather, and communications bases and the quarters and facilities left behind by previous researchers.

The pronounced shift of military attention to the Arctic islands (and beyond) was a result of a fundamental change in the strategy for continental defence. Continuous advances in aircraft, computer technology, and rocket propulsion – dramatically advertised by the first orbiting satellite of the USSR in 1957 – were sharply reducing attack times to minutes instead of hours and forcing military planners to look beyond the manned bomber to the long-range ballistic missile as the principal means of attack. A special system was needed to detect the high-flying missiles of an attacking force at the earliest instant. The upshot was the building of three powerful stations of the Ballistic Missile Early Warning System (BMEWS) at Fylingdales Moor (England), Thule (Greenland), and Clear (Alaska), pointing giant radar dishes skyward that could "see" around the curvature of the earth and sweep such vast arcs that they covered all the northern approaches to the North American continent.

The growing missile threat also increased interest in utilizing the Arctic Ocean, whose location, largely unmapped waters and seabeds, and ice-covered surfaces were ideal for purposes of attack or defence in the missile age. Soviet scientists and strategists had been active in the Arctic Basin since the 1930s, and Americans began their own studies by occupying certain ice islands, notably T-3 (Fletcher's Ice Island) between 1952 and 1961, as they circled slowly around the basin, including the "Canadian Sector." Such islands were floating airfields and mobile bases for mapping undersea terrain, studying oceanography, meteorology, and climate and for radio communication and radar detection purposes. They were evacuated while they were drifting north of the USSR, whose scientists did the same when their ice islands reached positions north of North America.

Nuclear-powered submarines began making undersea voyages in the basin, the best advertised of which included, in 1958, the transit of SS *Nautilus* from Hawaii to England via the North Pole (reached August 3), and two voyages of SS *Skate*, testing methods of surfacing through varying thicknesses and kinds of ice. On the first of these, *Skate* made contact with the staff on T-3, then surfaced several times at or near the North Pole on March 17, 1959, almost exactly half a century after Peary's visit (April 6, 1909), to hold a memorial service for the recently deceased Sir Hubert Wilkins and to scatter his ashes there, as he had instructed. Outside public view, unknown numbers of nuclear-powered missile-carrying submarines of both major powers continued to ply the Arctic waters on missions of surveillance and deterrence. The intercontinental ballistic missile was converting the Arctic Ocean into the front line of the Cold War and relegating the Canadian North, even the Arctic Archipelago, to something approaching back-up, second-line status.

With the new strategic orientation wrought by the missile, the continent-spanning radar lines and heavily armed SAC bases were outdated almost as soon as the DEW Line was finished. Much of the recently built apparatus for detecting manned planes became redundant. Technological advances (such as transistorized circuitry) that improved efficiency, considerations of costs, and by 1963 the thaw in the Cold War also contributed to the U.S. re-evaluation of the earlier system and drastic reductions in the Northern Canada program.

Moreover, it may be that Canadians' protests against the large American military presence in the North affected the U.S. decision to trim its forces and reduce the scale of its operations. From the outset these activities had attracted a great deal of attention, prompting visits by politicians, journalists, and students in search of information and local colour. The travellers were irritated (and said so) by the prominently displayed U.S. flags and the difficulties they experienced if they attempted to visit DEW Line stations without having first secured authorization from Federal Electric's New Jersey head office. Much of the hostility directed against that company was really a powerful resentment against the northern defence program and a widespread feeling of helplessness at Canada's inability to control military activities of the United States in the North that might, it was feared, invite retaliatory attacks on Canadian territory and draw Canada willy-nilly into nuclear war. In fact, opponents contended that the SAC and DEW Line bases had been located in Northern Canada to keep the effects of any nuclear war as far away as possible from the United States, whatever the damage to Canada. They urged the Canadian government to adopt a neutralist "open skies" policy, which they felt would remove the reason for anyone to attack Canadian territory and enable Canada to regain its autonomy in defence and foreign affairs, and eventually, perhaps, make a significant contribution toward reducing world tensions. Northern Canada, for instance, could become a centre for international inspection and scientific co-operation, including exchanges with Soviet scientists in permafrost research and other areas of their expertise.

Whatever the Canadian influence, the changing strategic situation led the United States in 1960 to begin replacing the USAF fighter and bomber squadrons at Churchill, Goose Bay, and Frobisher Bay with squadrons of large fuel-carrying tanker planes. These performed around-the-clock patrols to refuel the huge hydrogen-bomb-carrying B-52 planes in mid-air and keep them in constant readiness to fulfil their role as the main deterrent force. The new strategy reduced the numbers of American servicemen and the scale of construction required at those stations, to say nothing of the local employment and spending they generated. These air-refuelling operations were further reduced in 1963–64 by the closing of the USAF bases at Churchill and Frobisher Bay altogether; only the Goose Bay SAC station was retained. At the same time no fewer than twenty of the smaller DEW Line stations in Canada were closed because it was felt that their functions could be handled by the remainder. Canada for its part dismantled the entire Mid-Canada Line in 1964–65, writing off its $227-million investment in favour of relying on an improved Pinetree Line farther south. The relaxation of the Cold War mentality and reliance on massive retaliation as the principal means of averting a third World War were leading the United States in the sixties to loosen its grip on Northern Canada and return primary defence of that region to the Canadian government.

Canada's reaction to the new situation was to reduce the Canadian military presence in the North and lower its military profile there. Thus the RCAF closed its stations at Fort Nelson, Fort Chimo, Coral Harbour, Resolute, Whitehorse, and Churchill, and control of the Alaska Highway was taken from the Canadian Army. Icebreaking work, maintaining and managing the Alaska Highway and the airports, and providing radio and telephone service were transferred from military to civilian operators, among which were the Departments of Transport and of Public Works, the National Research Council (NRC), and commercial telephone companies. One commentator saw these actions as "in part, a reflection of diminished military importance and political development of the Canadian North which has occurred during the past decade."[12] As a result, full-time employment by the Department of National Defence in the North plummeted to 645 in 1967, barely a quarter of the 1961 level (2,484).

The remaining servicemen were engaged more fully on the traditional tasks associated with upholding the territorial integrity of Canada, defined in the *White Paper on Defence* of March 1964 as including "the ability to maintain surveillance of Canadian territory, airspace and territorial waters; [and] the ability to deal with military incidents on Canadian territory."[13] To help meet these objectives permanent forces were stationed at Inuvik (some 200 men in 1969) and Alert (about 180), small detachments were placed at each of the four main DEW Line stations, and, starting in 1970, headquarters units were opened at Yellowknife and Whitehorse to serve as liaison with the territorial governments. Other servicemen spent short periods in the North each year with scientific and similar operations to gain Arctic experience and participated in formal military training exercises such as Operation New Viking (1970), which involved transporting platoons from Churchill to Baker Lake and Rankin Inlet, and from "Crystal City" near Resolute to Eureka and Mould Bay. Contingents, mainly of paratroopers, also began participating in large-scale joint exercises conducted in Alaska. Unfortunately, the surveillance role over Canada's northern seas, which was soon to become so important, was almost entirely neglected. Canada in 1967 still had no warships or submarines capable of operating in Arctic waters and only limited icebreaking capability; occasional aerial surveillance was provided by long-range Argus patrol aircraft from stations in Nova Scotia and Prince Edward Island.

The curtailment of the direct American presence in Northern Canada meant that equipment in quantity, installations, and facilities were transferred to Canada for disposition and future use. Disposal of the movables was overseen by the Crown Assets Disposal Corporation, and many vehicles and motorized barges eventually were to be found serving the freighting needs of northern communities. Both CNT and Bell Canada examined the communications facilities with an eye to expanding their operations into the Arctic. Most of the airstrips, roads, docks, buildings, and other facilities at the closed DEW Line stations were taken over and kept in operation by the Department of Transport and other departments.

The main bases were a more serious concern. The unexpected American withdrawal from Frobisher Bay in 1963 left behind a $20-million airbase with 9,000 feet of paved runways and facilities for maintaining and refuelling the six aerial tankers that had been based there. These were of little use to long-distance commercial flying operations except as an emergency landing field. The town faced the exodus of about half its white population – the American servicemen and their families, and 140 Canadians employed at the base and townsite – for whom no immediate employment prospect remained. At Churchill, where a large defence establishment and Arctic research station had been built up since 1946, the situation was not so bleak. Some research operations continued, using the facilities for advanced meteorological and high atmospheric researches that DRB, NRC, and other authorized Canadian, U.S., and NATO bodies conducted by means of high-altitude balloons and rockets. Many of the 3,000 military and civilian personnel departed, but the older railway, port, and shipping activities remained as the economic mainstay of the community.

The federal government immediately arranged to use the surrendered sites by establishing regional headquarters at each station. The surplus buildings at Churchill were to be used by the departments that administered the District of Keewatin and possibly for a future university of the North. At Frobisher Bay, the recently built American administration and housing block, renamed "Federal Building," was remodelled and redecorated by the Department of Public Works, and turned over to the Department of Northern Affairs and National Resources to become its administrative centre for the Eastern Arctic. A major concern at both centres was what to do with the large native settlements that had grown up around the bases. The administration, like administrators elsewhere, was forced to devise community development programs suited to the needs of the increasing number of newly urbanized native persons.

IV

The modern settlers of both northern territories appreciated the rapid increase in government services and spending but found many grounds for complaint over the way these were provided and managed. They argued that federal programs were often too elaborate or expensive for current or foreseeable needs and that public funds were mismanaged or wasted in installation or implementation. They said that programs designed in Ottawa by civil servants did not make sufficient allowance for northern conditions, were imposed without consultation or notice, and were woodenly administered by the agents in the field. They contended that southerners, not northerners, derived the lion's share of the benefits from government expenditures in the territories, demanding that northerners should be employed as far as possible in installing and operating facilities and services and that contracts should be awarded in ways that did not discriminate against northern businessmen or suppliers. The Glassco Commission echoed many of their criticisms in recommending greater local control of government services and fuller participation by northerners in administering the programs for efficiency and other reasons. It urged that residents (including natives) be employed in the management of the federal government's northern operations instead of being the objects almost exclusively of "efforts to create special work for them."[14]

All this led, in the years after 1958, to vigorous political activity. Local spokesmen strove to make their territorial councils more representative of the resident populations, to increase the role of the elective element in the legislative process, to widen the range of services controlled and administered by the councils, and to make the territorial governments equal with the provinces in matters that concerned them. Fuller responsible government for the Yukon and the District of Mackenzie, the constitutions of the Northwest Territories and the Yukon, and the splitting of the Territories were issues that commanded lengthy discussion in Parliament. The future of the Northwest Territories was made the subject of a comprehensive inquiry by an advisory commission, and the eventful decade closed with the establishment of a territorial capital and government at Yellowknife in 1967.

As a result of pressure from northerners (and, to be fair, encouragement and support from federal administrators), the territorial councils had made considerable advances by 1967, though disappointingly little progress toward the coveted goals of responsible government and provincial status. In the area of social services, they moved appreciably toward the position occupied by the provincial governments. Assisted by the five-year financial agreements with the federal government (1957–62 and 1962–67) and by special federal grants, the territorial councils participated in shared-cost social programs, including besides the various pensions and allowances, unemployment assistance (relief), winter works, fitness and amateur sport, the Canada centenary, and especially hospital insurance. Federal initiatives and financial incentives drew the councils into enacting labour and workers' compensation legislation, providing vocational training, juvenile delinquency, and correctional institution programs, accepting policing by the RCMP under contracts similar to those made by other provinces, instituting fire prevention services, and numerous other reforms.

These many federally financed and inspired programs led the territorial councils into activities undreamed of only a decade earlier. The progressive character of the territorial councils' operations may be grasped from the sessional reports of their work during the 1960s. By the mid-sixties, indeed, the territorial councils had become as much concerned with social services as the provinces, or even more. No less than three-quarters of the Northwest Territories Council's expenditures of $6.2 million for 1965–66 (excluding the costs of the liquor system, which were offset by larger revenues) went to social purposes – education, hospital insurance, and health and welfare. Many of the remaining expenditures also had social implications: police and justice, municipal affairs, development services, fitness and amateur sport, administering workers' compensation, and library services. In the Yukon, too, social services accounted for over 54 per cent of the territorial government's expenditure of $8.147 million in 1966–67.

The process of transferring social services from the federal to the territorial authorities had much farther to go in the Northwest Territories than in the Yukon, where most such services (for non-native persons at least) had long been administered by the territory. For the Northwest Territories, the devolution had to start almost from scratch, since the administration in 1958 was still based in Ottawa and was conducted in the North by the federal agencies. The first stages were to transfer nominal control over education, health, and social services for non-native settlers, together with corresponding financial aids, to the Territorial Council, even while the services themselves continued to be delivered by the federal agencies. As late as 1965, for instance, employees of the Northern Administration Branch were providing the educational, welfare, municipal, engineering, hospital insurance, and even game management services: the Northern Health Service supplied the medical services, and the Department of Justice the RCMP and legal services. The one service directly operated by the Northwest Territories government (as it had been since the 1930s) was the very profitable liquor system, which employed a score or so employees and contributed over half the locally raised revenues. Not until the territorial government was installed in the North did actual conduct of most services begin to pass into its hands: public works, tourism, municipal affairs in 1967–68, education in 1969 (District of Mackenzie) and 1970 (Eastern Arctic).

The Yukon's civil service, dating from gold rush days, already controlled most of the services to non-natives that the Northern Administration Branch provided in the Northwest Territories, and so the main advances were to expand small-scale activities to levels prevailing elsewhere. The size of the territorial civil service reached 464 in 1967. The broadened range of its activities in that year included new departments and agencies: legal adviser, territorial treasurer, engineering, municipal affairs, social welfare, corrections, personnel, and travel and publicity. The Yukon's expenditures far exceeded the $2.775 million of territorial revenue raised locally, the remainder being derived from the federal government as the territorial share of joint programs ($3.125 million), an operating deficit grant taken from the federal-territorial financial grant ($1.823 million), plus "surplus funds accumulated over previous years."[15]

In the early 1960s the territories' political pot began boiling furiously as members of both councils came to feel a stronger sense of the rightness of the autonomist cause and greater confidence in their ability to manage the affairs of their regions. The Northwest Territories Council, calculating that the undeveloped eastern and northern parts of the Territories retarded the chances of settlers in the District of Mackenzie winning greater self-government, recommended splitting the Northwest Territories into two territories along the 105th meridian. The western part, made up of the District of Mackenzie with its capital at Fort Smith and named Mackenzie Territory, would retain the existing government, a council of five members elected from local constituencies and four appointed members, that would evolve into a territorial legislature with lawmaking and administrative powers comparable with those of the provinces. The Districts of Keewatin and Franklin together, largely populated by Inuit, for which the name "Nunassiaq" was eventually selected, would also receive a council to consist of seven members, two of whom would be elected from South Keewatin and South Baffin, which would progress to greater autonomy at its own pace. Transmitted to the federal cabinet in January 1962, the proposal was enshrined in the Speech from the Throne of September 27, 1962:

> Measures will be placed before you to provide for the division of the Northwest Territories into two territories, and to provide more self government for the residents of that area as a step toward the ultimate creation of new provinces in Canada's great north.[16]

In keeping with these plans, the Territories Council at its January 1963 session proposed to add a fifth elected member to give it an elected majority and considered other matters relating to the proposed division of the Northwest Territories.

The collapse of the Diefenbaker government and dissolution of Parliament meant the legislation for the division was left to the Liberals to deal with. The resolutions modifying the territorial boundaries were introduced by Laing on May 21, 1963, and Bills C-83 and C-84 embodying the division on July 8. Though the measures appeared to have the support of both major parties, vigorous opposition was speedily raised by the Conservative M.P.s from the territories and by the small Créditiste party. The former complained that the bills did not provide sufficiently democratic institutions for either new territory or any assistance for the Yukon in its struggle for increased autonomy and that the legislation had not been referred to the people of the Eastern Arctic and did not enjoy the support of most northerners. As for the Créditistes, they strenuously objected to Bill C-84 and demanded that the boundaries of Nunassiaq be redrawn to give Quebec a three-mile seaward zone on the north and west and possession of various offshore islands instead of the boundary of 1912 that confined Quebec to the sea margin.

The Liberal government struggled with these demands and even tried to proceed with Bill C-83 alone. But the opposition proved unrelenting, and in the end both bills were referred (in November 1963) to the Standing Committee on Mines, Forests and Waters. Over the ensuing months the committee heard many witnesses, including members of the council, spokesmen from the larger communities, and individuals, among them Justice Sissons, whose combined testimonies amply demonstrated the lack of accord among northerners on the division question. The government found the whole matter (which had been inherited from its predecessor) distasteful and quietly removed it from its agenda. Though Laing as late as April 16, 1964, promised that the legislation would be proceeded with, the government let the matter hang fire. The failure to enact the bills forced the Northwest Territories Council to hold an emergency session to rush through supply and arrange for new territorial elections before its term expired on November 21, 1963. These elections, held on May 11, 1964, were followed by the naming of the appointed members, a notable newcomer being Stuart M. Hodgson, a British Columbia union executive and political associate of the minister. In the following year Hodgson was promoted to deputy commissioner after the existing appointee resigned for health reasons, and a first native member, Abraham Okpik, took his place among the appointed councillors.

Okpik's appointment in 1965 was a long overdue recognition that the council did not truly represent or attend to the concerns of the native sector that with the Métis comprised a majority in the Territories. The lack of trained native leaders had made administration the exclusive preserve of white officials and settlers. By 1965, however, native leaders were at last emerging from the schools and co-operatives, and when predominantly native constituencies were created, as they were in 1965, they would be in a position to rally their ethnic fellows. Thus an abrupt emergence of new political forces and issues in the Northwest Territories was foreshadowed.

For native discontent was rising in the territories as elsewhere, though native brotherhoods were not organized in the Territories and Yukon until after 1967. Till then the main source of unrest was the deterioration of the wildlife industries, and most complaints concerned how the game resource was handled. A new grievance was emerging, however, in the form of native land rights, and the failure to provide the reserves in the Northwest Territories promised by Treaty No. 8 (1899) and Treaty No. 11 (1921) was the catalyst. The administration had simply considered them unnecessary in view of the limited economic development of the Territories and the special arrangements that had given the natives a virtual monopoly of the wildlife resource. Moreover, there was growing doubt whether reserves were really in the best interests of mid-twentieth-century Indians and Métis and a sentiment that the 640 acres per family of five offered by the treaties were inappropriate for the needs of largely nomadic hunting people. The delay in awarding the reserves made it all the more difficult to proceed with any settlement of the claims.

These views emerged during testimony before the Nelson Commission (named for its chairman, W.H. Nelson, a Prince Albert barrister) appointed in 1959 to investigate the unfulfilled provisions of the treaties as they applied to the District of Mackenzie. The commission found that "a large proportion" of the 4,502 Indians wished merely "to be allowed to continue to live as they now do."[17] They were reported to be woefully unprepared for and uninterested in reserves, highly suspicious of government actions, and afraid that any change might curtail their fishing, hunting, and trapping rights. The report was emphatically opposed to granting reserves except for land required for residential purposes. It recommended, instead, cash compensation ($20 an acre for the 576,016 acres of "land credit") to be added to the various band funds plus an annual payment of half of 1 per cent of the Crown revenues derived from extraction of the minerals and fossil fuels of the areas surrendered.

The failure to create Indian reserves came to be regarded by some as a gross violation providing justifiable grounds for new negotiations with the Indians and Métis over their aboriginal rights. The Nelson Commission "found it impossible to make the Indians understand that it is possible to separate mineral or hunting rights from actual ownership of land" and reported that some bands had "expressed the view that since they had the right to hunt, fish and trap over all the land in the Northwest Territories, the land belonged to the Indians."[18] Such an attitude closely paralleled the view derived from U.S. political theory, and followed by the courts and Indian administration in that country, that Indians in the absence of formal treaties remained sovereign entities. That emerging view of aboriginal land claims and of self-governing rights of the Indians, Métis, and Inuit of the Northwest Territories completely altered the shape and direction of native-white relations in the territories, perhaps for all time.

The federal government early in 1964 moved to establish a government of the Northwest Territories separate from the Northern Administration Branch. B.G. Sivertz, previously director of that branch, became full-time head of a small Territories government office in Ottawa with his own clerical and legal staff "as a step in establishing the Government of the Northwest Territories as a separate entity."[19] A year later, after the Territories Council passed a public service ordinance "providing a statutory basis for the establishment of a Territorial Public Service,"[20] the staff responsible to the commissioner was rapidly increased, the numbers of those stationed full-time in the Territories rising from twenty-nine in 1965 to 188 in 1967.

The controversies over the political future of the Northwest Territories added fuel to the Yukon Council's strivings for greater self-government, which Erik Nielsen, the territory's M.P., used in his attacks on the Liberal government in Ottawa. The council, whose membership had been increased from five to seven in 1961, represented the interests of independent-minded small businessmen, artisans, and labourers. At its spring and autumn sessions in 1963, it made several significant moves to assert control over the territorial administration headed by the federally appointed commissioner. Objecting to the report of a liquor committee set up by F.H. Collins, the commissioner, the council insisted on appointing its own committee to reconsider the matter, and it demanded a greater voice in the establishment of a territorial prison. Above all, it refused to enact the agreement under which the RCMP provided law enforcement for the territory (for which, incidentally, it had already voted funds) by way of protesting the federal government's delay in appointing a senior legal officer for the territory.

The contest grew more heated in the ensuing session (March-April 1964) when a four-member group headed by the Speaker, J.O. Livesey, determined to attack the administration, the tone being set by Livesey's remaining seated while the current commissioner, G.R. Cameron, read his opening address. Once again the RCMP agreement was rejected, and the administration's legal officer was subjected to personal attack. The Speaker rejected the commissioner's demand for an apology with the assertion that the council was the judge of its procedures. The same issue of council control over administration arose over representation at intergovernmental conferences dealing with matters that concerned the territories. The principle of representation was conceded by Prime Minister Pearson, but the federal government insisted that the commissioner, as head of the administration, not the council, should appoint the representatives. The territories were represented in this fashion at national conferences on pensions and on Indian affairs in 1964. More success was achieved with joint programs; the federal Student Loan Bill, for instance, was amended to ensure that the territorial commissioners would administer that legislation in consultation with their councils.

The Yukon Council's policy of opposition and obstruction became the main issue of the triennial territorial election on September 8, 1964. Two of the ringleaders (one of them Livesey) were defeated, and a new council was elected that was prepared to co-operate with the administration. The ensuing session accepted the previously criticized legal official, implemented the RCMP agreement, established a public utilities commission to manage power franchise matters, and passed other useful measures. This harmony, which made one veteran member call the session "the most productive and cooperative I have ever spent as a member of the Yukon Territorial Council,"[21] was the exception in council-administration relations during the mid-sixties.

Subsequently, however, the council moved increasingly into confrontation that featured much bickering, with frequent attacks on administration personnel and programs. In 1966, the council refused to pass the Justice estimates in an effort to bring the federal department's legal personnel in the territory under council control, and the next year a new council (to which Livesey and two of his former supporters were returned) rejected three bills in order to press the minister into giving council more fiscal control. A measure of the intensity of the controversy was the unexpected resignation in 1966 of the popular commissioner, G.R. Cameron. Cameron, a local businessman, apparently resigned because of the impossibility of conducting his office: the myriad tasks were more than one person could manage, bitter challenges from council over any administrative action seemed inevitable, and yet he was held accountable by the minister in Ottawa for administering the federal programs and maintaining necessary council support for them.

Meanwhile, the Yukon Council made efforts to secure control over areas of local concern such as Crown lands and inland fisheries and strongly criticized certain federal programs as unduly elaborate and likely to involve the territory in needless future expense. One issue that pitted the council against Ottawa was territorial finance. The fiscal agreement of 1962–67 had not met the territory's needs because of unexpected demands and inflation: the council therefore looked for increased grants during the next fiscal term. But the federal government intended to reduce the amounts in line with the slowed tempo of Yukon development and of the national economy. The pressure it put on the council to increase some local taxes or suffer reduction of the federal payments roused vigorous protest from all sides against interference with territorial rights.

The campaign to promote the council to rank with the legislatures drew inspiration from a brief foray of Premier W.A.C. Bennett into the Yukon in 1964 with a grandiose plan of annexing the territory to British Columbia. By arousing widespread opposition and heightening the settlers' faith in the future of their territory the visit only strengthened the position of the council as the embodiment of Yukon identity. In 1965 the council unanimously resolved that the Yukon should be advanced gradually to provincial status within a decade or two after 1967. A later council resolution of May 6, 1966, put forward by Nielsen and the Yukon Conservative party, was more precise, calling for the membership of the "Yukon Legislative Assembly" to be increased to fifteen and an appointed executive committee of five members to take charge of the main territorial administrative departments, followed after a dozen years by provincial status and a twenty-one-member legislature. The first small step in this direction did not occur until 1970, when an executive committee of five members (two of them council members) was formed to advise the commissioner in the exercise of his responsibilities and assist with the budget and legislative programs.

The Northwest Territories Council behaved far differently. The proposal for division having fallen by the wayside, it called on the minister to appoint a judicial commission "to examine and recommend on the future of the North economically, socially and politically."[22] It did show a certain independence on local matters, however; the February 1965 session saw the members defy administrators' advice by deciding to locate the territorial library at Hay River instead of in Yellowknife, voting a forty-dollar bounty on wolves (for economic reasons) in defiance of wildlife experts' advice to the contrary, and passing a motion to subsidize high electricity rates, which the commissioner accepted only as advice because it affected the revenue.

The federal government after a year's delay took up the suggestion of a judicial inquiry and appointed the Advisory Commission on the Development of Government in the Northwest Territories to study the Territories' political future. The three-member commission consisted of A.W.R. Carrothers, Dean of the Faculty of Law, University of Western Ontario, as chairman; Jean Beetz, a rising constitutional lawyer of Montreal and future justice of the Supreme Court of Canada; and John H. Parker, a geological engineer, mayor of Yellowknife, and future commissioner of the Northwest Territories. Over the summer and winter of 1965–66 the commission held hearings in Ottawa and throughout the Territories, the first inquiry to set out expressly to visit as many settlements and elicit the views of as many inhabitants as possible. The report was submitted on August 30 and tabled in the House of Commons on October 5, 1966.

The main recommendation of the Carrothers Report was to maintain the Northwest Territories as a single jurisdiction for the time being, since the District of Mackenzie was not yet ready for any large political step and even basic political institutions were lacking in the other districts. An ingenious scenario was proposed for the political evolution of the Territories: the Territorial Council (renamed legislative assembly) should be enlarged to eighteen members, fourteen of them elected, the remainder appointed as before. An executive council, appointed from the members by the commissioner, would prepare legislation, co-ordinate finance, and advise the commissioner: individual members would take charge of seven departments administering the fields of territorial jurisdiction. Full responsible government would come about gradually. The commissioner would continue as a federal agent, but at an appropriate time he would be instructed to exercise his powers "as though he were partially responsible to the legislative assembly," like a lieutenant-governor. In similar fashion, the position of deputy commissioner could be reserved for the member "who has the confidence of the legislature, in a parliamentary sense," whom the commissioner would designate as premier to head the executive council, and responsible government would be fully achieved when "the commissioner elects not to attend the sessions of the legislative assembly."[23]

The new territorial government would eventually administer a range of powers similar to those of the provincial governments, with appropriate financial aids, but without power to alter its constitution or to control its natural resources except as transferred by the minister – for example, authority over lands in or adjacent to settlements. A short period – the commission suggested two years – should suffice for the transfers of powers, and a territorial civil service should be built up quickly by transferring federal employees and hiring as many northerners as possible. On the question of the seat of government, which was of greater concern to the inhabitants than any other recommendation, the commission came down on the side of Yellowknife because of its size and facilities and its relatively central location in the Northwest Territories. The commission also recommended delegating authority to the Territories' communities and greatly increased federal spending on the native sector and on assistance to economic development. Lastly, it suggested that a second commission be appointed after a ten-year interval to review the situation and make changes indicated by past experience.

While the Carrothers Commission was proceeding with its business, the Northwest Territories Council took steps to make its jurisdiction co-terminous with the Territories by extending the territorial franchise to all residents and establishing three new ridings of Keewatin, Central Arctic, and Eastern Arctic (June 1965). Parliament enacted these changes in 1966, so that the council at last had a majority of elected members when the new ridings had chosen their members, one of whom was an Inuk, Simonie Michael (Eastern Arctic). The council carefully followed the advisory commission's proceedings and prepared its own brief (eventually presented as a sessional paper to its January 1966 session) calling for evolution of the Northwest Territories (like the Yukon) to full provincial status in four stages over the next ten or twelve years.

Some recommendations had to be applied seriatim, but the transfer of the seat of government from Ottawa to the North could be proceeded with forthwith. In addition to creating the new constituencies the 1966 federal legislation started a consolidated revenue fund for the Territories, enabling that government to begin operating separately from the Department of Indian Affairs and Northern Development on April 1, 1967. A number of important changes of personnel were made in 1967, for B.G. Sivertz retired from the commissionership and Stuart Hodgson became commissioner in his place. John Parker, late of the Carrothers Commission, succeeded to the vacated deputy commissionership and a decade later followed Hodgson as Commissioner of the Territories. The summer of 1967 brought several new faces as a result of the first Territories-wide elections and new appointments to council, one of whom, following the pattern set in the previous council, was a native of the Territories, Chief John Tetlichi of Fort McPherson.

Planning the administrative transfer had been started in 1965, and by the summer of 1967 the territorial government was beginning to take shape as department heads were appointed and staffs were being recruited to replace the headquarters staff of the Northern Administration Branch. Because the federal-territorial financial agreement of 1962–67 had not allowed for the move, a special grant was required to cover the costs of the transfer, mostly related to constructing facilities and accommodations in Yellowknife. In 1966–67, twenty-four houses and an apartment building were completed for some of the incoming staff while work proceeded on a five-storey headquarters building. In the interim, "private homes, the curling club, a partially used school and a bowling alley" were pressed into service as temporary government offices.

The promised move took place on September 18, 1967, when seventy-five government employees, including the commissioner and staff members, and their families boarded a chartered DC-7 aircraft in Ottawa "to the tune of the bagpipes," while a second chartered plane hauled some thirty tons of books, records, reports, paper, and other supplies for the new offices. At Churchill, where the planes stopped to refuel, the travellers received "a rousing reception" from residents and Inuit pupils at the vocational school; at Yellowknife "a red carpet was rolled out and about 1,000 people greeted the arrival of the government" as Commissioner Hodgson proclaimed, "At last we are home!"[24] A century after the inauguration of the Dominion of Canada its youngest regional government was in place and ready to begin developing a distinctive northern jurisdictional persona for the Northwest Territories.

CHAPTER 13

Some Reflections on Northward Expansion – Canadian-Style

The northward sweep of the industrial, social, and administrative frontiers has radically altered the complexion of Canada. In 1914 Canada was more geographical expression than reality. Among the states of the world its area was surpassed only by those of Russia and China, and the Mercator Projection commonly used for world maps exaggerated it, coloured red by convention, to second place. With fewer than eight million inhabitants, Canada's developed territory, practically speaking, was confined to narrow strips of settlement fronting on the Atlantic, the St. Lawrence and the Great Lakes, the southern parts of the four western provinces, and patches along the Canadian Pacific Railway to the Pacific Ocean. Other transcontinental railways were being built to broaden the developed sections of the country, but by 1914 these still were unfinished, and the process of developing the resources of their hinterlands had scarcely begun. Only in the Prairie sector had agricultural settlement penetrated more than two hundred miles north of the United States border.

By 1967, however, Canada's population had passed twenty million, and the agricultural, forestry, hydro, and mining frontiers had been pushed to their economic and nearly to their physical limits. Expansion based on the development of natural resources, or responding to administrative and defence imperatives, had been propelled northward by the technological and commercial revolutions that made developing more remote resources increasingly feasible, by the favourable price and marketing situations that prevailed at intervals between 1914 and 1967, and by a plethora of aids that governments showered on resource developers. These attracted entrepreneurs, capital, and settlers to the many economic opportunities latent in Canada's Subarctic and Arctic territories. Enormous tracts that had once supported only hunters and trappers became crisscrossed with survey lines, trails, power lines, and railways and overflown by aircraft. Great areas had been transformed into pastures and cultivated lands or centres of forestry and mining operations. By 1967 approximately one million Canadians were settled on territories occupied after 1914, and permanent communities could be found almost at the northern limits of Canada.

Development of the country's natural resources, in keeping with Sir Wilfrid Laurier's most-quoted dictum, "The twentieth century belongs to Canada," continued to be the mainspring of national growth, as it had been from earliest times. In that spirit entrepreneurs and settlers exploited arable lands and other resources capable of development, and Canadians, conditioned by the country's vast extent, expected the process to continue indefinitely. When the development drive was resumed after the Great War, it was strengthened by new-found confidence based on the nation's wartime achievements and reinforced by welcome reports from Stefansson and others that the natural resource base was even greater than previously believed. The Depression of the 1930s, however, drove home the lesson that natural resources in themselves are not automatically sources of wealth but only as current economic and technological conditions allow them to be utilized – a state of affairs that gave rise, in the parlance of that day, to the paradox of "poverty in the midst of plenty." The concept of "economic" rather than "absolute" resources still prevailed when a "Canada Unlimited" ideology resurfaced after the Second World War. Nonetheless, a buoyant post-war economy, apparently limitless markets, innovative technology, and big-spending governments sustained expansion based on natural resource exploitation until most of the national endowment was brought under development. Reminders of the distinction between "economic" and "absolute" resources awaited the bouts of hard times that set in after 1967.

In the main, northward economic expansion followed the occupation or depletion of the richest, most accessible areas of each type of natural resource and advanced toward the limits of its profitable exploitation. The societies of the several resource and administrative frontiers that ensued were shaped largely by their economic bases. Wildlife exploitation, for instance, could sustain only small, widely scattered populations of individuals or family groups whose nomadic habits restricted them to a humble economic and social station. On the other hand, agriculture, exploiting a renewable and improvable resource, gave rise to relatively permanent settlements that radically altered the social as well as the physical nature of whole regions. Although farming was conducted by thousands of individual proprietors whose past experience, skills, goals, and cultural baggage coloured their economic, social, and institutional progress, the total of their efforts was subsumed in a densely settled advancing agricultural frontier.

While forests also are capable of renewal and even of betterment, the industry unfortunately tended to follow "cut and run" and clear-cutting methods that after exhausting the timber of a locality moved on to undepleted areas. Employment in lumber towns and pulp and paper centres was sustained only with difficulty by drawing supplies from farther afield. Similarly, many mining operations have eventually had to be abandoned through exhaustion of ore bodies, since minerals are a non-renewable resource.

Mining, as opposed to prospecting for minerals, creates high-value operations on tightly concentrated sites, a characteristic that permit-ted the industry to leapfrog over great distances when air transport became available. Mines could be readily established far beyond the limits of agriculture and forestry, and mining accordingly became the main northward-driving industry for the period of this study. The changing resources base of Subarctic and Arctic Canada also helped give mining its leading role in northern development. Since climatic and soil conditions are poorer as the latitude climbs, the sorts of nat-ural resources that are capable of commercial exploitation become fewer also until beyond the 60th parallel only minerals remain on which to base a self-sustaining industrial economy. Notwithstanding the efforts of administrators and others to improve the utilization of the wildlife resources, expand tourism, and increase spending on transportation, government services, or national defence, the eco-nomic and social future of the northern territories depends primarily on healthy mining industries.

Northward expansion was furthered at every step by improving technology. For instance, the legion of innovations and improvements in transportation and communications in the period 1914 to 1967 had an impact on the North that was completely past calculating. One need only consider the most obvious advances in this category – the air-plane, automobile, motorboat, paved road, high-voltage line, oil or natural gas pipeline, wireless telegraphy, radio, television, communi-cations satellite – to recognize the vital role of technology. The same is true of the several resource-based frontiers, including even the wild-life industries, as the preceding chapters have shown. Another sort of technical advance was evident in the application of improved knowl-edge to surveying, resource evaluation, and scientific research, the devising and application of better social and administrative programs, the management of relations with persons of different cultures and stages of acculturation, and the like. Each innovation improved the efficiency of operating in the North, lowered production costs, or enhanced the value of products and thereby made it more feasible to undertake development of previously undeveloped resources.

But technological change is a two-edged sword: although the innovator gained an advantage over his rival, his innovation speedily became the industry norm, and competition was renewed on a lower, more vital, cost-cutting plane. Before the relentless drive to reduce costs other economic and non-economic considerations were pushed aside, with deplorable effects on workers and others, and on the environment. Hence governments were compelled to set aside their laissez-faire approach to development and intervene on the side of employees by setting standards for work and pay. As for the ecological question, governments and public had simply taken the environment as a given to be used freely by authorized persons or corporations in their own interests. Only in the 1960s, after ignorance, indifference, or carelessness had done such massive damage through flooding, discharging of noxious fumes, and chemically polluting soils, waters, and the air did governments begin to move to protect the environment against abuses by the few to the detriment of the many.

How should Canada's twentieth-century frontier experience be evaluated? It resembled the classical American nineteenth-century example in that individualistic private enterprise was the motive engine driving development forward, but in other respects it differed radically from that model. The prominent place held by forestry and mining, rather than agriculture, in Northern Canada meant that hierarchical corporations more often than individuals were the main agents promoting northward expansion. Whereas expansion in the United States followed a parallel course westward from several seaboard centres, in Canada it followed a metropolitan path mostly northward from already populated, developed districts in the St. Lawrence Lowland and the southern prairies. Since the frontier districts failed to achieve as full a development as the metropolitan heartlands from which they sprang, they also proved unable to emancipate themselves from heartland economic, social, and political hegemonies as the American West had been able to do. A particularly Canadian consideration working against such advance was the long-standing colonialist tradition that control over newly settled territories remain firmly in the hands of the appropriate federal or provincial government. Above all, expansion was far less free and open than in the U.S. example, for on-the-spot administration by policemen and various officials, already well-established practice in Canada, became increasingly powerful because of the enhanced power of the twentieth-century state, the characteristics of the resource-using industries, and the nature of the territories being settled.

Indeed, a main feature of frontier expansion in Canada was the large, increasingly ubiquitous part governments played in the process from 1914 onward. By 1967 Canadian systems of administration, taxation, law enforcement and justice, local and regional government, scientific, social, and other services had been extended over the whole of Canada's territory and population. Governments, particularly after 1945, had participated actively in development by undertaking vigorous surveying, advertising, and other activities to encourage the taking up of the natural resources; by offering easy, generous, loosely controlled grants and tax concessions to developers; by providing transportation, hydro-electric power, and other infrastructures; and by assisting settlers with an increasing variety of social services and welfare aids.

To foster occupation and development of their vast territory Canadian governments relied on domestic and foreign sources of capital, entrepreneurship, and manpower. Participation by American citizens and firms was welcomed without question until the very close of the period, though the government of the United States, by contrast, was regarded more ambiguously – as a threat to Canada's sovereignty over the Arctic islands until that question was resolved in 1930, and since 1945, when U.S. programs of hemispheric defence have periodically aroused Canadians over possible encroachments on Canada's sovereignty. Southern Canadians, indeed, seemed to prefer to treat U.S. activities not as helpful steps enhancing the prosperity and security of the North but as affronts to the national dignity, useful for whipping up anti-American sentiments to help strengthen their own Canadian patriotism. On the other side, the outstanding material successes of the United States in exploiting the resources of its share of the continent were held out as an encouraging model for development-minded Canadians, while its presence in Northern Canada during the Second World War set an example and gave a lead to greatly increased official Canadian involvement with the territories.

Another significant difference between the frontier experiences of the two nations lay in the more prominent place of native people and native policies in Canadian expansion. In the United States, Indians became settled on their reservations; in Northern Canada, they remained nomadic. But the native bands found their livelihoods challenged by the agricultural advances and inroads of non-native trappers and fishermen into the Subarctic forests in the 1920s, and after 1945 their sustenance was threatened by the havoc wreaked on wildlife by the rapid onslaught of resource-developing industries. Even in the face of these threats the federal government left the northern natives largely alone to pursue their traditional lives. Unimaginatively and routinely it administered the provisions of the Indian Act and treaties, extending to the natives cash annuities, social and other commitments. Activities of competing whites were strictly regulated, large areas were set aside for the exclusive use of native hunters, and efforts were made to enhance the wildlife resource.

Unfortunately, this approach could not save the natives from the economic calamity of the thirties, and it failed utterly to prepare them for the revolution in their economic and social environment after 1950. Indian legislation was belatedly reformed after 1945 to help guide native groups in the new age of settled existence, wage employment, and a money-based economy. The sole unquestioned benefit before 1967 was in the health field, but otherwise native people were almost completely overwhelmed by the economic, cultural, sociological, and psychological difficulties that confronted them. It is still a little too early to tell whether the many programs of the 1945–67 period were truly useful in helping native persons adapt to the conditions of the modern world. Nonetheless, the emergence of native organizations and leaders toward the end of the period did give hope of fuller native participation in the economic and political life of Canada.

This uncertainty was part and parcel of a long-time ambiguity in Canadians' attitudes toward the North, which had been characterized by turns by attention and indifference, attraction and withdrawal. On the one hand, as in the period 1900–1920, the North was regarded as a doorway of opportunity and "opening the North" as the route to future national greatness. On the other, as in the period since 1967, the wish has existed to guard it jealously against outsiders and preserve it from abrupt change. After Canadians had lost interest in it during the interwar decades, the region's involvement in the Second World War made them more aware of its features and the need to make the land and its people a regular, equal part of the nation. A torrent of publicity on various aspects of the region, plus the North's continuing role in North American defence, made Canadians aware of the territories as never before and set natural and social scientists, artists and writers to work on northern topics. The sense of movement from 1945 to 1967 – industrial development, introduction of settlers and modern communities, rapid, troubled changes in the native population, and real advances in political self-determination – sustained Canadians' interest in the North at high pitch throughout the period. Since then, however, economic conditions in the North and changing social conditions in the South have deflected the attention of the public and seemingly drawn its main focus to the difficulties and burdens rather than to the opportunities present in northern development.

The year 1967, in fact, has been an important milestone in the emergence of new forces whose sharply differing approaches to northern development continue to challenge the long-standing, single-minded drive to extend the modern economy, society, and polity of Southern Canada ever northward. During the fifties, economic nationalists had begun seriously to doubt the wisdom of encouraging rapid, large-scale development by foreign as well as domestic corporations. Although environmentalists and advocates of native rights had started questioning the course of northern development in the early 1960s, their impact became significant only after 1967 when their causes captured the attention of the media. Governments began catering to these pressure groups by enacting environmental protection and similar regulatory legislation and by subsidizing the organizational and legal expenses of the groups. As the vehemence of the activist onslaught grew, governments found it increasingly difficult to promote natural resource development. Saddled with contradictory mandates, they struggled unhappily to conciliate the warring forces, with one hand imposing further protective restraints on development, with the other increasing financial and administrative aids to stimulate the developers' efforts. In any event, the development drive was running out of momentum for economic reasons even more than from the new controls. Developing remote resource sites acquired during the preceding expansionary phase or those not yet awarded had become too costly and too risky in the prevailing recessionary climate. The disappointing results many investors and developers had experienced since 1945 may also have made them more aware of the difficulties and hesitant about exploiting northern natural resources.

From time to time boosters of northern development injected the more successful record of the USSR into the argument and implied that it proved deficiencies of faith, knowledge, or effort on the part of Canadians and entrepreneurs. The comparison was unfair because it ignored the sharply different physical, climatic, and locational circumstances of the two northlands that make development a much more difficult task in the Canadian North. Furthermore the Soviet Union had the great advantages of a far larger population and economic base, the earlier start of its effort, and finally, its very different approach to northern development. In the Soviet North the state invested capital and deployed labour according to national priorities, the ideal being to develop to their fullest the resources of every part of the state, human as well as natural – fish, fur, reindeer, and other animals by the aboriginal peoples, the forests, arable soils, gold, nickel, oil, or diamonds by new as well as original settlers. Then the state arranged local, national, or export markets for the resulting products. The system was relatively immune to economic vicissitudes, and it offered the native population a secure place in the regional economy. At the same time, to further their integration into Soviet society the state co-opted individual natives to the official bureaucracy and party and displayed tolerance of the material, artistic, and linguistic sides of their cultures. Whether there is anything Canadians should have learned from this different approach to northern development is an open question.

In Northern Canada, by contrast, resource development proceeded under an open market system in which there were usually more profitable outlets elsewhere for investment and labour and northern products had to compete on even terms with those from more efficient, better-positioned sources. Hence economic development proceeded slowly, painfully, all too often in an exaggerated boom-and-bust pattern in which prosperity arrived near the close of an expansionary economic phase and dissipated at the first sign of oncoming recession. Entrepreneurs selected for development resources that could generate profits, especially the minerals and fossil fuels that could be produced in large volume by heavily capitalized, highly mechanized, labour-saving techniques. Resources that did not lend themselves to that treatment were simply left for the traditional economy to use as best it could. Thus two economies grew up side by side in the Canadian North: one modern, efficient, geared to external markets, employing specialist personnel recruited from outside; the other small scale, carried on by individuals using hand methods to harvest the land's resources. The modern economy afforded employment to only a small fraction of the swelling indigenous population while the traditional economy could no longer continue to fill their main needs. Many natives faced the unappetizing alternatives of accepting endless social assistance or moving to centres where employment was to be had and adapting on their own to the radically different lifestyle. Thus extending Southern Canada's economic hegemony over the North failed almost completely to serve the needs of the original peoples.

In the two generations after 1914 the developmental drive had marched northward in step with expanding transportation and other infrastructures, governmental administrative agencies and social programs, and the imperatives of continental defence all the way to the Polar Sea. Many thousands of workers and professional persons, with their families, had taken up places tilling fields, harvesting forests, digging minerals from the earth, and founding new communities and societies along the expanding resource frontiers. Well-meant but tragically inadequate efforts were being made to protect native inhabitants and wildlife from the worst effects of the invasion of their homelands and to help the peoples adapt as painlessly as possible to the requirements of the changing times. Notwithstanding these difficult and probably insoluble problems, the great progress in developing, settling, and organizing so much of Canada's frontierlands since 1914 should give all Canadians well-merited pride in their peaceful achievements as a nation, coupled with the determination to deal more justly with the people and the land of the North.

NOTES

Notes to Chapter One

1. The quotation is from an account of Stefansson's Empire Club lecture as given in the *Globe*, 12 Nov. 1918, p. 9. A copy of that address, "The Canadian Arctic Region," is found in PAC [Public Archives of Canada], RG85 [Northern Administration Branch], Vol. 584, File 571, No. 5, item 7. In it Stefansson asserts (p. 12) that by cultivating musk-ox and reindeer "we can turn the whole northern half of Canada into grazing lands that shall produce to the square mile as much meat, tallow, milk and wool as do the grazing lands of the Argentine and Australia." Another account (of sorts) of this luncheon address at the King Edward Hotel by "the intrepid explorer Vladmir Steffansson" appears in the *Toronto Daily Star* of the afternoon of 11 Nov., p. 4. The *Globe* of 12 Nov., p. 8, carries a further account of the Stefansson evening address of a more popular kind at Massey Hall. Stefansson's autobiography, *Discovery* (New York, 1964), pp. 214-15, published over forty years later, creates a minor mystery by referring only to an evening lecture at Massey Hall presided over by Sir Edmund Walker.

2. K.J. Rea, *The Political Economy of Northern Development*, Science Council of Canada, Background Study No. 36 (Ottawa, 1976), p. 92.

3. K.E. Dalzell, *The Queen Charlotte Islands, 1774-1966* (Terrace, B.C., 1968), p. 214, quoting a diary entry by T.L. Williams.

4. PAC, MG9 [Provincial, Local and Territorial Records], G3 (2), Journal of St. Matthew's Mission, Fort McPherson, Mackenzie River, entry for 3 Sept. 1914.

5. Hudson's Bay Company, Annual Meeting, 2 Aug. 1916, *Report*, p. 10.

6. See M. Zaslow, *The Opening of the Canadian North, 1870-1914* (Toronto, 1971), pp. 272-76.

7. RNWMP, *Annual Report*, 1916-17, p. 11.

8. Ibid., 1919-20, p. 26.

9. Ibid., 1920-21, p. 43.

10. PAC, MG26 [Prime Ministers Papers] (H) [Sir Robert Borden Papers], Vol. 185, pp. 101532-35 (Reel C4384), "Stefansson

Expedition 1914-20,'' letter from Insp. G.L. Jennings, RNWMP, Edmonton, 11 April 1914.

11. See *Opening of the Canadian North*, pp. 197-98.

12. Canada, *Statutes*, 7-8 Geo. V (1917), Chap. 36, Sec. 4 (3).

13. See *Opening of the Canadian North*, pp. 242-43.

14. RNWMP, *Annual Report*, 1918-19, p. 15.

15. PAC, RG15 [Dept. of the Interior], A2 [Miscellaneous Records], Vol. 2 "Arctic Islands, 1920,'' a collection of relevant documents on the area compiled by J.B. Harkin for the Advisory Technical Board on Canadian Sovereignty, p. 2A. It is just possible that the comment was intended to apply only to Greenland.

16. Ibid., p. 3A. Also published in L.C. Clark, ed., *Documents on Canadian External Relations, III: 1919-1925* (Ottawa, 1970), p. 569.

17. "Arctic Islands, 1920,'' p. 8A. Invited to a special meeting of the Advisory Technical Board, 1 Oct. 1920, Stefansson described Rasmussen as desiring to complete the exploration and occupation of the Queen Elizabeth Islands and colonize them with Greenland Eskimos (PAC, RG85, Vol. 584, File 571, No. 5, item 6).

18. PAC, RG7 [Governors General Files], G21, Vol. 411, File 10045, Part 1b (reel T2297), "Exploration Expeditions in the Arctic Regions, 1907-1925,'' Governor General to Colonial Secretary, 23 April 1921.

19. Senate, *Journals*, 1920, p. 294, report of committee, 4 June 1920.

20. By PC 2887, 21 Jan. 1921. There is a copy in PAC, MG26 (I) [Arthur Meighen Papers], Vol. 13 (or reel C3219), "Arctic Islands,'' pp. 7406-7.

21. See *Opening of the Canadian North*, pp. 273-74.

22. Borden Papers, "Stefansson Expedition 1914-20,'' p. 101610, Stefansson to Borden from "N. Lat 77°30', W. Long. 113° approximately,'' 21 June 1915.

23. R.J. Diubaldo, "Wrangling over Wrangel Island,'' *Canadian Historical Review* [CHR] 48, no. 3 (1967), p. 204, quoting Stefansson to Loring Christie, 25 Sept. 1920.

24. Meighen Papers, "Arctic Islands,'' p. 7381, Memorandum from Sir J. Pope to Meighen, 25 Nov. 1920.

25. Ibid., p. 7381; also in Clark, *Documents on Canadian External Relations, III*, p. 569.

26. "Arctic Islands, 1920,'' pp. 2'A', 3'A' (really pp. 24 and 25 of Part A).

27. Meighen Papers, "Arctic Islands,'' p. 7416, copy of letter, Meighen to Stefansson, 19 Feb. 1921.

28. Diubaldo, "Wrangling,'' p. 206, quoting Stefansson to C.V. Sale, 23 Feb. 1921.

29. Meighen Papers, "Arctic Islands,'' p. 7419, copy of letter, Capt. Armstrong (Meighen's private secretary) to Stefansson.

30. Governors General, "Exploration Expeditions,'' Colonial Secretary to Governor General, 9 June 1921.

31. Meighen Papers, "Arctic Islands,'' p. 7426, Sir E. Shackleton to Meighen, 5 April 1921.

32. Ibid., pp. 7479, 7484, copies

of cables to Shackleton, 9 May and 16 May 1921.

33. Toronto *Globe*, 19 Oct. 1920, p. 6.

34. Dept. of the Interior, *Annual Report*, 1921-22, p. 19.

35. Notice in *Canada Gazette* 54, no. 39 (26 Mar. 1921), p. 3972, signed by Commissioner W.W. Cory. A copy is included in the Minutes of the Council of the NWT, Session 2, 14 June 1922, p. 13 (PAC, MG9, G1, or reel M811).

36. Government of Canada, *Treaty No. 11 (June 27, 1921) and Adhesion (July 17, 1922), with Reports, etc.*, reprinted from the edition of 1926 (Ottawa, 1957), pp. 6-8.

37. Ibid., p. 3.

38. H. Daniel in *World's Work*, 43, nos. 5 and 6 (1921), pp. 77-88, 201-11.

39. J. Ness, "Canada's Northern Oilfields," address to 3rd Annual Convention of the Natural Gas and Petroleum Association of Canada, Hamilton, Ont., 1 Oct. 1921, p. 25.

Notes to Chapter Two

1. House of Commons, *Debates*, 1928, p. 1215, K.A. Blatchford, Edmonton East.

2. Ibid., 1929, p. 2740, Robert Forke, Brandon.

3. I. Bowman, *The Pioneer Fringe* (New York, 1931), p. 165.

4. Dept. of the Interior, *Annual Report*, 1930-31, p. 19.

5. Bowman, *Pioneer Fringe*, p. 6.

6. M.P. Jackson, *On the Last Frontier* (London, 1933), p. 60.

7. C.A. Dawson and R.W. Murchie, *The Settlement of the Peace River Country*, Canadian Frontiers of Settlement, Vol. 6 (Toronto, 1934), p. 7.

8. C.A. Dawson, "The Social Structure of a Pioneer Area as Illustrated by the Peace River District," in W.L.G. Joerg, ed., *Pioneer Settlement* (New York, 1932), p. 38.

9. J.K. MacKenzie, "Iron Hands," *Country Guide*, 15 Jan. 1929, p. 39.

10. R.W. Murchie, *Agricultural Progress on the Prairie Frontier*, Canadian Frontiers of Settlement, Vol. 5 (Toronto, 1936), p. 329.

11. Jackson, *On the Last Frontier*, p. 100.

12. *Canadian Annual Review* [*CAR*], 1916, p. 485, report of press interview of 30 June 1916.

13. *L'Action Française*, 16, no. 3 (1926), p. 138.

14. R. England, *The Colonization of Western Canada* (London, 1936), p. 95.

15. W.L. Morton, *Manitoba, A History* (Toronto, 1957), p. 401.

16. H.M. Leppard, "Settlement of the Peace River Country," *Geographical Review*, 25, no. 1 (1935), p. 69.

17. House of Commons, Select Standing Committee on Railways, Canals and Telegraph Lines, "Various Proposed Railway Routes for a Western Outlet to the Pacific from the Peace River District," 1927, *Minutes*

of *Proceedings and Evidence*, p. 93, evidence of Premier J.E. Brownlee, 8 April 1927.
18. Alberta, Dept. of Agriculture, *Annual Report*, 1926, p. 8.
19. R.W. Murchie, "Agricultural Land Utilization in Western Canada," in Joerg, ed., *Pioneer Settlement*, p. 17.
20. A.R.M. Lower, "The Case Against Immigration," *Queen's Quarterly*, 37, no. 3 (1930), pp. 569, 571.
21. Quoted in N.F. Priestley and E.B. Swindlehurst, *Furrows, Faith and Fellowship* (Edmonton, 1967), p. 88.
22. *L'Action Française*, 16, no. 3 (1926), p. 132, "Par la colonisation," by A. Dugré, S.J.
23. D.A. McArthur, "Immigration and Colonization in Canada," in Joerg, ed., *Pioneer Settlement*, p. 30.
24. *CAR*, 1927-28, p. 189, citing "several papers on Apr. 28, 1929." See also *CAR*, 1928-29, pp. 162-63.
25. Saskatchewan, *Sessional Papers*, 1921-22, no. 21, p. 90. From an address to the legislature on the customs tariff, 25 Jan. 1922, by the Minister of Education.

26. *CAR*, 1926-27, p. 185, attributes the phrase to T.O.F. Herzer, manager of the Canadian Colonization Association, at its annual meeting in Winnipeg, 6 Nov. 1926.
27. *CAR*, 1927-28, p. 186, quoting a *Toronto Daily Star* interview of 10 Sept. 1927.
28. R.S. Lambert and P. Pross, *Renewing Nature's Wealth* (Toronto, 1967), p. 308.
29. C.A. Dawson, *Group Settlement: Ethnic Communities in Western Canada*, Canadian Frontiers of Settlement, Vol. 7 (Toronto, 1936), p. 380.
30. C.A. Dawson and E.R. Younge, *Pioneering in the Prairie Provinces: The Social Side of the Settlement Process*, Canadian Frontiers of Settlement, Vol. 8 (Toronto, 1940), p. 159.
31. House of Commons, *Debates*, 1929, p. 2738.
32. *The Year Book and Clergy List of the Church of England in the Dominion of Canada, 1930* (Toronto, 1930), p. 38, report of Bishop H.A. Gray, Edmonton.
33. C.C. McLaurin, *Pioneering in Western Canada* (Calgary, 1939), p. 217.

Notes to Chapter Three

1. *Canada Year Book*, 1941, p. 195.
2. R.D. Craig, "The Lumber Industry in Canada," *Canadian Geographical Journal* [*CGJ*], 15, no. 5 (1937), p. 229.
3. A.R.M. Lower, *Settlement and*

the Forest Frontier, Canadian Frontiers of Settlement, Vol. 9 (Toronto, 1936), p. 127.
4. Ontario, Dept. of Lands and Forests, *Annual Report*, 1934, p. 18.

Notes to Chapter Four

1. Ontario, Committee of Inquiry into the Economics of the Gold Mining Industry, 1953, *Gold Mining in Ontario* (Toronto, 1955), p. 12.

2. Dr. E.L. Bruce report cited in M. Zaslow, *Reading the Rocks, the Story of the Geological Survey of Canada, 1842-1972* (Toronto, 1975), pp. 367-68. An earlier, typed version may be found in PAC, RG45 [Geological Survey], Vol. 22, file 176 (1), 2 Nov. 1921.

3. B.J. Young, "C. George McCullagh and the Leadership League," *CHR*, 47, no. 3 (1966), p. 202.

4. *New York Times*, 14 Sept. 1955, p. 49.

5. H.A. Innis, *Settlement and the Mining Frontier*, Canadian Frontiers of Settlement, Vol. 9 (Toronto, 1936), p. 401.

6. J.P. Williamson, *Securities Regulation in Canada* (Toronto, 1960), p. 22.

Notes to Chapter Five

1. Canada, Advisory Committee on Reconstruction, Subcommittee II: Conservation and Development of Natural Resources, *Final Report*, 29 Sept. 1943 (Ottawa, 1944), p. 23.

2. P.H. Godsell, *Arctic Trader* (New York, 1934), pp. 196, 202.

3. Hudson's Bay Company, Annual Meeting, 30 July 1920, *Report*, p. 5.

4. R.M. Anderson, "The Present Status and Future Prospects of the Larger Mammals of Canada," *Scottish Geographical Magazine*, 40, no. 6 (1924), p. 322.

5. Ibid.

6. Alberta, Dept. of Agriculture, *Annual Report*, 1933, p. 47.

7. M.J. and J.L. Robinson, "Fur Production in the Northwest Territories," *CGJ*, 32, no. 1 (1946), pp. 40, 39.

8. Dept. of Indian Affairs, *Annual Report*, 1932-33, p. 7.

9. Bishop G. Breynat, "Canada's Blackest Blot," *Toronto Star Weekly*, 28 May 1938, p. 3.

Reprinted in R. Fumoleau, *As Long as This Land Shall Last* (Toronto, 1973), p. 382.

10. RCMP, *Annual Report*, 1925-26, p. 71.

11. British Columbia, Game Commissioner, *Annual Report*, 1939, p. L-7.

12. C.H.D. Clarke, "Terrestrial Wildlife and Northern Development," in D.H. Pimlott, K.M. Vincent, and C.E. McKnight, eds., *Arctic Alternatives* (Ottawa, 1973), p. 230.

13. Northwest Territories, Tourist Office, *Canada's Northwest Territories* (Ottawa, 1962), p. [16].

14. E.L. Paynter, "Wildlife Trends and Management in Saskatchewan," in Dept. of Northern Affairs and National Resources [NANR], National Parks Branch, *Minutes of the 23rd Federal-Provincial Wildlife Conference, Ottawa June 1959*, p. 49.

15. V.E.F. Solman, "Wildlife

Research in Canada," in NANR, National Parks Branch, *Minutes of the 23rd Federal-Provincial Wildlife Conference*, p. 53.
16. H.F. Lewis, "Wildlife as a Recreational Resource in the Atlantic Provinces," in Canada, Resources for Tomorrow Conference, Montreal, 1961, *Background Papers*, Vol. 2 (Ottawa, 1961), p. 858.

Notes to Chapter Six

1. M.P. Jackson, *On the Last Frontier* (London, 1933), p. 105.
2. L.T. Burwash, *Canada's Western Arctic, Report on Investigations in 1925-26, 1928-29 and 1930* (Ottawa, 1931), p. 67.
3. Louise Rourke, *The Land of the Frozen Tide* (London, [1930]), p. 239.
4. F.H. Kitto, *The Northwest Territories, 1930* (Ottawa, 1930), p. 68, quoting W.H.B. Hoare, "Investigator for the Northwest Territories and Yukon Branch, who has spent many years among them."
5. Bishop G. Breynat, "Canada's Blackest Blot," *Toronto Star Weekly*, 28 May 1938, p. 6.
6. C. Bourget, *Douze Ans Chez les Sauvages* (Ste Anne de Beaupré, 1938), pp. 112-13.
7. G. Breynat, *Cinquante Ans aux Pays de Neiges,* III: *L'Eveque Volant* (Montréal, 1948), p. 74.
8. Ibid., II: *Voyageur du Christ* (Montréal, 1947), pp. 194-95.
9. Canada, North Pacific Planning Project, *Canada's New Northwest* (Ottawa, 1947), p. 17.
10. Dept. of Indian Affairs, *Annual Report*, 1926-27, p. 10.

The same and similar passages occur in earlier annual reports.
11. Ibid., 1919-20, p. 7.
12. Ibid., 1919-20, p. 31, quoting the recent (1918) amendment to the Indian Act adding Sec. 122A.
13. Canada, *Statutes*, 8-9 Geo. V (1918), Chap. 26, Sec. 4 (2).
14. Dept. of Indian Affairs, *Annual Report*, 1919-20, p. 13.
15. Canada, *Statutes*, 20-21 Geo. V (1930), Chap. 25, Sec. 16.
16. *League of Nations Official Journal*, 5, no. 6 (1924), p. 829.
17. Canada, Special Joint Committee of the Senate and House of Commons Appointed to Inquire into the Claims of the Allied Indian Tribes of British Columbia, 1927, *Report and Evidence*, p. x.
18. *Canadian Magazine*, 66, no. 4 (1926), p. 9.
19. W.H. Nevin, "Policing the Far North," *The Beaver*, Outfit 276, no. 3 (1945), p. 9.
20. *Victoria Daily Colonist*, 22 Dec. 1936, p. 2 (T.A. Crerar).
21. House of Commons, *Debates*, 1932, p. 2574 (T.G. Murphy, Neepawa).
22. Dept. of Mines and Resources [M & R], Indian Affairs Branch [IAB], *Annual Report*, 1937-38, p. 190.

Notes to Chapter Seven

1. *Canadian Aviation*, 9, no. 3 (1936), p. 7.
2. F.H. Kitto, *The Northwest Territories, 1930* (Ottawa, 1930), p. 61.
3. RCMP, *Annual Report*, 1930-31, pp. 32-33.
4. L.C. Clark, ed., *Documents on Canadian External Relations, III: 1919-1925* (Ottawa, 1970), p. 582. For this episode, see correspondence in PAC, RG25 [Dept. of External Affairs], D1, Files 318 and 319, and D. Dinwoody, "Arctic Controversy: The 1925 Byrd-MacMillan Expedition Example," CHR, 53, no. 1 (1972), pp. 56-65.
5. A.I. Inglis, ed., *Documents on Canadian External Relations, IV: 1926-1930* (Ottawa, 1971), p. 950.
6. Ibid., pp. 972, 979.

Notes to Chapter Eight

1. D.P. Fitzgerald, "Pioneer Settlement in Northern Saskatchewan," Ph.D. dissertation in Geography, Univ. of Minnesota, 1966, p. 489.
2. House of Commons, *Sessional Papers*, 1940, No. 137, "The Alaska Highway," p. 6.
3. Ibid., p. 9.
4. *Vancouver Province*, 21 Oct. 1941, p. 1.
5. W.G. Carr, *Checkmate in the North* (Toronto, 1944), p. 84.
6. Dept. of External Affairs, *Treaty Series*, 1943, No. 17, p. 4.
7. United States, Senate, *The Canol Project, Hearings . . . 78th Congress, 1st Session, under Senate Resol. 6 (78th Congress), A Resolution Authorizing and Directing an Investigation of the National Defense Program* (Washington, 1944), p. 9294 (sitting at Whitehorse, 11 Sept. 1943).
8. Quoted in *Vancouver Province*, 7 Mar. 1942, p. 2.
9. Ibid., p. 8.
10. *Edmonton Journal*, 4 Dec. 1943, p. 1, quoting Rep. Leon H. Gavin of Pennsylvania.
11. La Guardia to Roosevelt, 28 May 1942, quoted in C.P. Stacey, *Arms, Men and Governments: The War Policies of Canada, 1939-1945* (Ottawa, 1970), p. 375.
12. S.W. Dziuban, *Military Relations between the United States and Canada, 1939-1945*, The United States Army in World War Two, Special Studies (Washington, 1959), p. 193.
13. R.J. Diubaldo, "The Canol Project in Canadian-American Relations," *Canadian Historical Association Historical Papers*, 1977, p. 183.
14. C.R. Nordman, "The Army of Occupation: Malcolm MacDonald and U.S. Military Involvement in the Canadian Northwest," in K. Coates, ed., *The Alaska Highway: Papers of the 40th Anniversary Symposium* (Vancouver, 1985), p. 98.

15. B.H. Kizer, *The U.S.-Canadian Northwest* (Princeton, N.J., 1944), p. 2.
16. J.W. Pickersgill, *The Mackenzie King Record*, Vol. 1 (Toronto, 1960), p. 436.
17. Dept. of External Affairs, *Treaty Series*, 1943, No. 17, p. 4.

18. D. Jenness, *Eskimo Administration: II, Canada*, Arctic Institute of North America, Technical Paper No. 14 (Montreal, 1964), p. 73.
19. M. Bridge, "The Arctic Institute of North America," *CGJ*, 29, no. 6 (1944), p. 275.

Notes to Chapter Nine

1. J.L. Robinson, "Northward by Road and Rail," *The Beaver*, Outfit 285, no. 1 (1954), p. 45.
2. *CAR*, 1964, p. 310.
3. *Canada Year Book*, 1965, p. 22.
4. Saskatchewan, Dept. of Natural Resources, *Annual Report*, 1951-52, p. 168.
5. P. Mathias, *Forced Growth* (Toronto, 1971), p. 102.
6. Ibid., p. vii (Introduction, by A. Rotstein).
7. Canada, Royal Commission on Canada's Economic Prospects, 1955, *Final Report*, 1957, p. 389.
8. Canada, Resources for Tomorrow Conference, Montreal, 1961, *Background Papers*, Vol. 1 (Ottawa, 1961), statement on front cover of volume.
9. P.H. Pearse, "Public Management and Mismanagement of Natural Resources in Canada," *Queen's Quarterly*, 73, no. 1 (1966), p. 98.

Notes to Chapter Ten

1. Saskatchewan, Dept. of Natural Resources, Northern Affairs Branch, *Annual Report*, 1958-59, p. 7.
2. H. Brody, *Maps and Dreams: Indians on the British Columbia Frontier* (Vancouver, 1981), pp. 190-213.
3. P. Godt, "The Canadian Eskimo Co-operative Movement," *Polar Record*, 12, no. 77 (1964), p. 159.
4. Dept. of Citizenship and Immigration [C & I], Indian Affairs Branch [IAB], *Annual Report*, 1956-57, p. 71.
5. Ibid., 1959-60, p. 69.
6. Ibid., 1957-58, p. 78.
7. Ibid., 1959-60, p. 84.
8. Ibid., 1958-59, p. 51.
9. H.B. Hawthorn and M.-A. Tremblay, *A Survey of the Contemporary Indians of Canada*, Vol. 1 (Ottawa, 1966), p. 46.
10. C & I, IAB, *Annual Report*, 1959-60, p. 69.
11. C.C. Hanks, G. Granzberg, and J. Steinbring, "Social Changes and the Mass Media: The Oxford House Cree, 1909-83," *Polar Record*, 21, no. 134 (1983), p. 459.
12. Ibid., p. 460.
13. Hawthorn and Tremblay,

Contemporary Indians, Vol. 1, p. 112.

14. C & I, IAB, *Annual Report*, 1960-61, p. 45.

15. Hawthorn and Tremblay, *Contemporary Indians*, Vol. 1, p. 63.

16. Ibid., p. 166.

17. Ibid., p. 167.

18. Ibid.

19. Ibid., p. 168.

20. V.C. Serl, *An Overview of Provincial Policies, Programs, and Agencies in Northern Saskatchewan*, Economic and Social Survey of Northern Saskatchewan, June 1963 (Regina, 1963), p. 7.

21. Department of Mines and Resources [M & R], Indian Affairs Branch [IAB], *Annual Report*, 1944-45, p. 170.

22. C & I, IAB, *Annual Report*, 1955-56, p. 54.

23. Ibid., 1960-61, p. 45.

24. D. Jenness, *Eskimo Administration: II, Canada*, Arctic Institute of North America, Technical Paper No. 14 (Montreal, 1964), p. 159, fn. 1.

25. G.W. Rowley, "The Canadian Eskimo Today," *Polar Record*, 16, no. 101 (1972), p. 203.

26. Jenness, *Eskimo Administration: II, Canada*, p. 144.

27. L. Black, "Morbidity, Mortality and Medical Care in the Keewatin Area of the Central Arctic – 1967," *Canadian Medical Association Journal*, 101, no. 10 (1969), p. 35.

28. Dept. of National Health and Welfare, *Annual Report*, 1966-67, p. 127.

29. Ibid., 1968-69, p. 121.

30. Canada, Royal Commission on Health Services, 1961, *Report*, Vol. 2 (1965), p. 273.

31. Dept. of Northern Affairs and National Resources [NANR], *Annual Report*, 1961-62, p. 44.

32. NANR, *Government Activities in the North*, 1965, p. 146.

33. T. Yatsushiro, "The Changing Eskimo Economy: Wage Employment and Its Consequences among the Eskimos of Frobisher Bay, Baffin Island, 1960," p. 10. Report prepared for presentation at the annual meetings of the American Anthropological Association in Minneapolis, Nov. 1960, copy in the library of the Arctic Institute of North America, Calgary.

34. Rowley, "Canadian Eskimo Today," p. 203.

35. C & I, IAB, *Annual Report*, 1956-57, p. 49.

36. Ibid., 1954-55, p. 51.

37. Ibid., 1958-59, p. 60.

38. NANR, *Annual Report*, 1954-55, p. 19.

39. R.E. Johns, "History of Administration of Schools, N.W.T.," *The Musk-ox*, no. 18 (1976), p. 50.

40. Dept. of Indian Affairs and Northern Development [IAND], *Annual Report*, 1966-67, p. 25.

41. Hawthorn and Tremblay, *Contemporary Indians*, Vol. 1, p. 209.

42. The quotations in this and the two succeeding paragraphs are derived from Parliament, Special Joint Committee of the Senate and House of Commons on the Indian Act, *Fourth Report* (22 June 1948), pp. 187-88.

43. House of Commons, *Debates*, 1949 (Second Session), p. 2285.

44. Ibid.
45. Ibid., p. 2290.
46. Ibid., pp. 2288, 2298.
47. Hawthorn and Tremblay, *Contemporary Indians*, Vol. 1, p. 61.

48. NANR, *Annual Report*, 1954-55, p. 17.
49. S. Weaver, *Making Canadian Indian Policy: The Hidden Agenda, 1968-1970* (Toronto, 1981), p. 15.
50. Ibid., p. 28.

Notes to Chapter Eleven

1. G.W. Rowley, "Northern Canada Today," in M. Zaslow, ed., *A Century of Canada's Arctic Islands, 1880-1980* (Ottawa, 1981), p. 304.
2. Department of Northern Affairs and National Resources [NANR], *Annual Report*, 1954-55, p. 20.
3. Ibid., 1955-56, p. 25.
4. NANR, *The Northwest Territories Today*, revised edition (Ottawa, 1965), p. 81.
5. Ibid.
6. P.F. Cooper, Jr., "Application of Modern Technology in an Arctic Environment," *Polar Record*, 14, no. 89 (1968), p. 144.
7. J.T. Wilson, "Exercise Muskox, 1946," *Polar Record*, 5, no. 33-34 (1947), p. 24.
8. F.H. Soward, *Canada in World Affairs,* IV: *1944-1946* (Toronto, 1950), p. 273, quoting *Financial Post*, 29 June 1946.
9. Statement of C.D. Howe on the proposed establishment of weather stations in the Arctic, 4 March 1947, in R.A. MacKay, ed., *Canadian Foreign Policy 1945-1954: Selected Speeches and Documents* (Toronto, 1970), p. 236.
10. R.B. Wybou, "The DEW Line," *The Roundel*, 12, no. 4 (1960), p. 6.
11. D.F. Pelly, "The DEW Line, a Journalist's Visit to Military Isolation Posts," *North*, 29, no. 1 (1982), p. 18.
12. D.E. Rodger, "A Week at Fox Bravo DEW Line Station," ibid., p. 49.
13. J.R.K. Main, *Voyageurs of the Air* (Ottawa, 1967), p. 230.
14. H. LaFay, "Dew Line," *National Geographic Magazine*, 114, no. 1 (1958), p. 146.
15. E. Cowan, "Good-doing Won't Replace Traplines," *Globe Magazine*, 18 Jan. 1969, p. 8.

Notes to Chapter Twelve

1. P.G. Nixon, "Eskimo Housing Programmes, 1954-1965: A Case Study in Representative Bureaucracy," Ph.D. dissertation, Political Science, Univ. of Western Ontario, 1984, p. 171.
2. W.A. Kupsch, ed., *Proceedings of the First National Northern Research Conference, Saskatoon, Oct. 30-31, 1967* (Saskatoon, 1967), p. 69.
3. Canada, Royal Commission on

Government   Organization,
1960, *Report*, Vol. 4 (Ottawa,
1963), p. 172.

4. Ibid., p. 171.

5. Blair Fraser, "Our Double
Image of the North," *Maclean's
Magazine*, 77, no. 20 (Oct. 17,
1964), pp. 17, 79, reprinted in J.
Fraser and G. Fraser, eds., *Blair
Fraser Reports, Selections 1944-
1968* (Toronto, 1969), pp. 289-
90.

6. *Whitehorse Star*, 23 Sept.
1963.

7. Ibid., 29 Aug. 1963.

8. *Edmonton Journal*, 18 Sept.
1963, p. 12.

9. *Whitehorse Star*, 23 Sept.
1963.

10. *Edmonton Journal*, 11 Jan.
1964, p. 29.

11. *Whitehorse Star*, 7 Oct.
1964.

12. R.J. Sutherland, "The Strategic Significance of the Canadian Arctic," in R. St. J.
MacDonald, ed., *The Arctic
Frontier* (Toronto, 1966), p.
275.

13. Dept. of National Defence,
*The White Paper on Defence,
March 1964* (Ottawa, 1964), p.
13.

14. Royal Commission on Government Organization, *Report*,
Vol. 4, p. 174.

15. Government of Yukon Territory, *Public Accounts*, 1966-
67, p. 3.

16. House   of   Commons,
Debates, 1962-63, p. 7.

17. Canada, Commission Appointed to Investigate the Unfulfilled
Provision of Treaties 8 and 11
as They Apply to the Indians of
the Mackenzie District, *Report*,
1959 (as reprinted by Indian-
Eskimo Association of Canada,
1970), p. 4.

18. Ibid.

19. Department of Northern
Affairs and National Resources
[NANR], *Government Activities
in the North*, 1964, p. 122.

20. NANR, Commissioner of
Northwest Territories, *Annual
Report*, 1965-66, p. 7.

21. *Whitehorse Star*, 7 Dec.
1964, quoting John Watt,
Whitehorse West.

22. NANR, Commissioner of NWT,
Annual Report, 1964-65, p. 9.

23. Canada, Advisory Commission on the Development of
Government in the Northwest
Territories, 1965, *Report*, Vol.
1, 1966, pp. 159, 161.

24. Department of Indian Affairs
and   Northern   Development
[IAND], Commissioner of Northwest   Territories,   *Annual
Report*, 1967-68, p. 5.

Bibliographical Note

Because this book is concerned with the fairly recent past and with general trends more than with individuals, the sources that were consulted in preparing it were mainly government publications, newspapers, periodicals, specialized studies, and only to a lesser degree archival materials. The wide range of government publications used included the annual reports of the principal federal departments concerned with northern administration: Interior, Indian Affairs, RCMP, Citizenship and Immigration, National Health and Welfare, National Defence, Transport, External Affairs, Mines and Resources, Resources and Development, Northern Affairs and National Resources, and Indian Affairs and Northern Development. The debates and journals of the House of Commons and Senate and some of the reports of their standing committees were consulted, in addition to the reports and commissioned studies of several royal commissions: Dominion-Provincial Relations (1940), Canada's Economic Prospects (1957), Energy (1959), Government Organization (1962–63), Health Services (1964–65), and Government of the Northwest Territories (1966). So, too, were the special publications of certain agencies such as the Dominion Bureau of Statistics (*Canada Year Book* and annual reports on particular topics), the *Treaty Series* of the Department of External Affairs, the many reports issued by the Northern Co-ordination and Research Centre [NCRC], and two or three special studies of the Science Council of Canada. A number of histories of federal government agencies were also useful, notably those on surveying and mapping, geological surveying, the coast guard, civil air transport, and grain marketing. Provincial and territorial governments' reports and special publications consulted included the annual reports of agencies and departments that grant and administer resources, and of public works, municipal affairs, education, health and welfare, and northern administration. Reliance on these government publications has limitations as well as merits. They are generally very accurate, and at the same time their point of view is obvious enough that it can easily be discounted. But they also tend to avoid controversial or inconvenient matters, which must therefore be sought elsewhere – in archives that may supply material left out of the published versions or in sources outside government altogether. Because annual reports are based on fiscal rather than calendar years it is sometimes uncertain whether a particular incident occurred in one year or the next. Unfortunately, in recent times reports have been purposely kept so vague and general and have been turned into such public relations exercises that their value is sharply reduced for researchers. Many agencies overcome this trend by publishing more detailed reports directed at serious users. One such example, particularly valuable for this volume, was the NCRC's *Government Activities in the North*, issued annually after 1953.

The newspapers examined for periods of one to thirty years include the *Globe and Mail*, *Financial Post*, *London Free Press*, *Edmonton Journal*, *Calgary Herald*, *Ottawa Citizen*, and for shorter periods as they came to hand, the *Montreal Gazette*, *Winnipeg Free Press*, *Victoria Colonist*, and others. Northern newspapers, each followed for long periods, included the *Whitehorse Star*, *News of the North* (Yellowknife), *Peace River Record*, *Peace River Block News* (Dawson Creek), and *Le Progrès du Saguenay* (Chicoutimi). A useful source for the twenties was the little-known *Natural Resources Canada*, a four-page monthly published for a dozen years by the Natural Resources Intelligence Branch of the Department of the Interior. By subscribing to several journals and the magazines *Maclean's* and *Saturday Night* and casting a wide subjects net, I was able to collect tens of thousands of news items and some hundreds of feature pieces that outlined the topics treated in this volume in somewhat the way iron filings delineate the shape of a magnet and its force field. Clippings and notes sorted by subjects and reviewed in chronological fashion afford a panorama of how events unfolded, an excellent way to study history in the making and a good basis for writing history "as it really happened." Of course, information based on a source of this kind must be carefully checked for accuracy and for possible bias on the part of reporters or editors. But contemporary feature pieces are unrivalled in providing lively, often perceptive, eyewitness accounts that can hardly be matched by other sources.

Periodicals also were sometimes sources of news items, but more especially they offered articles whose value for research purposes varied according to their scholarly goals. Those used for both purposes included *Polar Record*, *Arctic*, *Musk-Ox*, *Arctic Circular*, and *North/Nord*, and for occasional articles the *Canadian Historical Review*, *Canadian Historical Association Historical Papers*, the quarterlies of the various provincial historical societies, *The Beaver*, *Canadian Journal of Economics and Political Science* and its successors, *International Journal*, *Canadian Geographer*, *Canadian Geographical Journal*, and *National Geographic*. A number of trade publications such as *Canadian Transportation*, *Canadian Aviation*, *Canadian*

Forestry, Northern Miner, Forces (Hydro-Québec), *Imperial Oil Review*, and *Roundel* also were consulted.

Even more useful for many topics were the two or threescore unpublished theses in several academic disciplines I encountered in departmental and university libraries but more especially at the Institute of Northern Studies (University of Saskatchewan), the Boreal Institute (University of Alberta), the Arctic Institute of North America [AINA] (now at the University of Calgary), and the Northern Affairs Library (Ottawa/Hull), which hold sizeable collections of theses on northern subjects. Other unpublished manuscripts include "Geography and Administration of Canada's Northlands" by Trevor Lloyd (at the Canadian Institute of International Affairs [CIIA] library), the "Encyclopedia Arctica" at the AINA library, and a dozen or so book manuscripts (some of them still unpublished) that I was privileged to read. These are particularly good sources for my researches because of the authors' care, accuracy, and objectivity and the insights with which they were written.

Reliance on these essentially secondary materials does not mean that primary sources were overlooked. Indeed, these were used extensively for most of the chapters down to 1945. I spent many days at the Public Archives of Canada examining files in the MG9 and 26 Manuscript Groups and the RG7, 15, 25, 45, 85, and 91 Record Groups, including prime ministers' and governors' general correspondence, minutes of the Northwest Territories Council, and files relating to associations and individuals collected by the Northern Affairs Branch (under various titles) and the Indian Affairs, RCMP, and Interior departments. Similar collections were examined at the public archives of British Columbia, Yukon, and Northwest Territories, among others, and university libraries across Canada from Memorial University to the University of British Columbia; at the Scott Polar Research Institute (Cambridge), Dartmouth College (Stefansson Collection), Glenbow Foundation (Calgary); in Washington, D.C. (for narrative histories of the U.S. Army units in the Canadian North during the Second World War); and in London (for the Church Missionary Society Archives, now transferred to the University of Birmingham, and for the Public Record Office at Kew).

The particular sources used for the chapters on the industrial frontiers (2, 3, 4, and 9) included reports of pertinent federal and provincial government departments and their special studies, the *Canada Year Book* and other DBS reports, annuals such as the *Statistical Year Book of Quebec/Annuaire de Québec, Mining in Canada*, articles from periodicals and journals, news notes and clippings from the newspapers listed, and the volumes of the *Canadian Annual Review*. Particularly helpful for the period between the wars were volumes of the Canadian Frontiers of Settlement Series by C.A. Dawson, W.A. Mackintosh, R.W. Murchie, A.R.M. Lower, and H.A. Innis. Other general monographs included Pierre Biays, *Marges de l'oekoumène dans l'est du Canada* (Québec, 1964), and J. Lewis Robinson, *Resources of the Canadian Shield* (Toronto, 1969). Those for the specific frontiers included Robert England, *The Colonization of Western Canada* (London, 1936), and Mary P. Jackson, *On the Last Frontier* (London, 1933), for agriculture; Arnold D. Hoffman, *Free Gold* (Toronto, 1955), and Eric J. Hanson, *Dynamic Decade* (Toronto, 1958), for mining; Carl Wiegman, *Trees to News* (Toronto, 1953), and R.S. Lambert and Paul Pross, *Renewing Nature's Wealth* (Toronto, 1967), on forestry; J.H. Dales, *Hydroelectricity and Industrial Development: Quebec, 1895–1940* (Cambridge, Mass., 1957), and Merrill Denison, *The People's Power* (Toronto, 1960), for hydro-power; George R. Stevens, *Canadian National Railways*, II: *1896–1922* (Toronto, 1962), Robert F. Legget, *Railroads of Canada* (New York, 1973), Frank H. Ellis, *Canada's Flying Heritage* (Toronto, 1961), Walter E. Gilbert and K. Shackleton, *Arctic Pilot* (London, New York, 1942), and J.R.K. Main, *Voyageurs of the Air* (Ottawa, 1967), for transportation. Works that focused on specific regions include the agricultural, forestry, and mining volumes of Esdras Minville's "Etudes sur notre milieu" (Montréal, 1942–46), P.-Y. Pepin, *Le Royaume du Saguenay en 1968* (Ottawa, 1969), William L. Morton, *Manitoba, A History* (Toronto, 1957), Margaret A. Ormsby, *British Columbia, A History* (Toronto, 1958), H. Vivian Nelles, *The Politics of Development* (Toronto, 1974), Robert Rumilly, *Histoire de la province de Québec*, volumes 25 to 37 (Montréal and Ottawa, between 1940 and 1968), and Peter N. Oliver, *G. Howard Ferguson* (Toronto, 1977). For the period since 1945 one should add the monthly reports of the Bank of Nova Scotia during the 1950s, Paddy Sherman, *Bennett* (Toronto, 1966), Philip Mathias, *Forced Growth* (Toronto, 1977), and Rex A. Lucas, *Minetown, Milltown, Railtown* (Toronto, 1971), representing the several works on the single-industry community so characteristic of resource development in Northern Canada.

The main books consulted for the military history sections included Stanley W. Dziuban, *Military Relations between the United States and Canada, 1939–1945* (Washington, 1959), and other volumes of the series The United States Army in World War Two; Charles P. Stacey, *Arms, Men and Governments* (Ottawa, 1970); Kenneth Coates, ed., *The Alaska Highway: Papers* . . . (Vancouver, 1985); Gertrude Baskine, *Hitch-Hiking the Alaska Highway* (Toronto, 1944); Richard Finnie, *Canol* (San Francisco, 1945); and for the period since the Second

World War, Melvin Conant, *The Long Polar Watch* (New York, 1962), James Eayrs, *In Defence of Canada*, Vol. III: *Peacemaking and Deterrence* (Toronto, 1972), and the several biennial volumes of *Canada in World Affairs* by various authors, published by the CIIA.

For the chapters on the wildlife industries and the native peoples (5, 6, and 10), the works used were the *Background Papers* (four volumes) for the Resources for Tomorrow Conference, Montreal, 1961 (Ottawa, 1961–62), Janet Foster, *Working for Wildlife* (Toronto, 1978), C. Gordon Hewitt, *The Conservation of the Wildlife of Canada* (New York, 1921), Roderick L. Haig-Brown, *The Living Land* (Toronto, 1961), Anthony D. Scott, *Natural Resources: The Economics of Conservation* (Toronto, 1954), and on the modern fur trade, Philip H. Godsell, *Arctic Trader* (New York, 1934), James W. Anderson, *Fur Trader's Story* (Toronto, 1961), and Duncan Pryde, *Nunaga* (New York, 1971).

A vast literature on the native peoples of the North has grown up in the past thirty years. The main sources used for this history included Diamond Jenness, *Eskimo Administration, II: Canada, III: Labrador*, and *V: Analysis and Reflections* (Montreal, 1962–68), in addition to his *The Indians of Canada*, 1955 edition, Ottawa, and Henry B. Hawthorn and Marc-Adélard Tremblay, *A Survey of the Contemporary Indians of Canada*, 2 vols. (Ottawa, 1966–67). Other works that should be singled out are Sally M. Weaver, *Making Canadian Indian Policy . . . 1968–1970* (Toronto, 1981); R.G. Moyles, *British Law and Arctic Men* (Saskatoon, 1975); René Fumoleau, *As Long As This Land Shall Last* (Toronto, 1967); a trio by Hugh Brody: *Indians on Skid Row* (Ottawa, 1971), *The People's Land* (Harmondsworth, 1975), and *Maps and Dreams* (Vancouver, 1981); Richard Slobodin, *Metis of the Mackenzie District* (Ottawa, 1966); Heather Robertson, *Reservations Are for Indians* (Toronto, 1970); and Minnie A. Freeman, *Life Among the Qallunaat* (Edmonton, 1978).

A very selective list of the many biographical, travel, and other books on the Canadian North that went into the making of the chapters on the Yukon and Northwest Territories (1, 7, 11, and 12) includes Vilhjalmur Stefansson, *Discovery* (New York, 1964), Richard J. Diubaldo, *Stefansson and the Canadian North* (Montreal, 1978), George Whalley, *The Legend of John Hornby* (Toronto, 1962), Knud J.V. Rasmussen, *Across Arctic America* (New York, London, 1927), Helge M. Ingstad, *The Land of Feast and Famine* (New York, 1933), Richard Finnie, *Lure of the North* (Philadelphia, 1940), Erik Munsterhjelm, *Fool's Gold* (Toronto, 1957), Edgar Laytha, *North Again for Gold* (New York, 1939), Archibald L. Fleming, *Archibald the Arctic* (New York, 1956), Gabriel J.E. Breynat, *Cinquante ans au pays de neiges*, 3 vols. (Montréal, 1945–48), William R. Morrison, *Showing the Flag: The Mounted Police and Canadian Sovereignty* . . . (Vancouver, 1985), Harwood Steele, *Policing the Arctic* (Toronto, 1935), Ernie Lyall, *An Arctic Man* (Edmonton, 1979), Dudley Copland, *Livingstone of the Arctic* (Ottawa, 1967), and Jack H. Sissons, *Judge of the Far North* (Toronto, 1968). More general works include Louis-Edmond Hamelin, *Canadian Nordicity* (Montreal, 1979), William C. Wonders, ed., *Canada's Changing North* (Toronto, 1971), Kenneth J. Rea, *The Political Economy of the Canadian North* (Toronto, 1968), Morris Zaslow, ed., *A Century of Canada's Arctic Islands* (Ottawa, 1981), Carl A. Dawson, ed., *The New North-West* (Toronto, 1947), Richard Finnie, *Canada Moves North* (Toronto, 1948), Robert A.J. Phillips, *Canada's North* (Toronto, 1967), Jim R. Lotz, *Northern Realities* (Toronto, 1970), and Terence E. Armstrong, Graham W. Rowley, and George Rogers, *The Circumpolar North* (London, New York, 1978). On international relations there are Lovell C. Clark, ed., *Documents on Canadian External Relations*, III: *1919–1925* (Ottawa, 1970), and in the same series, Alex I. Inglis, IV: *1926–30* (Ottawa, 1971), Donat Pharand, *The Law of the Sea of the Arctic* (Ottawa, 1973), Ronald S. Macdonald, ed., *The Arctic Frontier* (Toronto, 1966), and Edgar J. Dosman, ed., *The Arctic in Question* (Toronto, 1976).

Index

Abasand Oils Co., 112, 205
Abitibi district, Que., 5, 45, 54, 56, 78, 81, 95, 98, 100, 118, 122, 154, 250, 285
Abitibi Power and Paper Co., 79, 82, 84, 85, 91, 98, 234, 245
Abitibi River, 91, 95, 247; Canyon, 84, 91, 93, 96
Advisory Board on Wildlife Protection, 11, 13, 143
Advisory Comm. on Development of Government in N.W.T., *see* Carrothers Commission
Advisory Technical Board on Canadian Sovereignty, 17–18
Aero Timber Products Co., 205
Agriculture, 31–69, 249–50; natural conditions for, 34–35, 38, 41; surveys and squatters, 36–37, 53; incentives to settlers, 31, 35–36, 38–41, 44, 52, 55, 249–50; farm development, 31, 35–37, 43–46, 48, 59–60; settlement, 5, 31, 34–36, 43–46, 47–50, 52–59, 151, 203, 249–50; abandonment and relocation, 44, 46, 48, 52–53, 56, 57, 60, 208, 250; farm produce: wheat culture, 42, 46, 48–49, 208; seed-growing, 41, 49; mixed farming, 35, 41, 42, 46–48, 54, 55, 207–8; non-farm income, 34, 95, 132, 244; markets and prices, 41, 43–44, 46–48, 52, 54, 207–8; mechanization, 5, 42–43, 46, 48, 60, 249; transportation, 37–39, 54; organizations, 39, 50, 60–61, 69; wheat pools, 61; research and training, 34, 35, 42, 47; social aspects: group settlements, 49, 60–62; local government, 63–64; education, 62, 64–66; health services, 66–67; and religion, 61–62, 67–69; language questions, 62, 68; civilizing role of, 69, 368–

69; impact of, 69, 151
Aguasabon River, 93
Aircraft, 23, 236; advances in, 104; types of, 23, 74, 104, 105, 325, 327, 328, 353, 354
Air services, 74, 86, 236, 248; airmail, 105, 122, 177, 180, 184, 212; air photography, 74–75, 104, 236, 313–14. *See also* Aviation
Aklavik, N.W.T., 156–57, 159, 176–77, 184, 194–95, 198, 317, 319
Alaska, 9, 14, 23, 145, 201, 211, 215–19, 221–23, 225, 229, 354; Railroad, 175
Albany River, 93, 114
Alberta, 9, 143, 225, 285; agriculture, 37, 48, 58, 60, 249; forestry, 77, 245; oil and natural gas, 112, 260, 265–66; railways, 9, 23, 38, 184, 260; highways, 38, 195, 253; frontier health service, 66; Métis rehabilitation, 170–71; interest in Mackenzie district, 191
Alberta and Arctic Transportation System, 136, 138
Alberta Research Council, 37
Alberta Resources Railway, 260
Albright, W.D., 34
Alert, N.W.T., 325, 327, 330, 354
Alert Bay, B.C., 162
Aleutian Islands, 221, 222
Alexander hydro development, 92
Algoma Steel Corp., 92, 116
Alikomiak, 12
Allied Indian Tribes of British Columbia, 165
Alma, Que., 89
Alsib Movement, 223
Aluminium Co. of Canada (Alcan), 89, 96, 112, 203, 239
Aluminum, production of, 89, 96, 112, 203, 239
Aluminum Co. of America, 89

Canada (cont.)

Northern Affairs and National
Resources, 304, 309, 311, 334,
335, 336, 339, 355; activities on
behalf of Inuit, 273, 275–76,
284, 301, 305
Public Works, 195, 312, 315, 318,
343, 354, 355
Railways and Canals, 176
Resources and Development, 301,
309
Trade and Commerce, 336
Transport, 195, 213, 223, 248,
312, 315, 335, 336, 342, 354,
355
Agencies, Bureaus, and Services:
Astronomical Service, 314; Canadian Radio Broadcasting Comm.,
187; Canadian Wildlife Service,
140, 147, 150, 313, 350; Domin-
ion Lands Agencies, 40, 48–49;
Dominion Experimental Farms,
34; Dominion Forest Service,
309, 313; Dominion Observatory,
313, 314; Dominion Water and
Power Bureau, 313; Indian Health
Service, 287; National Employ-
ment Service, 279; Northern
Health Service, 286–88, 297, 299,
301; Unemployment Insurance
Comm., 279
Boards: Canadian Air, 23, 74;
Canadian Wheat, 46; Defence
Research (DRB), 349, 355; National
Advisory, 201; National Energy,
266
Branches: Civil Aviation, 105, 212;
Development Services, 309;
Dominion Parks (later National),
26, 29, 344; Land Settlement, 52;
Lands, Parks and Forests, 308,
309; Meteorological, 342; Mines
and Geology, 213, 309; Mining
Land and Yukon, 25; National
Historic Sites, 344; Northwest
Territories, 24–26; Surveys and
Engineering, 309. See also Indian
Affairs Branch, Northern Admin-
istration Branch
Corporations: Canada Develop-
ment, 265; Canadian Broadcast-
ing, 342; Central Mortgage and

Canada (cont.)

Housing (CMHC), 261, 319, 343;
Crown Assets Disposal, 354
Crown corporations, 205, 240,
251
Canada Power and Paper Co., 82, 84
Canada Tungsten Co., 346
Canadian Airways, 105, 106, 107,
184
Canadian Arctic Expedition (1913–
18), 9, 15–16
Canadian Arctic Producers Ltd., 278
Canadian Assoc. in Support of
Native Peoples, 303
Canadian Car and Foundry Co., 4
Canadian Eskimo Art Comm., 276
Canadian Forestry Corps, 3
Canadian Handicrafts Guild, 171,
275
Canadian International Paper Co.,
82, 83, 84, 88, 90
Canadian National Railways (CNR),
38, 59; branch lines, 78, 110,
122, 215, 239–40, 247, 253, 260,
341
Canadian National Telecommunica-
tions (CNT), 342, 355
Canadian Northern Railway, 9, 77,
122
Canadian Pacific Air Lines, 105, 223
Canadian Pacific Railway (CPR), 38,
52, 71, 349, 367
Canadian Shield, 34, 86, 101, 102,
105, 123, 180, 241
Canadian snowshoe rabbit inquiries,
140
Canalaska Trading Co., 136, 137
Canol Project, 217–19, 222, 225,
226, 229, 315, 320
Cape Dorset, N.W.T., 159, 287
Cape Dyer, N.W.T., 326
Cape Perry, N.W.T., 326
Carcross, Y.T., 219, 293
Cariboo district, B.C., 114, 123
Caribou, 10, 34, 142, 143, 144, 272,
274, 313
Carr, Emily, 167
Carrot River, 48
Carrothers, A.W.R., 364
Carrothers Commission, 363–65
Carter, F.A.G., 335
Cassiar Asbestos Co., 347

Negus Gold Mine Co., 182, 186,
320–21
Nelson, W.H., and commission on
Indian reserves question, 360
Nelson River, 91, 255
Ness, John, 28
New Aklavik, *see* Inuvik
New Brunswick, 207
Newfoundland, 79, 213, 214, 237,
256; leased bases, 213–14
New Helen Iron Mine, 116
New Imperial Mines Co., 347
New Liskeard, Ont., 42
Newsprint Assoc. of Canada, 83, 85
New Westminster, B.C., 71
New York, 8, 83, 109, 132
New York News, 79
New York Times, 81, 222
Niagara Falls, Ont., 93; district, 6
Nielsen, Erik, 361, 363
Nipigon River, 92, 96
Nipissing Mining Co., 115, 116, 180
Noranda, Que., 109
Noranda Mines Co., 111–12, 118,
124, 349
Norman Dam, 91
Norman Wells, N.W.T., 102, 182,
185, 187, 217, 218, 219, 222,
228, 229, 243, 320, 322, 324
North American Air Defence Com-
mand (NORAD), 337
North Atlantic Treaty Organization
(NATO), 355
North Bay, Ont., 44, 148, 277, 337
Northern Administration Branch/
Division, 301, 304–5, 316–17,
318, 338, 339, 357, 361, 365;
educational activities, 282, 295–
97, 357; native peoples programs,
272, 274, 277, 280, 284–85,
286–87, 301, 302–3, 311; housing programs, 290–91, 334, 343;
and co-operatives, 277–78; community programs, 318–20, 330;
structural changes in, 308–10,
335–36, 340
Northern Aerial Mineral Exploration
Co. (NAME), 105, 107, 180
Northern Alberta Railways (NAR), 38,
184, 248
Northern British Columbia Power
Co., 91

Northern Canada Power Comm.
(NCPC), 316, 342–43
Northern Construction Co., 326
Northern development: and natural
resource industries, 69, 96–97,
100, 117–18, 128–29, 236–37,
238, 251, 343–44, 367–70; focus
of Canadian interest, 233, 306,
332, 372. *See also* Northern
Vision
Northern Development Loan Fund,
343
Northern Messenger Service, 187
Northern Miner, 181
Northern Ontario Properties Agree-
ment Act, 93
Northern Traders Co., 136
Northern Trading Co., 9, 138
Northern Transportation Co., 122,
181, 183, 206, 226, 315, 328,
336, 342
Northern Vision, 253, 332–34, 338,
339, 345, 348, 350
North Pacific Planning Project, 157–
58, 171, 225, 232, 267, 312
North Pole, 19, 201, 352; Magnetic,
313, 325
North Vancouver, B.C., 248
North Water Project, 350
Northwest Company, 22
North-West Passage, 231
North-West Staging Route (NWSR),
212–13, 215, 219, 222–23, 227,
228
Northwest Territories: administration of, 22–26, 28–29; wildlife
industries in, 9–11, 130–39 *passim*, 141–46, 190; fishery in,
147–48, 323; mining, oil, and gas
in, 22–23, 28, 180–83, 206, 226,
241, 243, 320–23, 343–44, 345–
46, 348–49; hydro development
in, 316, 342–43; transportation,
9, 23–24, 177–80, 183–85, 195,
219, 220–21, 228, 231, 248, 253,
315–16, 327–28, 340–42; modern settlers and communities,
172, 176–77, 185–88, 229, 318–
20, 329–30, 343, 347, 355; native
peoples, 26–28, 151, 152, 153,
154, 232, 272, 308, 320, 329–31,
359–61; proposal to divide, 358,

Rogers, Will, 166
Rohmer, Richard, 267–68
Roman Catholic church, 67–69, 157, 159
Romanet, Louis, 3
Roosevelt, Capt. Elliott, 214
Ross, Sir George, 58
Ross River district, 315, 339, 340, 345, 347
Rouvière, Father J.B., 159
Rouyn, Que., 106, 107, 113, 114, 117, 118, 122, 126; Township, 111
Rowatt, H.H., 25
Rowley, Graham, 286, 292
Royal Air Force, 221
Royal Canadian Air Force (RCAF), 75, 213, 214, 220, 313, 314, 324, 327, 329, 349, 354; Air Transport Command, 327; Northwest Air Command, 223
Royal Canadian Corps of Signals (RCCS), 176, 185, 186, 187, 194, 195, 223
Royal Canadian Mounted Police (RCMP), 21, 25, 29, 135, 154–56, 336; northern posts and detachments, 16, 17, 18, 20, 25, 29, 132, 154, 176, 185–86, 192–93, 198, 200, 201, 202, 230, 231, 327; northern duties, 12, 26, 147, 155–56, 169–70, 192–94, 196, 197–98, 201–2, 226, 231, 272; and Arctic sovereignty, 20–21, 201–2; relations with native peoples, 132, 155, 156, 163, 164, 166; under contract to Territorial councils, 357, 361, 362
Royal Flying Corps, 104
Royal Geographical Society, 20
Royal Naval Assoc., 47
Royal Northwest Mounted Police (RNWMP), 10, 22
Rudnicki, Walter, 335
Rupert House, Que., 279
Rupert River, 115, 146
Rupert's Land, Anglican Archdiocese of, 159
Ryan, Mickey, 9
Ryan, Patrick, 9

Sabellum Trading Co., 10

Saguenay district, 45, 54, 80, 81, 89, 203–5
Saguenay-Lac St Jean area, 71, 79, 88, 96, 250
Saguenay Power Co., 89
Saguenay River, 245
Ste Anne de la Pocatière, Que., 55
St. Elias Mountains, 217, 344
St Félicien, Que., 107, 247
St Hyacinthe, Que., 42
St. John's, Nfld., 213
St. Laurent, Louis S., 298
St. Lawrence Corp., 82
St. Lawrence River, 367; lower, 59, 94, 97; basin, 86. See also Quebec North Shore
St. Lawrence Seaway, 239, 247
St. Maurice Lumber Co., 80
St Maurice River, 4, 45, 79, 81; district, 71, 82, 88, 89
Sale, Charles, 137
Salmon River, B.C., 112
Salt River settlement, Alta., 169
Salvation Army, 47
San Antonio Gold Mine, 114
Sandys Wunsch, T.V., 155
Saskatchewan: and First World War, 4; agriculture, 38, 40, 41, 48, 59, 60; aids to settlers, 53–54; forestry, 55, 259; hydro development, 91, 110, 255; prospecting and mining, 106, 107, 114, 241, 242; wildlife and trapping, 132, 149–50; Indians, 151–52, 154, 155, 271, 273, 276–77; and Second World War, 208; northern development, 249, 252, 253, 258–59, 267; administrations, CCF, 258–59, 267, 276–77; Liberal, 251, 259; Crown corporations, 258; Fur Marketing Service, 276; Northern Administration District, 258; Northern Affairs Branch, 258; Northern Settlers Re-Establishment Branch, 54; Rehabilitation Branch, 54
Saskatchewan Liquor Comm., 196
Saskatchewan Power Comm., 255
Saskatchewan River, 59, 71, 255; estuary, 146; North, 38
Saskatchewan Timber Board, 259
Sault Ste Marie, Ont., 3, 4, 71, 74,

Timmins, Jules, 237
Timmins family, 113, 125
Timmins, Ont., 91, 115, 120, 206, 244
Torbay, Nfld., 213, 214
Torch River, 48
Toronto, 1, 86, 88, 118, 123–24; and mining industry, 109, 123–24, 126–27, 181, 182; stock exchanges, 113, 126–27, 182
Toronto Stock Exchange, 126–27
Tourism, 150, 166–67, 175, 193, 273–74, 344–45; tourist-hunters, 141, 149, 150, 274, 344
Tractor trains, introduction of, 87, 96, 184–85
Trail, B.C., 341
Transair Air Lines, 328
Trans-Canada Pipe Lines Co., 266
Transpolar flights, 325, 327
Transportation, see under modes of, industries, and regions
Treadwell Yukon Mining Co., 175
Tree River, N.W.T., 10, 12
Trelle, Herman, 48
Trois-Rivières, Que., 80, 82, 90
Tuktoyaktuk, N.W.T., 138, 159, 296, 312, 319, 328, 329, 342
Tundra Gold Mines Co., 346
Tungsten, N.W.T., 340
Tununuk Point, N.W.T., 345
Turquetil, Father Arsène, 159
Twin Falls, Nfld., 238
Twin Falls, N.W.T., 342
Twin Falls, Ont., 91
Tyrrell, Edith, 1
Tyrrell, Joseph, 1

Uluksuk, 12
Ungava Bay, 238; district, 277
Uniate Church, 68
Union Catholique des Cultivateurs (UCC), 61
Union of Soviet Socialist Republics (USSR), 215, 223, 267, 325, 351, 352, 353, 367, 373–74
United Air Transport, 107, 223
United Brotherhood of Carpenters and Joiners of America (AFL), 98
United Church of Canada, 47, 68
United Farmers of Alberta, 50

United Keno Hill Mines, 125, 321, 346, 347
United Nations, 267
United States, 45, 127, 216, 304, 361; expansion contrasted with Canada's, 370–71; and Canadian industries: investment, 6, 79–80, 81, 82, 88, 89, 109–10, 124–25, 127, 237–38, 250, 263–65; as market, 6, 8, 78–81, 83, 87, 110, 113, 125, 128, 236, 239, 240–41, 252, 265–66; Canadian promotions in U.S., 127; part in St. Lawrence Seaway, 239; and Arctic exploration, 12, 200–1; and Arctic sovereignty, 200–21, 352–53; Second World War military involvements with Canada: 209–27 passim, 229; military agreements with Canada, 216, 225–27; Alaska Highway Commission, 211–12; Joint Economic Committees, 225; Canol Project, 217–19, 221–22; expenditures, 215, 219, 221, 228, 230, 233; Senate Subcommittee Investigating the United States National Defense Program (Truman Committee), 216, 218; post-1945 military involvements with Northern Canada, 324–30 passim, 337, 351–53; impact of involvements on Canada, 327–30, 352–54, 371 (see also Joint Air Weather Stations, Radar, Distant Early Warning Line, Strategic Air Command); Lend Lease Act, 83; National Recovery Act (NRA), 83; Treasury Department, 113, 243; Navy Department, 200–1, 215; War Department, 212, 215; Army Air Force, 23; Securities and Exchange Commission, 127; Atomic Energy Commission, 241, 251; Office of Naval Research, 349
United States Steel Corp., 238
University of Saskatchewan, 335
University of Toronto, 20
Uranium City, Sask., 241, 249, 252, 253
Uranium oxide, 236; industry, 237, 240–42, 251–52, 320, 321

THE CANADIAN CENTENARY SERIES

A History of Canada in Nineteen Volumes

The Canadian Centenary Series is a comprehensive history of the peoples and lands which form the Dominion of Canada.

Although the series is designed as a unified whole so that no part of the story is left untold, each volume is complete in itself. Written for the general reader as well as for the scholar, each of the nineteen volumes of *The Canadian Centenary Series* is the work of a leading Canadian historian who is an authority on the period covered in his volume. Their combined efforts have made a new and significant contribution to the understanding of the history of Canada and of Canada today.

W.L. Morton (d. 1980), Vanier Professor of History, Trent University, was the Executive Editor of *The Canadian Centenary Series*. A graduate of the Universities of Manitoba and Oxford, he was the author of *The Kingdom of Canada; Manitoba: A History; The Progressive Party in Canada; The Critical Years: The Union of British North America, 1857-1873;* and other writings. He also edited *The Journal of Alexander Begg and Other Documents Relevant to the Red River Resistance*. Holder of the honorary degrees of LL.D. and D.LITT., he was awarded the Tyrrell Medal of the Royal Society of Canada and the Governor General's Award for Non-Fiction.

D.G. Creighton (d. 1979), former Chairman of the Department of History, University of Toronto, was the Advisory Editor of *The Canadian Centenary Series*. A graduate of the Universities of Toronto and Oxford, he was the author of *John A. Macdonald: The Young Politician; John A. Macdonald: the Old Chieftain; Dominion of the North; The Empire of the St. Lawrence* and many other works. Holder of numerous honorary degrees, LL.D. and D.LITT., he twice won the Governor General's Award for Non-Fiction. He had also been awarded the Tyrrell Medal of the Royal Society of Canada, the University of Alberta National Award in Letters, the University of British Columbia Medal for Popular Biography, and the Molson Prize of the Canada Council.

Ramsay Cook, Professor of History, York University, co-author with R.C. Brown of *Canada 1896-1921*, volume 14 of the series, is the Executive Editor of *The Canadian Centenary Series*, 1983.